Canon® EOS Rebel T5i/700D

Digital Field Guide

Rosh Sillars

WILEY

Canon® EOS Rebel T5i/700D Digital Field Guide

Published by
John Wiley & Sons, Inc.
10475 Crosspoint Boulevard
Indianapolis, IN 46256
www.wiley.com

Published simultaneously in Canada

ISBN: 978-1-118-71164-4

Manufactured in the United States of America

10 9 8 7 6 5 4 3 2 1

Library of Congress Control Number: 2013936838

Credits

Acquisitions Editor
Courtney Allen

Project Editor
Amanda Gambill

Technical Editor
George Maginnis

Senior Copy Editor
Kim Heusel

Editorial Director
Robyn Siesky

Business Manager
Amy Knies

Senior Marketing Manager
Sandy Smith

Vice President and Executive Group Publisher
Richard Swadley

Vice President and Executive Publisher
Barry Pruett

Project Coordinator
Sheree Montgomery

Graphics and Production Specialists
Jennifer Creasey
Jennifer Goldsmith

Quality Control Technicians
Lindsay Amones
Susan Moritz
Dwight Ramsey
Rob Springer

Proofreading and Indexing
Chris Sabooni
Potomac Indexing, LLC

About the Author

Rosh Sillars is a veteran photographer with a background in photojournalism. He specializes in photographing people, food, and interiors. He earned a BFA in photography from the College of Creative Studies (CCS), Detroit. He owns the creative representation firm, The Rosh Group Inc.; works as a social media consultant for Synectics Media; teaches photojournalism at Wayne State University in Detroit; and is a digital photography instructor at the University of Detroit, Mercy. He is an active author, speaker, and consultant on photography and marketing.

Rosh's home photography studio, Octane Photographic, is located in Ferndale, Michigan, where he lives with his wife, Shirley, and their daughters, Ava and Kelly.

Acknowledgments

Thank you to my wife Shirley, and my children, Ava and Kelly, who demonstrated admirable patience during this process and its many deadlines. Thank you to the Synectics Media team for your support and for taking the time to model in my camera demonstrations: Jeffrey Huysentruyt, Sharon Stanton, Katy Hinz, Tim Kloote, and Steve Gualtieri.

Thank you to the photography social media community, without which I would have never connected with all of the great photographers who share their knowledge in this book. I'm grateful to everyone who took the time to submit tips and photos — you added a wonderful dimension to this book.

Appreciation for added support goes to Dean La Douceur, Greg Evans, April Pochmara, and Kevin Dolan.

Thank you to Courtney Allen for the opportunity to write this book, Amanda Gambill for her guidance, and to the entire Wiley team who really make this book shine.

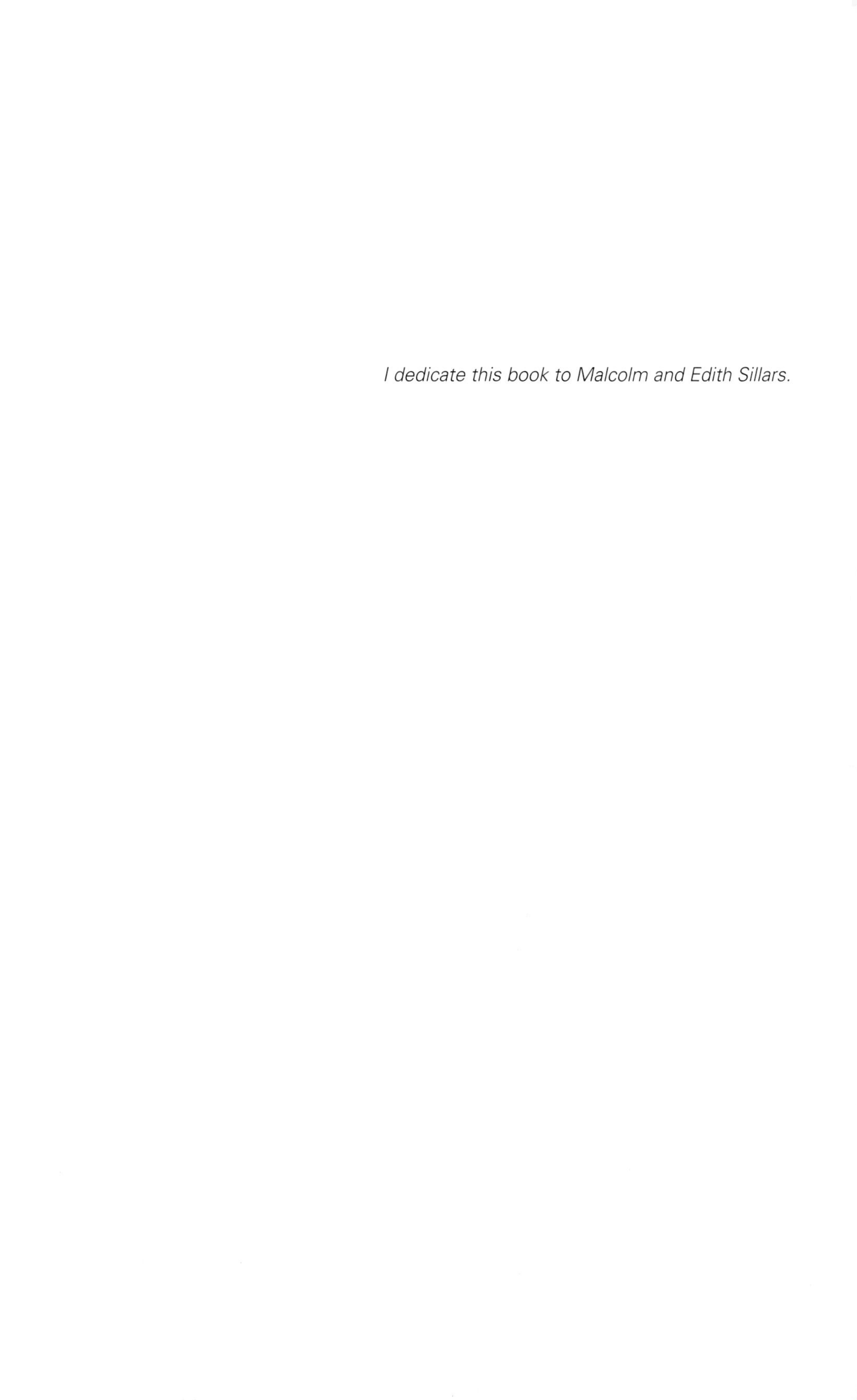

I dedicate this book to Malcolm and Edith Sillars.

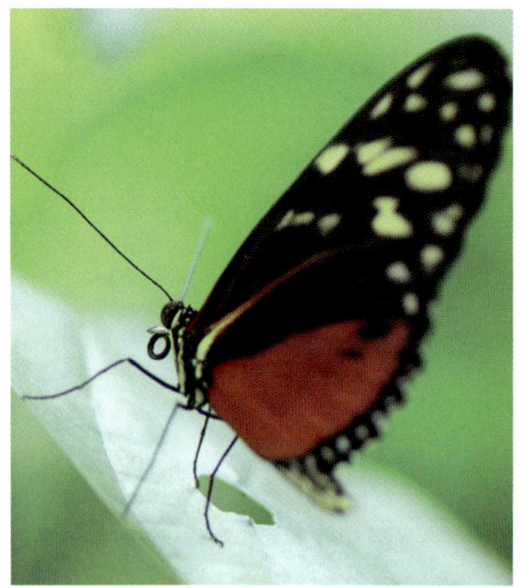

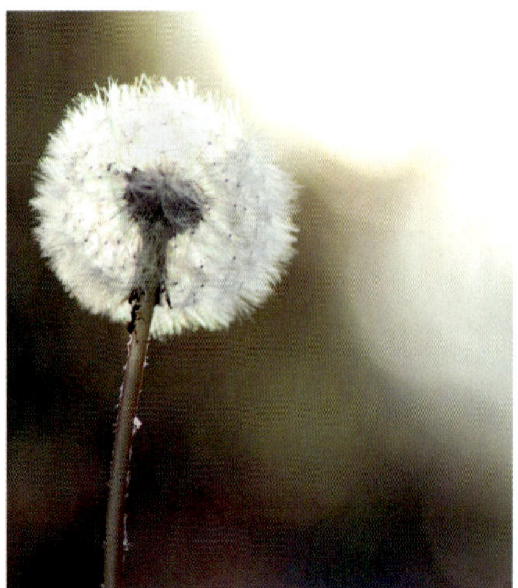

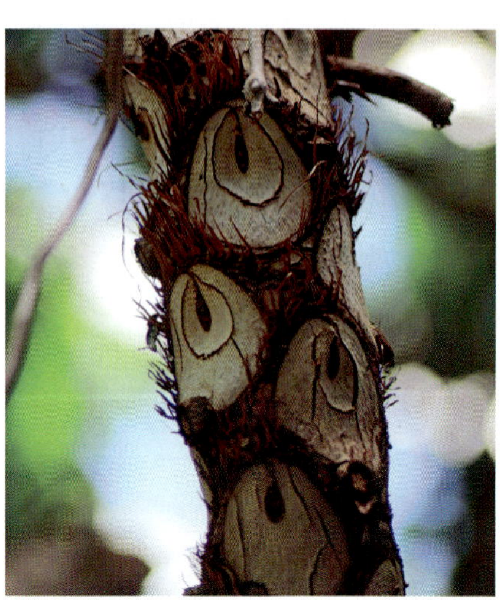

Contents

Introduction xii

QUICK TOUR

Getting Started 2

Camera Controls 3

The top of the camera 4

The back of the camera 5

Choosing Image Quality 6

Selecting a Focus Mode 7

Using Flash 8

Reviewing Images or Video. 9

Taking Better Photos 9

CHAPTER 1
Exploring the Canon EOS Rebel T5i/700D **11**

The Top of the Camera 12

The Bottom of the Camera 15

The Front of the Camera 16

The Back of the Camera 17

The Sides of the Camera. 22

Lens Controls 24

The Viewfinder Display 25

The LCD Touchscreen and Live View Mode. . . 27

CHAPTER 2
Setting Up the Canon EOS Rebel T5i/700D **31**

The Shooting Menus 32

Shooting menu 1 32

Settings and corrective functions 32

Flash control. 33

Shooting menu 2 35

Shooting menu 3 37

The Live View Shooting Menu 37

The Movie Shooting Menus 39

Movie shooting menu 1 39

Movie shooting menu 2 40

The Playback Menus 41
  Playback menu 1. 41
  Playback menu 2. 42
The Setup Menus 43
  Setup menu 1 43
  Setup menu 2 44
  Setup menu 3 45
  Setup menu 4 46
My Menu Settings. 48

CHAPTER 3
Choosing the Right Settings for Your Camera 49

The Basic Zone Modes 50
The Creative Zone Modes 55
Focus Modes. 57
Picture Styles. 61
Drive Modes 65
White Balance Settings 66
Flash Modes 71
ISO Settings 75
Choosing File Quality and Format 78
  Image size and file numbering 78
  The RAW file format. 79
  The JPEG file format. 79
Movie Mode 80
  Exposing for video 81
  Setting the file size and focus. 82

CHAPTER 4
Using Lenses with the Canon EOS Rebel T5i/700D 83

Choosing a Good Lens 84
  Focal lengths. 86
  Autofocus 89
  Aperture and depth of field. 89
  Image Stabilization (IS) 90
  Vignetting 91
Types of Lenses 92
Prime versus Zoom Lenses. 95
  Understanding prime lenses. 95
  Understanding zoom lenses 96
Specialty Lenses 96

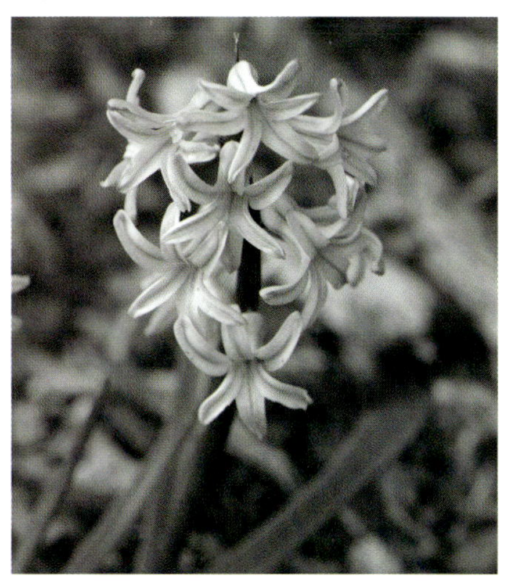

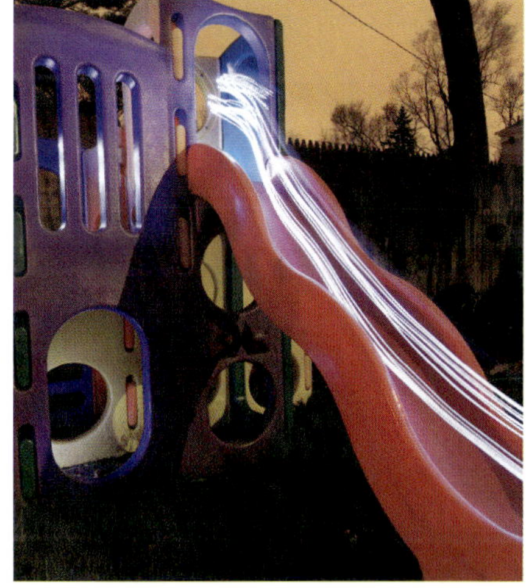

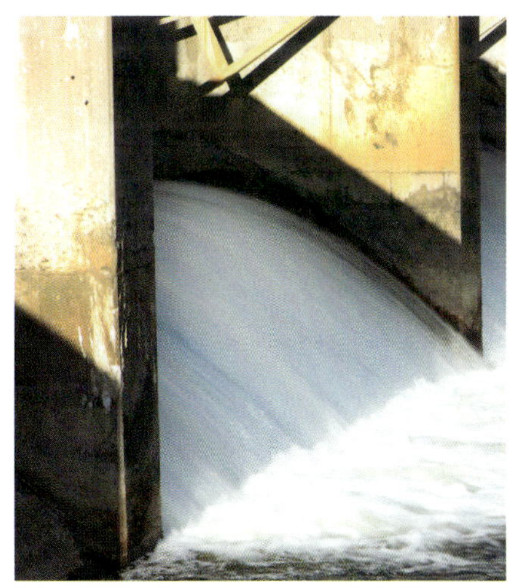

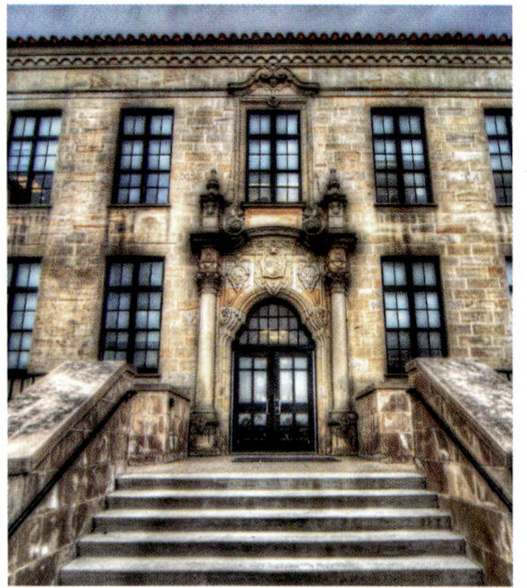

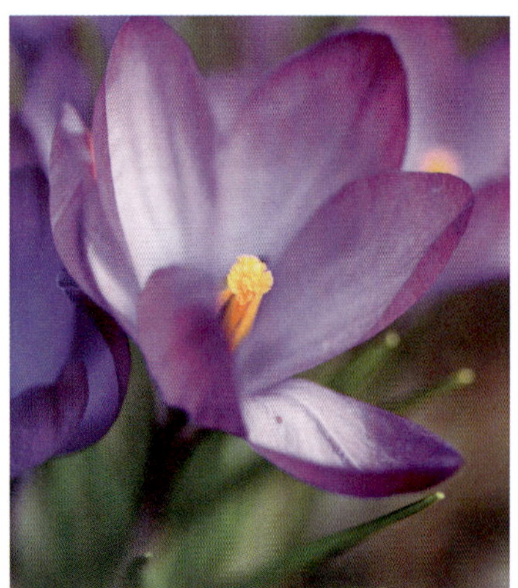

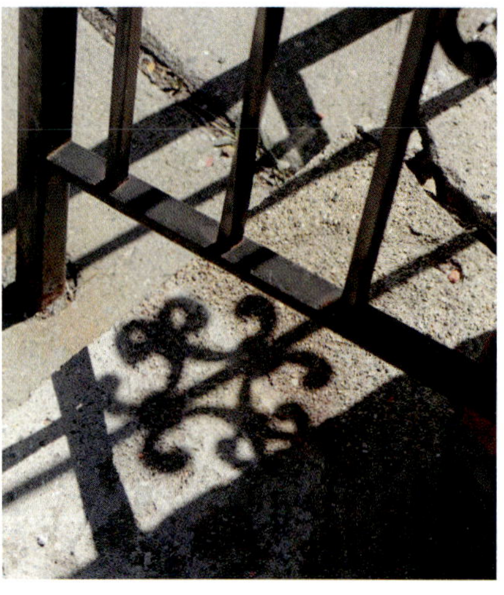

CHAPTER 5

Exploring Exposure and Composition 101

Choosing the Right Exposure 102
Setting the shutter speed 105
When to use fast shutter speeds . . . 106
When to use slow shutter speeds . . . 106
Night photography and painting with light 111
Setting the aperture 114
Setting the ISO 116
Using Exposure Compensation 118
High Dynamic Range Photography 119
Exposing for Video 121
Composition 122
The Rule of Thirds 123
Filling the frame 125
Lines and shapes 126
Foreground and background 127
Keeping it simple 127

CHAPTER 6

Working with Lighting and Flash 129

The Importance of Light and Shadow 130
The Direction of Light 131
Frontlighting 131
Sidelighting 131
Overhead lighting 134
Backlighting 134
The Quality of Light 136
Hard lighting 136
Soft lighting 137
Types of Light 138
Natural light 138
Continuous light 139
Flash 139
Shutter speed and flash 140
Aperture and flash 142
Manual mode and flash 142
The Color of Light 144
White balance options 145
Using Picture Styles 145
The Picture Style Editor 146
Ambience Effects 147
Choosing a color space 147

Measuring Light 148
Choosing the proper exposure 148
Metering modes 150
Evaluative metering mode 150
Center-weighted average metering mode 150
Spot metering mode 150
Partial metering mode 151
The Canon Flash System 151
The pop-up flash 152
Using an external flash 153
Using multiple flashes 154

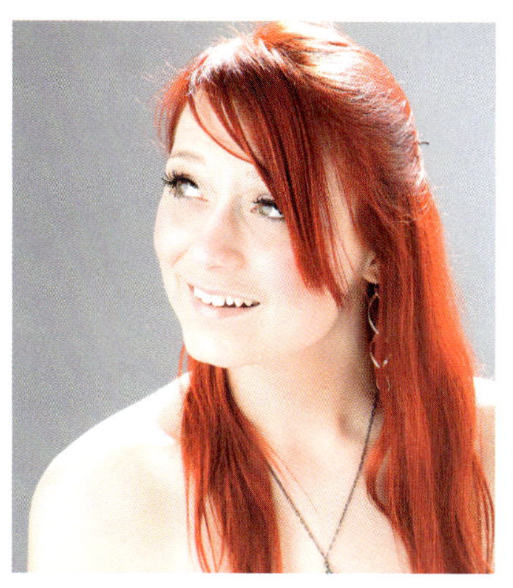

CHAPTER 7
Shooting Photos 157

Portrait Photography 158
Equipment 158
Best practices 160
Tips 162
Family Photography 166
Equipment 166
Best practices 167
Tips 167
Action and Sports Photography 169
Equipment 169
Best practices 170
Tips 172
Event Photography 172
Equipment 173
Best practices 173
Tips 174
Landscape and Nature Photography 176
Equipment 176
Best practices 178
Tips 179
Macro Photography 180
Equipment 180
Best practices 181
Tips 182
Night and Low-Light Photography 183
Equipment 183
Best practices 184
Tips 185

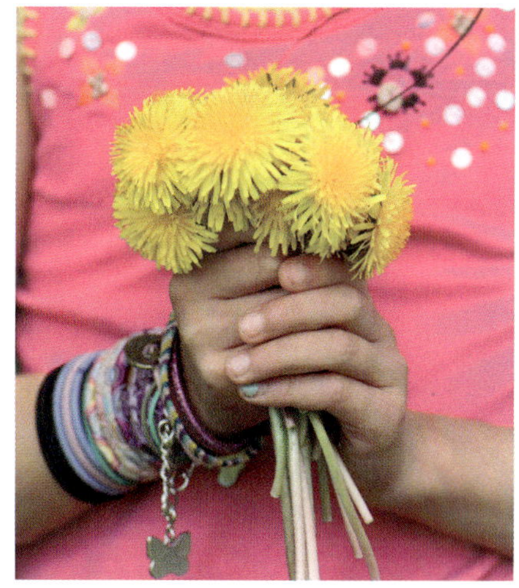

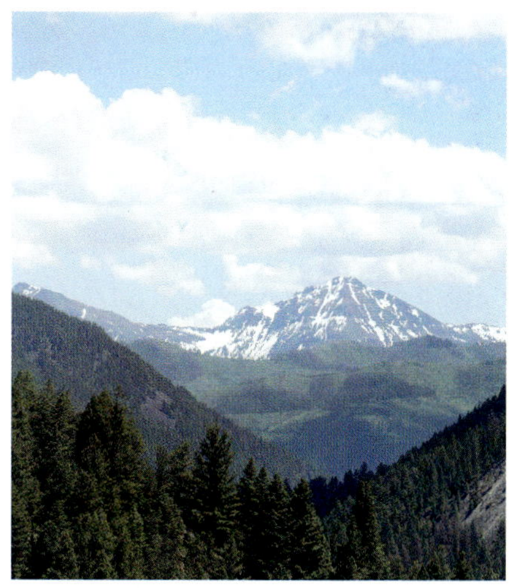

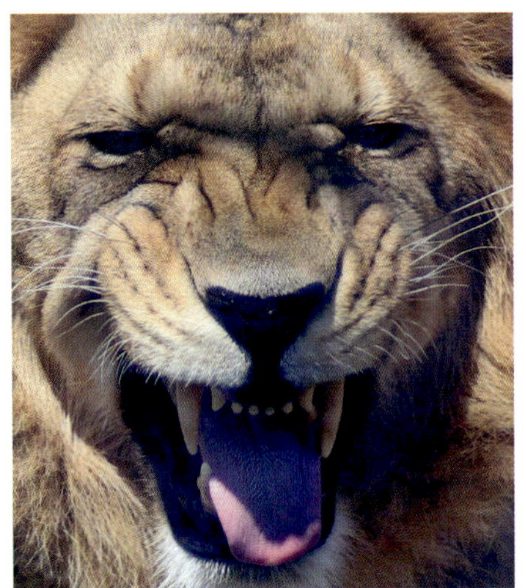

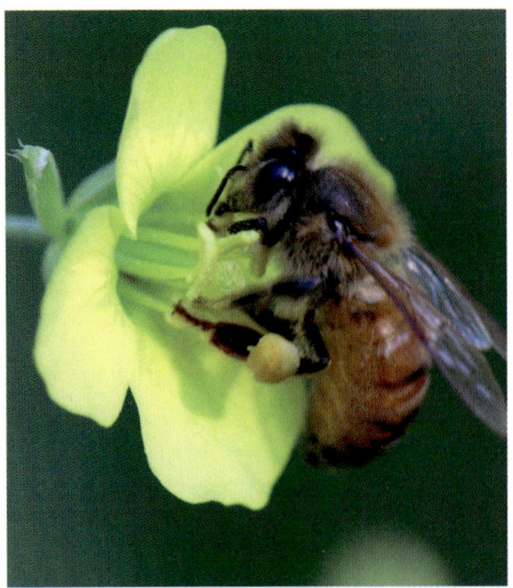

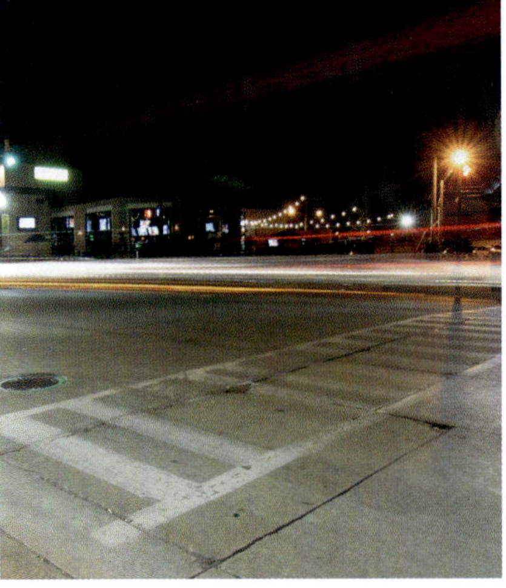

Travel Photography 186

Equipment 186

Best practices 187

Tips 189

CHAPTER 8
Shooting in the Live View and Movie Modes 191

Using the Live View Shooting Mode 192

The Quick Control/Print button 196

Shooting stills 196

Focus modes 197

Live View and video 198

Shooting Video 199

Setting up for a video shoot 201

The frame rate 202

The shutter speed 203

Lighting 205

Sound 206

Choosing a focus mode 208

Recording video 210

Creating video snapshots 211

Equipment 212

Types of video 213

CHAPTER 9
Viewing, Editing, and Sharing Your Content 217

Viewing Content 218

Viewing content on the camera 218

Playback 218

The Quick Control/Print and Info buttons 219

Viewing content on a TV or smart device 220

Downloading and Storing Your Images 221

Storage 221

The 3-2-1 rule 223

Editing and Adjusting Content on the Camera 223

Sharing Photos and Videos 225

E-mailing images. 225

Printing images 225

Uploading content to a website 226
Sharing content via social media 227

APPENDIX A
Postproduction 233

Photo-Editing Software 234
Digital Photo Professional. 236
Image Browser EX 239
Lightroom 241
iPhoto 242
Photoshop. 243
Video-Editing Software 245
Image Browser EX 247
iMovie. 248
Windows Live Movie Maker. 248
Other video-editing software 249

APPENDIX B
Accessories 251

Grips and Remotes 251
Video Accessories 253
Microphones 254
Tripods. 255
Bags. 257

APPENDIX C
How to Use the Gray Card and Color Checker 259

The Gray Card 259
The Color Checker. 260

Glossary 261

Index 267

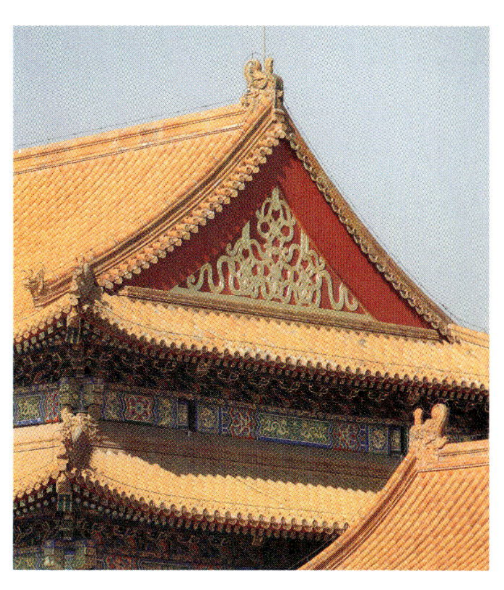

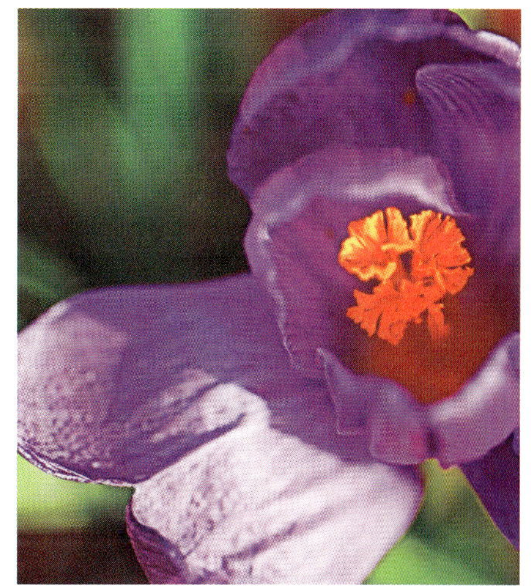

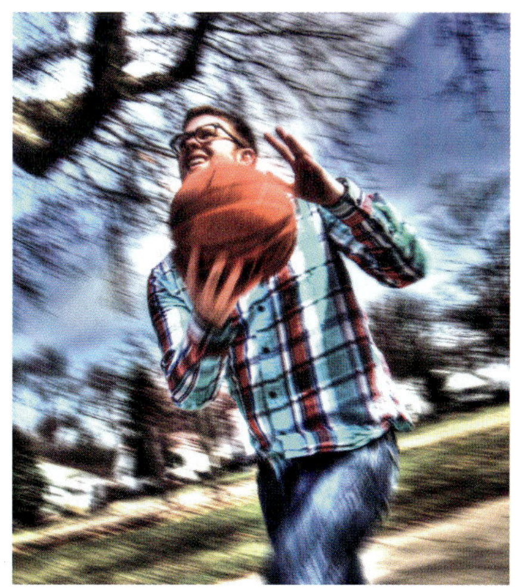

Introduction

For a photography enthusiast, there is nothing like opening a box and pulling out a new camera. Even if you purchased a used camera, it's still exciting. Soon, you'll discover the wonderful features the Canon T5i/700D offers for creating both still photography and video. Use this book to explore these features and learn how to take better photos. As I wrote this book, I reviewed every menu, pushed every button, and applied my 25 years of experience in photography to inform you about how this technology can benefit your photos. This book also features tips from other photographers on everything from how to compose your shots to best practices for shooting video.

The first part of this book covers the technical information, including how to use the camera's many menus, displays, and buttons. As you read further, you will discover more information on important topics, such as lenses, lighting, and accessories.

Your camera has some great features, including HDR and low-light modes. The LCD touch screen makes selecting features and settings from your camera's menus much easier. It also makes it possible for you to review your images and videos with the swipe of a finger.

This book is not intended to replace the owner's manual. In fact, it was written under the assumption that you have read the owner's manual and know the basics, like how to put the camera strap on and how to charge the battery. Even so, I do dig into plenty of basic information that you need to get started. I also take you through some mid-level and advanced ideas that you won't find in the manual, but that are meant to improve your photographs and experience with the Canon Rebel T5i/700D.

Quick Tour

I'm sure you are thinking about all the awesome photographs you will take as you open the box containing your new Canon Rebel T5i/700D. Of course, once you do get it out of the box, you realize there are many buttons and options on your new camera. This Quick Tour covers the basic features on your camera and a few photography tips to get you started. I dig deeper in the following chapters of this book, reviewing all of the menus, functions, and settings your camera offers. I also explore how to create better photographs. You can use this section as a go-to reference in the field, so make sure you always keep your *Canon EOS Rebel T5i/700D Digital Field Guide* in your camera bag.

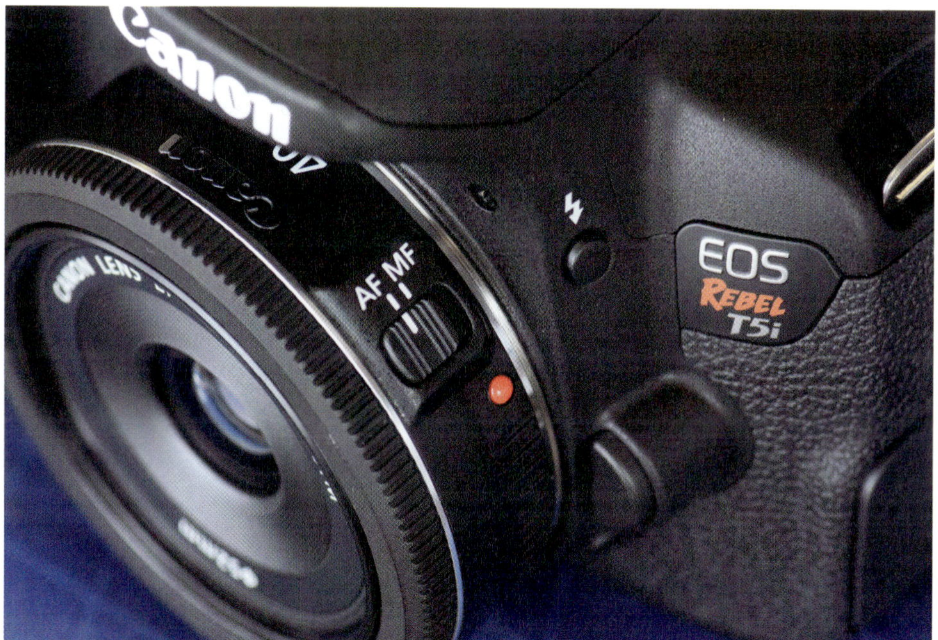

The Canon T5i/700D has many great features, including an LCD touchscreen, HDR capabilities, and continuous focus for shooting video.

Getting Started

If you want to take photos right now, follow these quick steps to get going. Your camera should be unpacked from the box. The camera battery, straight out of the box, should have some power; however, I recommend fully charging it before you use it for the first time. If you cannot wait that long, go ahead and take a few shots.

To begin shooting, you need a fully charged battery, a formatted memory card, and a Canon (or compatible third-party) lens attached to your camera. The battery door is on the bottom of the camera. Open it and insert the battery until you hear a click indicating that it is locked in place.

The memory card should also be formatted for your camera. To format the memory card, place it in the card slot (with the letters facing you) on the right side of the camera, as shown in Figure QT.1. You know you've inserted the card correctly when you hear a faint click. Turn on the camera by flipping the power button on the top, right side. Press the Menu button (**MENU**), select Setup menu 1 (🔧), select Format, and then press OK. The memory card is formatted within a few moments. The more memory the card has, the longer the formatting process takes.

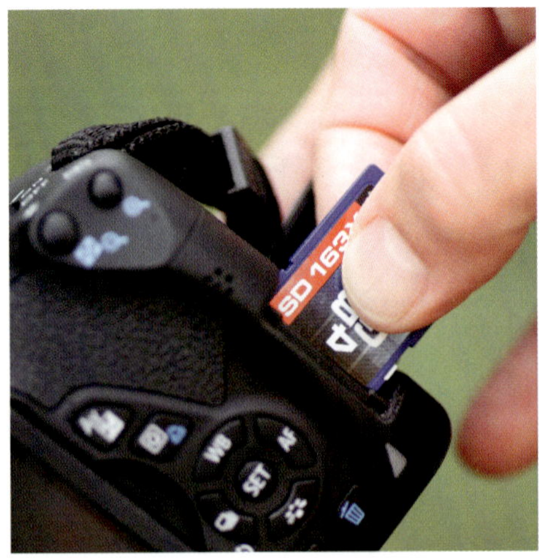

QT.1 The memory card fits into the slot on the right side of the camera.

To place a lens on the camera, match the red (or white) dots found on both the camera and lens, and then turn the lens to the left. Make sure that the camera lens is set to autofocus — you will find the Autofocus/Manual Focus option on the side of the lens.

On the top, right side of your camera is the Mode dial. I recommend that you set the camera to the Scene Intelligent Auto shooting mode (A+) for evaluative automatic program control. In other words, this mode lets the camera make all of the decisions.

Your job is to place your index finger on the shutter button, as shown in Figure QT.2, and your eye to the viewfinder to begin shooting photos.

To shoot videos, flip the power button (see Figure QT.3) to Movie mode (🎥). The LCD screen's Live View feature turns on and displays the view through the lens. For quick access to many of the camera's main movie options, press the Quick Control/Print button (Q) to get the options displayed on the screen. Use the Live View Shooting button (▣) to start and stop movie recording.

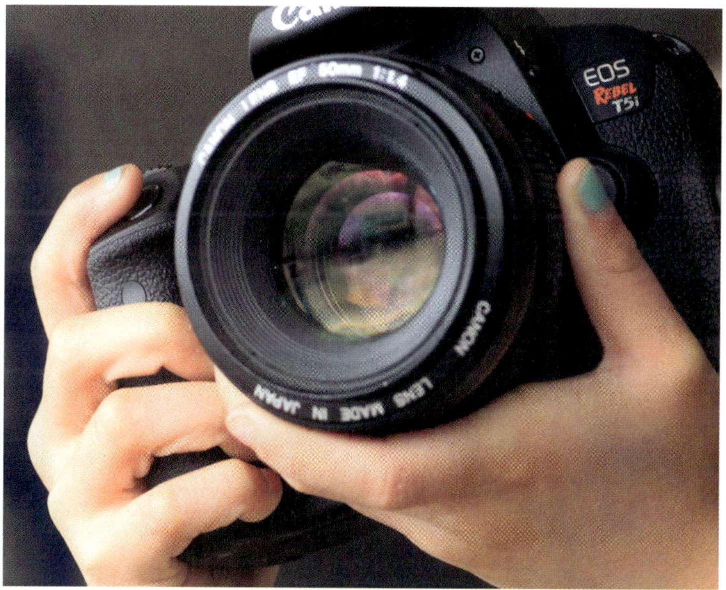

QT.2 Place your index finger on the shutter button to begin taking photos. Make sure that you support the camera securely with your other hand.

Camera Controls

This section covers some of the basic controls you need to know for the everyday use of your Canon T5i/700D. Most of these are found on the top and back of the camera. Many of the same controls can also be found on the LCD touchscreen. Press the Quick Control/Print button (Q) to view them.

CROSS REF A detailed list of all of the camera controls can be found in Chapter 1. Menu options are covered in Chapter 2.

The top of the camera

The top of the camera features the following buttons and dials:

- **ISO button (ISO).** ISO refers to the light sensitivity setting of your camera. The higher the ISO, the less light you need. The lower the ISO, the more light you need, but the less digital noise your image will contain (higher quality). Your camera has a range of ISO 100 to ISO 12,800, with an option to expand to ISO 25,600. This setting is found in Setup menu 4 (🔧) under Custom Function 1: Exposure.
- **Power button.** You have three power options: Movie shooting ('🎥), On, and Off. Turn the power button On when you want to take still photos. Turn it to the Movie shooting setting ('🎥) when you want to create videos.

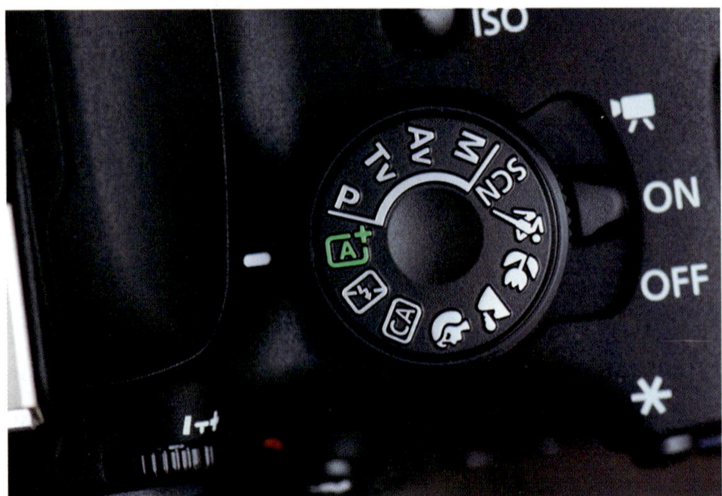

QT.3 The Mode dial and power switch are located on the top right side of the camera.

- **Mode dial.** This controls the 14 exposure modes. The dial is divided into two zones: Basic and Creative. The following Basic Zone modes offer a variety of automatic settings: Scene Intelli-gent Auto (A+), Flash off (⚡̸), Creative Auto (CA), Portrait (👤), Landscape (⛰), Close-up (🌷), Sports (🏃), and Special Scene (SCN). The Special Scene mode hosts three modes: Night Portrait (☆), Handheld Night Scene (▣), and HDR backlight control (▣). To select one of these options, look on the LCD screen. If the LCD screen is off, press the Quick Control/Print button (Q) on the back of your camera, and then use the Main dial (⚙) to select an option. The following Creative Zone modes offer more exposure freedom for advanced users: Program AE (**P**), Shutter-priority AE (**Tv**), Aperture-priority AE (**Av**), and Manual (manualc).

- **Shutter button.** Press the shutter button halfway to focus on your subject or check the exposure of the scene. Press it completely to take a photograph.

The back of the camera

The back of the camera features the following buttons and dials:

- **Menu button (MENU).** Pressing this button gives you access to the many options available to customize your camera.

CROSS REF The camera menus are covered in Chapter 2.

- **Info button (INFO.).** Press this button to activate the information display on the LCD screen. Depending on the mode you are using, the LCD screen displays information about the camera, the shooting mode settings, and the photograph or video.
- **Dioptric Adjustment dial.** Located to the right of the viewfinder, this dial adjusts the viewfinder's clarity.
- **Live View/Movie Shooting button (▣).** This button turns on the camera's LCD screen for the Live View feature, which allows you to see the scene as the lens reads it. This button also starts and stops recording during a video shoot.
- **Reduce/Exposure Lock (✱)/Flash Exposure Lock (ϟ✱)/Index button (⊞·🔍).** When viewing your images, you can press this button to Reduce the magnification of an image. When taking a photograph, pressing this button engages the Exposure (✱)/Flash Exposure (ϟ✱) Lock, which fixes the exposure with or without flash. If an image is not magnified during playback, pressing this button displays a scrollable index of the images on the memory card — use the Cross keys (✣▴▾◂▸) to maneuver through them.
- **Magnify (🔍)/Autofocus (AF) point select (⊞) button.** In Playback mode (▶), the Magnify button (🔍) allows you to magnify the displayed image. When taking a photograph in a Creative Zone Mode, the Autofocus (AF) point select feature displays and allows the selection of an AF point. The AF point selection appears on the LCD screen and in the viewfinder.
- **Aperture/Exposure Compensation (Av⊠) button.** When photographing in Manual mode (**M**), this button, used in combination with the Main dial (⚙),

controls the aperture. In the other Creative Zone modes, it controls exposure compensation.

- **Quick Control/Print button (Q).** Press this button to display important features quickly on the LCD screen to use in specific modes. You also press this button to print an image if your camera is connected to a printer.
- **Cross keys (✣).** These four buttons offer quick access to the White balance (**WB**), Autofocus mode (**AF**), Picture Styles, and Drive modes. Each of the quick access options display on the LCD screen on the back of your camera. They also serve as direction keys to navigate through menu options. When you land on the menu option that you want, press the Setting button (SET).

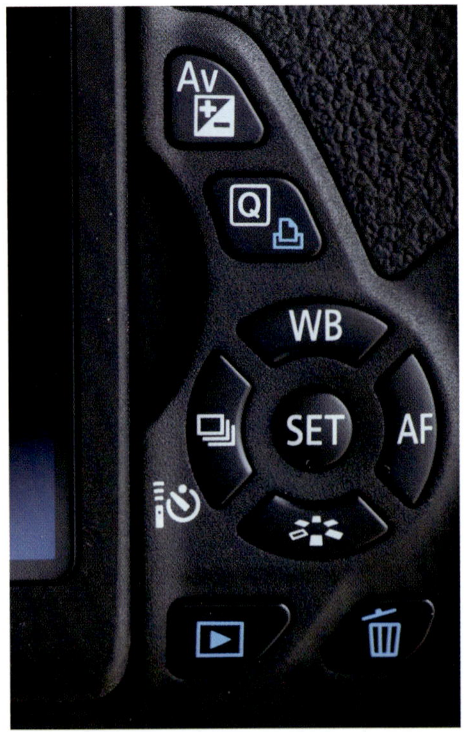

QT.4 The control center on the back of Canon Rebel T5i/700D.

- **Playback button (▶).** Press this button to display images and movies stored on the memory card. When you first press this button, the last recorded image or movie appears.
- **Delete button (🗑).** Press this button to erase unlocked images when viewing them in Playback mode (▶).
- **LCD touchscreen**. You use the vari-angle LCD touchscreen to view and set menu functions. You also use it to shoot images and video in the Live View and Movie shooting modes, and to review images and videos in Playback mode (▶).

Choosing Image Quality

Your camera has 10 image-quality options. The default is Large fine (◢ L), which is the largest JPEG size available on your camera at 5184 × 3456 pixels. This is the equivalent of a 72- × 48-inch image at 72 dpi (dots per inch), or a 17.28- × 11.52-inch image at

300 dpi. The RAW format (RAW) is the highest quality image available on your camera and Small 3 (S3) is the smallest file size. I recommend that you use the higher image-quality settings, such as the default Large fine (◢L), for regular use because you can always downsize your photos on your camera or in the Digital Photography Professional software that came with it. You cannot, however, increase a photograph's resolution without losing image quality. If you need more room for images, purchase a card with more memory, especially if you plan to shoot larger files and video.

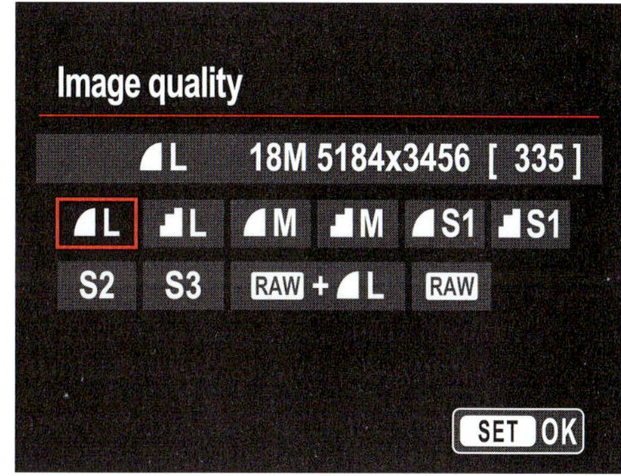

QT.5 The Image quality menu has 10 options.

Selecting a Focus Mode

To use autofocus, check the switch on the side of your lens and make sure that it is in the Autofocus (AF) position. Next, press the shutter button halfway to focus on your subject. If you are using a basic (automatic) zone mode, the camera selects the focus points for you. If you are using a Creative Zone mode, you have the option of nine focus points (31 if you are using the Live View FlexiZone Autofocus method options). The default is automatic autofocus, in which the camera selects the focus point based on nine AF points, usually focusing on the closest subject to your camera. To adjust the autofocus points manually, press the Magnify button (🔍) to view the camera's AF points. Adjust the points by using the Main dial (⌓) on top of the camera.

CROSS REF For more information about the Live View and Focus options, see Chapter 8.

You also have three options related to how your camera focuses. Press the Autofocus button (**AF**) to see your autofocus operation options. The default (and first) option is One-shot autofocus mode (**ONE SHOT**) and it does just that. When you press the shutter button halfway in this focus mode, the camera focuses on your subject once. It stays at that focus point until you lift your finger and press the shutter button again. AI focus (**AI FOCUS**) takes one shot unless the camera detects motion, and then it switches to the AI Servo mode (**AI SERVO**). AI Servo (**AI SERVO**) follow focuses as you or the subject moves.

The default focus setting for videos is Movie Servo AF mode (SERVO AF). This means that the camera follow focuses the closest object to the camera. This setting is only available when the camera is in the Movie shooting mode ('Ṝ). You can turn off Movie Servo AF (SERVO AF) by touching the icon in the lower-left corner of the LCD screen. When Movie Servo AF mode (SERVO AF) is turned off, your camera focuses once when you press the shutter button halfway. Manual focus is achieved by selecting the Manual Focus mode (**MF**) on your lens.

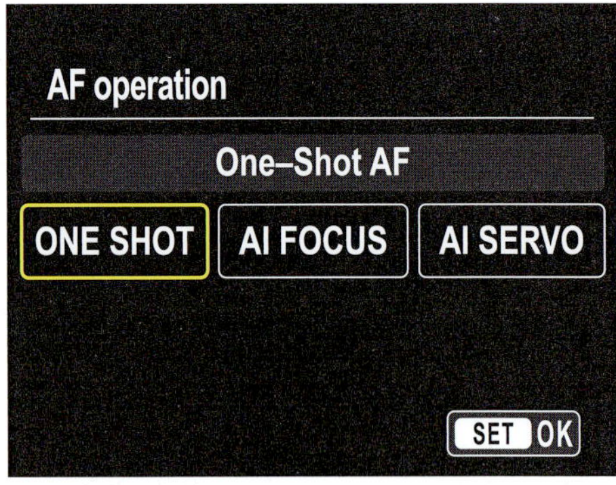

QT.6 The AF operation menu offers three focus options.

Using Flash

If you are using one of the Basic Zone modes, the flash pops up automatically when needed. When using one of the Creative Zone modes, the flash must be manually popped up by pressing the Flash button (ϟ) on the front of the camera (see Figure QT.7). If you are using an external flash, place it in the hot shoe on top of the camera. Flashes that are compatible with Evaluative Through-the-Lens (E-TTL) technology (that is, Canon's version of Through-the-Lens metering) synchronize seamlessly with your camera. This means that the flash and camera work together to create the best exposure using your camera's evaluative metering sensor. This type of metering is helpful for more accurate readings, especially if you have a filter on your lens, because the flash knows how much to adjust.

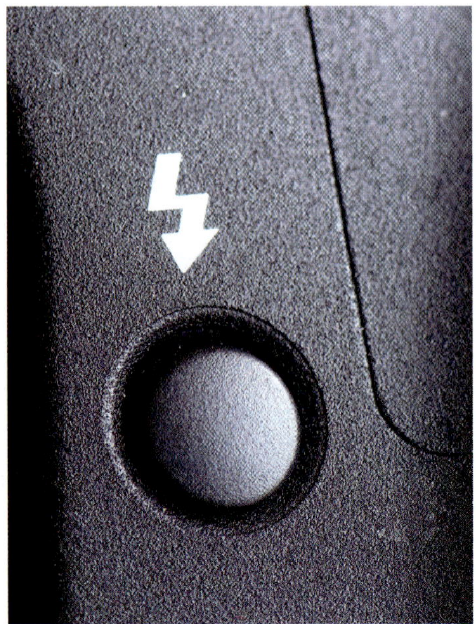

QT.7 The Flash button is on the left side of the camera.

QT

Reviewing Images or Video

Once you have taken some pictures, you will want to review them. To see your photos, press the Playback button (▶) while keeping the camera power on. You can use the left and right Cross keys (✣) to move forward and backward between images. This is where the LCD touchscreen is very convenient — you can also swipe your finger back and forth acros s the screen to review images. If you want to skip through a large number of images, use the Main dial (⚙) to scroll through 10 or more at a time.

To play a video, press the Setting button (SET) located in the middle of the Cross keys (✣) twice. The first time you press it, the camera displays the video playback and review options on the LCD screen. The second time you press it, the video plays if the Playback button (▶) is highlighted. An even easier option is to press the Playback button (▶) on the LCD screen.

NOTE Each time you press the Info button (**INFO.**), a different image display screen appears for either images or videos. There are four screen options.

Taking Better Photos

I have invited other professional photographers to share their tips and suggestions throughout this book; however, the following list includes a few of my own suggestions to help you get started:

- **Fill the frame.** Get close to your subject. Often, too much empty space or unrelated objects can lessen the impact of a great subject. Make sure that everything in the frame is necessary and supports your concept. To help compose your images, use the Live View mode (▣) to view your scene in larger form on the LCD screen. Consider using the grid option (located under the Live View menu ▣) to support your composition.
- **Light.** Light is everything in photography, so always make sure that you have a good source of it for your photographs. Early morning and late evening (referred to as the *Golden Hours*) are the prime times for photography. Experiment with light direction and shadows. If you turn on the Auto Lighting Optimizer located in Shooting menu 2 (📷), your camera will adjust your image automatically to optimal brightness when you are shooting in the basic modes.
- **Flash.** Don't be afraid of the built-in or external flashes; learn how to use them. I encourage you to use Canon E-TTL II flashes to ease the learning curve of flash photography. Additionally, your camera is designed to fire Canon flashes wirelessly, offering you more lighting options.

- **Variety.** Not every photograph has to be shot the same way — try out new lenses and accessories. Use your vari-angle LCD screen to get pictures from high and low angles. Place your subjects in different parts of the frame.
- **Experiment.** Try all of the exposure modes and special effects, such as Picture Styles, so that you know what your camera can do.

Before and After the Shoot

Trevor Current is a professional product photographer and graphic designer. He uses his images in the designs he creates for his clients. The following is Trevor's list of things you should consider before and after a photo shoot:

- **Purchase a battery grip.** It has two batteries for longer sessions and a shutter button for vertical shooting, which is helpful when taking portraits.
- **Make sure the camera batteries are charged.** Always carry fully charged backup batteries, as well.
- **Review all of the buttons and become familiar with your camera.** It is important to know what your camera is capable of doing, and how the features apply to different subjects.
- **Test your camera to make sure it is working.** Look through the viewfinder and press the shutter button. Check the light meter by pointing it toward, and then away from a light source, and make sure it's adjusting and metering light.
- **Check your lenses.** Make sure that the contacts are clean and connected to your camera properly.
- **Make sure there is enough room on the memory card to store everything you want to shoot.** Check your backup memory cards, too. A 2GB to 4GB memory card is good for most applications. If you plan to shoot video, though, you need at least a 16GB memory card.
- **Be prepared and know the environmental conditions.** Make sure you are prepared for any weather situation and know your surroundings.
- **After you finish shooting, copy your images from the memory card onto your computer immediately.** Don't risk losing all of your images.

Trevor Current's work has been used in exhibits, on product packaging, and in national advertising campaigns. He is the founder of http://currentphotographer.com and the co-host of the photography podcast Digital Photography Café.

CHAPTER 1

Exploring the Canon EOS Rebel T5i/700D

The Canon Rebel T5i/700D has many buttons and dials, and it's important that you take the time to review each control and option at least once. You may not need them all now, but as you become more familiar with your camera, it helps to know what options are available. In this chapter, I cover each side of the camera to help you understand the standard controls, as well as the viewfinder, LCD screen, and display options. I also review the camera exposure modes, where the tripod and connection sockets are, and how to use the dioptric adjustment dial. Once you understand the camera's controls, you can focus on taking photos.

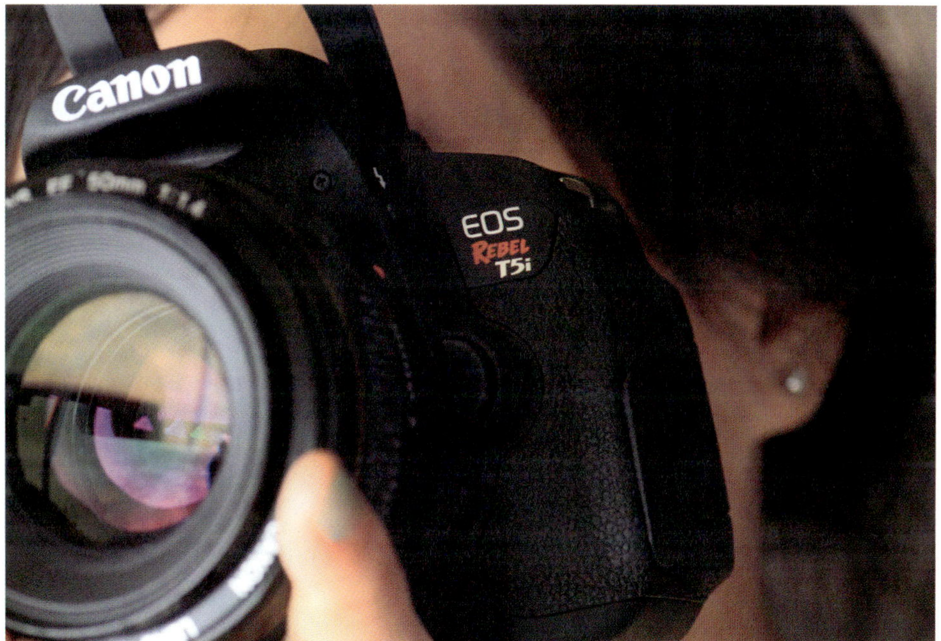

Make sure you understand the function of each of the buttons on your camera.

The Top of the Camera

The top of the camera houses the power switch, exposure modes, Main dial (Main dial icon), and the ISO (ISO) and shutter buttons. All of these play an integral role in creating photographs.

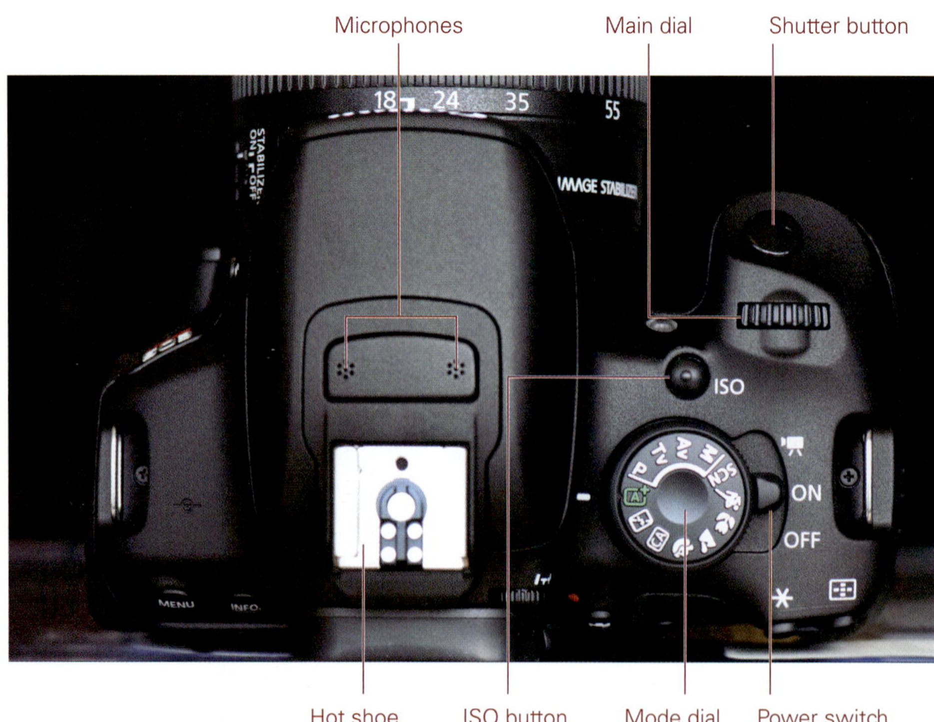

1.1 The top of the Canon EOS Rebel T5i/700D.

The following list explains what each switch and button does:

- **ISO button (ISO).** The ISO setting represents the camera's sensitivity to light. Your camera has a range of ISO 100 to ISO 12800. You also have the option of H, which if engaged increases the camera light sensitivity to ISO 25600. To turn this option on, use the Custom Function 2 ISO expansion.
- **Shutter button.** This button triggers the camera to take a photograph. Pressing the button halfway activates the focusing and exposure system. To view the shutter speed and aperture, look through the viewfinder. When using slower shutter speeds, press the shutter button slowly to avoid camera shake.

- **Main dial ( ).** Use this to move through different menus and options on your camera. For example, if you press the Menu button (**MENU**) and turn the Main dial ( ) either left or right, you scroll across the menu screen. If you select Shutter-priority AE mode (**Tv**), you use the Main dial ( ) to increase and decrease your shutter speed.
- **Power switch.** You have three options on the power switch: On, Off, and Movie ( ). On is for photographing still images; Movie ( ) is for creating videos.
- **Mode dial.** This dial houses the 12 exposure modes. The white line next to the Mode dial tells you which option is in use. Unlike previous models, the dial rotates 360 degrees to make it easier to change modes. There are also three additional options located under the Special Scene mode (SCN): Night Portrait ( ), Handheld Night Scene ( ), and HDR Backlight ( ). You can view the Special Scene mode (SCN) options on the LCD screen. If the LCD screen is off, press the Quick control/ Print button ( ) to view the three mode options.

1

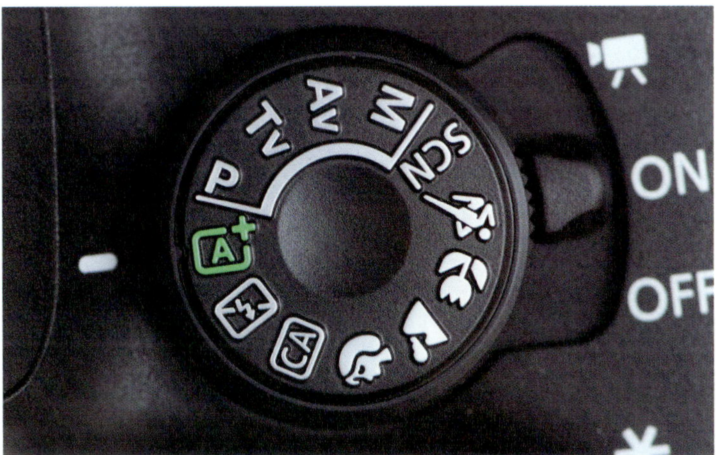

1.2 **The Canon T5i/700D has 12 exposure Modes on the Mode dial.**

- **Microphones.** There are two microphones on top of the camera to record audio for videos. The microphone controls are found under Movie shooting menu 2 ( ).
- **Hot shoe.** The hot shoe holds an external flash, such as the Canon Speedlite 430 EX II. It is also the connection point for flash-related accessories, such as the Canon OC-E3 off-camera shoe cord.

Table 1.1 lists the exposure modes available on your Canon T5i/700D. The Creative Zone modes offer greater flexibility. The automatic exposure options are located in the Basic Zone.

Table 1.1 The Exposure Modes

Mode	Description
Manual (**M**)	You set the shutter speed and aperture.
Aperture-priority AE (**Av**)	You set the aperture and the camera sets the shutter speed for proper exposure.
Shutter-priority AE (**Tv**)	You set the shutter speed and the camera sets the aperture for proper exposure.
Program AE (**P**)	The camera automatically sets the shutter speed and aperture.
Scene Intelligent Auto ()	The camera analyzes the scene and chooses the proper settings, such as shutter speed, aperture, ISO, and focus mode. It also activates the flash if needed.
Flash off ()	Performs the same function as the Scene Intelligent Auto mode () but does not activate the flash.
Creative Auto (CA)	The default setting is the same as Scene Intelligent Auto mode (), except that you have more options, such as depth-of-field adjustments, choosing the drive mode, and deciding whether to fire the flash. Press the Quick Control/Print button () to see the available options on the LCD screen.
Portrait ()	This mode blurs the background so that your subject is the central focus. This mode works best with a long lens.
Landscape ()	Use this mode when you want a large depth of field and crisp images. Note that it enhances the green and blue colors in your image. This mode works best with a wide-angle lens.
Close-up ()	This mode is for photographing small subjects that are close to your lens. A long or macro lens is optimal for this setting.
Sports ()	Ideal for action photography, this mode prevents the blurring of moving objects, such as active children or athletics.
Special Scene Mode (SCN)	This mode houses the Night Portrait (), Handheld Night Scene (), and HDR Backlight () modes. Press the Quick Control/Print button () to see these options on the LCD screen.
Night Portrait ()	When photographing people at night, this mode can help you capture as much of the background light as possible by slowing the shutter speed. Use a tripod to minimize camera shake or hold the camera as steady as possible.
Handheld Night Scene ()	When you don't have a tripod, this mode can help you capture handheld night shots. It accomplishes this by quickly shooting and combining four exposures.
HDR Backlight ()	This mode takes three quick shots at different exposures, and then combines them to create better highlight and shadow detail. For best results, use a tripod with this mode.

The Bottom of the Camera

The following items are located on the bottom of your camera:

- **Tripod socket.** Use this threaded hole to attach tripod plates or attachments.
- **Battery.** Your camera uses an LP-E8 battery pack. It takes approximately 2 hours to fully charge.

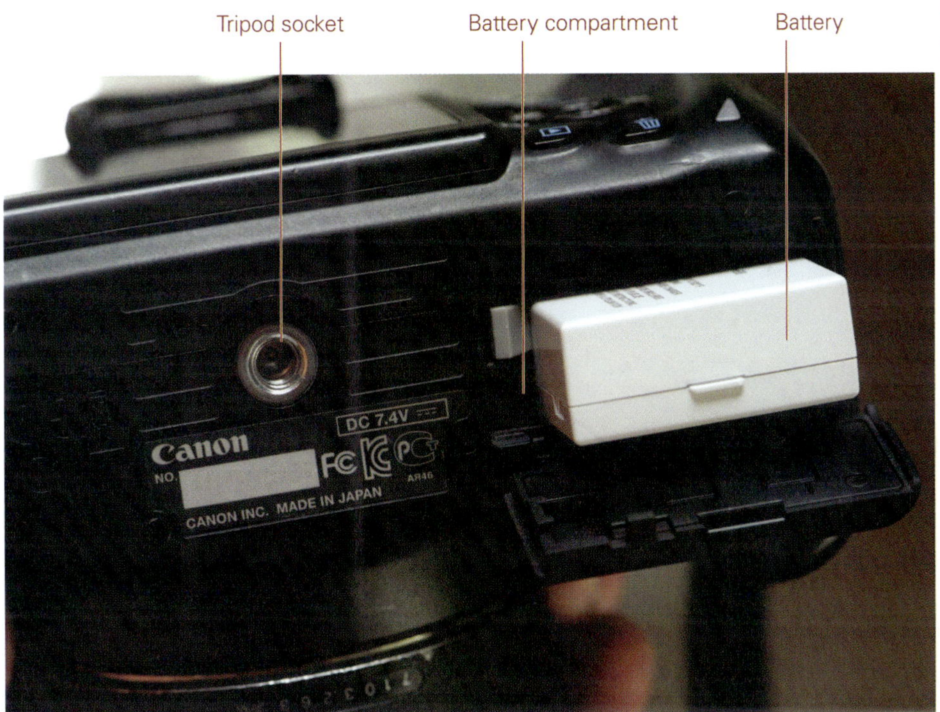

1.3 The bottom of the Canon EOS Rebel T5i/700D.

NOTE A battery grip (BG-E8) is available for your Canon T5i/700D. This accessory holds two LP-E8 battery packs and allows for easier vertical shooting.

The Front of the Camera

The front of the camera features important things like the lens, and the flash (ϟ) and Depth-of-Field Preview (⊠) buttons.

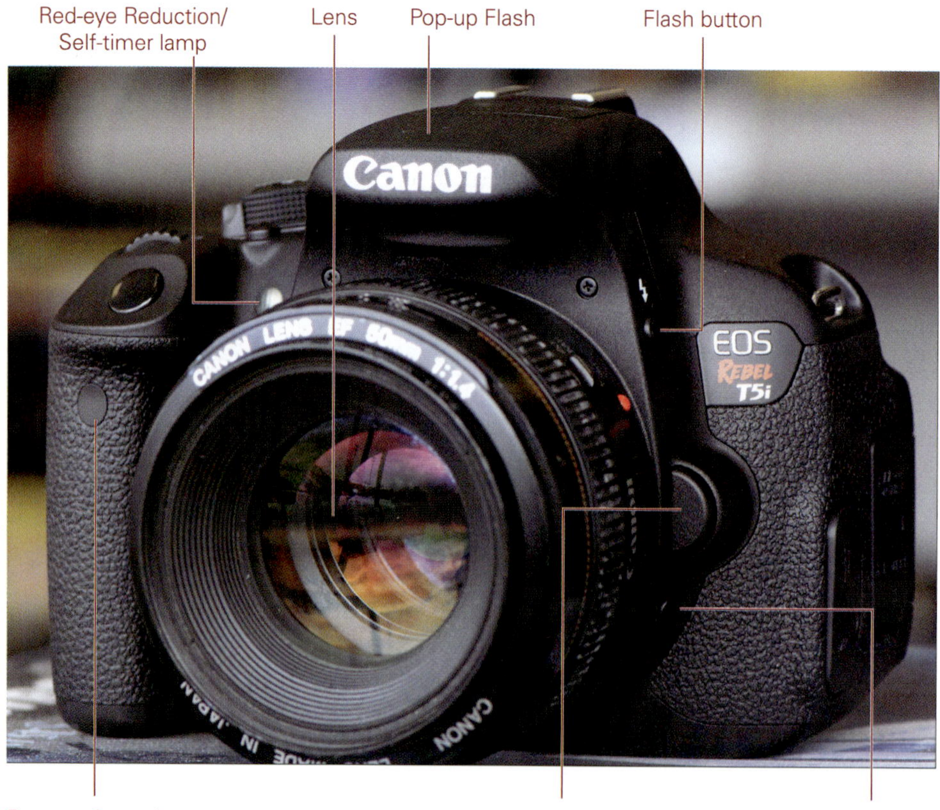

1.4 The front of the Canon EOS Rebel T5i/700D.

The following buttons and features are found on the front of your camera:

- **Flash.** The built-in pop-up flash is a handy feature in low- and backlit situations. It syncs between 1/60 and 1/200 second. The effective distance of the flash depends on the aperture and ISO settings and the lens that you are using. I don't recommend using flash for subjects farther than 12 feet from your camera.

- **Flash button (⚡).** You have more control over your camera when using the Creative Zone modes because they prevent the pop-up flash from activating, even if it's dark. If you need additional light and don't have an external flash, press the Flash button (⚡) to activate the built-in flash.
- **Depth-of-Field Preview button ().** It is sometimes helpful to know what the depth of field in your photo will look like in advance. The Depth-of-Field Preview button () closes down the aperture so you can see the depth of field before you take your picture. In other words, you can see which parts of your image are in and out of focus.
- **Red-eye Reduction/Self-timer lamp.** When Red-eye reduction is enabled, this lamp lights up when you press the shutter button. To enable this option, press the Menu button (**MENU**), and then select Red-eye reduc., located at the bottom of Shooting menu 1 (). This lamp also blinks during the Self-timer () exposure countdown if you enable that option.
- **Remote Control sensor.** Point a camera remote (such as the RC-6) at this location to trigger your camera's shutter.
- **Lens Release button.** Press this button (on the right side of the front of your camera) to release the lens, and then turn the lens counterclockwise to remove it. Remember to hold onto both the lens and the camera. To attach a Canon-dedicated lens, point the camera away from you. Rotate the lens until the red or white dots on both the camera and lens are aligned. Attach the lens to the camera lens mount, and then turn the lens to the left until you hear a click and the lens stops turning.

1

The Back of the Camera

The back of your camera is where the action takes place. Most of the options and controls are accessible from here, including menus, photo information, and standard functions. The LCD touchscreen adds additional functionality compared to other cameras — many standard functions are available just by touching an icon on the screen. The available menu options depend on which mode you are using. For example, you have fewer menu options when you use the Basic Zone modes.

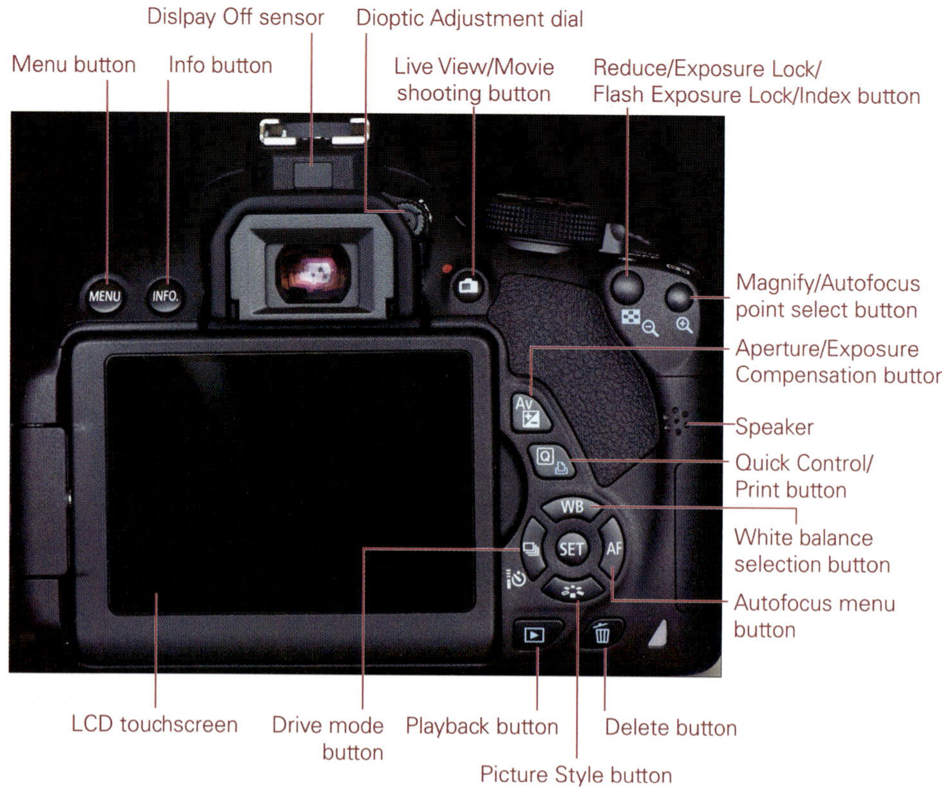

1.5 The back of the Canon EOS Rebel T5i/700D.

The following buttons and options are available on the back of your camera:

- **Menu button (MENU).** Pressing this button takes you to the menu screen. You have fewer menu options available when the camera is in the following Basic Zone modes: Scene Intelligent Auto (A+), Flash off (⚡̸), Creative Auto (CA), Portrait (👤), Landscape (⛰), Close-up (🌷), Sports (🏃), and Special Scene (SCN). There are three additional mode options located under Special Scene (SCN): Night Portrait (🌙), Handheld Night Scene (📷), and HDR backlight (☀). The menus are divided into the following six groups:
    - **The Shooting menu (📷).** This menu includes options for taking photographs.
    - **The Movie shooting menu (🎥).** Here is where you find the options for creating videos.
    - **The Live View shooting menu (▣).** These options are for setting the Live View functions.

- **The Playback menu (▶).** This menu contains options for reviewing images and postproduction.
- **The Setup menu (🔧).** This menu is packed with camera operation functions.
- **My Menu (★).** Here, you can set up your own menu of favorite settings.

CROSS REF Chapter 2 explains all of the menu options in detail.

- **Info button (INFO.).** Press the Playback button (▶), select an image using the Cross keys (✣), and then press the Info button (**INFO.**). It offers four informational display options about your photographs, including two with histograms. When you press the Info button (**INFO.**) when the LCD screen is blank, a display appears with statistics about your camera, including how much free space is on the memory card and which color space you are using. When using the Live View Shooting (◘) or Movie ('🎥) modes, press the Info button (**INFO.**) to display the available functions and mode options.
- **Display Off sensor.** This sensor detects your eye moving toward the viewfinder and turns off the LCD screen. When you move your eye away from the camera, the LCD screen turns back on. This helps prevent glare from hitting your eye when trying to look through the viewfinder. This feature does not work in the Live View Shooting mode (◘). You can turn the sensor off in Setup menu 2 (🔧).
- **Dioptric Adjustment dial.** This dial, located above and to the right of the viewfinder, adjusts the viewfinder's clarity. To customize the clarity to your requirements, focus on the nine autofocus (AF) points in the viewfinder, and then move the dial left or right until the points are sharp.
- **Live View Shooting button (◘).** This button activates the Live View shooting mode (◘) on the LCD screen. This option allows you to watch what's happening live through the lens without looking through the viewfinder. It is also used for starting and stopping movie capture when shooting in Movie mode ('🎥). You can also tap the Magnify button (🔍) in the Live View shooting mode (◘) to magnify a scene.
- **Aperture/Exposure Compensation Button (Av±).** This button has two options when you are shooting in any of the following Creative Zone modes: Manual (**M**), Aperture-priority AE (**Av**), Shutter-priority AE (**Tv**), or Program AE (**P**). When in Manual mode (**M**), use the Main dial to adjust the shutter speed. When you press the Aperture/Exposure Compensation button (Av±), the Main dial switches to aperture control. When you are shooting in the Program AE (**P**), Shutter-priority

AE (**Tv**), or Aperture-priority AE (**Av**) modes, press this button, and then use the Main dial (Main dial icon) to adjust the exposure compensation as many as 5 stops.

- **Reduce/Exposure Lock (✱)/Flash Exposure Lock (⚡✱)/Index button (Index icon).** This button has four uses. In Playback mode (▶), it reduces magnified images. It also allows you to lock an exposure when recomposing a shot, which is helpful in high-contrast or backlit situations. It also serves as the Flash Exposure Lock (⚡✱), preventing your flash from readjusting its exposure. This allows you to recompose your image without worrying that the flash will under- or overexpose your image. When you view your images in Playback mode (▶), this button serves as the Index Display and shows multiple photographs at one time on the LCD screen.
- **Magnify (Magnify icon)/Autofocus point select (AF point icon) button.** This button has two uses. First, it magnifies your photos when you review them in the Playback mode (▶). You also can magnify the scene on the LCD screen if the camera is not in Face Tracking mode (AF face tracking icon). If you are in a Creative Zone mode and Live View shooting mode (Live View icon) is turned off, this button can be used in conjunction with the Main dial (Main dial icon) to select autofocus (AF) points.

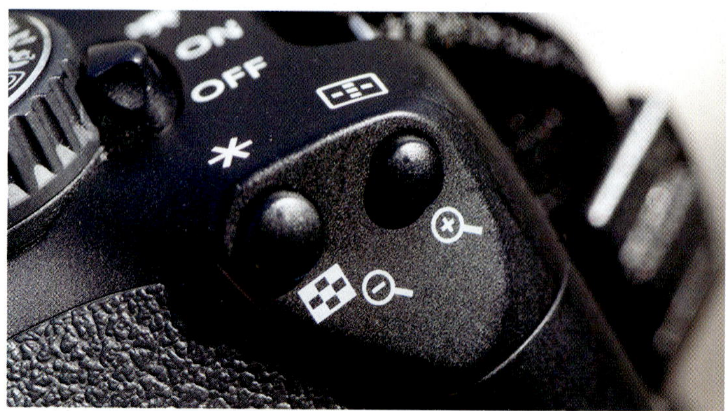

1.6 The Reduce/Exposure Lock/Flash Exposure Lock/Index and Magnify/Autofocus point select buttons are located on the back of your camera on the upper-right side.

- **Speaker.** The speaker plays the sound from videos and slide shows.
- **Setting button (SET).** This button works like a return or input button on a computer. It affirms the highlighted setting you want to engage on a menu, option, or function.
- **Delete button (🗑).** When you want to delete an image or video during playback, press the Delete button (🗑).

- **Autofocus menu button (AF).** In the Basic Zone modes, autofocus is set according to the mode and scene, and it cannot be adjusted. In Playback mode (▶) and when maneuvering through menus, this button acts as the right Cross key (✣) button. In the Creative Zone modes, the Autofocus menu button (AF) has the following three options:
  - **One-shot AF mode (ONE SHOT).** This locks on your subject after you press the shutter button halfway.
  - **AI Servo focusing mode (AI SERVO).** Use this mode to follow-focus on your subject.
  - **AI Focus (AI FOCUS).** This setting defaults to the One-shot AF mode (ONE SHOT) and switches to AI Servo focusing mode (AI SERVO) if the camera detects movement.
- **Access Lamp.** When this light is on, it means the camera is recording an image. Make sure this light is off before removing the memory card or opening the battery compartment.
- **Picture Style button ( ).** Your camera offers many options for creating stunning images. The Picture Styles are designed to enhance your photographs, depending on the type of scene you are photographing. For example, if you are shooting a landscape, using the Picture Style Landscape mode ( ) enhances the blues and greens, and increases the sharpness of your image. The Portrait Picture Style ( ) softens the image. You can also make your own Picture Styles in the Picture Style Editor software that is included with your camera. In Playback mode (▶) and when navigating through menus, this button acts as the down Cross key (✣) button.

CROSS REF Full descriptions of the Picture Style options can be found in Chapter 3.

- **Playback button (▶).** This option allows you to review your images. You can use the Main dial ( ) or a finger swipe on the LCD screen to advance to the next image.
- **Drive mode button ( ).** This button can be used in any exposure mode. It allows you to shoot one image at a time or take continuous shots of up to 5 frames per second (fps). You also have the following three self-timer options: 2 seconds, 10 seconds, and multiple shots with 10-second countdowns. In Playback mode (▶) and when navigating through menus, this button acts as the left Cross key (✣) button.

- **White balance selection button (WB).** This button lets you change color tones in your photographs when the camera is in a Creative Zone mode. Use it to adjust the color of the environment to appear more natural. For example, photographing in a room with tungsten bulbs as the main light source produces a yellow cast in in your photographs. If you select the Tungsten white balance setting (☀), the camera adds a blue filter to the scene to neutralize the yellow. In Playback mode (▶) and when navigating through menus, this button acts as the up Cross key (✥) button.

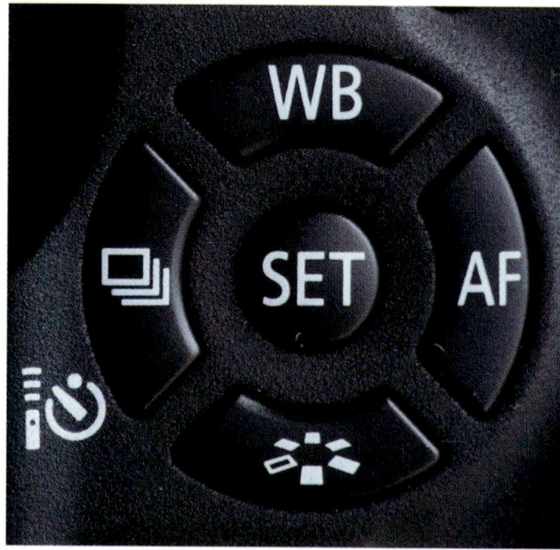

1.7 These buttons on the back of your camera are also used as Cross keys to navigate around the LCD screen.

CROSS REF For more about white balance, see Chapter 3.

- **Quick Control/Print button (Q).** When using either the Creative or Basic Zone modes, use the Quick Control/Print button (Q) to make active options available for that specific mode. For example, if you want to change your shutter speed while shooting in Shutter-priority AE mode (**Tv**), press the Quick Control/Print button (Q). The shutter speed options activate on the LCD screen. The Print function allows you to print directly to your home printer when the camera is connected to it with the supplied USB cable. If your printer is PictBridge-compatible, it is also compatible with your camera.
- **LCD touchscreen.** The screen on the back of your camera is a vari-angle LCD touchscreen. It is covered in detail later in this chapter.

The Sides of the Camera

The sides of your camera are dedicated to electronic and computer functions. With the lens pointing away from you, the input and output terminals are located on the left side. The memory card slot is on the right side. Use memory cards with as much space as possible. If you plan to shoot a lot of video, I recommend using cards with more than 8GB of memory. If you want to transfer photos and videos wirelessly to your computer, consider purchasing an Eye-Fi card. The settings for the Eye-Fi card are found under Setup menu 1 (🔧).

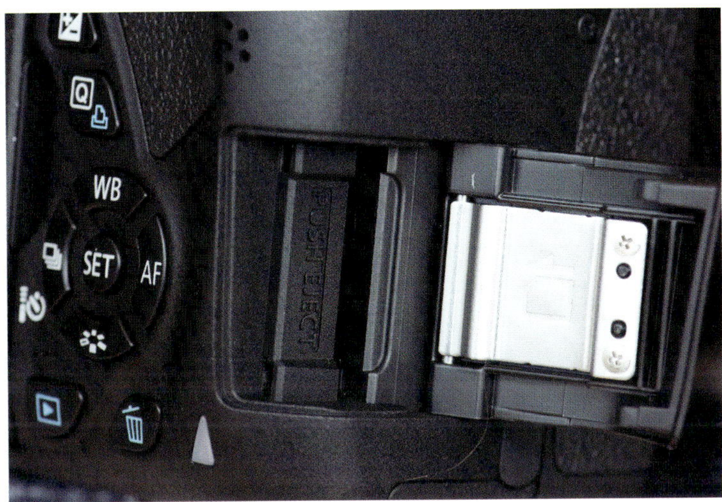

1.8 The memory card slot is located on the right side of the camera.

The following terminals are located on the left side of the camera:

- **A/V Out Digital.** This terminal is for connecting your camera to a non-HD television or monitor. An AVC-DC400ST cable is required.
- **HDMI out.** Use this socket to connect the camera to an HD television or monitor to view your photographs or movies on a larger screen. You will also need an HDMI cable HTC-100.
- **Remote terminal.** This is where you plug in a remote control, which allows you to keep the shutter open for long exposures. It is located above the microphone terminal.
- **External microphone terminal.** If you plan to produce professional-quality videos, you need an external microphone. Your camera has a built-in microphone, but it also picks up camera noise, which is unacceptable for a good video presentation.

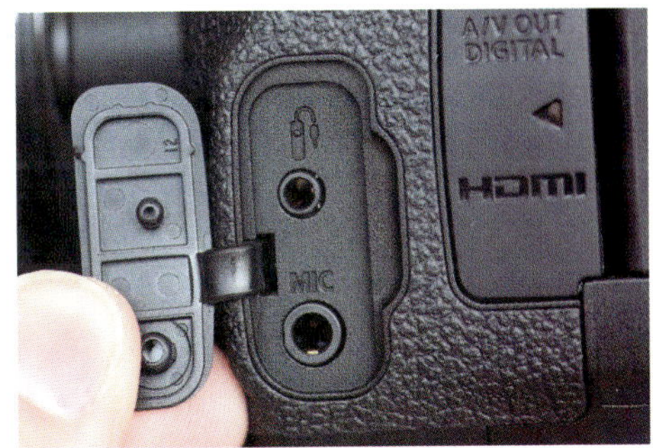

1.9 The connection terminals are located under the two covers on the left side of your camera.

CROSS REF The A/V and HDMI outputs are discussed in more detail in Chapter 9.

Lens Controls

Each lens has its own set of controls, and they vary depending on the purpose it was designed for and the company that manufactures it. You must use a lens with a dedicated Canon lens mount.

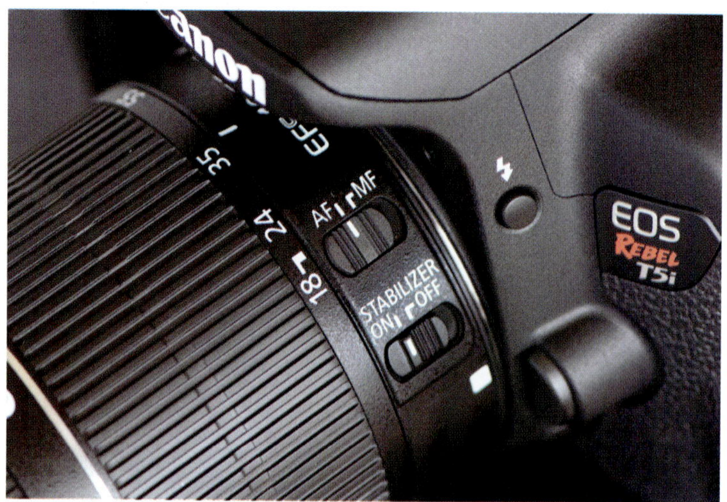

1.10 The Canon T5i/700D 18-55mm kit lens has Image Stabilization and focus switches on the left.

Here are a few common features and controls you find on lenses:

- **Focus mode.** The focus mode lets you switch back and forth between manual and autofocus.
- **Focus ring.** If you switch your lens to Manual focus mode (**MF**), you use this ring to focus.
- **Image Stabilization switch.** This switch turns Image Stabilization on or off in lenses that have it. Image Stabilization helps prevent blurring in images when handholding the camera and using slow shutter speeds; however, it will not prevent the blurring of a moving subject.
- **Distance scale.** Many lenses have a distance scale on top that can be used to estimate focus in feet or meters. The low number represents the closest your

lens can be to an object to focus properly. Infinity is used when you want to focus at a distance, such as when shooting a landscape.

- **Zoom ring.** If you are using a zoom lens, turning the zoom ring sets your desired lens focal length.

The Viewfinder Display

1

The viewfinder is your photographic dashboard. The display only shows information relevant to the scene or your choice of options. It lets you know if the flash is ready to fire, if the exposure is correct, and if your subject is in focus.

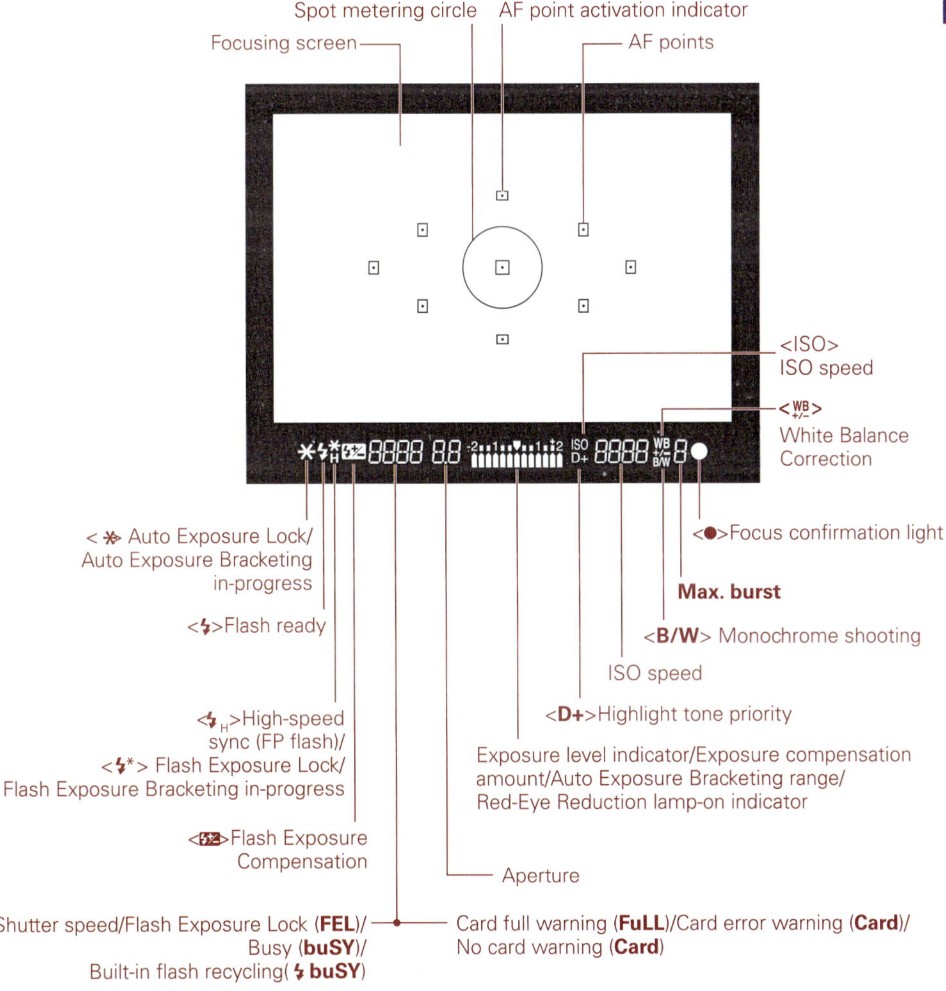

1.11 The information you see in the viewfinder.

The following are the indicators you see in the viewfinder (the options displayed depend on the mode you are using):

- **Focusing screen.** This is the electronic screen that you see when you look through the viewfinder to focus the camera.
- **Spot metering circle.** This is the area the Spot metering mode ([•]) reads to determine the proper exposure.
- **AF points.** There are nine autofocus points on the focus screen that can be used to focus the camera.
- **AF point activation indicator.** Each of the nine autofocus points light up round dot indicators as the AF points are activated.
- **ISO speed (ISO).** This setting displays the camera's ISO setting.
- **White Balance Correction (WB+/-).** This lets you know that a white balance correction is being applied.
- **Focus confirmation light.** This light indicates that the camera believes your image is in focus. This is especially helpful when focusing manually.
- **Max. burst.** This is the number of photographs your camera buffer can hold before it is full.
- **Monochrome shooting (B/W).** This lights up if you are using a black-and-white or monochromatic option.
- **Highlight tone priority (D+).** This lets you know that Custom Function 3, Highlight tone priority (D+) is on. This option improves highlight detail in your photos.
- **Exposure level indicator.** This lets you know how much your image is under- or overexposed based on the camera's internal light meter.
- **Exposure compensation amount.** This indicates how much of an increase or decrease in exposure is set.
- **Auto Exposure Bracketing range.** This lets you know how many stops under- and overexposed your bracket is set.
- **Red-eye Reduction lamp-on indicator.** This lets you know that the Red-eye Reduction option is on.
- **Aperture.** This tells you at what aperture your camera is set.

- **Card full warning.** When the memory card is full, this warning alerts you. You cannot take any more photographs until you delete some images or replace the card.
- **Card error or no card warning (Card).** When you see this warning, your camera is experiencing an error reading or writing to the memory card, or there is no card in your camera.
- **Shutter speed.** This tells you at which shutter speed the camera is set.
- **Flash Exposure Lock (ϟ*).** When this icon appears, it means that the Flash Exposure Lock is engaged.
- **Busy (buSY).** When you see this, the camera is still processing images.
- **Built-in flash recycling.** This indicates that the built-in flash is recharging.
- **Flash Exposure Compensation (ϟ±).** This light comes on when Flash Exposure Compensation is in use.
- **High-speed sync (ϟH).** This indicates that High-speed sync is engaged on your speedlite.
- **Flash Exposure Lock/Flash Exposure Bracketing in-progress (ϟ*).** This icon indicates that the Flash Exposure Lock and Flash Exposure Bracketing are in use.
- **Built-in flash recycling.** This indicates that the built-in flash is recharging.
- **Flash-ready (ϟ).** When your flash is ready to fire, this icon lights up.
- **Auto Exposure Lock/Auto Exposure Bracketing in progress (*).** This indicates that the Auto Exposure Lock or Auto Exposure Bracketing is in use.

1

The LCD Touchscreen and Live View Mode

The LCD touchscreen on your Canon Rebel T5i/700D adds a flexible dimension to your camera. It gives you a large, adjustable screen to use while shooting photos and video. The touchscreen also makes features easy to access. You use the LCD screen to review photos and videos the same way you would on a smartphone. Swipe your fingers across the LCD screen to view the next image. Pinch or spread your fingers to zoom in or out of an image.

NOTE The utility software that comes with your camera allows you to connect it to a computer and take photos remotely.

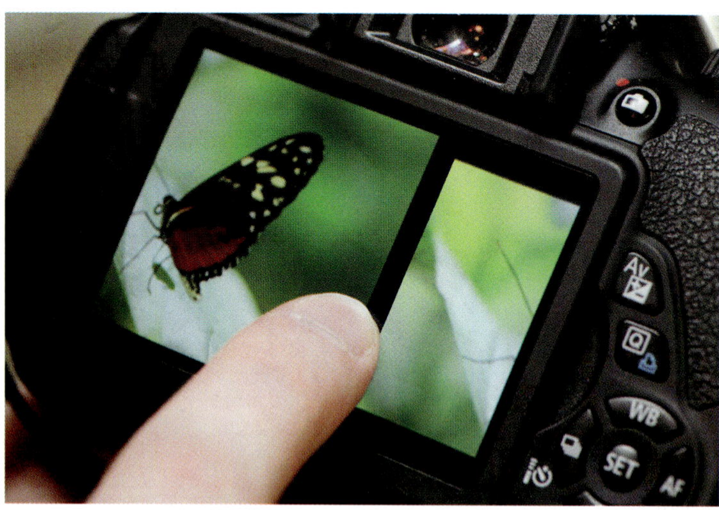

1.12 Use your finger to swipe to the next image.

The Live View shooting mode (▣) is a useful feature, particularly when you are shooting video, because the touchscreen menus are found on the edges of the LCD screen. To turn on Live View mode (▣), press the Live View button (▣) located to the right of your camera's eyepiece. The default focus system for Live View is Continuous autofocus. There are options to make adjustments using the four information displays. Each time that you press the Info button (**INFO.**) the display switches to the next option. If you don't want to use the Live View mode (▣), disable it by pressing the Menu button (**MENU**), and then select the Live View menu (▣).

CROSS REF For more information about the Live View Shooting mode (▣), see Chapter 8.

The following list covers how to navigate the options and views available in the Live View Shooting mode (▣):

- **Making selections.** Menu options differ from the Creative to Basic Zone modes. You have more options in Creative Zone modes. When you want to make a selection, touch the icon on the LCD screen, and additional options appear (if applicable).
- **Viewing photos.** To view your photos, press the Playback button (▶), which shows the last photograph you created. Swipe one finger across the screen to scroll back to the previous picture. Move your finger to the left to view the newest image, and to the right to view older photos or those with lower file

numbers. If you use two fingers when you swipe, the camera jumps the number of images set in Playback menu 2 (▶). When you place two fingers in the middle of the screen and spread them apart, you zoom in to the photograph. When you pinch your fingers together, you zoom out. You can also use the Cross keys (✥▴▾◂▸) to navigate through your photos.

- **Viewing videos.** Press the Playback button (▶). You will know which files are videos because they have a large Playback icon (▶) displayed on the LCD screen; press it and the video starts playing. There are additional options at the bottom of the LCD screen to fast-forward, rewind, turn the sound off, or edit the video. Use the Main dial (dial icon) to control the volume.
- **Still information display.** When shooting photos, there are standard information displays for the Creative and Basic Zone modes (these do not appear in the Live View shooting mode (Live View icon)). Press the Quick Control/Print button (Q icon) to adjust the available options.
- **Movie information display.** This display includes some of the same information that the still display does, including white balance, AF method, and Picture Styles. However, it also includes the video size and frame rate. Like the still information, you have a few more options when you use the Creative Zone modes. For example, you don't have white balance or Picture Style options available if you're using a Basic Zone mode.

1

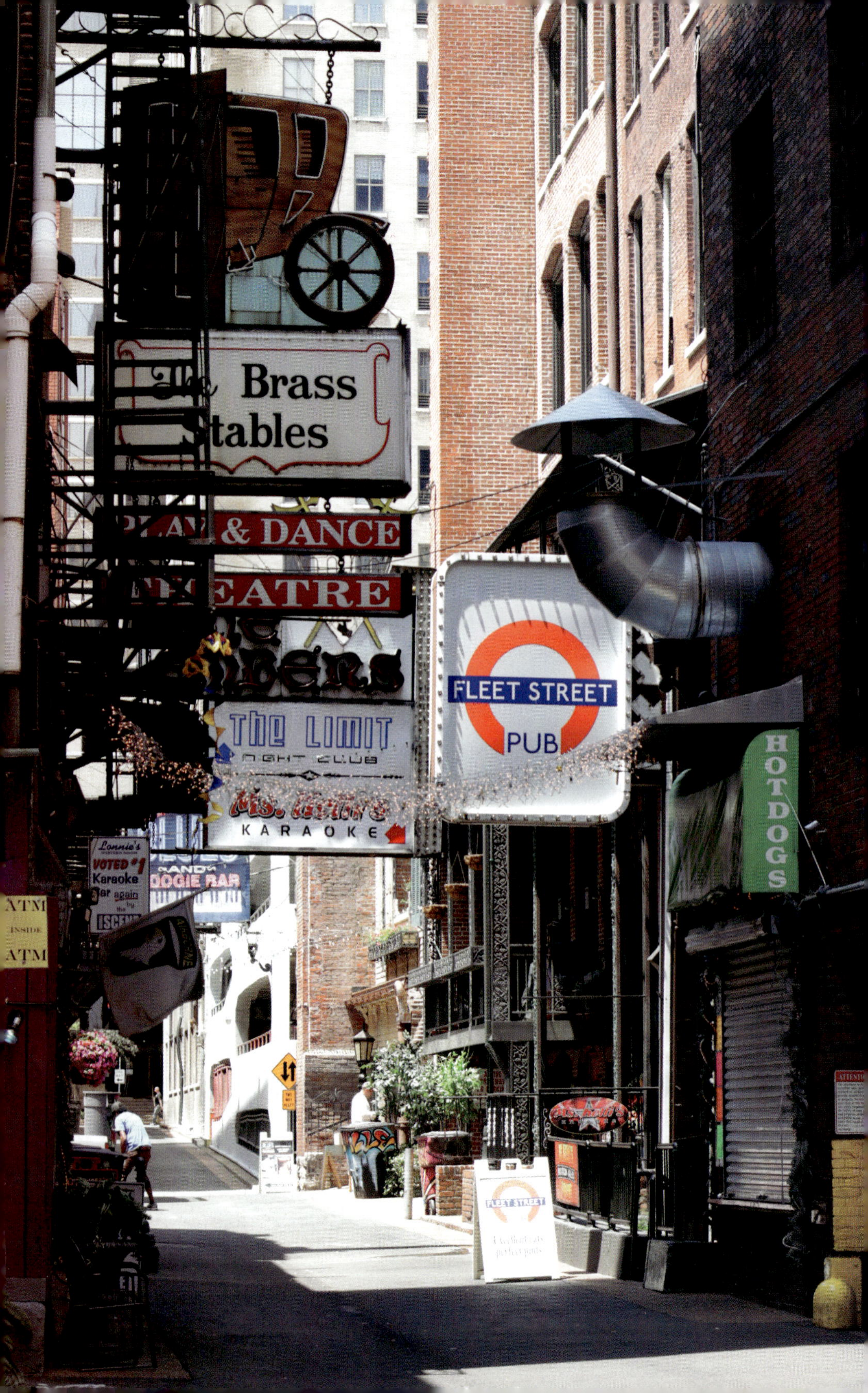
The Brass
Stables
& DANCE
EATRE
The LIMIT
NIGHT CLUB
KARAOKE
FLEET STREET
PUB
HOT
DOGS
VOTED #1
Karaoke
ATM
INSIDE
ATM
FLEET STREET

CHAPTER 2

Setting Up the Canon EOS Rebel T5i/700D

This chapter covers the menus displayed on the LCD screen when you press the menu button (**MENU**) on the back of the camera. I also share an overview of what each option does. Generally, each menu has a theme, such as the shooting, movie, setup, and playback menus. Some menus are visible only when using specific modes, such as movie shooting ('🎥). It's not easy to remember where all of the functions are located within the menus, so take some time to review where the key settings are, such as long exposure noise reduction, and the custom and wireless functions. The menu color codes can help you remember the locations of your favorite settings. If you continue to have trouble finding certain functions, make sure that you keep your *Digital Field Guide* with you for reference.

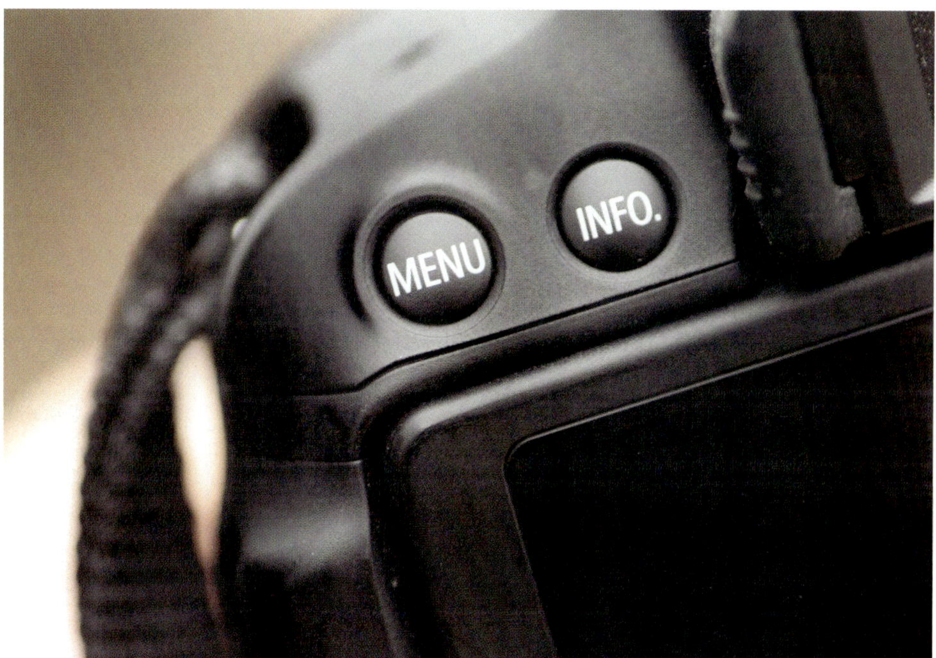

The Menu button is on the upper-left side on the back of your camera.

The Shooting Menus

If you use the Creative Zone modes — Program AE (**P**), Shutter-priority AE (**Tv**), Aperture-priority AE (**Av**), and Manual (**M**) — you have three shooting menus available to you. When you use the Basic Zone modes — Scene Intelligent Auto (icon), Flash off (icon), Creative Auto (CA), Portrait (icon), Landscape (icon), Close-up (icon), Sports (icon), Night Portrait (icon), Handheld Night Scene (icon), and HDR backlight (icon) — only Shooting menu 1 (icon) is available.

When you are using any of the shooting modes, you can press the Info button (**INFO.**) on the back of the camera next to the Menu button (**MENU**) to display a screen containing many of your camera's major functions.

Shooting menu 1

This first menu is for both the Basic and Creative Zone modes. Flash control is the only option not available when your camera is set to a Basic Zone mode. When you are in Movie shooting mode (icon), flash control and red-eye reduction are not available on the menu list. I find that Image quality is the most common option I select from this list.

Settings and corrective functions

The following list of options is available in Shooting menu 1 (icon):

- **Image quality.** You have 10 options here. RAW (RAW) is the option with the highest quality and Small 3 (S3) is the smallest. The RAW (RAW) and Large fine (L) combination creates both image types at the same time.
- **Beep.** The beep sounds when the camera has achieved focus, during self-timer countdown, and when you press a button on the LCD touchscreen. Select Enable or Disable to turn the beep on or off. You can also turn the beep off for the LCD touchscreen only, and leave it on for both the focus and self-timer.

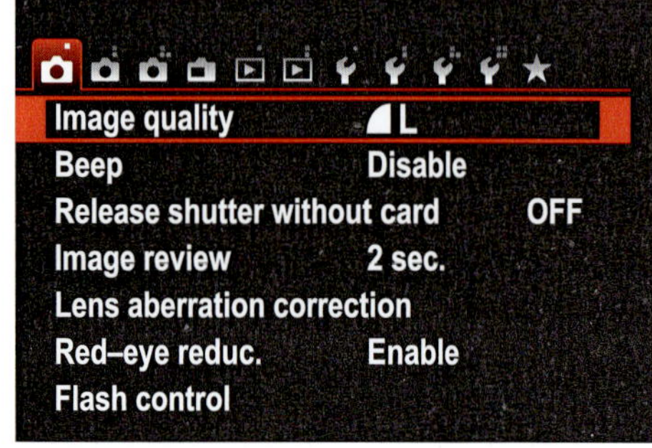

2.1 Shooting menu 1.

- **Release shutter without card.** This option allows you to shoot even if there is no memory card in your camera. The default is Off, which prevents you from taking a photograph without a card. I recommend leaving this off. It's no fun finding out later that you took a bunch of pictures without a card to record them.

- **Image review.** After you take a photograph, the image displays on the LCD screen. This option gives you the choice of turning Image review off, or setting the review time to 2, 4, or 8 seconds. There is also an option called hold. This leaves the image displayed until the Auto power off timer (found under Setup menu 2) turns off the display or you press a button on the camera, such as the shutter or Menu (**MENU**) button.
- **Lens aberration correction.** Some lenses produce images with peripheral light falloff, which creates darker corners in your photos. This is also known as *vignetting*. Other lenses create *chromatic aberration*, which means that the color fringes along light and dark (high-contrast) lines because the colors traveling through the lens are not able to focus on the same point. If you have these issues with your lens, this selection is an option to help correct it. If you photograph in the RAW file format, you can also make adjustments using the Canon Digital Photo Professional software that came with your camera.
- **Red-eye reduction.** When using flash indoors, the light from it reflects off of your subject's pupils and back into the lens of your camera, making your subject's eyes appear to be red. The closer the flash is to your lens, the greater the chance of red eye. When you enable Red-eye reduction, the camera's red-eye reduction lamp lights up to reduce the size of your subject's pupils, thereby decreasing the chance of red eye. Red-eye reduction does not work in the Flash off (), Landscape (), Sports (), or HDR backlight () modes.

2

Flash control

Selecting this option opens a new menu with the following flash controls:

- **Flash firing.** By default, this option is normally set to Enable, so select Disable when flash is not allowed. This prevents the flash from popping up and firing while using Basic Zone modes. It also disables an external speedlite connected to the camera.

NOTE Disabling the flash from firing does not prevent the AF-assist beam from illuminating in low-light situations.

- **E-TTL II Metering.** This is Through-the-Lens metering for your flash. You have two flash metering options: Evaluative and Average. Evaluative is the default metering option, and it sets the exposure based on the scene the camera reads. I recommend using this option because it allows you to take full advantage of the camera's technology. Average metering averages the light in the entire scene to determine the proper exposure.

- **Flash sync. speed in Av mode.** There are three flash sync options when using a Creative Zone mode in Aperture-priority AE mode (**Av**). Auto ranges from 1/200 second to 30 seconds; this can be an issue if you don't want any blur in your photographs caused by low light. The 1/200 second to 1/60 second auto option prevents the camera from setting the shutter speed below 1/60 second. This helps prevent camera shake and ghosting, which happens when using slower shutter speeds. The third option is a fixed 1/200 second shutter speed. In low light, this setting tends to create a dark or black background.
- **Built-in flash settings.** When you select this option, you are taken to another menu with more options. Normal firing is the default for most flash photography using the pop-up, built-in flash. Easy wireless lets you set the channel you want to use to trigger an external speedlite when it is set to Slave, as shown in Figure 2.2. CustWireless offers more options to set up the camera's built-in flash to your specifications.

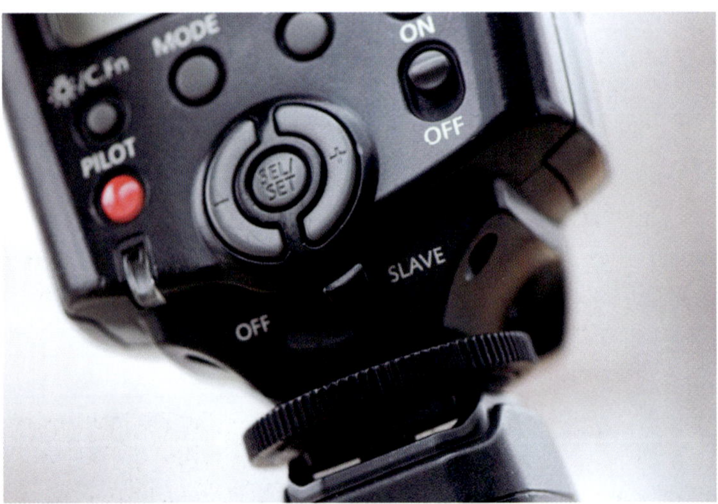

2.2 The switch to turn a speedlite to Slave mode is often found at the base, as shown here on the Canon 430EX.

- **Flash mode E-TTL II.** This option, available under CustWireless, gives you the choice of using Canon's E-TTL II flash metering system or manual metering. Manual is for controlled flash output. This option is recommended for advanced users.
- **Shutter sync.** This selection gives you two curtain sync options. First-curtain sync is the standard option, meaning that the flash triggers immediately after the shutter button is fully pressed. Second-curtain sync delays the curtain until the end of the shutter cycle.

- **Wireless func.** You have three wireless options. The first sets the built-in flash to extend only enough to trigger the external speedlite. The second is designed to trigger multiple speedlites. The third uses the internal flash and external speedlites for exposure. Each wireless function setting adds dedicated options to the menu, such as flash ratio setup and group firing options.
- **Channel.** You have four channels from which to choose for wireless to trigger an external speedlite using the Slave option. Make sure that both the camera and the speedlite are set on the same channel.
- **Exp. comp.** This gives you the opportunity to manually increase or decrease the flash output by 2 stops.
- **External flash func. Setting.** You can set some of your external flash settings from your camera's menu using this setting.
- **External flash C.Fn Setting.** This custom function setting varies depending on your flash model.
- **Clear settings.** If you want to set the camera's flash settings back to the defaults, select clear settings. You have the option of clearing the built-in and external flash settings, as well as the flash Custom Functions.

2

Shooting menu 2

Exposure, color, and contrast options are found under Shooting menu 2 (). Some of the most helpful options are Auto Exposure Bracketing (AEB), Picture Style, and Metering mode. These options are only available in the Creative Zone modes. You find the following options in Shooting menu 2 ():

- **Expo.comp./AEB.** This option has two settings. The first (top) is for exposure compensation, which allows you to increase the camera's exposure settings by plus or minus 5 stops. Use the Cross keys () to adjust exposure compensation. The bottom setting is the stop range between exposures for Auto Exposure Bracketing (AEB). Use the main dial () to adjust the stop range between brackets.

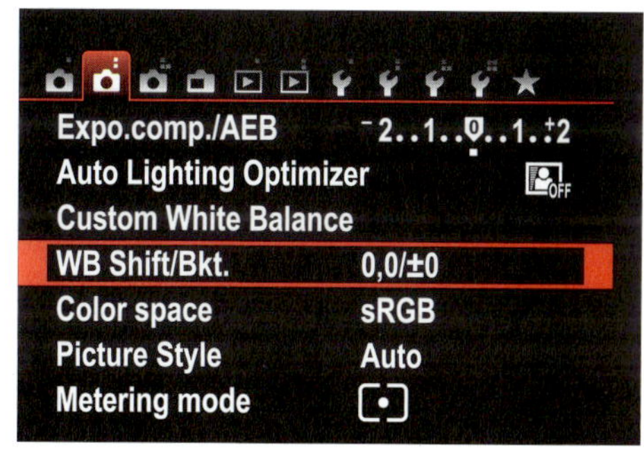

2.3 **Shooting menu 2.**

- **Auto Lighting Optimizer.** This setting automatically corrects the brightness and contrast of your image when you create JPEG files. You have four choices: Off, Low, Standard, and High. The default setting is Standard. This feature improves underexposed images. It helps bring out shadow detail in the dark areas of an image and automatically adds contrast without blowing out highlights. I recommend that you turn this option off or leave it on Standard, depending on your exposure preferences.
- **Custom White Balance.** Use Custom White Balance when you want to set white balance based on the light of a specific environment. For example, you may want to balance the greenish light found in many school gymnasiums. To do this, fill the frame with a white piece of paper and take a photograph of it in the same lighting you are balancing. Using the Custom White Balance setting, select the image of the white piece of paper (which will reflect the color of the light in the room), and the camera sets the custom white balance based on the selected image.
- **WB Shift/Bkt.** Just like bracketing for exposure, you can bracket for white balance. This selection is best for advanced users who are familiar with color temperature conversion. It gives you bracketing options between blue and amber, or green and magenta. So, in one shot you create three images with different color balances.
- **Color space.** You have two color spaces from which to choose: sRGB (the default) and Adobe RGB. sRGB is a good choice for e-mail, digital media, and Internet use. Adobe RGB has a larger gamut (that is number of colors) available and is a good choice if your photographs are going to be printed.
- **Picture Style.** These settings are designed to enhance various photographic scenes with sharpness, contrast, saturation, and tone adjustments. The Picture Styles menu and the Picture Styles button on the back of the camera offer the same options. You may select a specific style, adjust a preset style, or create your own style to be stored in the user-defined section.

CROSS REF For more information about Picture Styles, see Chapter 3.

- **Metering mode.** The Canon T5i/700D has four metering modes — the default is Evaluative ([⊙]). This is the recommended option because it sets the exposure for the scene in front of you. The other three options are Partial ([○]), Spot ([·]), and Center-weighted ([ ]) metering.

Shooting menu 3

The third Shooting menu (📷) houses the ISO, noise reduction, and image-quality options. You can only use these options in Creative Zone modes. The following options are available in Shooting menu 3 (📷):

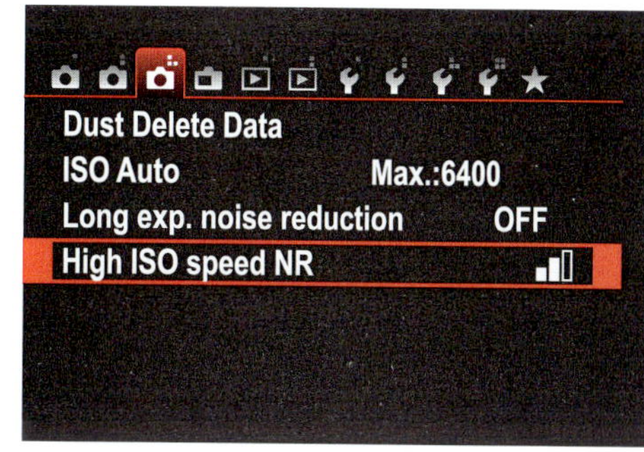

2.4 Shooting menu 3 on your Canon T5i/700D.

- **Dust Delete Data.** This option helps collect data on dust not removed by the self-cleaning sensor. Once you go through the data collection process, it attaches the information to your JPEG and RAW files. This option works in conjunction with the Canon Digital Photo Professional software that comes with your camera to automatically remove dust from your photographs.
- **ISO Auto.** If you don't want your automatic settings to exceed a specific ISO setting, you can set the maximum ISO within the range of ISO 400 to ISO 6400.
- **Long exp. noise reduction.** Long exposures tend to create a lot of noise in photographs. Noise is like visual static. It appears as specks in your image. When enabled, this setting can reduce the noise produced in your images by exposures of 1 second or more. When set on Auto, the camera detects and applies the setting as needed.
- **High ISO speed NR.** This is a Noise Reduction (NR) option. It can remove noise in shadow detail at all ISO settings, but the effect is more noticeable at higher ISO settings.

The Live View Shooting Menu

Press the Live View Shooting mode button (▣) to the right of the viewfinder to view the scene in front of your lens. The LCD touchscreen can swivel 180 degrees horizontally from the camera, which is helpful when shooting self- or family portraits. The screen can also swivel up or down to capture high or low angles. This section covers the options available under the Live View Shooting menu (▣), including the autofocus tracking method, touch options, and grid display.

2

You find the following options in the Live View Shooting menu (■):

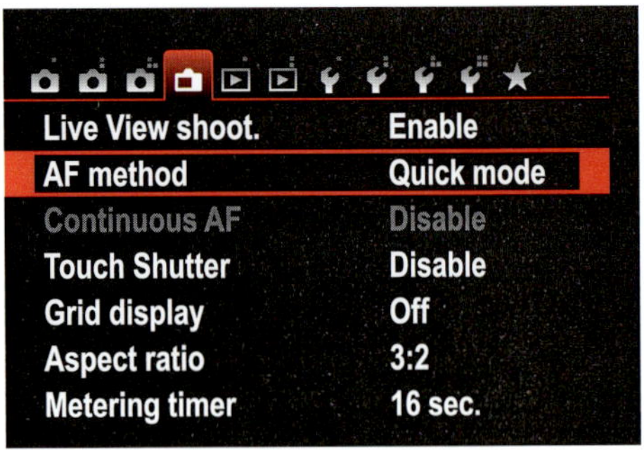

2.5 The Live View shooting menu.

- **Live View shoot.** Here, you can enable or disable Live View.
- **AF method.** This setting offers four focus modes. All of them (except the Quick focus mode AFQuick) use the image sensor to autofocus. The first option is the Face Tracking mode (AF☺), in which the camera focuses on and follows any face it detects. The second is the FlexiZone-Multi mode (AF( )), which uses 31 focal points that also may be manually divided (using the LCD touchscreen or the Setting button (SET)) into one of nine zones. The third is the FlexiZone-Single mode (AF□), in which you can select one of the 31 focal points as the point of focus for your photograph. The last option is the Quick focus mode (AFQuick). It is the fastest focusing option because it uses only nine AF points to focus.
- **Continuous AF.** When the Quick focus mode (AFQuick) is enabled, Continuous AF is automatically turned off.
- **Touch Shutter.** If you enable Touch Shutter, all you have to do is touch the LCD screen to focus and take a photograph. If it is disabled, there is an icon on the bottom left of your screen to enable the option at any time. This option works in all shooting modes.
- **Grid display.** You have two grid display options to help level your camera in comparison to your scene. One is shaped like a tic-tac-toe board, with two horizontal and two vertical lines resulting in nine squares in the grid. The second option contains 24 squares and 15 line intersections to help you compose your image.
- **Aspect ratio.** The *aspect ratio* is the shape in which the camera frames a scene. There are four options available on the T5i: 3:2 (35mm film), 4:3 (old television), 16:9 (HD video standard), and 1:1 (square). The aspect ratio option is only available in the Creative Zone modes.

NOTE RAW images always save at the 3:2 aspect ratio.

- **Metering timer.** Choose this option to select how long exposure settings are displayed on the LCD screen. You can select 4 sec., 16 sec., 30 sec., 1 min., 10 min., or 30 min. This option is available only in the Creative Zone modes (in the Basic Zone modes, the default is 16 sec.).

The Movie Shooting Menus

Your camera has two Movie shooting menus (). These options only display when your camera is set to Movie shooting mode ().

Movie shooting menu 1

The first Movie shooting menu () contains options such as autofocus, grid display, and meter timer. The following list covers all available options in Movie shooting menu 1 ():

2

- **AF method.** These are the same as the AF methods in the Live View shooting menu (), except that you don't have an option for the Quick focus mode (AFQuick). Face tracking (AF) detects a human face and places a focus point over it. FlexiZone-Multi (AF( )) uses multiple points to focus on the subject. FlexiZone-Single (AF□) uses one of the 31 available points of focus. You can use the Setting button (SET) to reset your focus to the center of your screen.

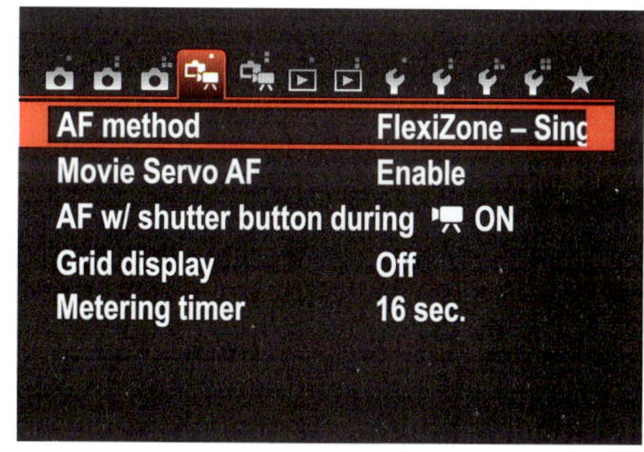

2.6 The five choices available in Movie shooting menu 1.

- **Movie Servo AF.** This selection turns the Movie Servo AF feature (SERVO AF) on or off — it is on by default. If either you or your subject is moving, the Movie Servo AF (SERVO AF) will follow-focus on your subject. If you are concerned about focusing noise from your lens, consider using one of the Canon STM lenses designed to limit noise.

NOTE When the Movie Servo AF setting (SERVO AF) is enabled, turn off the camera before switching the lens to Manual focus mode (**MF**).

- **AF w/shutter button during 'ᴿ.** Your camera allows you to take still photos while shooting in Movie mode ('ᴿ). The One shot selection (the default) is activated by pressing the shutter button halfway. It then refocuses for your still photograph while you are shooting your video. When this option is turned off, you can still take photographs, but the camera will not refocus.
- **Grid display.** Your camera has two grid display options useful for leveling your scenes. The grids are displayed on the LCD screen. This option is turned off by default.
- **Metering timer.** This sets how long the exposure settings are displayed on the LCD screen. This option is only available in the Creative Zone modes. In the Basic Zone modes, the default is automatically set to 16 seconds.

Movie shooting menu 2

The following options are available in Movie shooting menu 2 ( ):

- **Movie rec. size.** You have four movie recording options for each of the two video systems: NTSC and PAL. *NTSC (National Television System Committee)* is the standard video system used in North America and Japan (among other countries). *PAL (Phase Alternating Line)* is the standard recording format for Europe, much of Africa, and China (among other countries). Each of these settings gives you a combination of movie image sizes in pixels and frame rate (frames per second). The frame rate options for NTSC are based on recording at 30 frames per second (29.97). PAL is based on 25 frames per second. The third statistic displayed is how much recording time you have before you run out of storage space on your memory card. The maximum recording time is 29 minutes, 59 seconds.

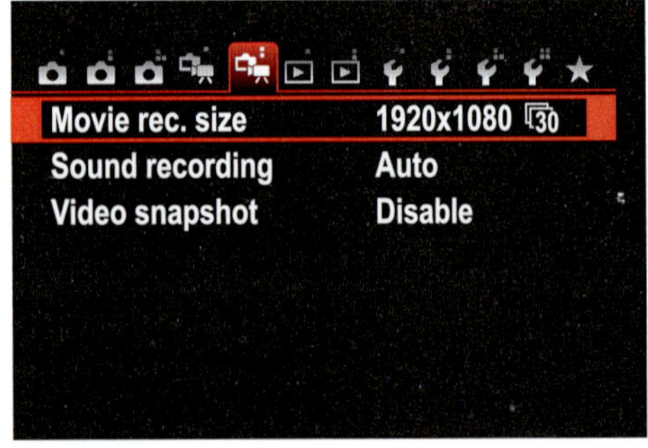

2.7 Movie shooting menu 2.

- **Sound recording.** This selection turns the microphone (located on top of the camera) on or off. You have five sound recording options: Auto, Manual, Disable, Wind filter, and Attenuator. If an external microphone is plugged into the camera, it is given priority.
- **Video snapshot.** Your camera can create quick snapshots and save them to albums. When this setting is turned on, you can adjust the length of your clips to

2, 4, or 8 seconds. Disable this option if you want to create movies longer than your selected short clip length.

CROSS REF For more information about the Video snapshot option, see Chapter 8.

The Playback Menus

The two Playback menus (▶) are where you find the options for viewing your photographs. The first menu focuses on postproduction and the second is where you find the image review options.

Playback menu 1

2

Playback menu 1 (▶) contains postproduction features, including options to print your photographs, create books, and protect or erase images. You also find the camera's creative filters here. The options are:

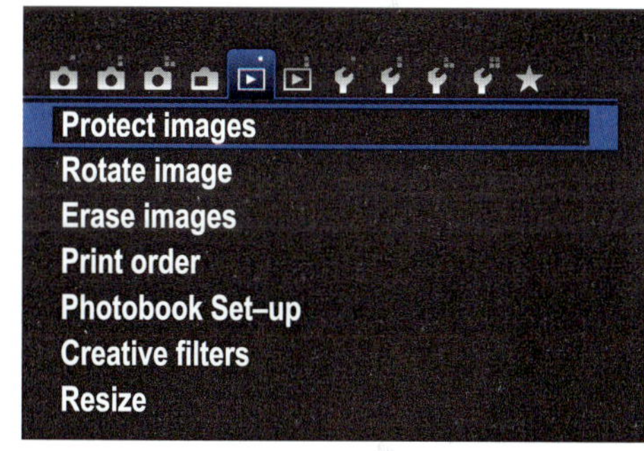

2.8 Playback menu 1 has seven options.

- **Protect images.** This option protects images from being erased from the memory card or unlocks images on the memory card.
- **Rotate image.** If you are not using Auto rotate (found in Setup menu 1 🔧), then you can manually rotate your images using this option.
- **Erase images.** This option lets you erase selected (checkmarked) images. You have three options: Erase selected images, Erase images from a specific folder, or Erase all images on your memory card. Protected images are not erased.

CAUTION If you use the RAW (RAW) and Large Fine (◢ L) image settings, the Erase option removes both images.

- **Print order.** If you use the digital print order format (DPOF) available with your camera, this option helps you select the print type, and date or file number imprint for your orders. The settings are applied to all print-ordered images.

- **Photobook Set-up.** If you want to create a photobook, this option helps you select images. The images are placed in a dedicated folder that is accessible using the EOS utility provided with your camera. You may select up to 998 images.
- **Creative filters.** Use this selection to apply creative filters to existing images. The options include Grainy B&W, Soft focus, Fish-eye effect, Art bold effect, Water painting effect, Toy camera effect, and Miniature effect. When you apply a filter, the camera creates a new file and leaves the original unaltered.

CROSS REF See Chapter 9 for examples of the Creative filters.

- **Resize.** Use this option to create smaller image files in-camera. Resize creates a new file so that your original is not erased. However, note that you cannot resize JPEG S3 (S3) or RAW (RAW) images, or make larger images from smaller JPEGs.

Playback menu 2

Playback menu 2 (▶) focuses on photograph review. Options such as histogram display, slide show, and photograph rating options are located here. The following options are available:

- **Histogram disp.** A *histogram* is a visual representation of the tones in a photograph. The left side represents black, the right side represents white, and the middle represents gray tones. This selection gives you the option of displaying either the brightness or RGB histogram when reviewing your photographs. Press the Info button (**INFO.**) to see the histogram of your photographs.

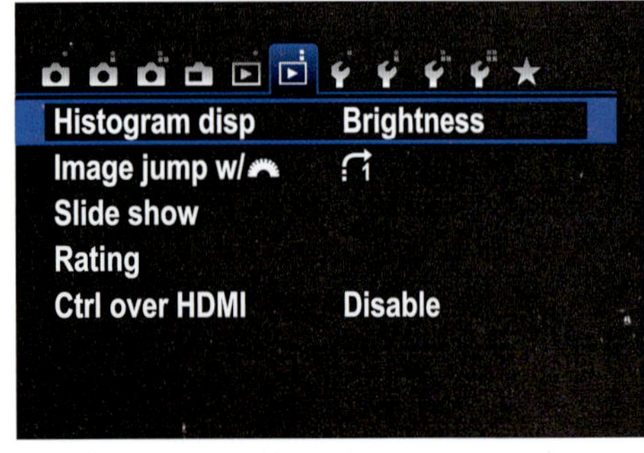

2.9 The options in Playback menu 2.

- **Image jump w/ .** Increase the image jump number when you want to move through your photos faster. The default setting is to browse one image at a time, but here you can adjust it to move between 10 or 100 images. This is useful when you have a lot of photographs and videos on your memory card. You can also set up your browsing based on different jump methods, such as by date, folder, movies only, stills only, or image rating.

- **Slide show.** You can share your images as a slide show on the LCD screen, or use the HDMI output to show them on an external TV or monitor. You can select specific images, or select them by date, folder, rating, or whether they are stills or movies. You also have a choice of five transitions and music options.
- **Rating.** Choose this option to rate your images and movies. This makes it easier to sort your photographs when using the Image jump or Slide show options.
- **Ctrl over HDMI.** When you connect your camera to an HDTV using an HDMI cable, you can use a remote control to activate your Canon T5i/700D's playback functions. You do this by selecting Enable and following the directions. Not all televisions allow this function. If yours does not, return to the default Disable setting.

The Setup Menus

The Setup menus are full of options to customize your camera the way you like it. There are four menus from which to choose when using the Creative Zone modes, which are Manual (**M**), Aperture-priority AE (**Av**), and Shutter-priority AE (**Tv**). There are three options available in the Basic Zone modes, which are Scene Intelligent Auto (A+), Flash off ( ), Creative Auto (CA), Portrait ( ), Landscape ( ), Close-up ( ), Sports ( ), Night Portrait ( ), Handheld Night Scene ( ), and HDR backlight ( ).

Setup menu 1

The following options are available in Setup menu 1 ( ):

- **Select folder.** This option allows you to select the folder where your captured photographs are saved. You can also create new folders here. This is helpful for organizing your photos in the field. For example, you can create a specific folder to contain images you want to delete when clearing your memory card.

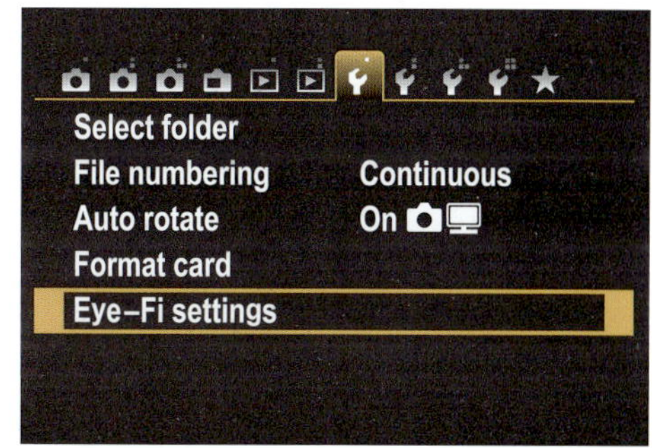

2.10 Setup menu 1.

- **File numbering.** You have three options when it comes to file numbering. Continuous numbers your files from 0001–9999. Auto reset reverts the file number to 0001 with each new memory card you insert or new folder you create. Manual reset gives you the opportunity to reset your file numbers to 0001 at any time. I find that the Continuous numbers option makes it easier to keep track of images and prevent overwriting photos.

NOTE A new folder is automatically created when your file numbers reset using the Continuous file numbering setting.

- **Auto rotate.** When this option is on, the camera rotates vertical images to display them in the horizontal frame of the LCD screen or computer. You also have the option to not have your images rotate during playback; they still rotate when viewed on the computer, however. You can also turn the Auto rotate option off.

NOTE A vertical image does not rotate automatically after you take a photo. Images only rotate in Playback mode (▶).

- **Format card.** When you purchase a new memory card or use one that was initialized by another camera, you should format the card for the Canon T5i/700D. After formatting the card, you may not be able to recover any images that were on the card. To ensure complete formatting of all sectors of the memory card, select Low-level formatting. This takes longer to execute than the Normal formatting, but it completely clears the card of recoverable data. There are many reasons a photographer might want to permanently remove all data from a memory card, such as to erase photos of a sensitive or security-related nature.
- **Eye-Fi setting.** You have two options under this selection: Enable or Disable. An Eye-Fi card allows you to automatically transfer images to your personal computer or an online hosting service. Although the option to enable an Eye-Fi card is in the T5i/700D firmware, Eye-Fi cards aren't officially supported by Canon. This option is only available when an Eye-Fi card is placed in the memory card slot.

Setup menu 2

Setup menu 2 (🔧) addresses power, the LCD screen, date/time, language, and video systems. The following seven options are available:

- **Auto power off.** You can set the camera to shut off automatically if left untouched for 30 seconds or 15 minutes. You can disable this option, but if you do (or if you set it for a longer period of time), you risk wearing down the battery before its next use.
- **LCD brightness.** This option controls the brightness of the LCD screen.

- **LCD auto off.** This setting disables the eye sensor from turning off the LCD screen, which it does when you bring your eye to the viewfinder. It turns on again when you remove your eye from the eyepiece.
- **Time zone.** This option lets you set the time zone based on a major city in your zone. The sun icon allows you to turn daylight saving time on or off.

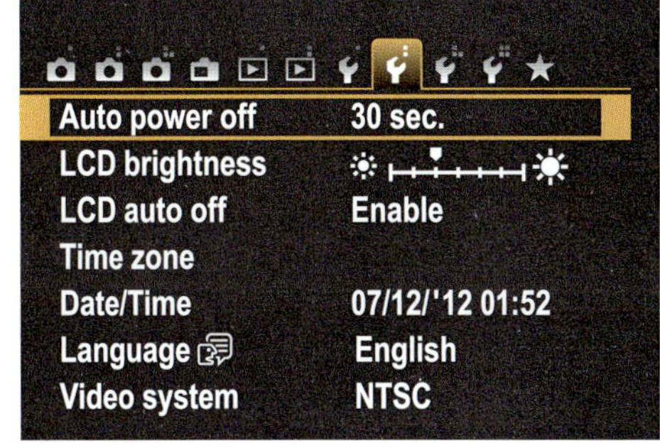

2.11 Setup menu 2.

- **Date/Time.** Use this option to set the date and time on your camera.
- **Language.** This option lets you select the language you want your camera to display.
- **Video system.** Use this option to select the video recording standard you want to use for your movies, NTSC (the default), or PAL.

2

Setup menu 3

Setup menu 3 (🔧) gives you options for screen color, the feature guide, touch control, sensor cleaning, and GPS device settings. The following menu options are available:

- **Screen color.** Your camera has five screen color options: Black, light gray, dark gray, blue, and red. Red is often used for night photography to help prevent the loss of night vision.
- **Feature guide.** The Feature guide is like an in-camera tutorial that explains different features as you review them. This is helpful when you are new to the camera. You can choose to enable or disable this option here.

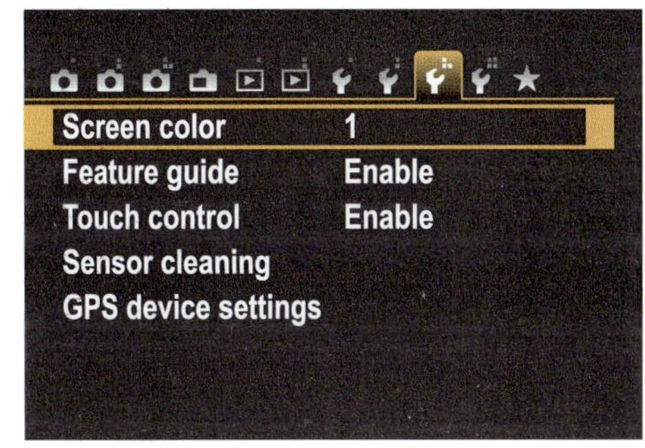

2.12 Setup menu 3.

- **Touch control.** This option turns the Touch control for the LCD screen on or off.
- **Sensor cleaning.** When you turn the power switch On or Off, you can activate the camera's sensor cleaner. The cleaner shakes dust off of the camera's front sensor. This setting gives you three options: Enable or Disable the auto sensor cleaning, Clean your sensor now, or Clean manually. If you choose manual cleaning, the camera locks the mirror up for easier sensor access. I recommend that you leave the auto sensor cleaning on.

CAUTION You should always use the proper tools or have an experienced professional clean the camera sensor; otherwise, you risk creating unwanted scratches.

- **GPS device settings.** If you purchase GPS accessories for your camera, this is where you control the settings for them. This menu option is only available if you are connected to a GPS device, such as the Canon GP-E2.

Setup menu 4

In Setup menu 4 (🔧), there are options for Custom Functions, copyright, clearing settings, and firmware updates. The options are:

- **Certification Logo Display.** Highlight this menu option and press the Settings button (SET). The camera displays some of the manufacturer certifications.
- **Custom Functions (C.Fn).** This selection allows you to control all eight of the camera's Custom Functions individually. The following four Custom Function groupings are available on the Canon T5i/700D:

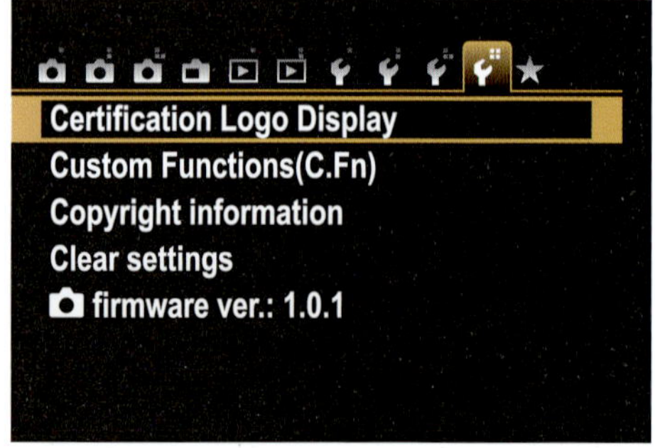

2.13 Setup menu 4.

  - **C.Fn I: Exposure.** Here, you can adjust the exposure level in 1/3- or 1/2-stop increments. If you prefer more refined increments for your exposure settings, such as shutter speed, aperture, and exposure compensation, use the 1/3-stop option. The other option under this function is turning ISO expansion on or off. ISO expansion allows you to shoot at the equivalent of ISO 12800 for stills or ISO 6400 for videos. This option is helpful in low light, but remember that high ISO settings produce more noise in digital files.

- **C.Fn II: Image.** In this menu, you can turn the Highlight tone priority function on or off. This option expands the camera's dynamic range into brighter areas, improving the highlight detail in your images.
- **C.Fn III: Autofocus/Drive.** There are two options here: AF-assist beam firing and Mirror lockup. The AF-assist beam supports the pop-up and external E-TTL flashes to properly expose your subject. I recommend that you leave this option on. The Mirror lockup function locks the camera mirror to help prevent vibration during long exposures when using telephoto and macro lenses.
- **C.Fn IV: Operation/Others.** You can adjust three settings here. The Shutter A/E lock button can be assigned different functions, such as autofocus lock, exposure lock (without autofocus lock), and autofocus lock (without exposure lock). Assign Set button allows you to assign a specific function to the Setting button (SET), such as image quality, flash exposure compensation, or ISO speed. You can enable the LCD display when power on function if you want the LCD screen to turn on automatically when the camera's power switch is turned on (this is the default). To save power, use the Previous display status option. To activate it, with the LCD screen turned off, press the Info button (**INFO.**) before turning off the camera. When you turn the camera back on, the LCD screen will not turn on automatically. To return to the default setting, press the Info button (**INFO.**).

- **Copyright information.** This option inserts copyright information into your files. There are four menu options here. The first is to turn the Copyright information option on or off. The second option allows you to list the author's name (your name). The third option allows you to add more information, and the final option is to delete copyright information. When you select options two and three, a keyboard displays on the LCD screen so you may type the information. You can then view this information under File Info in standard photo-editing programs.
- **Clear settings.** Use this option if you want to clear all of the camera's settings and return them to their default status. You can clear all settings or only the Custom Settings.
- **firmware ver.** This setting displays the camera's current *firmware* version (that is, the software running your camera). Make sure that you register your camera because Canon will send you notifications about firmware updates. You then activate those updates here. To do so, you use your computer to download the latest firmware to a clean, formatted memory card. The Format memory card option is in Setup menu 1 (🔧).

NOTE The LCD touchscreen is disabled during firmware updates.

My Menu Settings

Over time, you will discover which settings you use most often. My Menu (★), designated by the star, is customizable. It gives you six locations in which you can register your favorite options. My favorites listed under My Menu (★) include Image quality, Format card, and Custom functions. Follow these steps to customize your My Menu (★) settings:

1. **Select My Menu settings under My Menu (★).**
2. **Select Register to My Menu.** All of the available options are displayed. You can move through the options using the Cross keys (✣▲▼◀▶). If an option is grayed out, this means that it is already on the list.
3. **Press the Setting button (SET) to register your option.** Repeat this process until all six locations are filled.

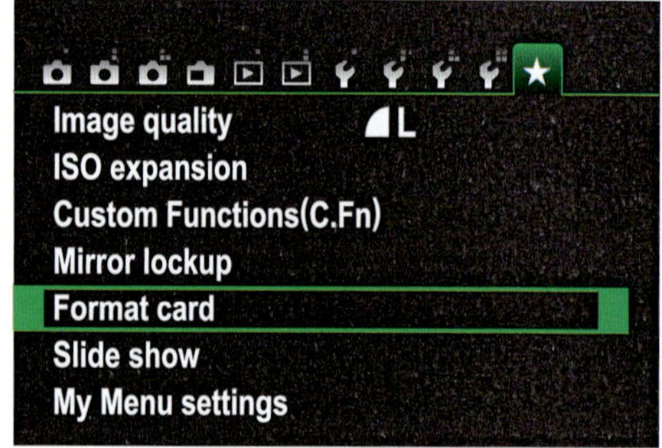

2.14 The options I selected for My Menu.

These settings are not permanent — you can sort (move a registered option up and down the list) or Delete them at any time in My Menu (★).

CHAPTER 3

Choosing the Right Settings for Your Camera

This chapter covers the buttons and modes available on your camera. Some options adjust the exposure, focus, drive, and white balance. Your camera has 12 mode options on the dial, and another three are available under Special Scene mode (SCN). The Creative Zone modes are for the more advanced photographer, while the Basic Zone modes were designed for the beginner, or photographers who prefer to point and shoot. Each mode is best for a particular scene or situation, so it is helpful to understand what they do and how they benefit your photographs. Some types of photography look best with a large depth of field, while others require fast shutter speeds. Focus modes help keep your subject in or out of focus. White balance enables you to get the best colors out of a scene. Flash modes help you control the most important element in photography — light.

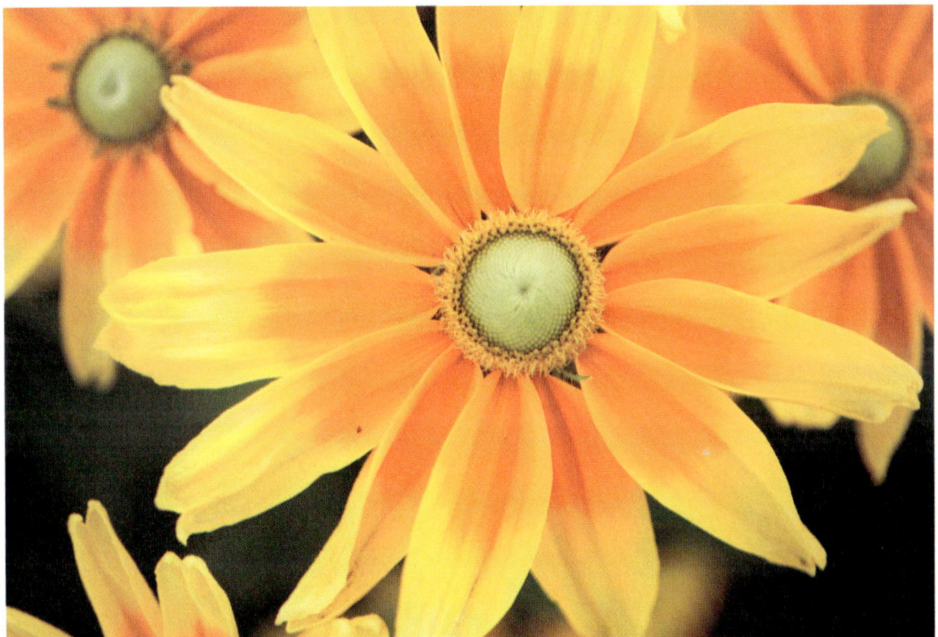

The right camera settings help you accurately capture the world around you.

The Basic Zone Modes

Portraits, landscapes, and sports photography all require different settings to create the best photograph. Your camera has some excellent modes to help you achieve this. The automatic modes are easily identified by their corresponding icons. Each Basic Zone mode allows you to adjust some functions, such as the drive mode. To review which options are available, press the Quick Control/Print button (Q). The Basic Zone modes are easy to use — just press the shutter button for a proper exposure.

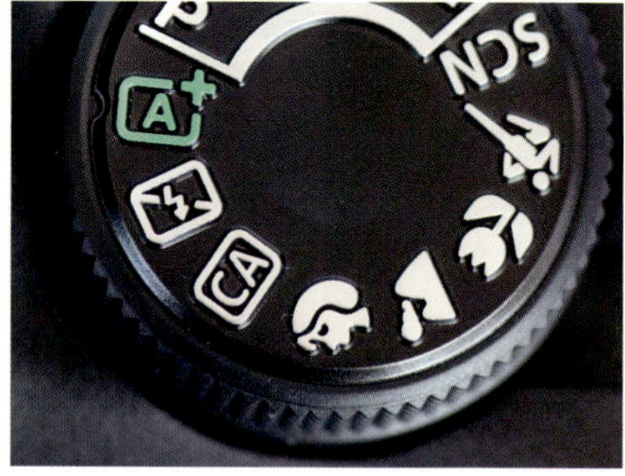

3.1 The Basic Zone modes make it easy for you to take a photo — all you have to do is press the shutter button.

The following are the Basic Zone modes on the Canon T5i/700D:

- **Scene Intelligent Auto mode** (A+). This is the ultimate program mode. It analyzes the scene and sets the shutter, aperture, ISO, white balance, and focus modes to take the best photograph. It uses all nine focus zones to focus on the closest object in the frame. If the camera detects a moving subject, it switches to the AI Servo AF mode (**AI SERVO**) to follow focus. *Follow focus* means that as you follow a moving subject, the camera continues to refocus to keep the subject sharp. The camera uses the flash when necessary, such as when it is dark and in backlit situations. If you want to lock focus, press the shutter button halfway and recompose.

  TIP When using the pop-up flash, you should stand at least 3.3 feet away from the subject to expose it properly. If you are too close, the bottom of the photo may be dark, especially if you are using a lens hood.

- **Flash Off mode (Flash Off).** If you don't want your flash to turn on at any time, use the Flash Off mode (Flash Off). This mode is the same as the Scene Intelligent Auto shooting mode (A+) without the flash. It is helpful when shooting in places where flash is distracting or not allowed, such as at a museum. If the shutter speed display is blinking, you may want to consider using a tripod to prevent camera shake, which is common in low-light situations.
- **Creative Auto mode (CA).** This setting uses the Scene Intelligent Auto mode (A+) as a default setting, but gives you a host of creative options. Press the

Quick Control/Print button (Q) to view a screen with the Creative Auto (CA) options. From there, make adjustments using the touchscreen or traditional controls. This mode allows you to change the ambience options and control the depth of field with a convenient slider to adjust the amount of blur you want in the background. The Drive mode (), Self-timer drive mode (), and flash controls are also available.

NOTE Ambience effects are available in all Basic Zone modes except Scene Intelligent Auto (A+), Flash Off (), and HDR backlight ().

- **Portrait mode ().** This mode () sets your aperture to the lowest possible number to create a shallow depth of field. A shallow depth of field blurs the background to separate the subject from it, which keeps the focus on your subject. This mode is for more than portraits, though. Any time you need a shallow depth of field for food, product, or pet photography, use the Portrait mode (). Use the Quick Control/Print button (Q) to adjust ambience settings, color scene filters for white balance, and drive modes. The default drive mode is Continuous shooting ().

  TIP If you want to preview what the depth of field looks like, press the Depth-of-Field Preview button () on the front of your camera.

- **Landscape mode ().** The goal of this mode is to give you the largest depth of field possible. It also boosts the blue and green saturation. In this mode, you have control over the ambience setting, color scene filters for white balance, and drive modes. Please note that Tungsten and Fluorescent options are not available in this mode.

  NOTE The built-in flash is turned off in Landscape mode ().

CAUTION When shooting landscapes, the shutter speed greatly slows down as the sun sets. Make sure that you use a tripod if the shutter speed goes below 1/30 second.

- **Close-up mode ().** This mode is designed for close-up photography, like the image shown in Figure 3.2. It is designed to strike a balance between a wide depth of field and a fast enough shutter speed to prevent camera shake. In this mode, you have control over the ambience setting, color scene filters for white balance, and shooting modes. If you are too close to your subject for the lens you are using, the Focus Confirmation light will blink.

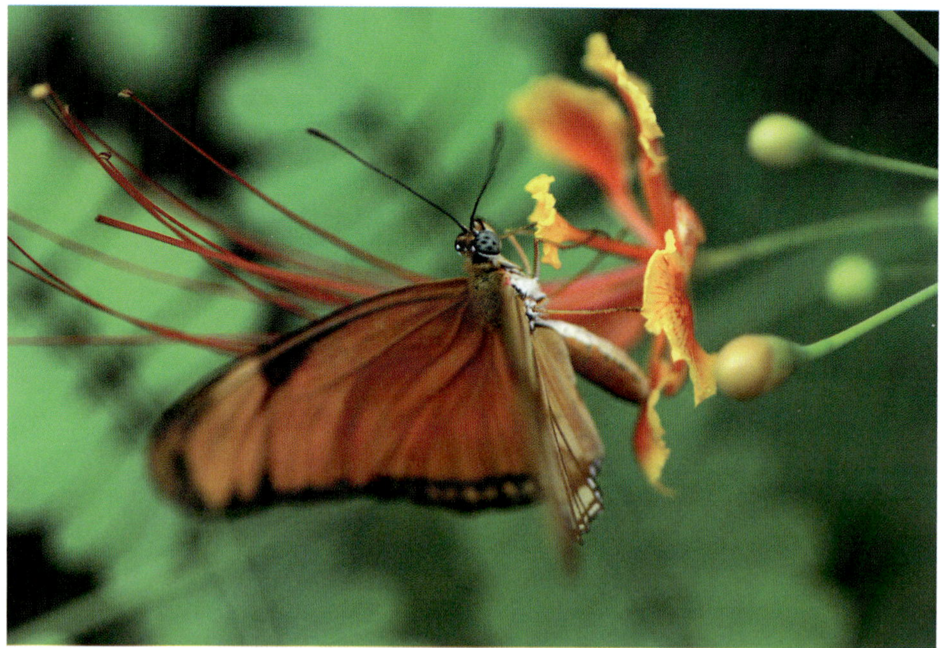

3.2 Use Close-up mode for small subjects like this butterfly. Exposure: ISO 800, f/2.8, 1/500 second, 100mm f/2.8 macro lens.

- **Sports mode (🏃).** This mode is a good option any time you are shooting fast-moving subjects. Sports photographers like to keep the shutter at the highest speed possible with the fastest frame rate possible. The default drive mode is Continuous (⧉), which photographs at a rate of about 5 frames per second. You can also use Sports mode (🏃) to photograph active children. In this mode, you have control over the ambience setting, color scene filters for white balance, and drive modes.
- **Special Scene mode (SCN).** To access the modes available here, press the Quick Control/Print button (Q), and then use the Main dial (⚙) to scroll through the options. The following three modes are available:
    - **Night Portrait mode (🌙).** This mode combines flash to freeze your subject with a lower shutter speed to expose for available light in the background. In this mode, you have control over the ambience settings and drive modes. Moving your camera while creating an exposure creates a ghosting effect. *Ghosting* is motion blur that often occurs when the photographer moves the camera while using a slow shutter speed with flash.

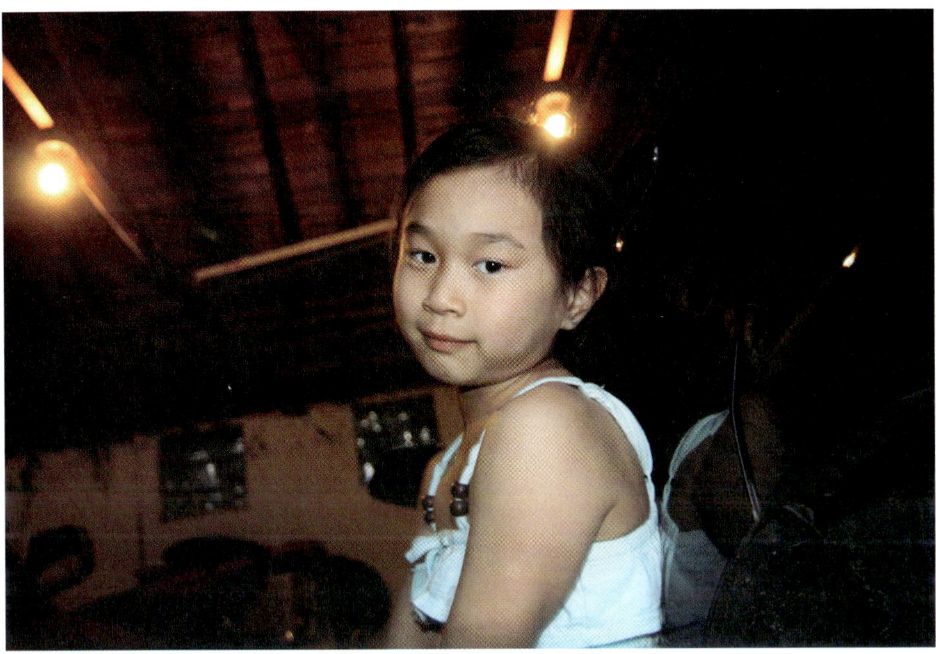

3.3 In Night Portrait mode, the camera slows the shutter speed enough to capture the lights and details in the background. It is a good option for indoor situations. Exposure: ISO 800, f/4.0, 1/25 second, 12-24mm f/4.0 lens at 20mm.

- **Handheld Night Scene mode ( ).** It is difficult to shoot at night because there are many dark areas that turn black in images and bright lights that easily blow out. This makes it hard to create a well-exposed image. In most cases, a tripod is necessary. The Canon T5i/700D Handheld Night Scene mode ( ) is helpful when shooting at night. When you press the shutter button, the camera takes four consecutive

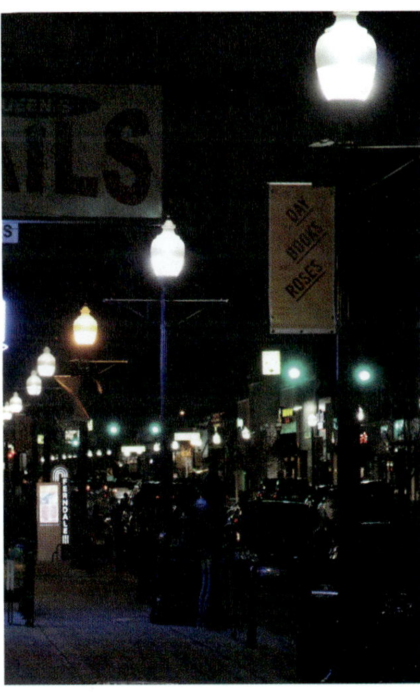

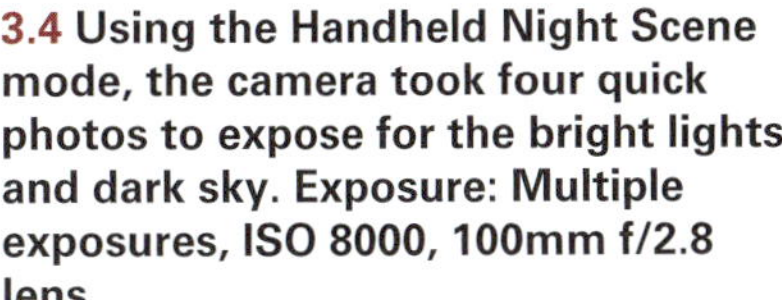

3.4 Using the Handheld Night Scene mode, the camera took four quick photos to expose for the bright lights and dark sky. Exposure: Multiple exposures, ISO 8000, 100mm f/2.8 lens.

shots. The camera then combines the four photographs to create one image. Perhaps the best part is that you don't need a tripod. This mode is also useful when photographing city scenes and skylines. The default flash setting in this mode is Flash Off (). If you want to take portraits in this mode, press the Quick Control/Print button () and turn on the flash. The first exposure triggers the flash, so make sure to tell your subject not to move during the additional three exposures. You also have control of color scene filters and shooting modes.

NOTE Although the flash fires only once when it is turned on in the Handheld Night Scene mode (), ask your subject to remain still until the camera takes all four shots.

- **HDR Backlight mode ().** High Dynamic Range (HDR) exposes for both highlights and shadow detail by combining multiple photographs at different exposures. The HDR Backlight mode () takes three quick exposures and combines them into one image to compensate for any intense light behind your subject. For example, if you're shooting a statue with the sun behind it and you don't want to create a silhouette, use the HDR Backlight mode () to improve both the highlight and shadow detail for a properly exposed photo. This mode doesn't work in all situations, especially in extreme conditions. For example, using HDR Backlight mode () with bright sun behind a dark object may not produce good results.

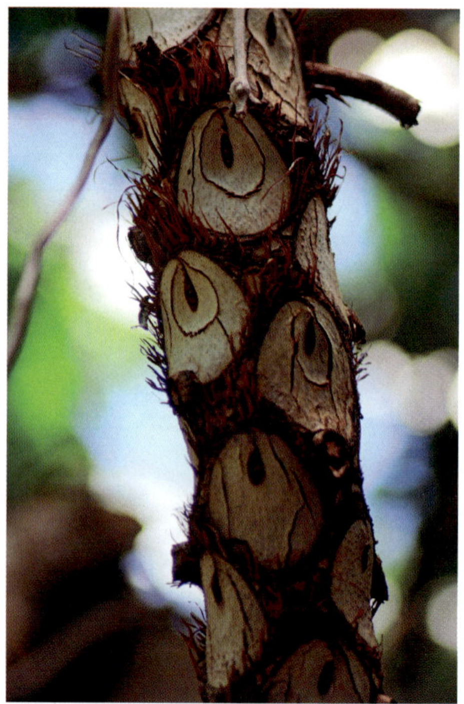

3.5 Three rapid shots were taken in the HDR Backlight mode and combined in the camera to create this image. Exposure: ISO 320, f/2.8, 1/640 second, 100mm f/2.8 lens.

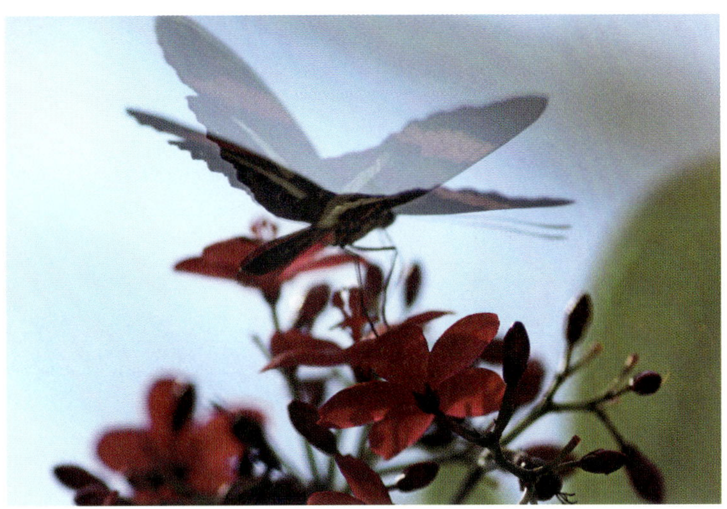

3.6 If you handhold your camera while photographing a moving object in the HDR Backlight mode, the three images may not line up. Exposure: ISO 100, f/3.5, 1/800 second, 100mm f/2.8 lens.

NOTE Although you can handhold your camera when using the HDR Backlight mode (), you must remain very still. Consider using a tripod whenever possible. If you move the camera, the three images might not align correctly.

The Creative Zone Modes

If you are looking for more flexibility, the Creative Zone modes are the place to be. Sometimes, you may want a shallow depth of field for a portrait or a fast shutter speed for sports. This exposure zone gives you the options necessary to control both the shutter and aperture. For times when you are unsure, you have the Program AE mode (**P**), which gives the camera the control, and allows it to use its technology to create a well-exposed photograph. None of the Creative Zone modes automatically set features such as Picture Styles, white balance, focusing modes, or the ISO (ISO).

When you want a little more control over the exposure, use one of the following Creative Zone modes:

- **Program AE mode (P).** When you don't know what to do or just don't want to think about the finer points of composition and light, use the Program AE mode (**P**). It gives you the confidence you need to take good photos with a little more control than the automatic Basic Zone modes. Program AE mode (**P**) sets the shutter speed and aperture for the proper exposure.

- **Aperture-priority AE mode (Av).** Some types of photography, such as landscape and portraiture, require that you control the depth of field. The Aperture-priority AE mode (**Av**) gives you control over the aperture, while the camera controls the shutter. The aperture allows light into the camera, so as you open it, more light hits the sensor. In response, the camera increases the shutter speed to compensate. When you close down the aperture, the camera does the opposite. For example, if you open your aperture from f/8.0 to f/5.6, the camera increases the shutter speed 1 stop, such as from 1/60 second to 1/125 second.

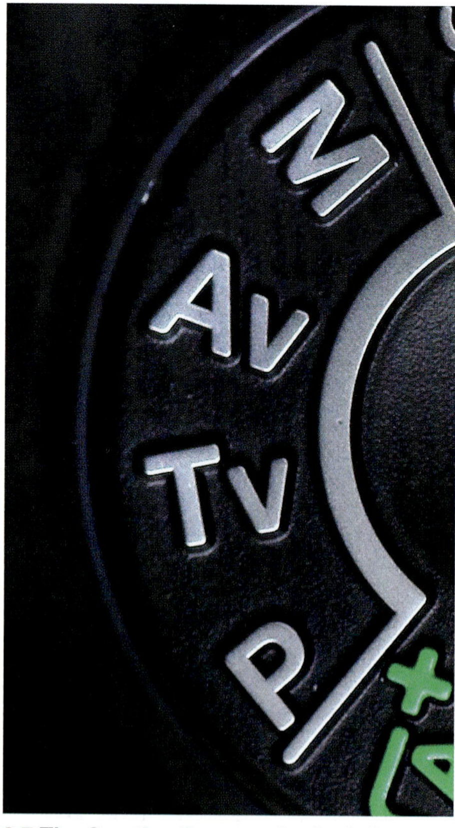

3.7 **The Creative Zone modes include Manual, Aperture-priority AE, Shutter-priority AE, and Program AE.**

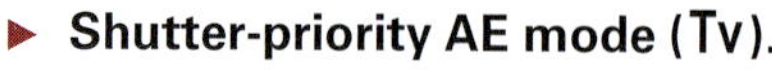

- **Shutter-priority AE mode (Tv).** When photographing sports or wildlife, you need a fast shutter speed to freeze the action. When shooting landscapes, you often need a slower shutter speed to achieve a larger depth of field. The Shutter-priority AE mode (**Tv**) gives you control of the shutter speed, while the camera controls the aperture. As you increase the shutter speed, such as when trying to capture moving subjects, the camera opens the aperture to allow in more light. When you lower the shutter speed, the camera closes the aperture.
- **Manual mode (M).** When you are comfortable with your camera, you may want to begin using Manual mode (**M**). It's not for everyone, but there may be times when you disagree with the camera's automatic settings, and you want to take full control of the shutter speed and aperture. It is especially useful in difficult lighting, such as backlighting or when shooting night scenes. The camera displays how under- or overexposed the image will be based on its exposure meter readings. You can make adjustments based on the camera's internal light meter information. As you gain more experience, you might decide to ignore the camera's recommendation.

Focus Modes

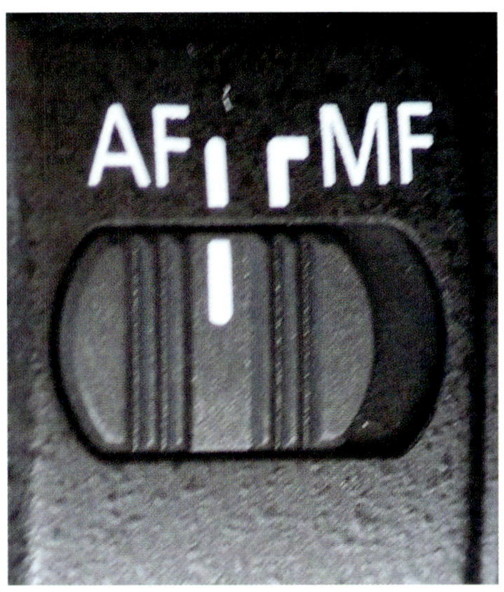

3.8 The Autofocus/Manual focus switch on a lens.

Camera manufacturers are improving autofocus system capabilities all the time. Lenses are faster and much quieter than earlier models (Canon's STM lenses are a good example). However, how to use these capabilities is often a mystery. The type of photography you plan to do usually determines the best autofocus solution. To change your autofocus mode, press the Autofocus button (AF), which is located to the right of the Setting button (SET). Next, select one of the three focus modes. You will know if your subject is in focus if the round focus confirmation light appears in the bottom-right corner of the viewfinder. Autofocus is not perfect — sometimes you just have to use Manual focus (**MF**). The Autofocus/Manual focus switch, as shown in Figure 3.8, is on the left side of your lens — don't be afraid to use it.

The following list includes the focusing options available on the Canon T5i/700D:

- **Autofocus mode (AF).** If you are using a Basic Zone mode, the optimal focus for that mode is automatically set. For example, in Sports mode (⛷), the camera sets the focus to the AI Servo focusing mode (**AI SERVO**) to follow focus on moving subjects. In the Creative Zone modes, you can change the focus mode or focus points at any time. If you see the round focus confirmation light blinking in the viewfinder, this means that the camera is having trouble focusing, and you may need to try one of the other focus modes.
- **Manual Focus mode (MF).** You will not always agree with your camera's choice of focus. When using the default automatic AF-point selection, it will focus on the largest object that is closest to the lens. This object is not always what you want to photograph. You can try using individual focus points to force your desired focus point but, in many cases, Manual Focus mode (**MF**) is your best bet. The following is a list of situations in which you might want to switch to the Manual Focus mode (**MF**) or select one of the nine focus points:
    - **When shooting low-contrast subjects, such as the sky or a gray wall.**
    - **When a subject is in low light.**

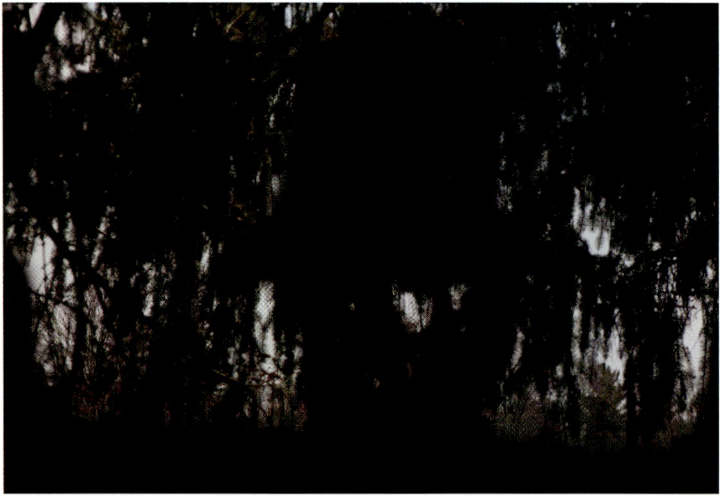

3.9 Sometimes, your camera has a tough time focusing in low-light situations.

- **When shooting repetitive patterns, such as rows of windows on a building.**
- **When shooting horizontal stripes.**
- **When shooting water or other reflective subjects.**
- **When an object is too close to the camera.** You may also need to back up or change lenses.

NOTE If focus cannot be achieved (because you are too close to the subject or the environment is too dark, for example), the round focus confirmation light blinks.

- **When shooting a subject with extreme backlighting, such as a small object with the sun behind it.**
- **When shooting very small subjects (use a macro lens).**
- **When a subject is too far away for the camera to detect.**

► **One-shot autofocus mode (ONE SHOT).** This is a good mode to use when you are photographing a still subject. Point your camera at the subject, and then press the shutter button halfway. The camera focus locks on the subject. When you see the round focus confirmation light in your viewfinder, you are free to recompose if necessary. If you need to refocus, lift your finger off the shutter button and focus again.

NOTE In One-shot autofocus mode (**ONE SHOT**), the camera takes its exposure settings at the same time that you lock focus.

- **AI Servo focusing mode (AI SERVO).** Photographing moving objects is not easy. The AI Servo focusing mode (**AI SERVO**) continuously refocuses on your subject until you fully press the shutter button to take a photograph. Pressing the shutter button halfway is a good idea so you can snap your picture quickly, but it doesn't stop the camera from refocusing as you move your lens or as the subject moves. This option is often used for sports and wildlife photography.

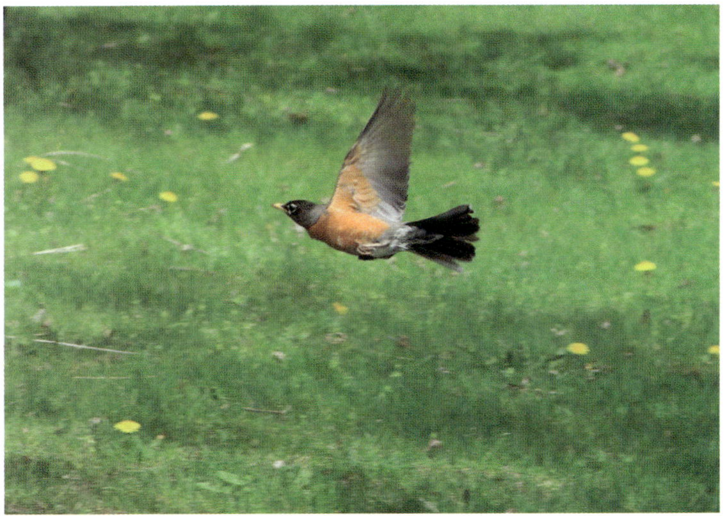

3.10 I followed this robin in the AI Servo mode to keep it in focus. Exposure: ISO 400, f/2.8, 1/000 second, 100mm f/2.8 lens.

NOTE The round focus confirmation light does not blink in the AI Servo focusing mode (**AI SERVO**), even if the subject is in focus.

- **AI focus (AI FOCUS).** If your subject starts to move while you are photographing in the One-shot autofocus mode (**ONE SHOT**), it may be out of focus by the time you press the shutter button. The AI focus mode (**AI FOCUS**) defaults to the One-shot autofocus mode (**ONE SHOT**), but switches to AI Servo mode (**AI SERVO**) if the subject moves. For example, if you are photographing an animal in the wild, the camera defaults to One-shot autofocus mode (**ONE SHOT**) if the subject remains still. If something spooks the creature and it moves, your camera switches to AI Servo mode (**AI SERVO**) as you follow the animal. When using the AI focus mode (**AI FOCUS**), the default One-shot autofocus mode (**ONE SHOT**) lights up the round focus confirmation light. When it switches to the AI Servo mode (**AI SERVO**) the light shuts off.

- **Focus points.** Your Canon Rebel T5i/700D uses nine focus points (in Live View shooting mode (◘) it has up to 31 focus points). If you are shooting in a Basic Zone mode, the camera automatically focuses on the subject closest to the lens using one of these points. If the camera doesn't focus on the main subject, switch to Manual Focus mode (**MF**) if you are using one of the Basic Zone modes. In the Program AE (**P**), Manual (**M**), Aperture-priority AE (**Av**), and Shutter-priority AE (**Tv**) modes, you can press the AF-point selection button (⊞) and manually select the focus point that you want with the Main dial (⚙). It is common to set the middle focus point as the default so that you can point the camera at the subject, lock the focus by pressing the shutter button halfway, and then recompose the scene. When all points of focus are lit, the camera is in AF-point selection mode and chooses the point of focus for you.
- **AF-assist beam (AF).** When light is low, this beam fires to help your camera focus on the subject. The beam is actually emitted from the flash quickly triggering in a rapid cycle. It works automatically in Basic Zone modes and only if the flash is popped up in Creative Zone modes. The AF-assist beam does not function in the Flash Off (⚡), Sports (⛷), or Landscape (▲) modes.

CAUTION Make sure that you warn your subjects not to move if the AF-assist beam fires. It is common for subjects to leave thinking that you already took the photo.

- **Tracking modes.** Your camera has three tracking modes in the Live View shooting mode (◘). The first option, Face Tracking mode (AF☺), looks for faces. If none are detected, it switches to FlexiZone-Multi AF (AF( )) and tracks whatever you point to on the LCD touchscreen. When the camera detects a face, it switches back to Face Tracking mode (AF☺) and follows it. In the FlexiZone-Multi AF mode (AF( )), you have 31 focusing touch zones. If you press the Setting button (SET), the camera toggles between automatic point selection and zone selection. Use the Cross keys (✥) for fine adjustments or the touchscreen to select a specific object in your frame. The FlexiZone-Single

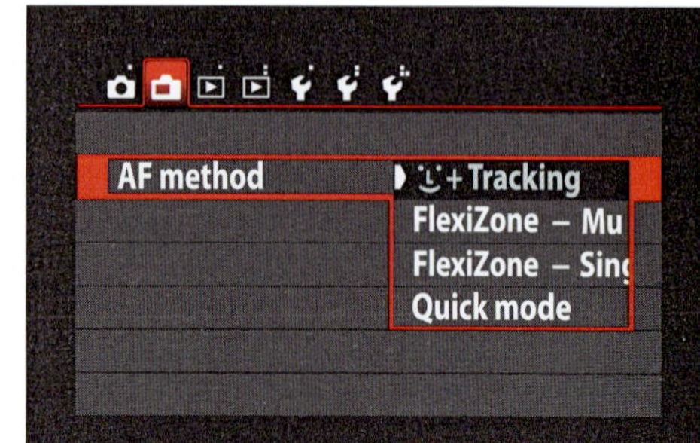

3.11 The AF tracking options in the Live View shooting menu.

AF mode (AF□) uses only one autofocus point and does not adjust with the movement of the camera or subject. You may adjust the focus point using the Cross keys (✣) or LCD touchscreen.

CAUTION If you press the shutter button halfway, even in a tracking mode, the camera refocuses.

- **Live View shooting mode (▣).** When your camera is in this mode, you have four focusing options. To get to them, press the Menu button (**MENU**) when the camera is in the Live View shooting mode (▣), and then select the autofocus method you want to use. You can adjust the focus method by pressing the Quick Control/Print button (Q) for options. The Quick focus mode (AFQuick) is a good default because it focuses quickly. If you are in a Basic Zone mode, such as Portrait (portrait icon), the camera selects the focus points. If you are using a Creative Zone mode, such as Aperture-priority AE (**Av**), you can select the focus zone via the LCD touchscreen or Cross keys (✣). Your other options are the slower (but useful) tracking methods of focus.

CROSS REF For more information about the Live View shooting mode (▣), see Chapter 8.

Picture Styles

3

Your camera has seven Picture Style options (picture style icon), plus three user-defined Picture Styles. Picture Styles can help when you want to optimize your photography for the type of subject you are shooting. For example, some Picture Styles are designed to enhance portraits and landscapes. All Picture Styles, including those that are user-defined, adjust sharpness, contrast, saturation, and color tone.

Picture Style options (picture style icon) only work in the Progam AE (**P**), Manual (**M**), Aperture-priority AE (**Av**), and Shutter-priority AE (**Tv**) modes. The following Picture Styles are available on the Canon T5i/700D by pressing the Picture Style button (picture style icon):

- **Auto (A).** This mode starts out as a neutral setting, but adjusts based on the detected scene. It is a good default if you don't want any specific adjustments applied to photographs.
- **Standard (S).** This is another good default Picture Style setting. It adds sharpness and produces vivid colors in your scene.

- **Portrait ([P]).** This Picture Style does not sharpen the image as much as others do. The default leaves all of the other tones in neutral settings, but you may want to adjust the skin tone to suit your style or subject. To do so, in the Picture Style menu, select Info and four options (Sharpness, Contrast, Saturation, and Color tone) appear. If you select Color tone, your subject looks more red the closer you get to the minus sign. The closer you get to the plus sign, the more yellow it appears.
- **Landscape ([L]).** Use this Picture Style to create impressive landscapes. It sharpens, adds contrast, and produces vivid blues and greens.
- **Neutral ([N]).** If you prefer to enhance your photos using software outside the camera, then the Neutral Picture Style ([N]) is a good choice. It is designed to produce natural-looking colors.
- **Faithful ([F]).** This is another Picture Style that is ideal for post-processing on a computer. Of all of the Picture Styles, it offers the best color representation based on a white light exposure of daylight.

NOTE *Kelvin* is the temperature measurement of the color of light. Temperatures between 5500K and 6000K are considered neutral (or white) light. Lower Kelvin temperatures produce light that appears warmer, and higher temperatures produce light that looks cooler.

- **Monochrome ([M]).** Choose the Monochrome Picture Style ([M]) if you want to take black-and-white photos, as shown in Figure 3.13. Because the Monochrome Picture Style ([M]) doesn't need saturation or color tone, those options are replaced in the menu with filter and toning effects. The filter effect works like a color filter over black-and-white film, with the following options: None, Yellow, Orange, Red, and Green. Each of these filters absorbs the color it represents. For example, the red filter absorbs the red in an apple, making it appear much lighter. The filters also enhance complimentary colors. For example, a yellow filter will darken a blue sky. Toning effects change the monochromatic color of the image. The options are None, Sepia, Blue, Purple, and Green.

CAUTION If you think that you might want to convert your photograph to a color image later, make sure that you use the RAW setting (RAW). Other image formats, such as JPEG, cannot be converted back to color.

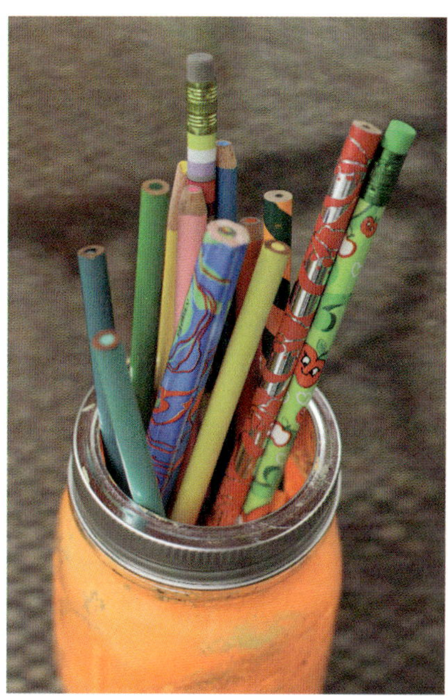

3.12 A color image before the Monochrome Picture Style is applied with filters. Exposure: f/3.5, 1/250 second, ISO 200, 50mm f/1.4 lens.

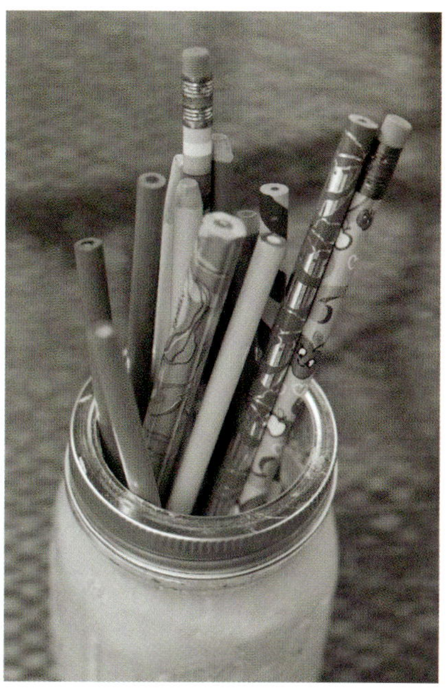

3.13 The Monochrome Picture Style with no filter. Exposure: f/3.5, 1/250 second, ISO 200, 50mm f/1.4 lens.

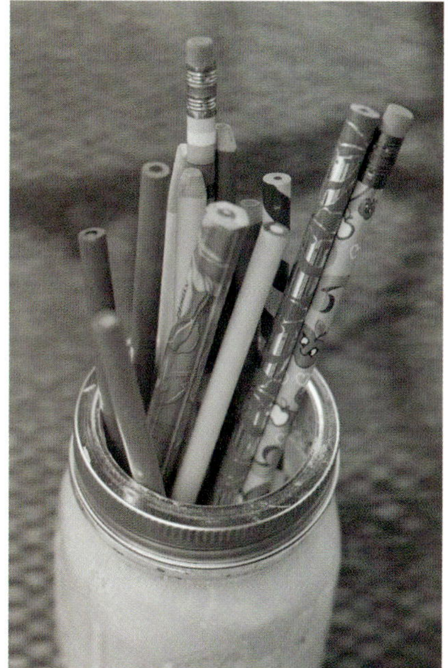

3.14 The Monochrome Picture Style with a yellow filter. Exposure: f/3.5, 1/250 second, ISO 200, 50mm f/1.4 lens.

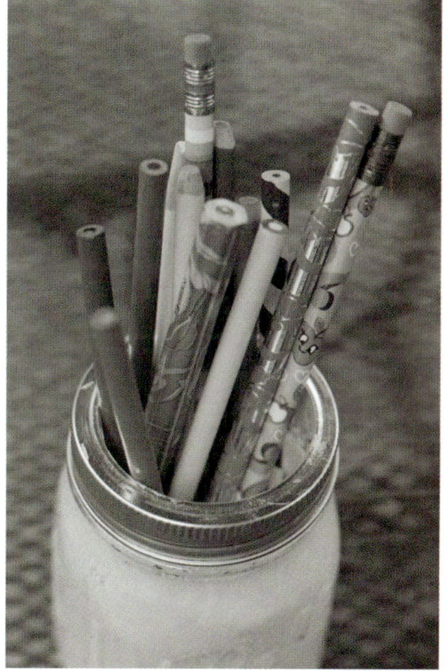

3.15 The Monochrome Picture Style with an orange filter. Exposure: f/3.5, 1/250 second, ISO 200, 50mm f/1.4 lens.

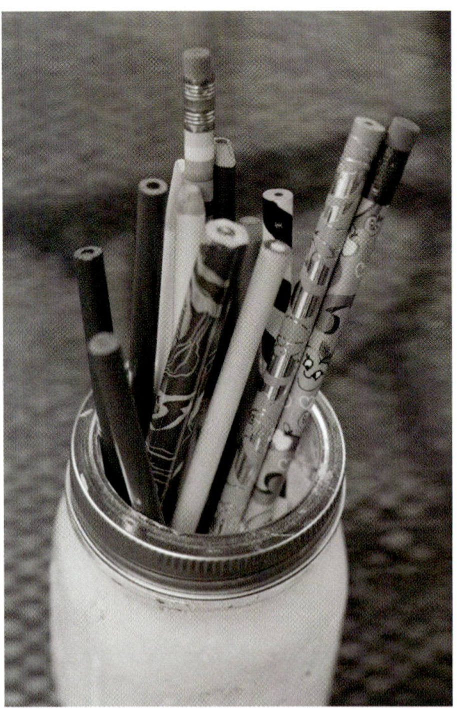

3.16 The Monochrome Picture Style with a red filter. Exposure: f/3.5, 1/250 second, ISO 200, 50mm f/1.4 lens.

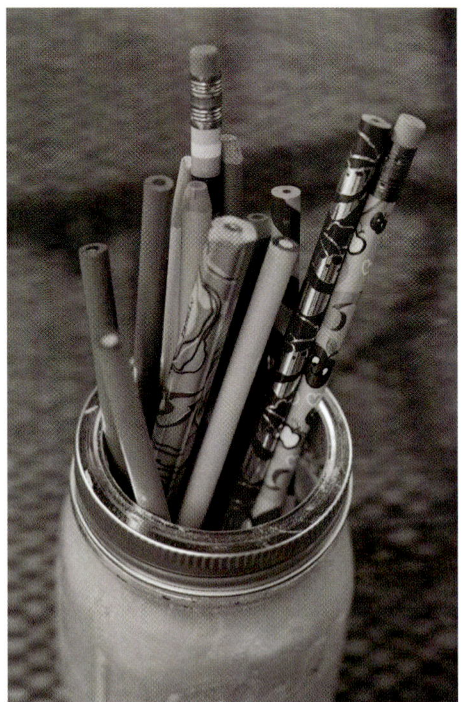

3.17 The Monochrome Picture Style with a green filter. Exposure: f/3.5, 1/250 second, ISO 200, 50mm f/1.4 lens.

- **User-defined Picture Styles 1 (1), 2 (2), and 3 (3).** Here, you can create your own Picture Styles. Unused Picture Styles default to the Auto Picture Style (A). You can use any of the camera's preset Picture Styles as a starting point to create your own custom styles. The following settings can be adjusted to create a custom style:
  - **Sharpness.** This adjusts the clarity of the image. You can adjust it from 0 (no sharpness) to 7 (sharpest).
  - **Contrast.** Use this setting to increase (+) or decrease (-) the contrast or vividness of the colors in your image. The neutral point is 0. The closer you move toward the minus sign (-), the duller the image; the closer you move to the plus sign (+), the more contrast and vividness the image has.
  - **Saturation.** This enhances the colors in your image. The closer to the minus sign (-) you move this setting, the more muted the colors become. The closer you move toward the plus sign (+), the bolder the colors become. The neutral setting is 0.

- **Color tone.** Use this setting to adjust skin tones. The closer to the minus sign (-) it is, the more red your subject's skin tones look. The closer it is to the plus sign (+), the more yellow skin tones appear.

CROSS REF For more information about creating User-defined Picture Styles, see Chapter 9.

Drive Modes

Depending on the type of photography you are doing, you might want to use a different Drive mode (⎘). Your camera has five drive modes and each has its benefits. To adjust the drive mode quickly, press the Drive mode button (⎘) located to the left of the Setting button (SET) on the back of your camera.

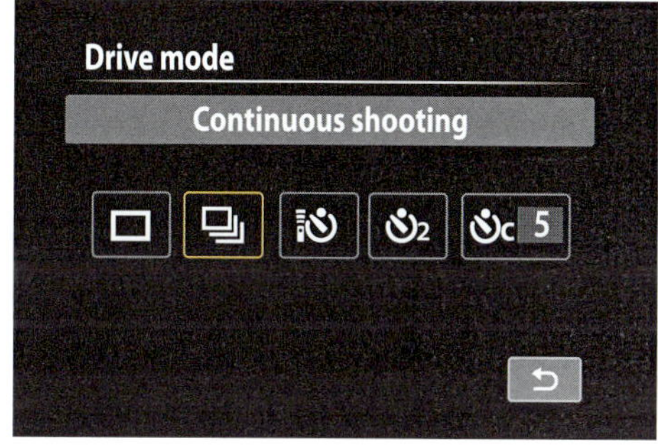

3.18 You have five drive modes to choose from, including three Self-timer options.

The following drive modes are available on the Canon T5i/700D:

- **Single-shooting mode (□).** In this mode, the camera takes only one photograph with each press of the shutter button. This is the default setting for most Basic Zone modes.
- **Continuous drive mode (⎘).** This mode is helpful when shooting action, such as sports, children, or wildlife. Use it when you need to take multiple photographs in quick succession — it shoots approximately 5 frames per second (fps). It is also helpful to have your camera on AI Servo (**AI SERVO**) or AI Focus (**AI FOCUS**) mode if your subject is moving.

  NOTE If you use flash, the frames-per-second (fps) rate is slower because the flash must recycle.

- **Self-timer drive modes (⏲).** When you press the Drive mode button (⎘), you see the following three self-timer options: 10 seconds (⏲), 2 seconds (⏲2), and a Multi-shot continuous timer (⏲c). The continuous timer starts as a 10-second timer, but takes up to 10 continuous photos. If you are triggering your camera with a remote, use the 10-second self-timer option (⏲).

3

White Balance Settings

You can use the white balance settings to adjust how the camera "sees" the color of light in your scene. The White Balance button (**WB**) is above the Setting button (SET) on the back of your camera. Each light source you encounter produces a different color or temperature. These are measured using the Kelvin scale. White light has a temperature between 5500K and 6000K (Kelvin). The higher the Kelvin temperature, the cooler the appearance. The lower the Kelvin temperature, the warmer the appearance. For example, an incandescent light bulb is around 3000K, which looks yellow. The goal of white balance is to make a white piece of paper (or any subject) look white under any lighting condition. Each white balance setting has a corresponding icon that represents the type of light or situation it is designed to correct.

You can choose from the following white balance settings:

- **Auto (AWB).** If you are unsure which white balance mode to use, set your camera to Auto (AWB). It's a good default for almost any scene because the camera adjusts to the light color automatically. If you are shooting in RAW format (RAW), you can make more adjustments in editing software, such as Adobe Photoshop Camera Raw or Lightroom, or the software that came with your camera.
- **Daylight (☀).** You can use this setting on bright days when the sun is high in the sky. It is a more neutral setting than others. Some photographers prefer it to the flash setting when using an on-camera or external flash.

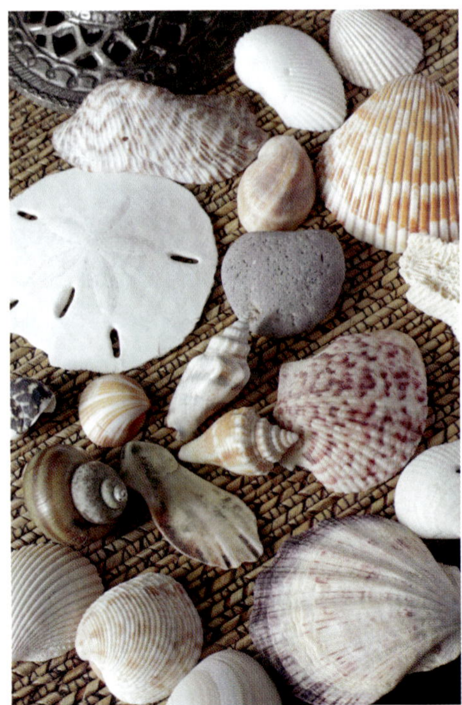

3.19 The result of the Auto white balance setting. Exposure: ISO 800, f/13, 1/10 second, 50mm f/1.4 lens, tripod.

- **Shade (🏠).** This white balance setting has a higher (bluer) Kelvin temperature, so the camera adjusts the color to make the image warmer. Use this adjustment when you find yourself in dark shade or shadows.
- **Cloudy (☁).** Like the Shade white balance setting (🏠), the Cloudy setting (☁) is based on a higher Kelvin temperature. Your camera is set to adjust a cool scene to make it look warmer. This is useful on cloudy days and in domed buildings where light penetrates the roof, such as a sports arena.

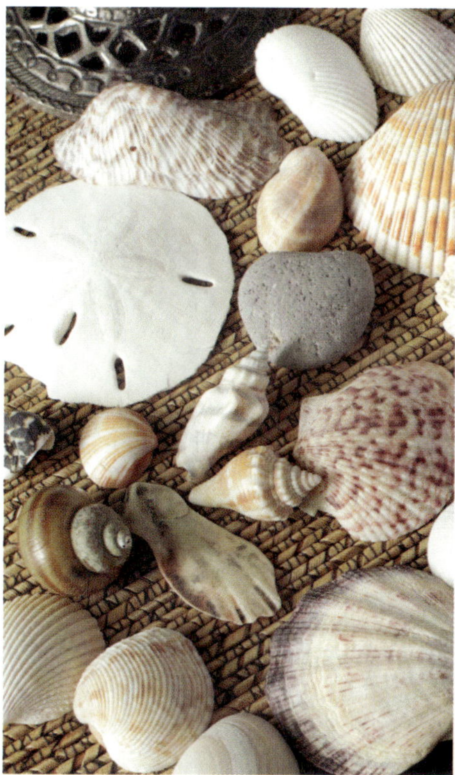

3.20 An example of the Daylight white balance setting. Exposure: ISO 800, f/13, 1/10 second, 50mm f/1.4 lens, tripod.

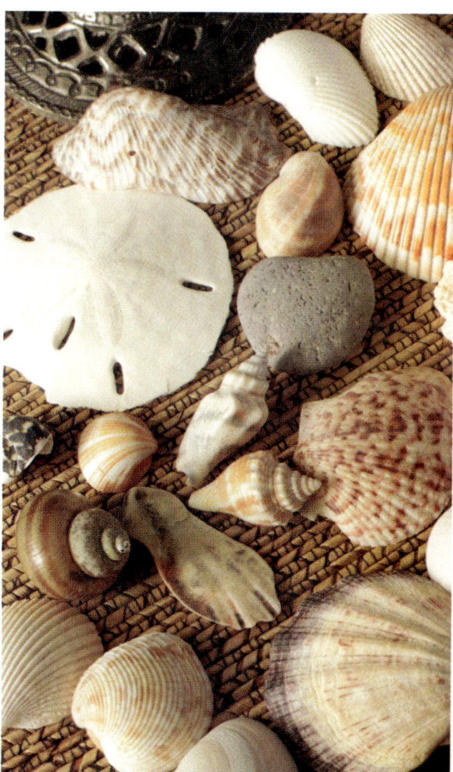

3.21 The effects of the Shade white balance setting. Exposure: ISO 800, f/13, 1/10 second, 50mm f/1.4 lens, tripod.

- **Tungsten (☀).** Tungsten (the traditional round light bulb) is an artificial light that emits a yellow cast. This white balance setting adjusts light that is around 3200K. Incandescent lights turn more yellow over time, so results vary.
- **Fluorescent (▦).** This is a good starting point to adjust fluorescent lights that are around 4000K (results depend on the type of fluorescent light used in your scene). Like incandescent bulbs, these change color over time, and there are many types on the market. If the Fluorescent white balance setting (▦) doesn't work to your satisfaction, consider using a Custom white balance setting (◪).

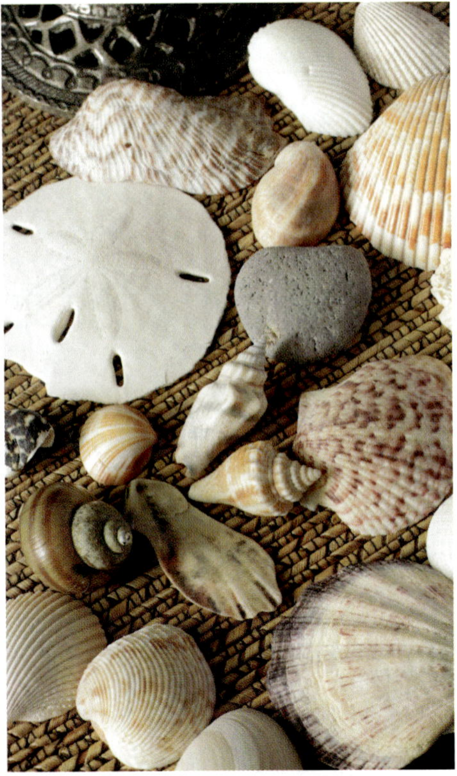

3.22 An example of the Cloudy white balance setting. Exposure: ISO 800, f/13, 1/10 second, 50mm f/1.4 lens, tripod.

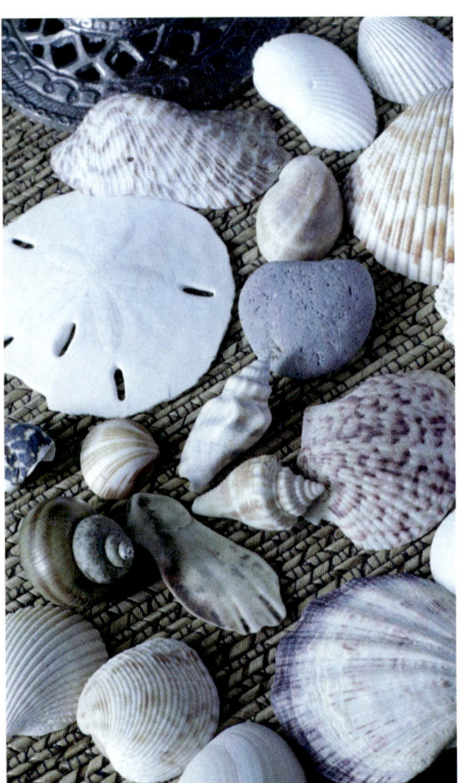

3.23 An example of Tungsten white balance setting. Exposure: ISO 800, f/13, 1/10 second, 50mm f/1.4 lens, tripod.

- **Flash (⚡).** This setting is designed for use with on-camera or external flashes. It is set to adjust light at 6000K to warm the cooler flash. If the image is too warm, you may want to consider using the Daylight white balance setting (☀).
- **Custom (custom icon).** This setting allows you to set your white balance to any temperature for a more precise light-color balance. You should adjust your custom setting under the lighting conditions in which you plan to work.

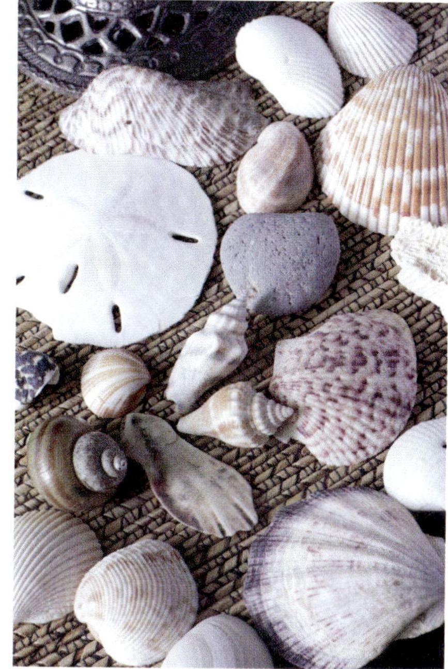

3.24 An example of the Fluorescent white balance setting. Exposure: ISO 800, f/13, 1/10 second, 50mm f/1.4 lens, tripod.

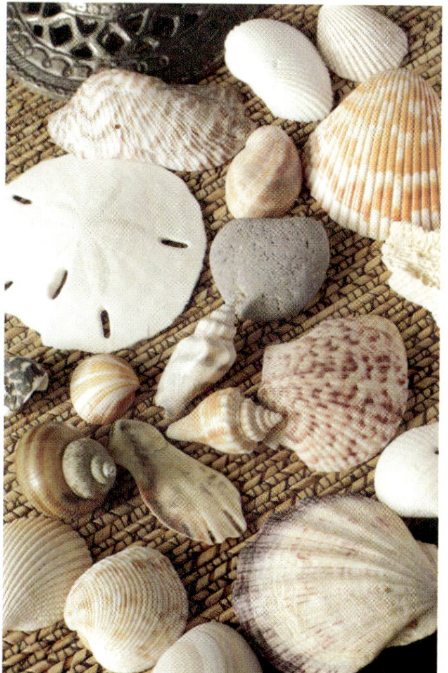

3.25 An example of the Flash white balance setting. Exposure: ISO 800, f/13, 1/10 second, 50mm f/1.4 lens, tripod.

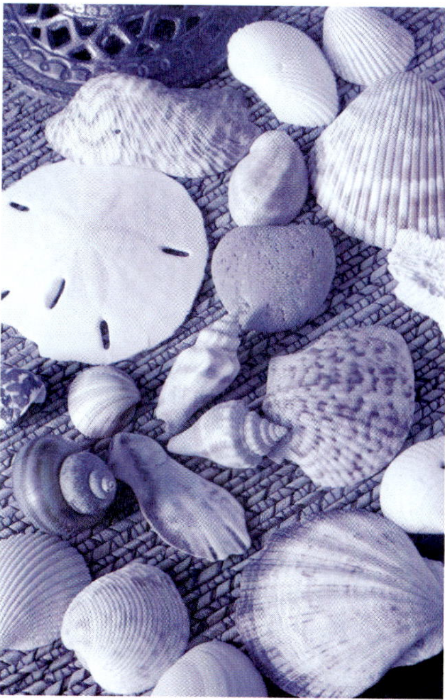

3.26 The Custom white balance set for tungsten correction in a daylight setting. Exposure: ISO 800, f/13, 1/10 second, 50mm f/1.4 lens, tripod.

3

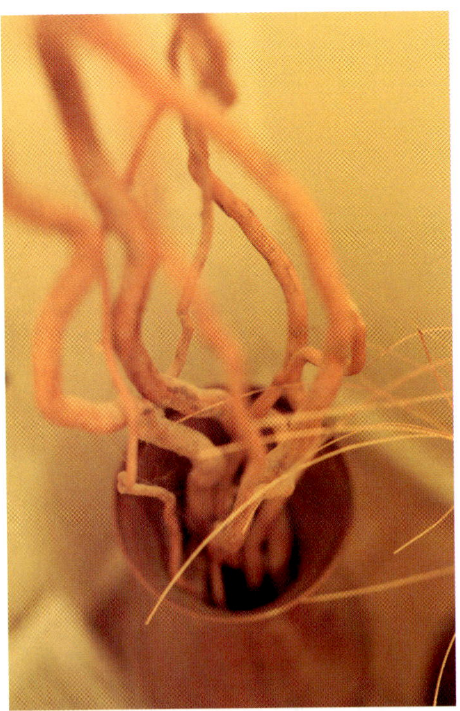

3.27 An example of the Custom White balance when not adjusted to the new environment. This setting can create fun color effects. Exposure: ISO 800, f/13, 1/10 second, 50mm f/1.4 lens, tripod.

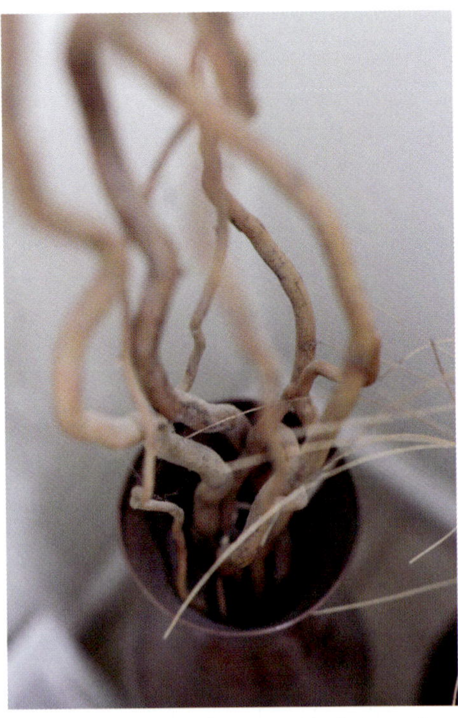

3.28 This image was created indoors using Custom white balance. Exposure: ISO 1600, f/3.5, 1/50 second, 50mm f/1.4 lens, tripod.

- **White Balance Auto Bracketing (WB).** If you are not sure about the white balance results the camera will deliver, you can use *White Balance Auto Bracketing* (WB). To do so, press the Menu button (**MENU**), select Shooting menu 2 (camera icon), and then select WB shift/bkt. The camera then displays the bracketing options shown in Figure 3.29. With one shot, three images with different color balances are recorded simultaneously.

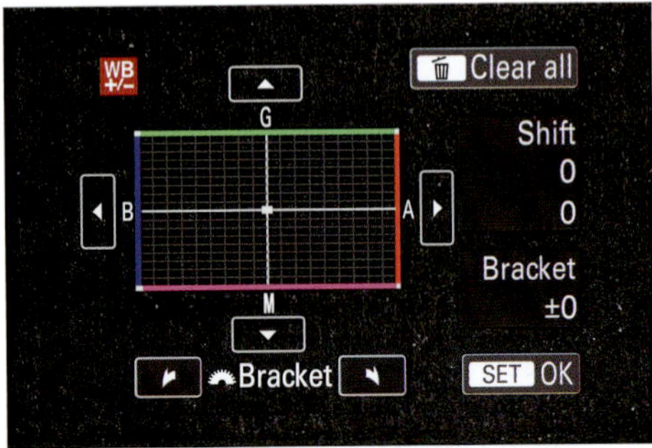

3.29 In the White Balance Auto Bracketing menu, you can choose blue (B) to auburn (A), or green (G) to magenta (M) bracketing depending on your needs.

Flash Modes

These modes are for the built-in, pop-up flash on top of your camera. Red-eye Reduction, fill-flash, and sync modes are useful tools when photographing — especially indoors, where it is often darker. The built-in flash is fine for casual use or when a larger one is not available, but I encourage you to purchase a more powerful flash with additional features for regular use.

CROSS REF More information about flash can be found in Chapter 6.

The following flash modes are available on your camera:

- **Auto.** Most of the Basic Zone modes use the pop-up flash in low light. It is not used in the Landscape (▲) or HDR backlight (▣) modes.
- **Red-eye Reduction.** The Red-eye Reduction feature is designed to prevent or minimize red-eye in your subjects when you photograph them in a dark or dimly lit environment. The same as the camera's aperture, pupils dilate in dark environments to let in more light. When this happens, more light from the flash reflects back to your camera. If your flash is close to the lens, your subjects will look like they have red eyes. When you press the shutter button halfway, the Red-eye Reduction lamp emits a light to shut the subject's pupils down and reduce red-eye when using a flash mode. The light turns off when the shutter button is pressed completely. The Red-eye Reduction setting does not work in the Flash Off (⚡), Landscape (▲), Sports (⛷), or HDR backlight (▣) modes.

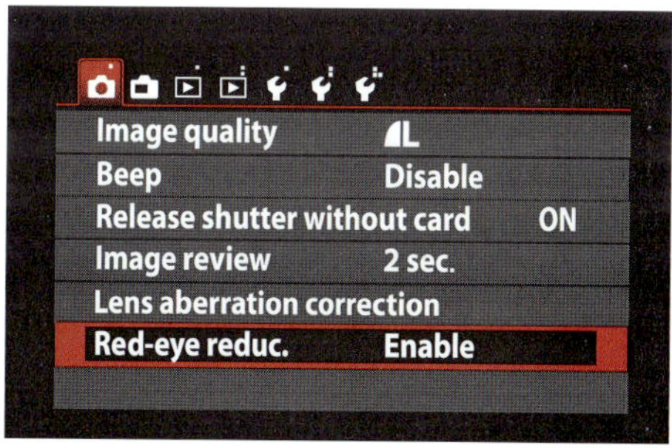

3.30 The Red-eye Reduction feature is found in Shooting menu 1 when you are using a Basic Zone mode.

- **Slow sync.** When using flash, your camera sets the shutter speed between 1/60 second and 1/200 second. If you are in a dark environment, in most cases the background appears black. If you want to see more of the environment or lights in the background, slow down the shutter speed while using flash. To do so, you can use the Shutter-priority AE (**Tv**) or Manual (**M**) modes to slow the shutter speed below 1/30 second. The best shutter speed depends on your ISO setting and how much light is in the background. The other option is to use the Night Portrait mode (▣).

- **Curtain sync.** Ghosting leaves movement trails (or lights) in front of or behind your subject, as shown in Figures 3.31 and 3.32. This occurs when you combine flash with a low shutter speed and available light. The flash freezes your subject and the camera records movement with the slow shutter. The default setting on all cameras is that the flash fires at the beginning of the shutter cycle, and then the slow shutter engages after leaving a front-moving trail. This is called using the front curtain. Your camera offers the option of either Front-curtain (first curtain) or Rear-curtain (second curtain) sync. In the Shooting menu 1 (📷), select Flash control. In that menu, select Built-in flash settings, and then select Shutter sync. Rear-curtain sync means that the slow shutter fires first, and then the flash fires at the end of the cycle. To get to this option, press the Menu button (**MENU**) and look in the first menu. Select flash control at the bottom, and then select Built-in flash settings. Go to Shutter Sync and choose your setting (First or Second curtain).

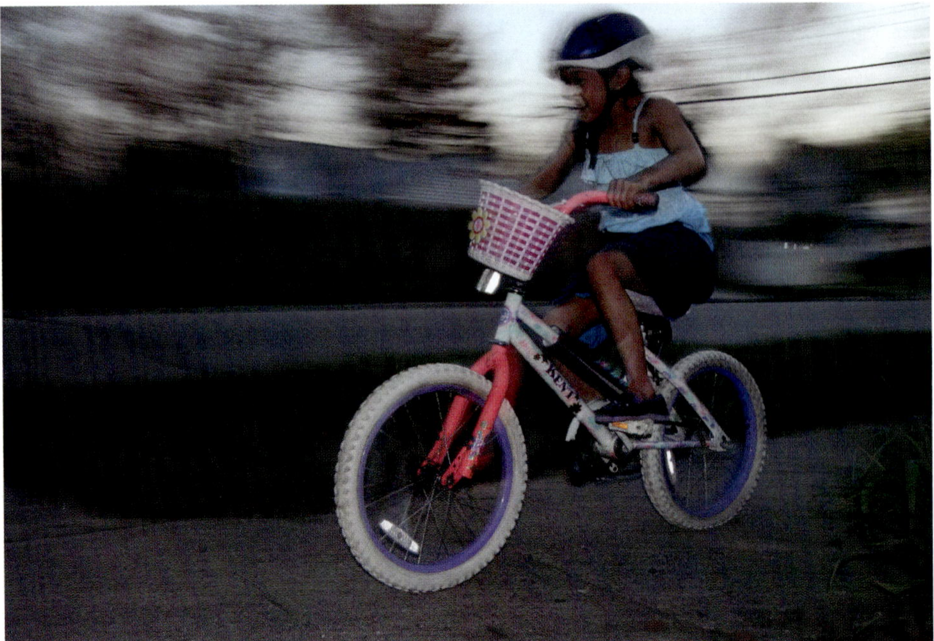

3.31 I used Front-curtain sync for this image. The flash fired immediately and the slow shutter speed left a trail moving in front of the subject. Exposure: ISO 100, f/13, 1/16 second, 12-24mm f/4.0 lens at 24mm.

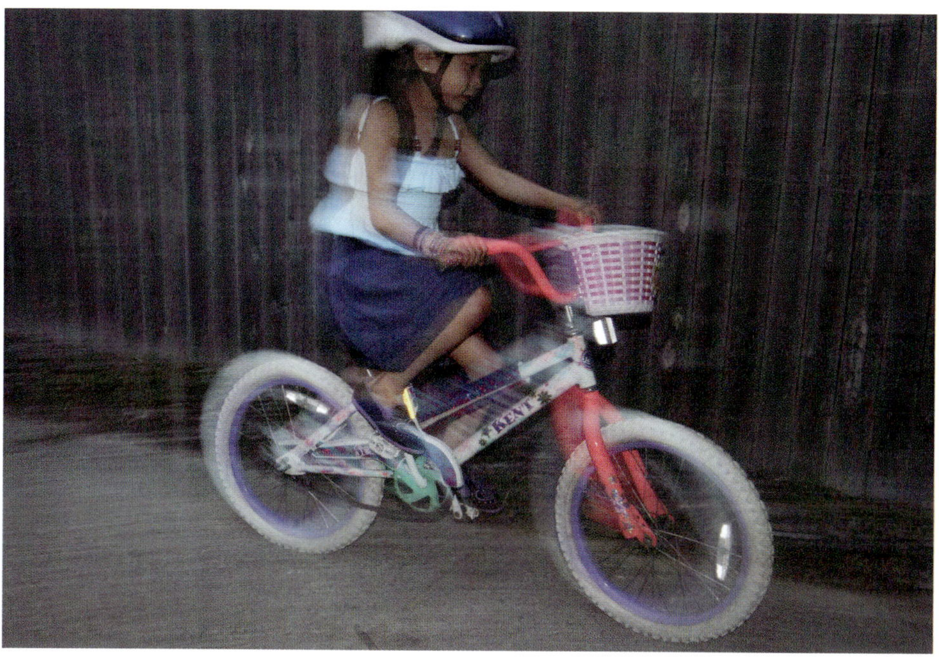

3.32 I used Rear-curtain sync for this image. The flash fired at the end of the slow shutter speed exposure, leaving a trail behind the subject. Exposure: ISO 100, f/14, 1/14 second, 12-24mm f/4.0 lens at 24mm.

- **Fill flash.** The sun can cast harsh shadows on your subject's face. You can use fill flash from the camera's pop-up or external flash to help minimize the shadows. If you place your subject in the shade with a bright background or in a direct backlight situation, use fill flash to prevent your subject from becoming a silhouette. If you are using a Basic Zone mode, your camera activates the built-in flash if it senses the need. When you are using the Creative Zone modes, if fill flash is necessary, press the Flash button (⚡) located below the pop-up flash on the left side of your camera, as shown in Figure 3.33.

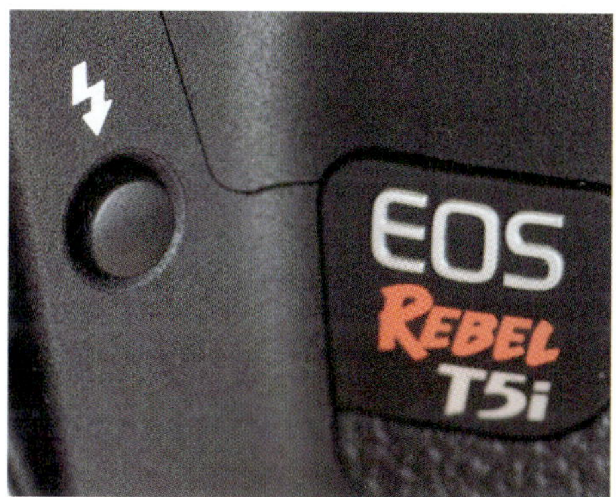

3.33 The button to activate the pop-up flash is on the front left of the Canon Rebel T5i/700D.

- **Wireless.** You can use the pop-up flash as a trigger for any external speedlites. To use your speedlite as an off-camera flash, switch it to Slave mode, and then press the Flash button (⚡) on the left side of your camera. For the camera and speedlite to sync, both have to be set to the same channel (speedlites default to channel 1). You have up to four channels from which to choose, but I recommend sticking with channel 1 unless you have a specific reason to switch, such as when using a more complex lighting setup or there is a conflict with another photographer using the same channel.

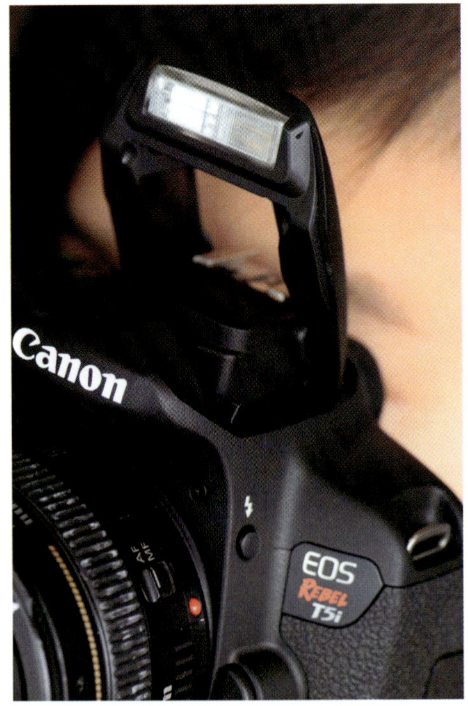

3.34 The Canon T5i/700D pop-up flash.

> **TIP** For easy wireless flash photographs, press the Quick Control/Print button (Q) (in the Creative Zone modes only), and then press the Flash button (⚡) on the right side of the LCD screen. Select the Easy Wireless Flash option ().

- **Flash Exposure Compensation.** Sometimes, you might disagree with the results that your camera and flash produce, and want your subject to appear a little lighter or darker. The Flash Exposure Compensation button (⚡±) lets you make adjustments in plus or minus 1/3-stop increments up to 2 stops. This option is useful in backlit situations. To adjust the Flash Exposure Compensation quickly when the camera is in a Creative Zone mode, press the Quick Control/Print button (Q), and then press the Flash Exposure Compensation button (⚡±) below the ISO setting. This option is not available in the Manual or Basic Zone modes.

NOTE If the Auto Light Optimizer is on any setting, photos with a negative stop adjustment may still appear bright.

CAUTION Don't forget to set the Flash Exposure Compensation setting (⚡) back to 0 when you finish using it.

ISO Settings

Your camera has eight ISO options ranging from ISO 100 to ISO 12800. ISO 25600 is available when Custom Function 2 is engaged. The ISO setting represents the camera sensor's sensitivity to light. Each step doubles or halves the amount of light sensitivity. For example, ISO 200 to ISO 400 doubles your camera's light sensitivity. This is the equivalent of adjusting the aperture or shutter 1 full stop. The lower the ISO setting, the more light you need, and the higher the quality and less digital noise will appear in your image. The higher the ISO setting, the less light you need, but your images will have more digital noise. To set the ISO, press the ISO button (ISO) on top of your camera.

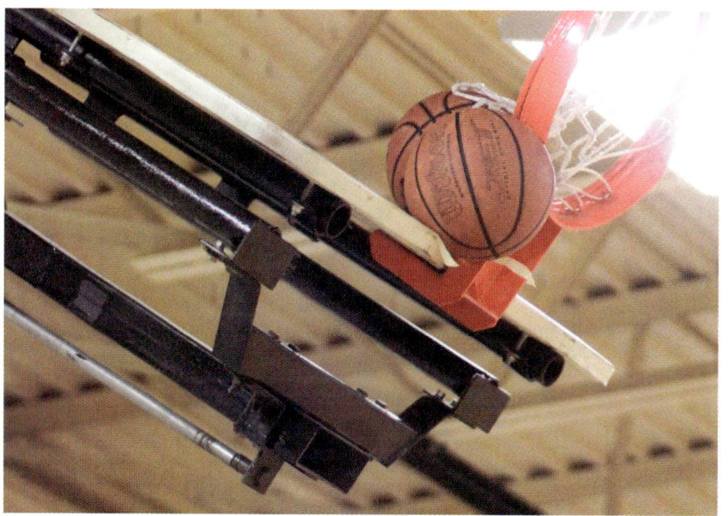

3.35 High ISO settings are helpful indoors when flash may not be effective or allowed. Exposure: ISO 6400, f/2.8, 1/500 second, 100mm f/2.8 lens.

3

The lower ISO settings — ISO 100, ISO 200, and ISO 400 — are good, all-purpose settings for use outside and in bright building interiors. Use ISO 800 and ISO 1600 when shooting in the evening, on overcast days, or indoors without a flash. When shooting at night or in a dark room, use ISO 3200, ISO 6400, ISO 12800, or ISO 25600. You can set the ISO at any point when using a Creative Zone mode. When your camera is set to a Basic Zone mode, the ISO is set automatically.

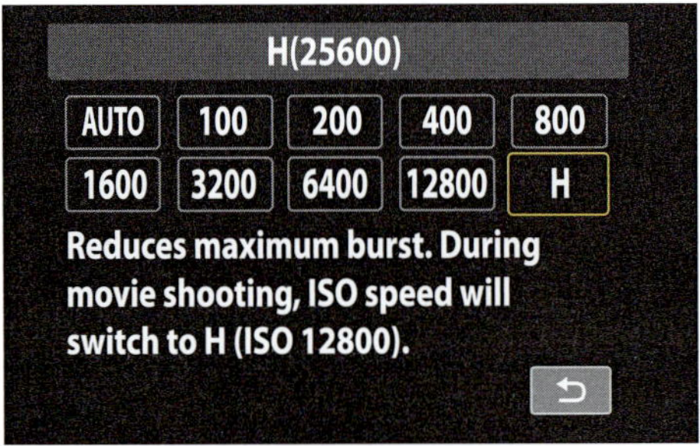

3.36 When Custom Function 2 is selected, the ISO range extends to ISO 25600.

NOTE In Portrait mode (portrait icon), your camera sets the ISO to 100. In the Bulb shooting mode (**B**), it sets the ISO to 400. The higher the ISO, the further away the camera can be and still make exposures using the dim light provided by the flash.

When Auto ISO is set on your camera, it selects the proper setting based on the shooting mode. In this mode, the ISO ranges from ISO 100 to ISO 6400 in most modes. You can limit this range by setting a maximum ISO. To do this, press the Menu button (**MENU**), choose menu 3 (third from the left), and then select Auto mode.

12 Things to Check After a Shoot

After you use your camera, it's a good idea to review the settings and make sure it's ready for your next photographic outing. Photographer Aaron Hockley likes to leave his camera in a known state so that he doesn't miss a photographic opportunity because his camera was left at an improper setting. The following is Aaron's list of 12 settings to check after a shoot:

- **Reset your ISO setting to your preferred sensitivity, such as ISO 200.** It's no fun realizing you unnecessarily took photographs on a bright, sunny day at ISO 6400.
- **Check your exposure mode.** Make sure you take your camera off modes you normally don't use. Place it back on Program AE (**P**) after experimenting on manual, for example.

- **Review your white balance.** If you shoot indoors one day and outside the next, your white balance will not be correct. Place it on Auto or your favorite setting during storage.
- **Make sure you clear your Picture Styles and modes that will alter a standard photograph.**
- **Make sure your drive mode is on Single (□) or Continuous (⧉).** You can lose a good photo opportunity if your self-timer is left on a 10-second countdown.
- **Return the exposure compensation to zero.**
- **If you set your camera to Manual focus (MF) during your shoot, make sure you return it to Autofocus mode (AF).**
- **Return your camera metering setting to your favorite position.**
- **Check the file size setting.** Always place it back to the largest size, such as RAW (RAW). You can always downsize, but you can't upsize.
- **Clear your memory card.** You don't want to risk losing your photos. Photographers lose good images by deleting files from their cards in the field.
- **Keep your camera and gear in the same place.** If you return your equipment to the same location, you will always know its location.
- **Check your support equipment, such as your flash.**

It may seem silly to worry about a few camera settings. However, with all the options you have on your Canon T5i/700D, you can waste precious time adjusting it, and that could cost you some fabulous images.

Aaron Hockley is an event, commercial, and portrait photographer from Vancouver, Washington. He shares commentary and information on his website: http://aaronhockley.com/.

3

The higher the ISO setting, the more noise you see in your images. *Noise* is the digital equivalent of grain in film. Camera companies, including Canon, have done a good job of limiting noise as they increase the ISO limits in cameras. The Canon T5i/700D is equipped with noise-reduction technology. In Shooting menu 3 (📷), you can select High ISO noise reduction to help reduce noise when you are photographing at a high ISO setting, such as ISO 12800. Another option in Shooting menu 3 (📷) is Long exp. noise reduction, which is used for exposures over 1 second. If you use this option, though, you will not be able to take another photograph until the noise reduction process is complete. Also, images shot over ISO 1600 may look grainier than normal, so use this feature in combination with lower ISOs.

Choosing File Quality and Format

The Canon Rebel T5i/700D has two file formats — RAW (one option) and JPEG (8 size/compression options) — and selecting the best one is not always easy. The best rule is to use the highest quality possible because you can always downsize, but you can't upsize and expect good results without specialized software. Even with good software, your results will vary. Don't be tempted by the large number of available photographs when you use a smaller file size and/or greater file compression. The number of photographs you can take may be impressive, but they will not be the best quality. If you need to take more images at one time, invest in larger memory cards. For the best quality results, set your camera to RAW (RAW).

The maximum camera resolution is approximately 17.9 megapixels, or 5182 × 3456 pixels (based on an aspect ratio of 3:2). This is the equivalent of a 17-1/4 × 11-1/2 photograph at 300 dpi (dots per inch). Your camera offers additional file size options that create file sizes as small as 720 × 480 pixels. Although larger files take up more room on a memory card, I recommend that you use the largest file size possible. It is always better to have the option of downsizing images rather than being stuck with files that are too small.

CAUTION The RAW (RAW) and Small 3 (S3) file formats cannot be resized. Also, resized images cannot be made larger later.

Image size and file numbering

Your camera's multiple image sizes range from 0.35 to 17.9 megapixels. It is best to use the largest size possible. Sometimes, you may want to downsize an image. This can be done in the Canon Digital Photo Professional software (which came with your camera on the EOS Digital Solutions Disk), Photoshop, or with software on the web. You also have the option of adjusting the image size in your camera. To do so, press the Playback button (▶), find the photograph you want to resize, and then press the Quick Control/Print button (Q). A menu appears on the left side of your screen and the bottom option is Image resize.

CROSS REF For more information about the Canon Digital Photo Professional software, see Appendix A.

The files in your camera are numbered from 0001 to 9999, and continue in this same order, even if you replace the memory card. If you want the number system to restart, you can set your camera to do so at any point. To select the numbering system, go to Shooting menu 1 (📷) and select File numbering.

NOTE You can create folders for more than one series of photos in Setup menu 1 (🔧).

The RAW file format

When you want the highest quality possible, RAW (RAW) is the best choice. However, you need special computer software to work with RAW files. Your camera comes with the EOS Digital Solutions Disk that includes the Canon Digital Photo Professional software. This program can handle RAW images and so can Photoshop, Lightroom, and Aperture.

The good thing about the RAW file setting (RAW) is that it stores the original data collected by your camera before a photograph is compressed into a Large fine (◢L) JPEG image. When you make adjustments to compressed files, such as JPEGs, the images lose quality with each adjustment. When you use the RAW format with the proper software to make adjustments, it is like re-exposing your image without losing quality.

The JPEG file format

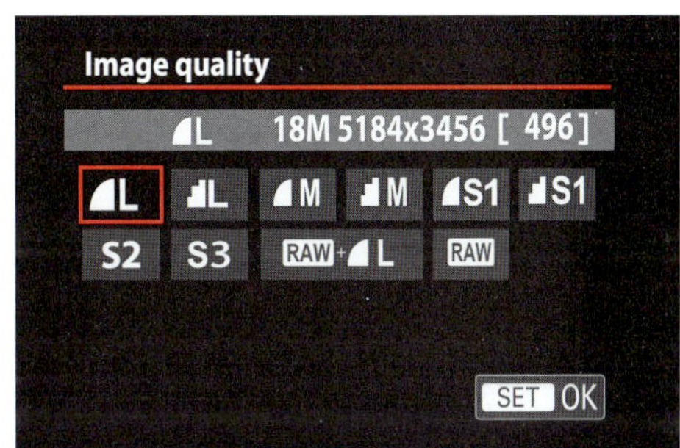

3.37 You have 10 image quality options; RAW is the highest and S3 is the lowest.

JPEG (Joint Photographic Experts Group) files are much smaller and easier to work with than RAW image files due to their size. This is the most common image file format used by photographers. One benefit of using JPEGs is the option to adjust the amount of compression applied to your photograph. The more a file is compressed, the smaller it is. However, the smaller a file is, the more information is lost. Your camera is capable of shooting in both the RAW (RAW) and Large fine (◢L) JPEG formats at the same time, giving you more options later in postproduction. However, this option also takes up more room on a memory card. If you are going to be shooting an event and taking many photos, JPEG is a good choice because the smaller file size is easier to work with in postproduction.

Your Canon Rebel T5i/700D offers the following eight JPEG size and compression options:

- **Large fine (◢ L).** Images at this setting are 17.9 megapixels. This is the highest-quality JPEG file setting your camera offers.
- **Large normal (▟ L).** These images are also 17.9 megapixels, but as they use additional compression, you can store about double the number of images versus the Large fine (◢ L) setting. Please note, though, that compression degrades the quality of an image.
- **Medium fine (◢ M).** Images at this setting are 8 megapixels. This average setting still produces large prints.
- **Medium normal (▟ M).** These images are also 8 megapixels. However, this setting produces about double the amount of images compared to the Medium fine setting (◢ M) by using additional compression. Remember, though, that compression degrades image quality.
- **Small fine (◢S1).** Images at this setting are 4.5 megapixels — a very small file size. This setting is useful for photographs created for websites, social media, or small 4 × 6 prints.
- **Small normal (▟S1).** Images at this setting are also 4.5 megapixels. However, additional compression means that it produces about double the amount of images compared to the Small fine setting (◢S1).
- **Small 2 (S2).** At 2.5 megapixels, images shot at this very small file size are best used for e-mail or the web.
- **Small 3 (S3).** Images shot at this setting are only 0.35 megapixels and, thus, are not ideal for most photography needs. However, this size is useful for special applications, such as web thumbnails or high-volume documentation.

Movie Mode

To shoot video, move the power switch to Movie mode (movie icon). The Canon T5i/700D is considered a full, High Definition (HD) camera. This means that it has the 1080 vertical pixels (or scanning lines) required for HD. When shooting video, I recommend that you use fast (class 6 or higher), large-capacity memory cards. Slower cards may not write as fast as the video is produced, which could affect the playback quality. When playing videos, connect your camera to a TV or monitor for better viewing.

CROSS REF See Chapter 9 for more info about how to connect your camera to a television.

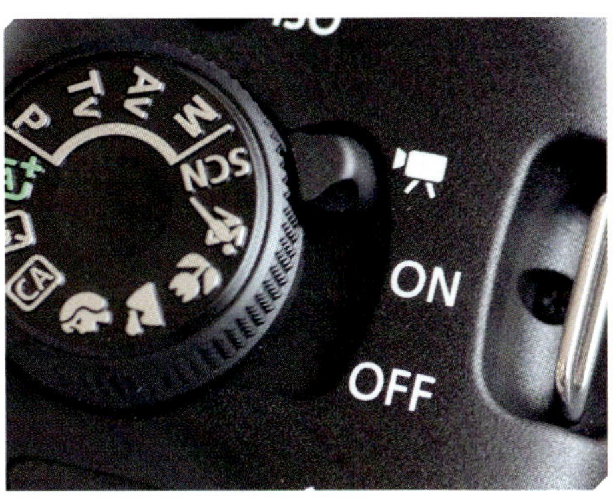

3.38 **The Movie mode is the top position on the power switch.**

Exposing for video

If your camera is set to any of the Basic Zone modes, it defaults to the Scene Intelligent Auto mode (A+). This means that the camera sets the shutter speed, aperture, and ISO. In Scene Intelligent Auto mode (A+), the camera also applies scene detection filters to enhance the video. The scene filter the camera detects appears on the LCD screen in the upper-left side of the frame. Auto exposure is fine for casual shooting, but when you want higher-quality video, experienced videographers recommend using the Manual shooting mode (**M**). This is because the camera tries to make adjustments as the scene changes in the automatic modes. This may seem convenient but, unfortunately, the results don't look very professional.

It is highly recommended that you use the Creative Zone modes when shooting video. The camera treats the Aperture-priority AE (**Av**) and Shutter-priority AE (**Tv**) modes the same as the Program AE mode (**P**). The Program AE mode (**P**) sets the camera shutter speed, aperture, and ISO. The biggest difference between the Scene Intelligent Auto (A+) and Program AE (**P**) modes is that Program AE mode (**P**) does not use scene detection. This means that you have more control over things like exposure compensation.

Manual (**M**) is the best mode for shooting high-quality video because it gives you control over the frame rate, shutter speed, aperture, and ISO. This is important because the other modes change the exposure settings while you are capturing video. If the exposure changes in the middle of a video clip, it is a sign of amateur work. The maximum ISO available for video is ISO 6400. Using Custom Function 1, option 2, you can set the ISO to High, which is the equivalent of ISO 12800. However, I wouldn't recommend using this setting because it creates a lot of digital noise in your video, and exposure compensation is not available when using the High ISO setting.

CROSS REF For more information about the relationship between shutter speed and frame rate, see Chapter 8.

Setting the file size and focus

The Canon Rebel T5i/700D has the following video size options:

- **1920 × 1080 (30 or 24 fps)**
- **1280 × 720 (60 fps)**
- **640 × 480 (30 fps)**

CROSS REF For more information about the effect frame rate has on your videos, see Chapter 8.

Your camera has a shooting time limit of 29 minutes and 59 seconds. If you use the highest file size (1920 × 1080), you need at least a 16GB memory card to record uninterrupted for the full time available. When you reach 29 minutes and 59 seconds, the camera automatically stops recording. Press the Live View shooting mode button (◘) and the camera begins recording again using a new video file.

NOTE Your camera turns on Live View Shooting mode (◘) for video capture and you have the same tracking options that you do when shooting still photography.

The default setting for video focus is Movie-servo AF (SERVO AF). This means that the camera focuses on the subject closest to it. You can turn this off by touching the Movie-servo AF (SERVO AF) icon in the lower-left corner of the LCD screen. When Movie-servo AF mode (SERVO AF) is off, your camera focuses once when you press the shutter button halfway. If you are not using a Canon STM lens, the audio of your video will likely include lens focus noise. Consider using Manual focus for higher-level video productions — to do so, select the Manual Focus mode (**MF**) on your lens.

NOTE If you press the shutter button all of the way, your camera takes a photo whether it is recording a movie or not.

CHAPTER 4

Using Lenses with the Canon EOS Rebel T5i/700D

Have you ever wondered how professional photographers get such beautiful, colorful, and sharp photographs? The photographer's skill plays an important role, but when it comes to equipment, the lens is the key to creating sharp images. No matter how good the camera body is, light travels through the lens before it reaches the camera's sensor. If you use a poor quality or defective lens, it is much harder to create high-quality imagery. The Canon EOS Rebel T5i/700D is a *dSLR* (digital single lens reflex) camera. This means you are not limited to the range and quality of a fixed camera lens. You can change the lens on a dSLR to suit your needs, vision, or photographic opportunities. In this chapter, I attempt to answer many of the most often asked questions about lenses.

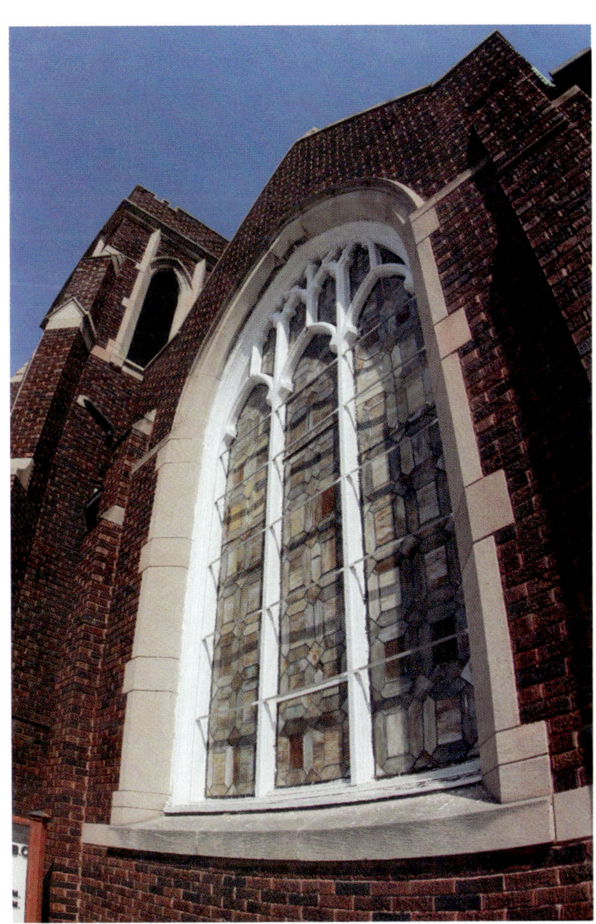

This photograph was taken using a fisheye lens.

Choosing a Good Lens

Before talking about lenses, I'll start with the basics. Understanding the proper way to attach a lens and hold your camera helps you take better photos. The idea is to use your hand as a base and your arm as a tripod to stabilize the camera and lens from the bottom. The larger the lens, the more important it is to properly support it, as shown in Figure 4.1. The EF (electrofocus) lens is Canon's standard model. EF-S lenses are designed for Canon cameras, such as your Rebel T5i/700D, because they have a mirror and sensor that is smaller than full-frame sensor cameras (resulting in a 1.6 crop factor). The *S* in *EF-S* stands for *short back-focus,* meaning that the back of the lens element is closer to the camera sensor. Most EF-S lenses are wide angle, allowing the photographer to use the full lens. The L (luxury) lens series is Canon's premium lens (with the price tag to match). When you want the highest quality possible, an L lens is a good choice.

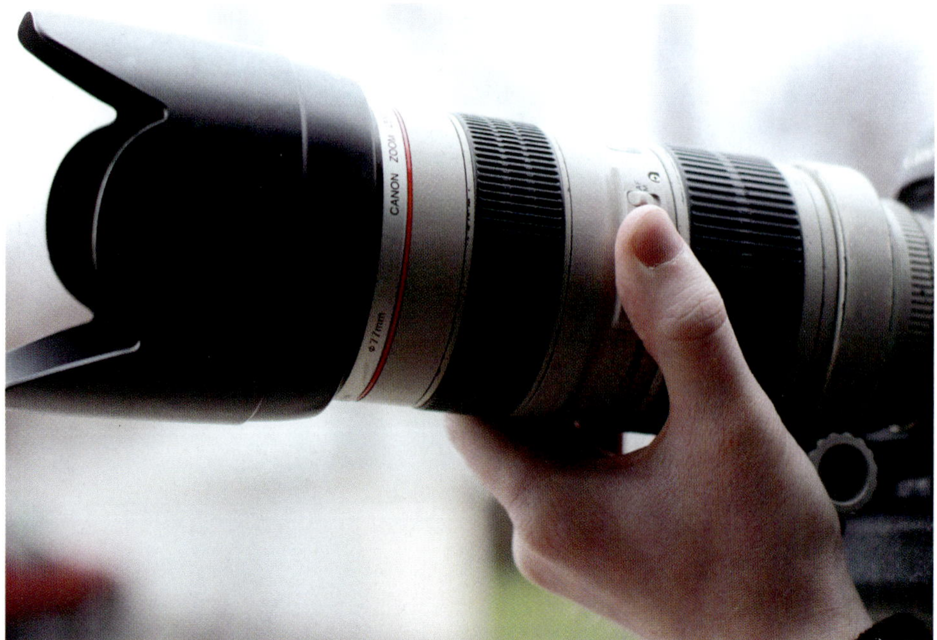

4.1 Always use your hand to support your lens and hold your elbows against your body for additional support.

To attach a Canon EF lens to your camera, align the red dot on the lens to the one on your camera. With the lens facing away from you, turn the lens to the left. For EF-S lenses, follow the same steps using the white squares. Remember, you can only use lenses with Canon-designated mounts on your camera.

Now for the big question: Why are lenses so expensive? It's because of the high cost of their design and manufacture. They have many parts that need to work with precision. It's safe to assume that the higher a lens is priced, the greater the quality of the glass and construction; an L series lens is a good example — it has a reputation for sharpness and clarity.

When choosing a lens, think about what type of pictures you want to take. Do you plan to shoot family events or take product shots for clients? Do you like to experiment with urban landscapes or document your travels? Making an informed choice about a lens saves you image quality and money. Buying lenses is an investment because, chances are, you will have your lenses longer than you will have your current camera.

NOTE Old EF lenses can be used with your Rebel T5i/700D, but older, manual FD-style lenses cannot.

So, how do you know if you have a good lens? As the lens is the eye of your camera, it needs to be sharp and offer good contrast. Low-quality lenses are not sharp around the edges, especially at lower apertures. Good lenses are well engineered and made with high-quality glass. High-quality lenses also have lower aperture numbers, which is good for shooting in low light. The best zoom lenses have the same aperture (usually f/2.8) at all focal lengths, are solidly constructed, and weatherproof. As a general rule, lower-quality zoom lenses have variable apertures, which means they change as you increase the focal length. For example, the Canon Rebel T5i kit lens (the EF-S 18-55mm f/3.5-5.6 IS STM) has an aperture of f/3.5 at 18mm and f/5.6 at 55mm. This doesn't mean it's a bad lens; it's just not as well constructed as higher-end lenses.

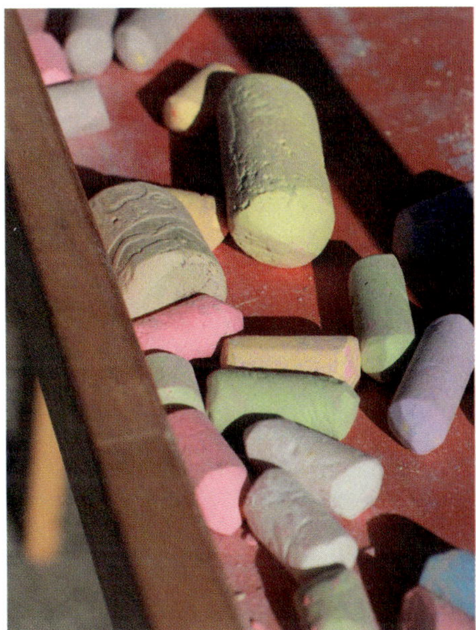

4.2 A good lens is sharp and has high-quality glass so you can easily see details in your images, as shown here. Exposure: ISO 100, f/9.0, 1/640 second, 50mm f/1.4 lens.

Your camera's lens is a combination of multiple glass elements. When a manufacturer describes a lens, it lists the number of elements in the lens. The idea is that the more elements there are, the better the image quality will be. On the other hand, a lens that has more elements also has more that can go wrong if it is not well made.

Many wide-angle lenses include an aspherical lens. An *aspheric lens* is designed to correct spherical and optical aberrations. In other words, they are used to correct lens distortion and blur that can occur around the edges. Much of what you pay for when you purchase a high-quality lens are the elements, which help decrease distortion in your images, such as a bubbled or bowing look. Quality lenses will increase the fine detail of your images, limit *vignetting* (dark edges), and improve contrast, which will improve the quality of whites and blacks in your image.

Focal lengths

When beginners ask me which lenses they should buy first, I usually recommend that they buy two zoom lenses to cover the full spectrum. For example, an 18-55mm lens and a 55-250mm lens cover most situations. If you are looking for an all-in-one solution, Canon offers lenses that range from wide to telephoto, such as the EF-S 18-135 f/3.5-5.6 IS STM kit lens. These simplistic options are not right for everyone, though. However, this chapter should help you figure out what combination will work best for the type of photography you want to pursue.

With the development of digital photography came the creation of the *crop factor,* or what the digital camera captures when compared to using the same EF lens on a 35mm film or full-frame digital camera. This is the result of a camera sensor being smaller than 35mm film. If a sensor is smaller than the traditional 35mm, it captures a portion of the image coming through the lens. This means you do not see as much of the scene as you would when using a full-frame dSLR with the same EF lens. It might seem cool that a 200mm lens is now working like a 300mm lens. Unfortunately, when it comes down to the wide-angle lens, such as the 24mm and 28mm, there is not as much to be enthusiastic about because the crop factor turns them into higher millimeter equivalents, too.

For the Canon T5i/700D, bear in mind what the effective focal lengths are for the lens you are considering. The crop factor for your camera is 1.6X. To figure out the effective focal length for your lens, multiply the lens value by 1.6. In other words, an EF 20mm lens is the equivalent of an EF 32mm lens, and an EF 200mm lens is the equivalent of an EF 320mm lens.

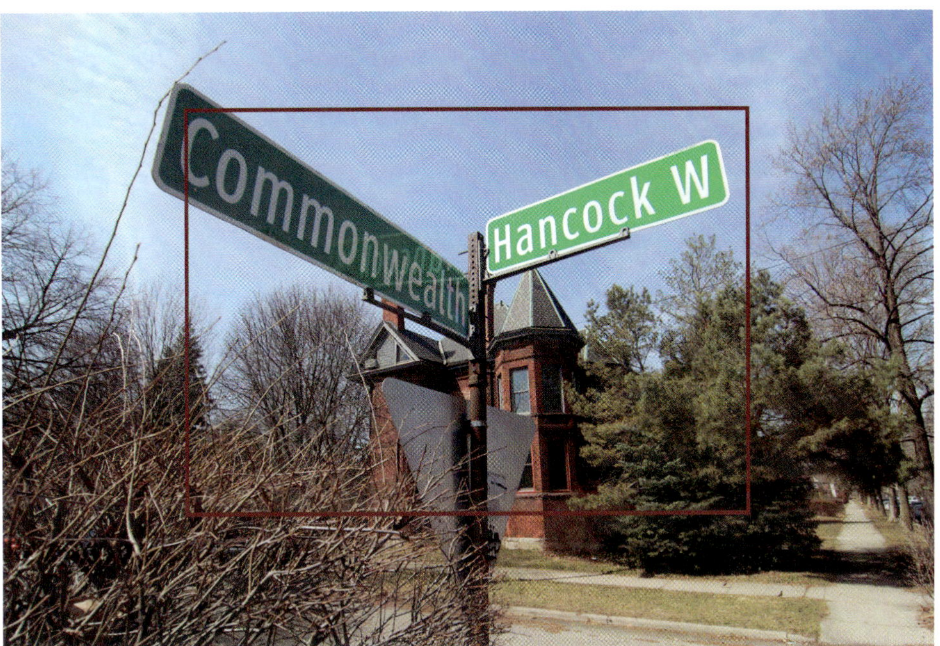

4.3 This shows the difference between an 18mm lens on a full-frame camera and the 1.6X crop factor with the Canon Rebel T5i/700D. Exposure: ISO 100, f/10, 1/200 second, 12-24mm f/4.0 lens at 12mm.

The following list covers the different types of lenses and how they can be used:

- **Ultrawide-angle.** Manufacturers have come to the rescue for cameras with crop factors, like the Canon Rebel T5i/700D, by creating ultrawide-angle lenses (under 20mm). These can be a blessing or a curse due to the distortion found along the edges. How much of an issue the distortion is depends on how you approach your subject. Take advantage of all of the real estate these lenses cover. Photojournalists regularly use ultrawide lenses to layer as much information into the frame as possible. When you use these lenses, make sure that your subject is not too far away and that you fill the frame. Canon produces four ultrawide zoom lenses. Three of them are L lenses, meaning they are high quality and expensive. The EF 17-40mm f/4.0L USM is a good, high-quality, all-purpose ultrawide lens worth considering for your Rebel T5i/700D.
- **Wide-angle.** Standard wide-angle lenses are the 24mm and 28mm. For a Rebel T5i/700D, they are closer to a standard (50mm) lens of equivalent focal length. So, if you are looking for a wide angle of view, I recommend an ultrawide-angle lens. Canon has eight standard prime lenses in the range of 20 to 35mm. The EF 24mm f/2.8 IS USM is a reasonably priced wide-angle lens to have in your bag.

If you want to step up to a higher-quality lens, the EF 24mm f/1.4L II USM is a good choice. Canon also offers an EF 15mm f/2.8 lens fisheye if you like the hemispherical distortion created by such lenses.

- **Standard.** Traditionally, the 50mm lens was considered the standard lens for a 35mm film or full-frame dSLR camera because it was the closest lens equivalent to the human eye. Anything below 50mm is considered wide-angle and anything above is considered a telephoto. It is a good all-purpose prime lens. For photography purists, a 50mm is standard equipment because it doesn't distort the image. For your T5i/700D, a 30mm or 35mm is a closer equivalent to the human eye. Canon makes three 50mm lenses, but the EF 50mm f/1.4 is priced in the middle. The Canon 40mm f/2.8 STM is a good choice for video use. It is not very expensive and is designed to be quiet.
- **Zoom.** These have multiple focal lengths and are good all-purpose lenses for everyday photography. Economy zooms have *variable apertures*, which means that the aperture increases as you increase the focal length. Higher-end zooms have the same aperture (such as f/2.8) at all focal lengths. Because your camera has the ability to follow-focus while shooting video, I would recommend the EF-S 18-135mm f/3.5-5.6 IS STM lens as a good all-purpose zoom lens. If you want to upgrade, the EF 24-70mm 2.8L USM and 24-105mm f/4L IS USM are both excellent choices.
- **Telephoto.** Bring the world closer to you with this type of lens. Sports, nature, and wildlife photographers prefer telephoto lenses from 200mm to 600mm. When using a telephoto lens, it is important to keep track of your shutter speed (over 1/500 second). A faster shutter speed keeps your subject sharp. If using a fast shutter speed is not possible, a tripod or monopod may be required.

One of my favorite Canon telephoto lenses is the EF 135mm f/2.8 with soft-focus portrait lens (I rarely use the soft-focus option, however). Portrait lenses are generally 70mm to 135mm. Unlike wide lenses, they do not distort or exaggerate your subject. I use this lens for many types of photography, including events, because it is light and easy to move around in stealth mode. The EF 70-200mm f/2.8L is considered a standard telephoto zoom and is an excellent high-quality lens to consider. Canon makes three variations of this lens, with and without Image Stabilization (IS), but it also has a wide variety of telephoto zooms available at every price point. Canon makes telephoto lenses ranging as high as 800mm (these are considered *super-telephoto lenses*). However, the larger ones cost thousands of dollars.

TIP *Lens extenders* increase the reach of a lens. Canon sells two models for its L series lenses: The EF 1.4x III increases the focal length of a lens by 40 percent; the EF 2x III doubles the focal length. However, extenders also decrease the amount of light reaching the sensor by 1 to 2 stops.

Autofocus

Most modern cameras are autofocus cameras. Autofocus is helpful when you are taking many photographs quickly, such as at an event, and don't want to think about focusing. Canon cameras have a fast autofocus system, but it really depends on the lens you use. For example, a prime lens often focuses faster than a long zoom lens. You don't have to keep your camera on autofocus all of the time. There is a switch on the side of the lens that turns autofocus on and off. I do this a lot, depending on the subject. Sometimes, if it's dark or I want to prefocus for an expected event, such as an athlete crossing the finish line, I turn off autofocus. Today's autofocus systems are very good and highly dependable.

NOTE Some Canon lenses have focus preset buttons. These are handy when shooting sports, or events with a goal or finish line.

NOTE It is easy to confuse lens speed and autofocus speed. Lens speed refers to the aperture of your lens.

Aperture and depth of field

When photographers talk lenses, they first mention the focal length and then the aperture. The *aperture* is the diaphragm opening in the lens that controls the amount of light allowed into the camera. High aperture numbers, such as f/22, produce a larger depth of field, increasing the amount of the scene or subject that is in focus. A traditional landscape is a good example of a scene with a large depth of field. Lower apertures, such as f/2.8, produce a shallower depth of field. Shallow depths of field are common in portraiture. Photographers also sometimes refer to lenses as *slow* or *fast*. A lens with a large maximum aperture, such as f/2.8, is considered fast because it allows more light into the camera compared to a maximum lens opening of f/4.5. More light means that you can increase your shutter speed, photograph in lower light, and see your image better with a brighter view. Slow lenses are generally darker, and don't have the low-light and speed advantages.

Quality zoom lenses have the same aperture at every focal length compared to lower-priced lenses with variable apertures. This means the more affordable lens aperture is smaller as you increase the focal length. It may be represented by f/3.5-5.6, which means that the lens starts out with a larger f/3.5 aperture at a shorter focal length, and then decreases to f/5.6 as the focal length increases. This is a disadvantage because you often need the larger apertures when photographing at a longer focal length to keep the shutter speed higher.

CROSS REF For more information on depth of field, see Chapter 5.

Depth of field is the area of focus around the subject. The larger the depth of field is, the larger the area around the subject that is in focus. The focal length of each lens has a different affect on depth of field. As a rule, the lower the aperture number, the higher the quality of the lens is when compared to equivalents. The EF 35mm f/1.4L USM is an example of a high-quality lens with a low aperture.

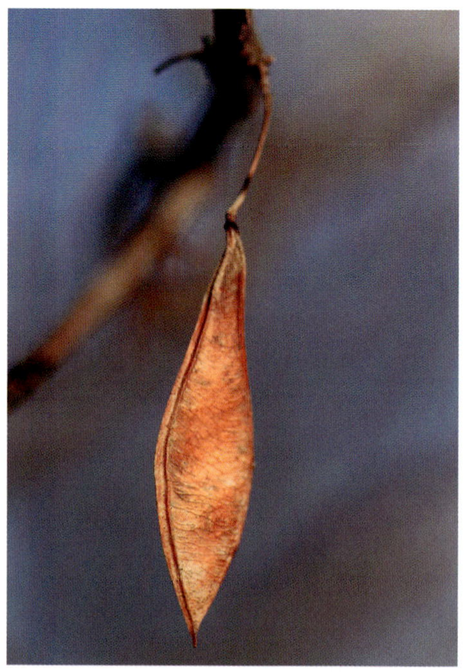

4.4 This image has a shallow depth of field, which blurs the background. Exposure: ISO 200, f/2.8, 1/1000 second, 100mm f/2.8 macro lens.

Image Stabilization (IS)

When you see IS in the name of a Canon lens, it means it has *Image Stabilization*. The lens detects camera shake using microchips and gyro sensors to help the camera provide sharper images at lower shutter speeds. In many situations, the photographer gains 1 to 4 stops. In other words, if you handhold your camera while photographing a stationary subject, you can use a lower than normal shutter speed. For example, when using a non-IS 200mm lens, the general recommendation is to set your shutter speed to at least 1/200 second. When using an IS lens, you might achieve similar results at 1/30 second.

However, this doesn't mean it fully eliminates blurring. Fast-moving subjects and very low shutter speeds still show movement, and IS does not correct the sharpness of subjects that are not in proper focus. Image Stabilization is designed for stationary subjects, but it's helpful when you have low light and don't want to use a higher ISO. You find Image Stabilization most often on longer lenses because camera shake is more of a problem at a lens tip far way from the focal plane. Also, consider Image stabilization lenses when recording video to help prevent frame-to-frame jitter.

NOTE Some Image Stabilization lenses have a panning mode option called Optical Image Stabilizer Mode 2 that automatically turns off if it detects a panning motion.

Vignetting

Vignetting happens when light falls away and doesn't reach the edges — notably the corners — of your frame. It is most noticeable with wide-angle lenses, but a good lens does not have this issue. With that in mind, vignetting is not always bad. It can be corrected to a point in Photoshop or your favorite photo-editing program by using dodging or anti-vignetting tools.

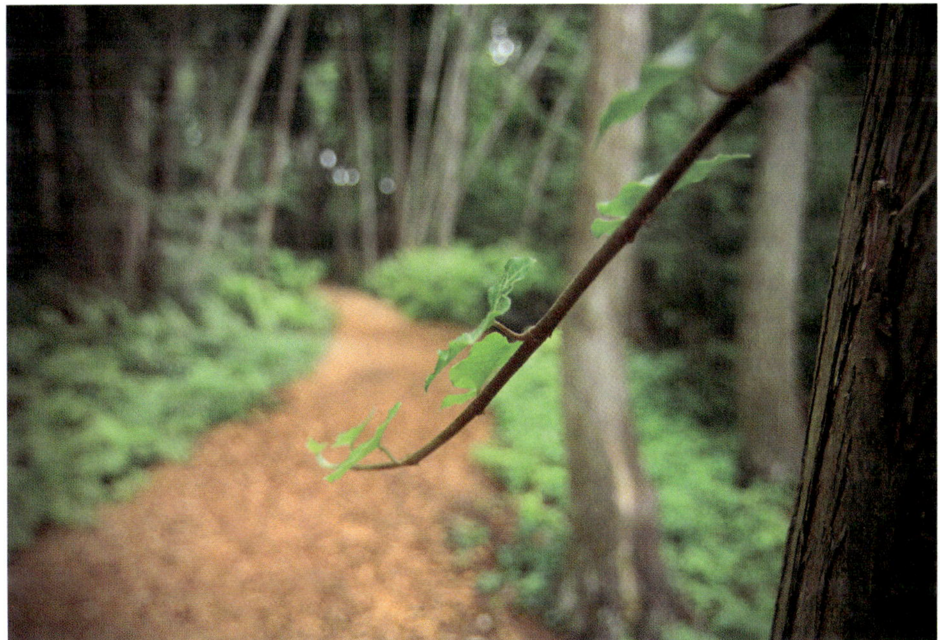

4.5 A dark area around the edges of a photo (especially in the corners) is called vignetting. Exposure: ISO 800, f/4.5, 1/100 second, 12-24mm f/4.0 lens at 20mm.

Some photographers like the effect it has on their images, and it is not uncommon to add it during postproduction. You can test your camera lens for vignetting by photographing a white piece of paper with the aperture wide open. Look for darkening corners to determine how much vingetting occurs with each lens.

NOTE Using lens shades on wide-angle lenses, using the incorrect lens shade, or stacking too many filters can cause vignetting.

Types of Lenses

A good lens for a beginning photographer is the kit lens that is available for purchase with your camera body. It is an inexpensive option to get you started when building a lens collection. Not all lenses are the same. On the contrary, each one is different and worth testing to make sure you get the sharpest picture. Even the same type of lens from the same manufacturer can produce different results. Some photographers test multiple lenses before they purchase one.

> **TIP** Test any lenses you are considering buying at your local photography store. You can also use websites like www.borrowlenses.com to rent one and see if you like it before you purchase it.

The following list covers different types of lenses and their uses:

- **Kit lenses.** A kit lens is one that is bundled for sale with a camera, like the one shown in Figure 4.6. Some kit lenses are better than others, but as a rule they tend to be lower quality. There are two kit lens options for the Canon Rebel T5i/700D: The EF-S 18-55 f/3.5-5.6 IS STM or the EF-S 18-135 f/3.5-5.6 IS STM (the more expensive option). These are intended to get you started without adding too much money to the price of the camera body. If you already have lenses that you like, a kit lens will not be an upgrade to your gear, and you should consider purchasing only the camera body.
- **Electrofocus (EF) lenses.** All modern Canon lenses are referred to as EF lenses (see Figure 4.7). They are good autofocus lenses and are priced much lower than the professional L lenses that Canon also manufactures.

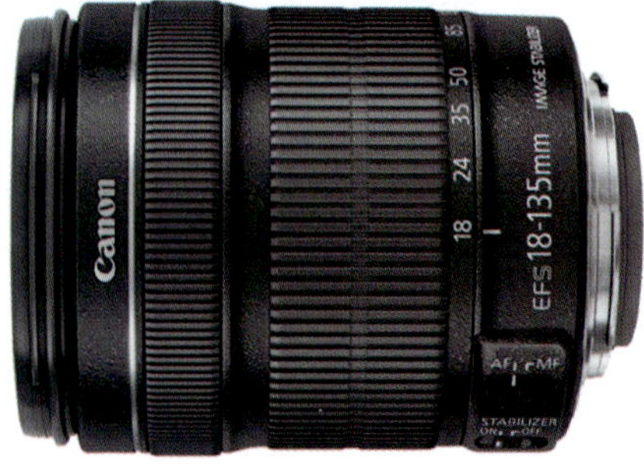

Image courtesy of Canon

4.6 The EF-S 18-135mm f/3.5-5.6 IS STM is one of two lenses that are available as the kit lens for the T5i/700D.

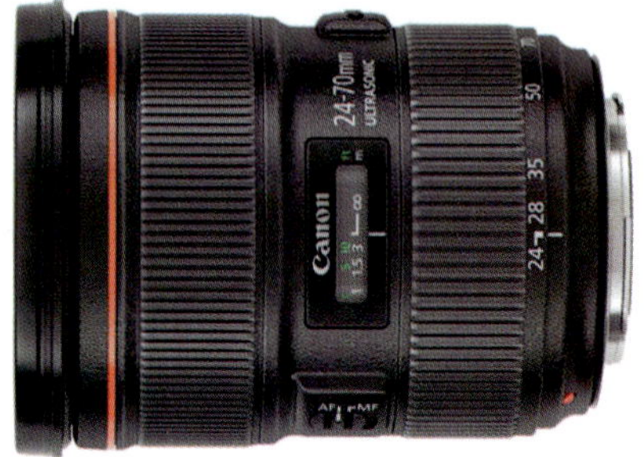

Image courtesy of Canon

4.7 The 24-70mm f/2.8 II USM lens is one of Canon's many EF lenses.

- **Electrofocus short back-focus (EF-S) lenses**. The S in EF-S stands for *short back-focus,* meaning that the back of the lens element is closer to the camera sensor. This lens, shown in Figure 4.8, is designed for digital crop cameras, like the Rebel T5i/700D, which has a 1.6 crop factor. The white square on the camera's lens mount means that it accepts EF-S lenses. However, this type of lens does not work on full-frame or film cameras. Consider this fact if you plan to upgrade to a full-frame camera in the future.
- **Luxury (L) lenses.** A red line around a Canon lens identifies it as a premium lens. They are constructed of excellent glass, which gives you sharp photos from edge to edge and good contrast. They are built for heavy use in all types of environments and weather. L lenses are expensive and, as such, a true investment in your photography.

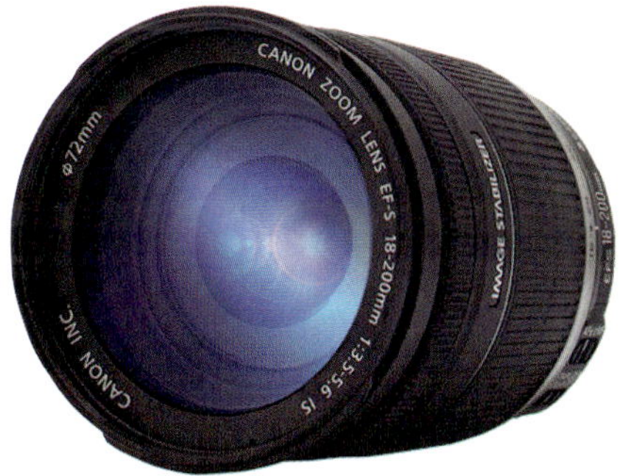

Image courtesy of Canon

4.8 The Canon EFS 18-200mm f/3.5-5.6 IS lens is designed for Canon cameras with a 1.6 crop factor.

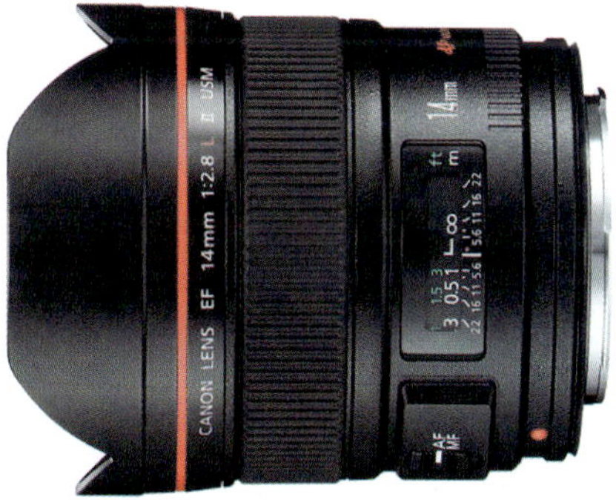

Image courtesy of Canon

4.9 You can tell that this 14mm lens is a premium Canon L lens by the red line around the barrel.

- **Stepper Motor (STM) lenses.** Autofocus lenses make noise, and this is a problem if you are shooting in Movie mode ('🎥) and using the Rebel T5i/700D continuous-focus technology. Most lenses for dSLR cameras are not designed with video in mind. However, the new Canon STM lens system uses *step* *motor technology* for quiet focusing while in Movie mode ('🎥). This is helpful for keeping the noise level down while the camera continues to focus in the AI Servo mode (**AI SERVO**).

- **Ultra Sonic Motor (USM) lenses.** These are ultra-quiet, fast-focusing lenses for Canon cameras. Many of the high-quality Canon lenses are USM lenses, such as the EF-S 17-55mm f/2.8L IS USM.

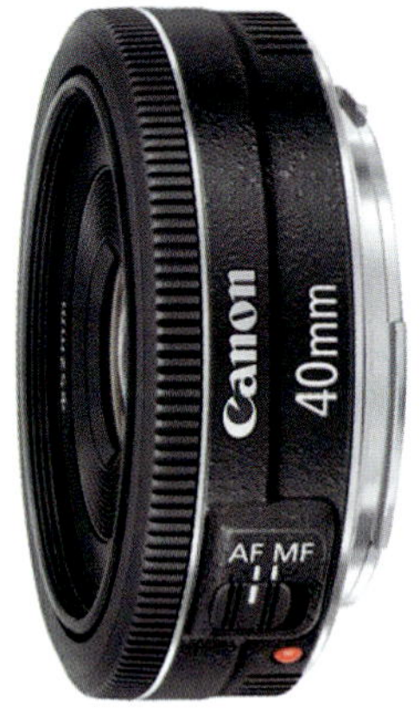

Image courtesy of Canon

4.10 The Canon 40mm f/2.8 was designed as a quiet lens for video.

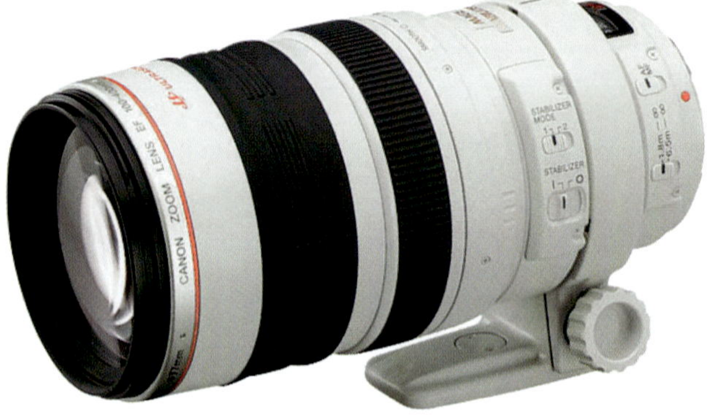

Image courtesy of Canon

4.11 This Canon EF 100-400L 4.5-5.6 is an ultra-quiet USM lens.

- **Third-party lenses.** You don't have to purchase all of your lenses from Canon. Third-party manufacturers make lenses for multiple camera brands, and often at a lower price point. The quality of third-party lenses has greatly improved over the years, and some even make lens types that are not available through Canon. The following companies make lenses for Canon bodies:
  - **Bower.** This company is known for specialty lenses, including a range of fisheye lenses.
  - **Rokinon.** This manufacturer is best known for its selection of wide-angle lenses at affordable prices.

- **Sigma.** This company has been one of the top third-party lens manufacturers for over 50 years.
- **Tokina.** One of my favorite third-party brands, Tokina offers sharp lenses at affordable prices. I use the Tokina 12-24 f/4.0 regularly.
- **Tamron.** This company offers a full line of zoom lenses in a competitive price range.

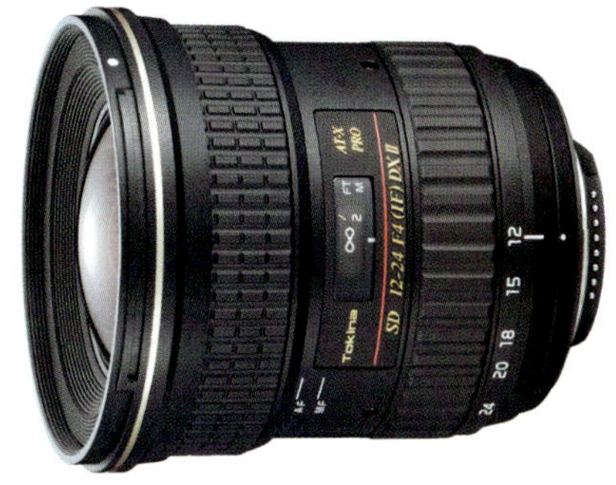

Image courtesy of Tokina

4.12 The Tokina 12-24mm f/4.0 is a good third-party lens.

- **Vivitar.** Best known for its flash accessories, Vivitar also has a full line of inexpensive, midrange lenses.
- **Zeiss.** This company has a long tradition of manufacturing high-quality lenses.

All lens manufacturers seem to go through phases in which they excel in one lens type over another. It is always important to read reviews, and test and evaluate a lens before you buy it.

CAUTION If a lens costs a lot less than a comparable Canon model, there is most likely something missing, such as Image Stabilization (IS).

Prime versus Zoom Lenses

A prime lens is a fixed-focal-length lens, such as a 28mm. A zoom lens offers you multiple focal lengths in one lens, such as a 70-200mm. Prime lenses are known for their ease of use, and they tend to be sharper, especially along the edge of your image frame. Zooms are good all-purpose lenses for everyday use. They are convenient for situations where the distance of your subject frequently changes.

Understanding prime lenses

A prime lens has a fixed focal length. I prefer prime lenses and use them as often as possible. They are lighter, faster, and traditionally sharper than zoom lenses. They are also less expensive than zooms and tend to be a good value for the money.

Photographers appreciate the shallow depth of field they gain with the larger aperture prime lenses offer. For example, the Canon EF 85 f/1.8 USM can produce an extremely shallow depth of field when set wide open at f/1.8.

Not every photographer takes advantage of prime lenses. Some purists only use a 50mm prime lens because it is nearly equivalent to what the human eye captures. Commercial photographers often use prime lenses, especially in a studio, to achieve the best possible focus and clarity. Many sports photographers like to use prime lenses because their low aperture allows them to maximize the shutter speed to stop action. The disadvantage is that you have to change your lens if you want a different focal length. If you plan to use many focal lengths in a short period of time, you should consider a zoom lens.

Understanding zoom lenses

Zoom lenses are an excellent choice for vacation photography — you only need to pack one or two to cover almost any situation. One moment you could be photographing a landscape and the next you could capture a candid portrait of an interesting local. If low light is not an issue, I like to use telephoto zoom lenses for sports photography so I can make adjustments as a play develops. You always want to be prepared, and a good zoom helps.

There are different types of zooms. Some, such as the Canon EF 16-35mm f/2.8L II USM, cover a short focal-length range. Others, such as the EF-S 18-200mm f/3.5-5.6 IS, cover a wide focal-length range. Telephoto zooms, such as the EF 70-300mm f/4-5.6 IS UM, cover higher focal lengths. Event photographers often use zoom lenses because they need to be ready for anything at any moment.

Specialty Lenses

Specialty lenses perform specific functions. You may not use them every day, but it is nice to know they are in your bag if needed. The following list includes some types of specialty lenses:

- **Fisheye.** The difference between the ultrawide-angle lens and a fisheye lens is the presentation of the wide view. A fisheye produces a highly distorted image, as shown in Figure 4.13.

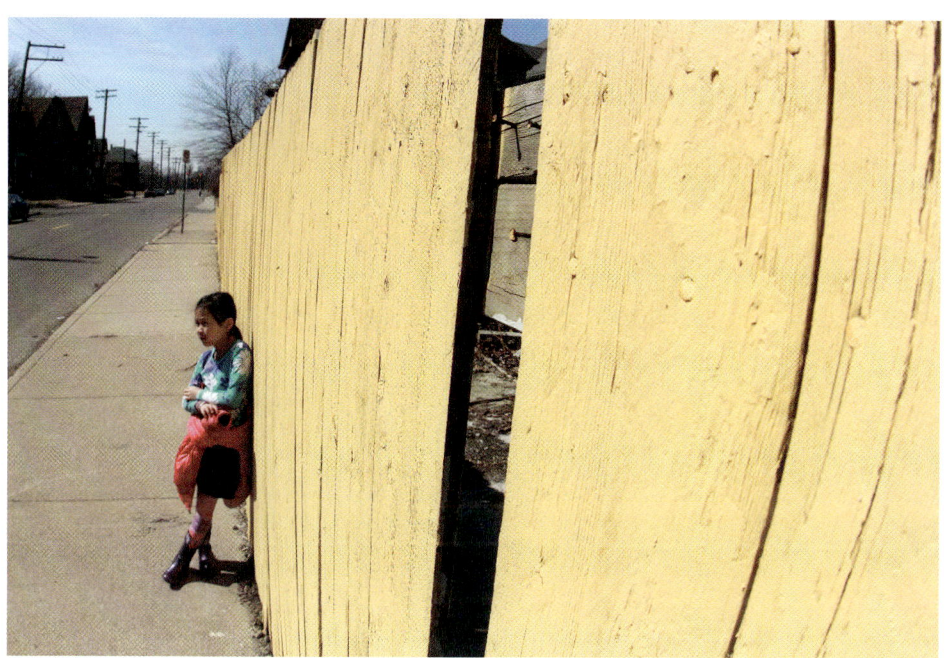

4.13 You can tell this image was created with a fisheye lens due to the distortion along the right side. Exposure: ISO 100, f/10, 1/400 second, 15mm f/2.8 fisheye lens.

- **Macro.** Macro lenses are built for photographing the world of the small. Most lenses are not able to focus close enough to create decent images of small objects. Macro lenses are designed to solve this problem. As always, you should test different lenses to see what type of macro you prefer. Some are dedicated to close-up photography, while others can also be used as regular lenses. Nature photographers often use a macro lens to photograph insects, flowers, and plants. This type of photography is a lot of fun because you get to see things that are often overlooked, or see something familiar in a new way. There

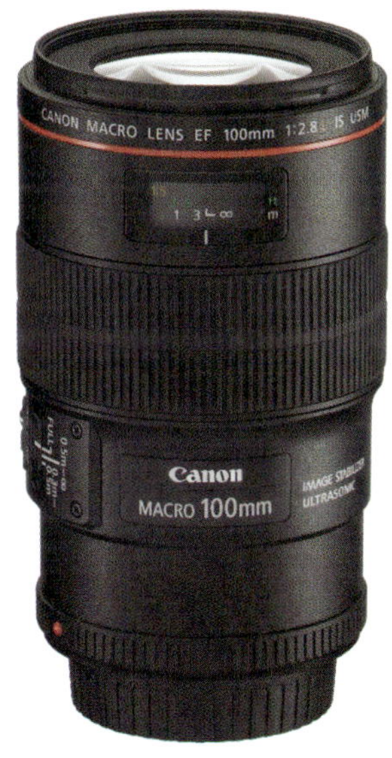

Image courtesy of Canon

4.14 The Canon 100mm f/2.8L Macro IS USM lens is for close-up photography.

are many subjects to photograph in your own backyard if you have a macro lens. Canon makes six macro lenses, but I recommend the 100mm f/2.8 Macro USM. It is versatile and, in my experience, can also be used as a portrait lens in a pinch.

NOTE Macro photography uses a very shallow depth of field, so a tripod is recommended for point-of-focus accuracy.

- **Tilt-shift.** When you photograph a building with a wide-angle lens, you will notice that the lines of the building lean in the image. A tilt-shift lens corrects this by allowing the photographer to shift the lens to create proper perspective and tilt it to alter the focus plain. These lenses have many advantages when correcting for perspective, as well as depth of field. While it's often suggested that a tilt-shift lens changes the depth of field, it doesn't. Rather, it moves the center point of the focal plane to match the subject instead of the plane of focus cutting through the subject, rendering part of it out of focus (due to a shallow depth of field). The photographer can adjust the focus plane to match the subject, keeping the subject in focus and the rest of the scene out of focus. Using a tilt-shift lens for panoramic photographs is an excellent way to keep lines straight while still having the advantage of a wide-angle lens. Canon has four tilt-shift lenses in its lineup ranging from 17mm to 90mm. All are high quality and expensive. If you need this type of lens, your biggest consideration is how wide you need it to be. For the T5i/700D, my recommendation is the wider the better.

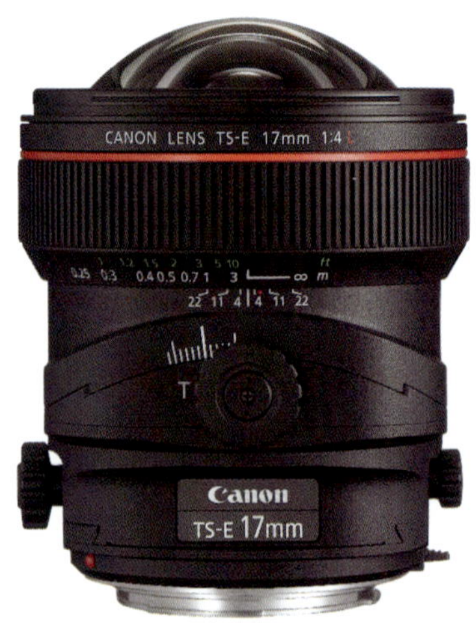

Image courtesy of Canon

4.15 The Canon TS-E 17mm f/4.0L tilt-shift lens is commonly used for correcting perspective.

The following list recommends the best lenses for specific types of photography:

- **Architecture.** Wide-angle lenses are most popular for architectural photography because the ability to get the entire structure in the shot is important. If you want to spend the extra money, a tilt-shift lens is the way to go.
- **Family.** I recommend that you have a good, all-purpose zoom lens for family photography. One moment you may be photographing a child and the next a group photo with all of your relatives.
- **Landscape.** This type of photography is similar to architecture, and wide-angle lenses are preferred. Of course, whenever you are in the field, you never know what you might find, so having a good telephoto lens is also highly recommended.
- **Portrait.** A good portrait lens is between 70mm to 135mm because they do not distort the subject. Plus, you don't have to be in the person's face to take the photo. Unless you are creating an environmental portrait, people prefer to be photographed by a longer lens because wider lenses distort and widen the subject. None of my portrait clients has ever asked to be widened. Larger lenses, such as a 70-200mm f/2.8, do work, but they can overwhelm your subject. Telephoto prime lenses have a lower aperture, which gives photographers the option to create a shallow depth of field. This is helpful for separating your subject from the background.
- **Environmental portraits.** When you want to tell a story about a person, an environmental portrait is an excellent option. Usually, the person is looking at or posing for the camera, which is different from a candid shot, in which the subject is either ignoring or unaware of the camera. These types of images can be taken with any lens, but a wide-angle is the traditional choice to better show the environment around your subject.
- **Food Photography.** The best food photography fills the frame with the subject. I prefer a good macro lens, like the Canon 100 f/2.8 Macro IS USM, for food work. The f/2.8 aperture is helpful for creating a shallow depth of field, which is preferred for editorial-style food photography.
- **Travel.** One or two good all-purpose zoom lenses are very helpful when traveling. A wide lens for landscapes and a telephoto to photograph people will do the trick. The less gear you need to think about during your trip, the happier you will be.
- **Sports.** Dark gymnasiums and arenas are not a photographer's best friend. This is why photographers who shoot action prefer lenses with lower apertures to deliver maximum shutter speeds. It is common to see sports photographers with longer telephoto lenses because they need to catch action across a long

field. They also use wide-angle lenses to capture action happening directly in front of them.

- **Street Photography.** Documentary artists or street photographers like to use 50mm or wide-angle lenses because they allow the photographer to remain inconspicuous. It is intuitive to think a long lens is the right choice, but big lenses are more likely to attract attention.
- **Wildlife and nature.** Wild animals don't like you to get too close, and there are some you probably don't want to get too close to anyway. This is why telephoto lenses are popular with wildlife photographers. Birds are a specialty and usually require at least a 300mm lens or longer. Also, consider bringing a macro lens with you to photograph the little things you find along the way.

CROSS REF For more information on different types of photography, see Chapter 7.

CHAPTER 5

Exploring Exposure and Composition

Which aperture to use is one of the most common issues discussed by photographers. Understanding how other photographers approach a subject is an important part of learning to improve your own photography. It is helpful to think about the process of taking a photograph. If you want to be a successful photographer, you need to understand the mechanics of exposure and composition. Your job, with the support of your camera's metering system, is to decide which combination is best for the scene in front of you. Although there are many automatic exposure options, I urge you to explore and learn more about how exposure works. Don't just point and shoot, and then settle for what the camera gives you. Take charge and compose your images to create the results you desire.

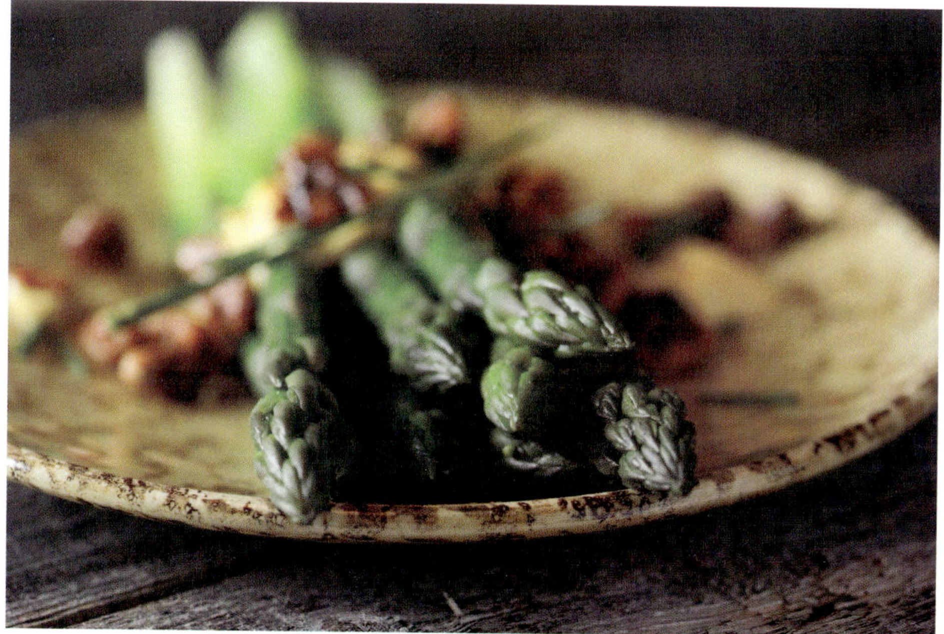

The shallow depth of field in this image was achieved by using a large aperture.

Choosing the Right Exposure

You can turn almost anything into a camera, which is just a lightproof box. Even the room you are in could be a camera if you cover the windows and keep out all of the light. If you place a large white piece of paper on one wall and drill a hole in the other, you see an image of the outside world reflected upside down on the paper. Light travels in a straight line, reflecting from its source. The piece of paper is the light-sensitive material that captures the image. In your camera, the light-sensitive material is electronic, and it is known as a sensor.

The hole in the wall is the aperture that allows light to pass through. If you let the light continuously hit the light-sensitive material, it overexposes the image. You need the shutter to start and stop the light from traveling into your camera. The intensity of light and the sensitivity of the light-sensitive material (the sensor) also determine how large or small the opening (the aperture) in the wall is, and how long the shutter must remain open. When using a dSLR, *exposure* is the amount of light that fills the camera sensor after you click the shutter button.

Fortunately, your camera makes all the complicated stuff easy. The advanced technology in the Canon Rebel T5i/700D makes creating a photograph as simple as pressing a button in the Basic Zone modes. If you want more control over the process, you can take the reins by using the Creative Zone modes. These modes give you full or partial control of the exposure.

Here are some quick tips to get you started (they are explained in more detail later in this chapter):

- **Use the Program AE mode (P).** Consider this the P for Panic mode. This mode sets the shutter speed and aperture for the proper exposure. You can also use Scene Intelligent Auto mode (A+) for the same purpose. This mode detects and applies settings to enhance your photo based on the scene. When you are not sure what to do and need to get the shot, let the camera do the thinking.
- **Select a high-enough shutter speed.** When you handhold your camera, use a shutter speed of 1/60 second or higher to prevent blur. If you want to stop the action, use a shutter speed of more than 1/500 second. The general rule is to use a shutter speed equal to or greater than the length of the lens. For example, if you are using a 100mm lens, your shutter speed should be at least 1/125.

- **Select the right aperture.** The higher the aperture number, the greater the depth of field. The lower the aperture number, the shallower the depth of field. If you want everything in focus, use a higher aperture number, such as f/22. If you want your subject to pop (that is, to appear separate from the background) use a low aperture number, such as f/2.8, to create a shallow depth field.
- **Select the right ISO setting.** The higher the ISO setting, the less light necessary for an exposure. If you want crisper and cleaner images (that is, with less noise), I recommend that you use a lower ISO, such as ISO 100, for better quality.
- **Use the Bulb shooting mode (B) for long exposures.** If you desire an exposure over 30 seconds, use Bulb mode (**B**). This setting holds the shutter open as long as you press the shutter button. Use a tripod and cable release to make this easier, and avoid camera shake when you press the shutter button. Your camera must be on Manual mode (**M**) to use the Bulb shooting mode (**B**).
- **Remember the dark side of filters.** When you put dark or color filters on the lens, they reduce the amount of light entering the lens, and the photograph needs more exposure. This also affects the shutter speed or aperture, depending on what exposure setting you use. The amount of light blocked by the filter is called the *filter factor*. Knowing how a filter affects your exposure helps you determine what support equipment you might need, such as a tripod.
- **Know how shutter speed and aperture work.** A fast shutter speed (like 1/1000 second) stops action. A slow shutter speed (like 1/8 second) shows motion. Increasing the shutter speed by 1 stop cuts the amount of light entering the camera by half; decreasing it by 1 stop doubles the amount of light entering the camera. Opening the aperture by 1 stop doubles the amount of light entering the camera; closing it by 1 stop cuts the amount of light in half. A high aperture (f/22) creates a large depth of field and a low aperture number (f/2.8) creates a shallow depth of field. Depth of field looks different depending on the lens you use.
- **Meter the exposure.** The combination of the intensity of the light source and camera ISO (sensitivity) setting determines the proper shutter speed and aperture necessary for a proper exposure. If you photograph a subject at a distance, handhold a gray card and meter off it under the same lighting conditions. Use the same meter reading off the gray card for the subject in the distance.

A photograph is *underexposed* when there is not enough light during the exposure process. This makes the photograph look too dark, as shown in Figure 5.1. A photograph that is *overexposed* has received too much light in the exposure process. This makes the picture look too bright, as shown in Figure 5.2.

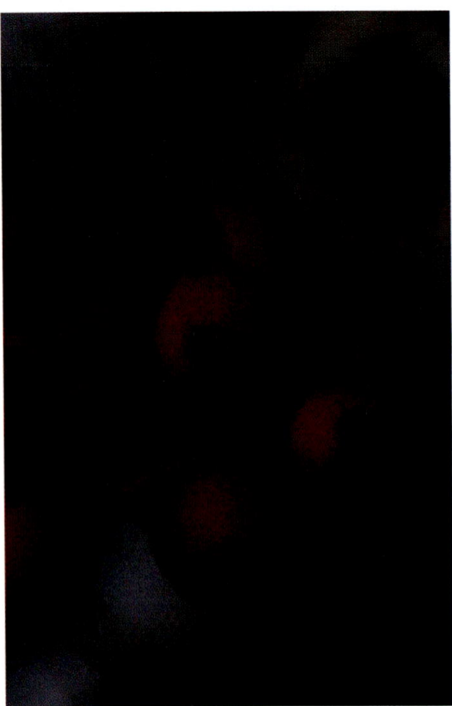

5.1 In this underexposed photo, the shadow details are lacking. Exposure: ISO 1600, f/2.8, 1/2000 second, 100mm f/2.8 lens.

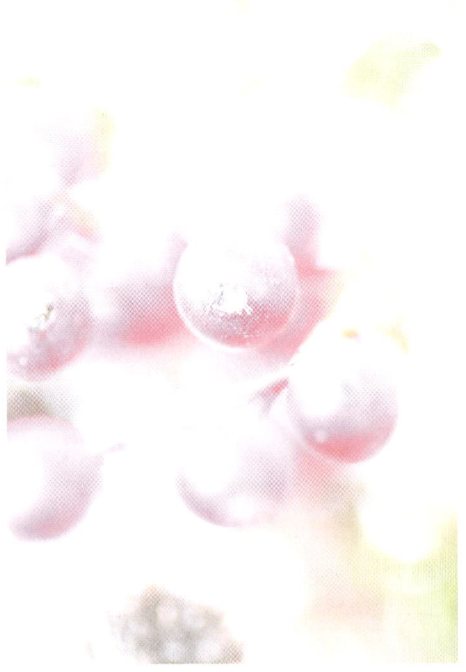

5.2 In this overexposed image, the highlight details are lacking. Exposure: ISO 1600, f/2.8, 1/30 second, 100mm f/2.8 lens.

The Basic Zones are automatic; you do not have to make any adjustments when using them. The following are the Basic Zone modes and when to use them:

- **Scene Intelligent Auto (A+).** You can use this all-purpose mode for everyday photography. It analyzes the scene and adjusts the shutter speed, aperture, and focus as needed. This mode is good for family events, travel, or changing scenes and weather conditions.
- **No flash (⚡).** When it is not appropriate or allowed, such as in a museum, this prevents the flash from firing. Otherwise, it is the same mode as Scene Intelligent Auto (A+).

- **Creative Auto (CA).** Unlike the Scene Intelligent Auto mode (A+), in which the camera sets everything for you, Creative Auto mode (CA) gives you some flexibility to adjust the depth of field, the drive mode, and flash firing. You can also add ambience settings to your photographs.
- **Portrait.** This mode creates a shallow depth of field, which is helpful for portraits. I recommend that you use a good portrait lens (70-135mm) in combination with this mode for maximum benefit.
- **Landscape.** This creates a large depth of field, which is helpful for panoramic shots. This mode works best when more light is available in the scene.
- **Close-up.** Use the macro setting to shoot close-ups or for small-object photography.
- **Sports.** This mode uses a fast shutter speed to stop action. It is commonly used for wildlife, sports, and fast-moving children.
- **Special Scene (SCN).** This mode also houses the following three additional modes that are available via the LCD touchscreen:
  - **Night Portrait.** This slow shutter speed mode helps capture background lights at night. Remember that the flash pops up if the camera detects the need.
  - **Handheld Night Scene.** It's hard to take good photographs at night, especially if you handhold the camera. This mode allows you to handhold the camera while it takes four consecutive shots and layers them. The result is a well-exposed nighttime image.
  - **HDR Backlight Control.** This mode takes three quick exposures and combines them into one image to compensate for any intense light behind your subject.

Setting the shutter speed

Photographs of fast-moving objects frozen in motion, such as a cheetah bounding through the grass toward its prey, are a result of a fast shutter speed. Likewise, a trail of stars advancing across the night sky is the result of a slow shutter speed.

Most of the time, shutter speed is measured in fractions of a second. Your camera has shutter speed settings that range anywhere from a 30-second exposure to 1/4000 second. In most cases, any speed more than 1/500 second stops action. You start to see more motion blur at 1/30 second or lower; the faster you or your subject is moving, the more blur you see.

When considering shutter speed, ask yourself whether you want to show motion or stop it. If stopping or showing motion is an important element of your photograph, consider using the Shutter-priority AE mode (**Tv**). This mode allows you to control the shutter speed, while the camera controls the aperture. Pay attention to the aperture number displayed next to the shutter speed in the viewfinder. If it is blinking, the shutter speed is too high or low for a proper exposure.

TIP The longer the camera lens, the higher the minimum shutter speed should be to avoid blur from lens movement.

When to use fast shutter speeds

You can stop action in your photographs by using a fast shutter speed. Sports and wildlife photographers generally use fast shutter speeds to create crisp images with little or no movement. A shutter speed over 1/125 second is considered a fast shutter speed. If you want to stop action and convey no movement in the image, a shutter speed over 1/500 second is required in most cases. The top shutter speed on your camera is 1/4000 second. It is rare that you will need such a fast shutter speed unless you are photographing in bright sunlight at a high ISO, such as ISO 1600.

Use the Shutter-priority AE mode (**Tv**) when photographing sports, wildlife, or any moving subject to help prevent blurring. If you prefer to use the Basic Zone modes, the Sports mode (🏃) is a good option because it keeps the shutter at the highest possible setting for every shot. If you are not getting a fast enough shutter speed to achieve the results you want, consider increasing the ISO setting.

CAUTION Increasing the ISO setting to achieve a higher shutter speed, although helpful, affects the quality of the image by increasing the amount of digital noise.

When to use slow shutter speeds

A slow shutter speed is required when you want to show movement. A slow shutter speed is required when you want to use photographic techniques, such as panning and ghosting. Using motion well in your photos can turn everyday pictures into action-filled images, as shown in Figure 5.4. It can also create a more ambient background light when using flash.

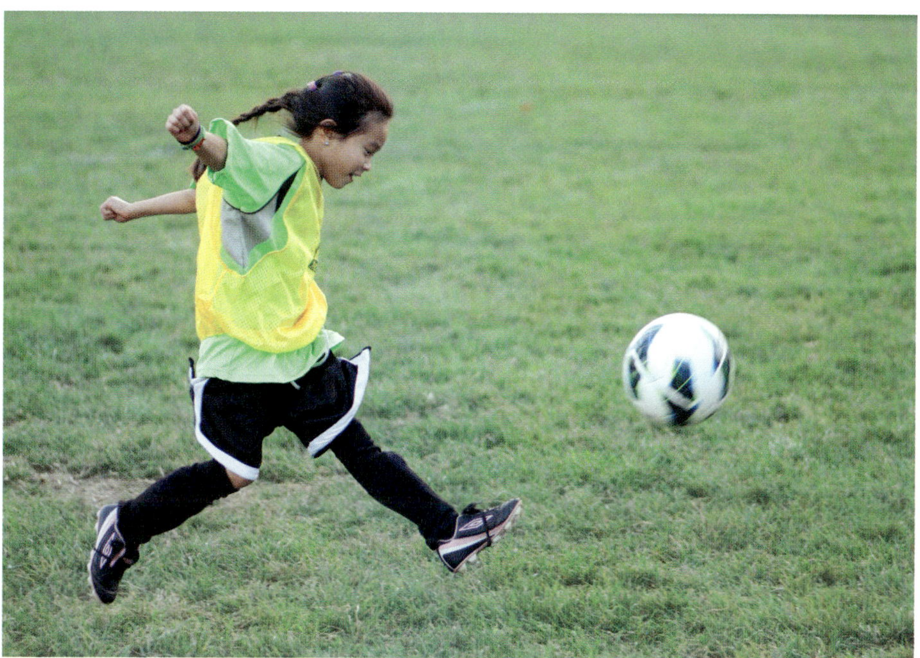

5.3 When shooting action or sports, a high shutter speed freezes the subject. Exposure: ISO 800, f/2.8, 1/400 second, 100mm f/2.8 lens.

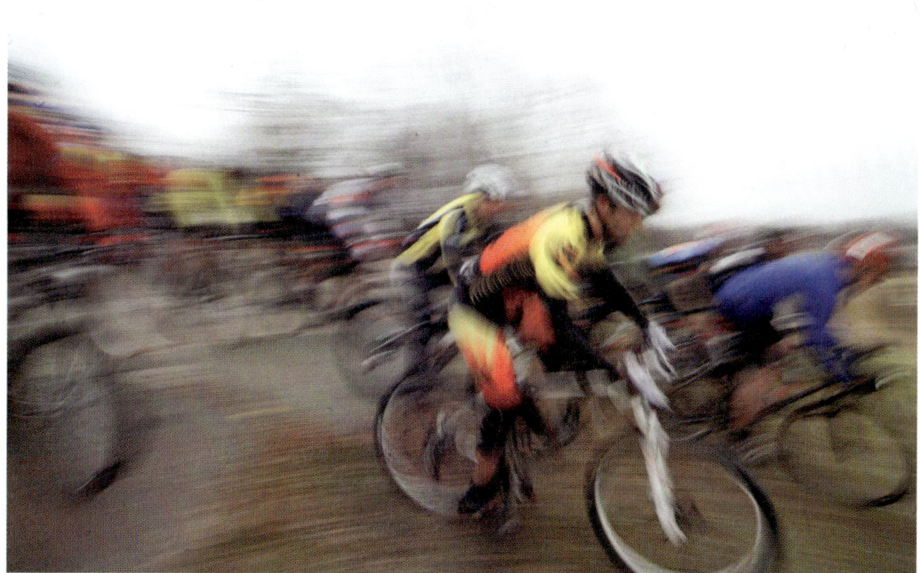

5.4 A slow shutter speed was used to show the movement of this bike race. Exposure: ISO 200, f/22, 1/25 second, 12-24mm f/4.0 lens at 20mm.

If you need a greater depth of field (which is explained later in this chapter), try slowing down the shutter speed until you reach the desired aperture. As the shutter speed decreases, the aperture number needs to increase to keep proper exposure. Landscape and architectural photographers often use very slow shutter speeds, especially in the early morning or late evening, to help keep the aperture numbers high for a greater depth of field. For this type of photography, use a tripod to steady the camera.

If the shutter speed falls below 1/60 second, you can use a tripod to prevent blurry photographs. A helpful guideline to remember — especially if the subject is still or moving toward you — is if the shutter speed is lower than the focal length of the lens, you should use a tripod. This isn't a perfect recipe for sharp images — there are other things to consider, such as the speed and movement of your subject. If your subject is moving side-to-side, you most likely need a faster shutter speed.

Moving water, such as waterfalls or crashing waves, is a great opportunity to influence the outcome of the image with the shutter speed. Use a fast shutter speed, such as 1/500 second, to capture individual water droplets cascading down a falls or to stop the action of breakers crashing onto rocks. Use a slow shutter speed, such as 1/8 second, to bring out the silken flow of the falling water or to create a peaceful seascape. You can use fast and slow shutter speeds to set different visual tones. For example, you can demonstrate speed using the motion blur of a fast-moving train, or convey the power of a hammer hitting a rock by using stop action at the point of impact.

If you need a slower shutter speed, but don't want to blur your photo, use the Handheld Night Scene mode (). Canon's Image Stabilization (IS) lenses are also helpful when lens shake might ruin a good photo opportunity. The stabilization technology cancels out much (if not all) of the blur by adding the equivalent of up to 4 full shutter speed stops.

CROSS REF For more details about lenses, see Chapter 4.

If you handhold your camera at a slow shutter speed (under 1/60 second), both the background and the subject will show motion in the image. How much motion depends on how slow the shutter is, how steady you handhold the camera, and the speed and movement of your subject. Try playing with the blur by moving the camera in different directions while you shoot to see what forms and shapes you can create.

When you use a tripod and set your camera to a slow shutter speed to shoot a moving object, the object shows blur but the background remains in focus. How much blur is created depends on how fast the object is moving and how slow you set the shutter.

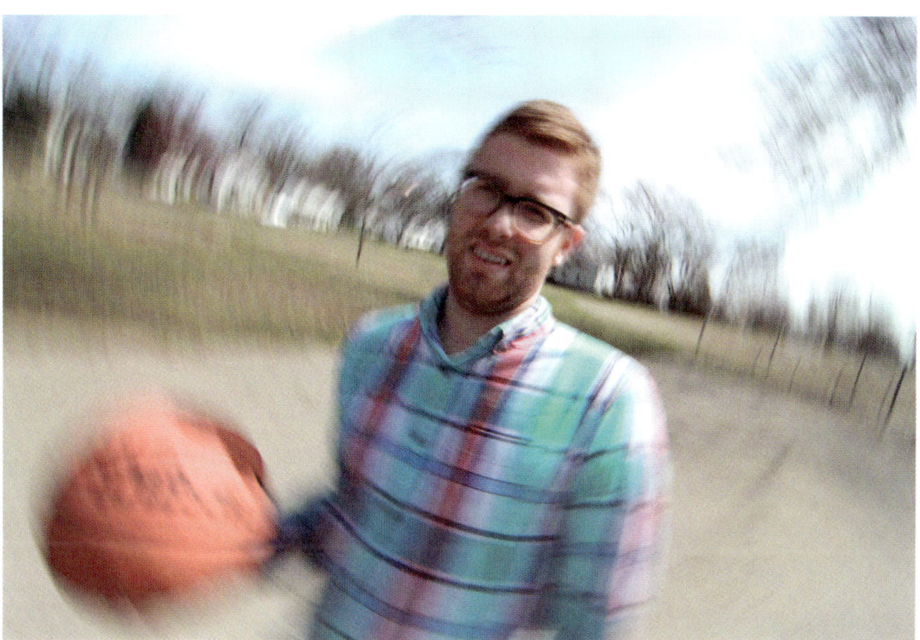

5.5 When shooting this image, I quickly turned the camera during the exposure to add movement. Exposure: ISO 200, f/18, 1/25 second, 12-24mm f/4.0 lens at 12mm.

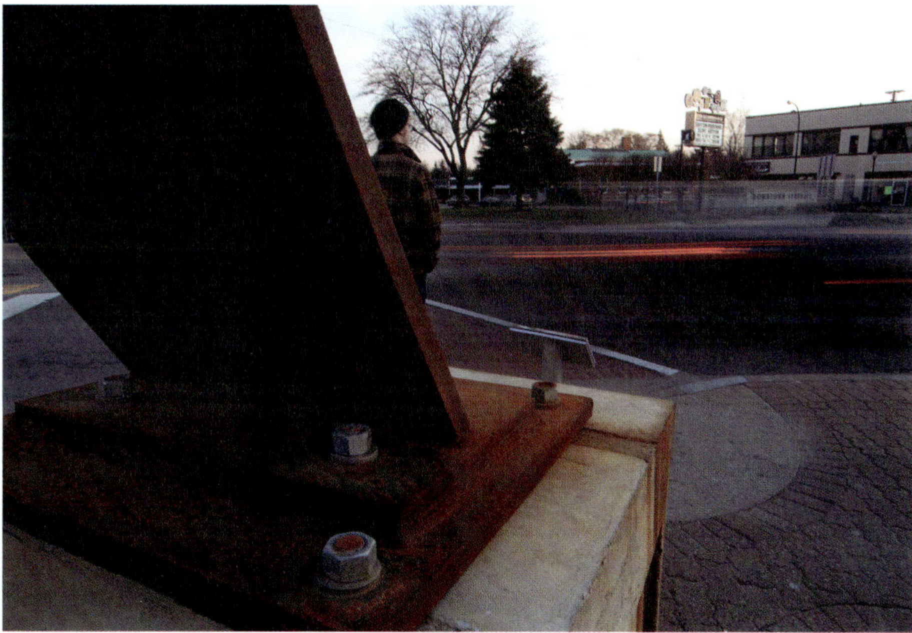

5.6 This shot was taken using a tripod while cars sped by. Exposure: ISO 100, f/22, 1/6 second, 12-24mm f/4.0 lens at 14mm.

Panning is a fun technique to use with a slower shutter speed. To do so, track a moving subject with your camera and use a slow shutter speed. This technique delivers an image with the subject in focus against a blurred background, as shown in Figure 5.7. Sports photographers use this technique for auto racing, biking, and track and field. Don't plan to get panning right the first time. Shoot multiple images using this technique for practice.

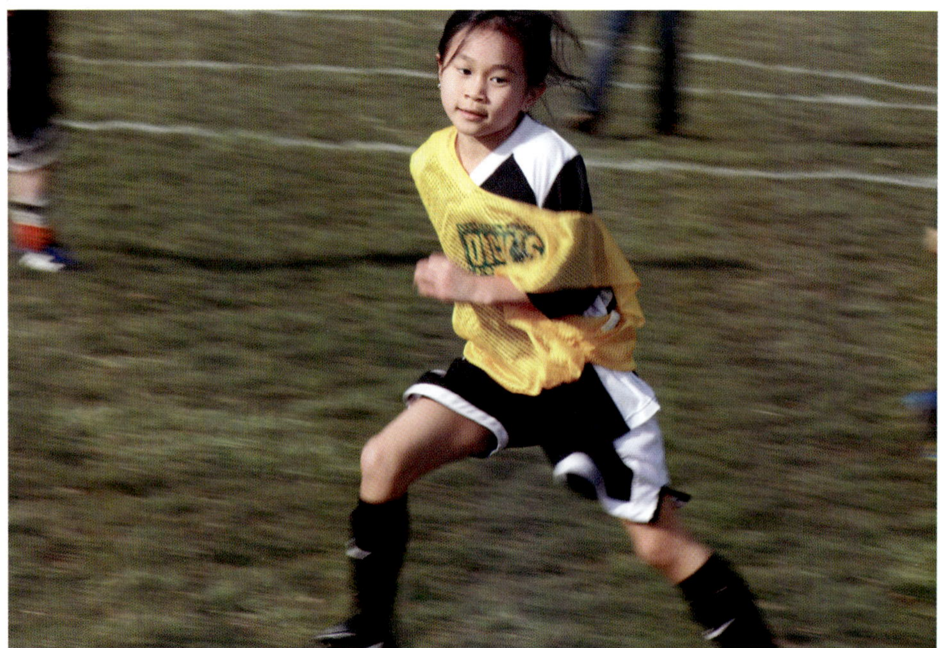

5.7 Panning creates an image in which the subject is in focus and the background is blurred. Exposure: ISO 100, f/11, 1/80 second, 100mm f/2.8 lens.

The Bulb setting (**B**) is commonly used for extra-long exposures to capture streaks of light, as shown in Figure 5.8. Use this setting when you are trying to capture car headlights on the highway, stars moving across the night sky, or the silky movement of water.

Your camera syncs with the flash up to 1/200 second. If you use a faster shutter speed, part of your image will be dark or black because the flash isn't synced with the shutter. Fortunately, you can prevent this from happening. Even if you set a higher shutter speed, as soon as you turn on the flash it reverts to 1/200 second.

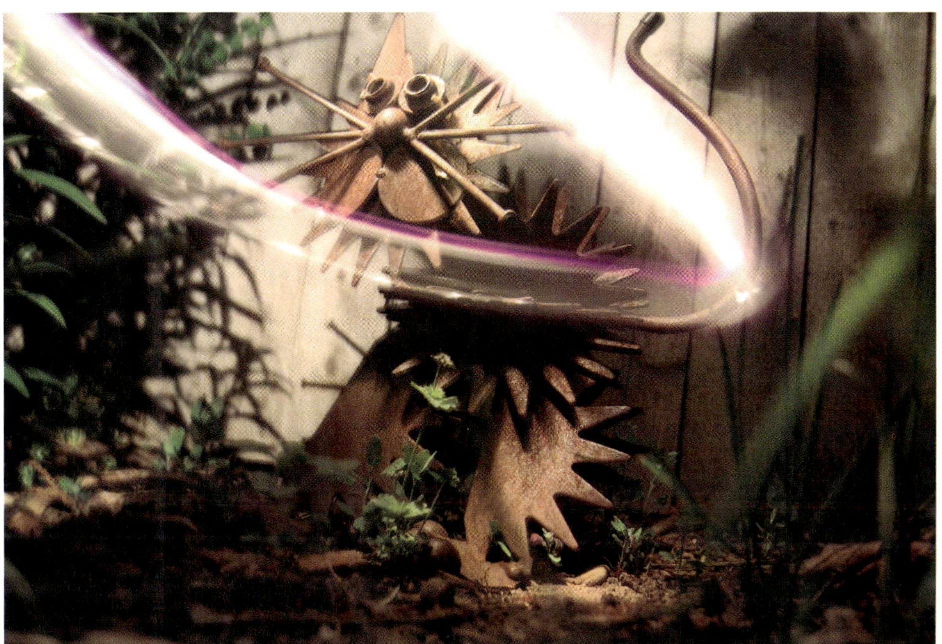

5.8 I set the camera on the ground, used the Bulb mode, and waved a flashlight to illuminate parts of this cat sculpture. Exposure: ISO 200, f/5.6, approximately 8 seconds, 12-24mm f/4.0 lens at 24mm.

The built-in flash on top of your camera has a maximum sync level of 1/200 second. You can slow down the shutter speed as much as you want. When you slow the shutter speed in combination with flash, you can create a *ghosting* effect. This means that the camera flash freezes the subject and the slow shutter speed continues to expose, causing a blur. The result is a motion-filled photograph.

NOTE If you use external flashes, such as the Canon Speedlite series, the top shutter speed is 1/4000 second using the High-speed sync feature.

CROSS REF See Chapter 6 for more details about ghosting.

Night photography and painting with light

Have you ever wanted to create one of those beautiful shots of a skyline at night, or capture a large moon rising over a landscape? Night photography offers many dramatic photographic opportunities — all you need is a little knowledge and the right tools. Two necessary accessories for night photography are a cable release (remote switch) and a tripod. A tripod is necessary to keep the camera steady for long exposures. You can use a cable release to trip the shutter at any shutter speed without touching the camera. This is especially helpful for extra-long exposures of more than 30 seconds.

When shooting nighttime photographs, it is tempting to use the camera's higher ISO settings, but if you are using a tripod, time is on your side. Consider using a slower setting, such as ISO 200, ISO 400, or ISO 800, for better image clarity, color, and less noise. Night photographs tend to have more digital noise, so consider using the camera's Long exposure noise reduction feature. You can find this setting under Custom Function 4.

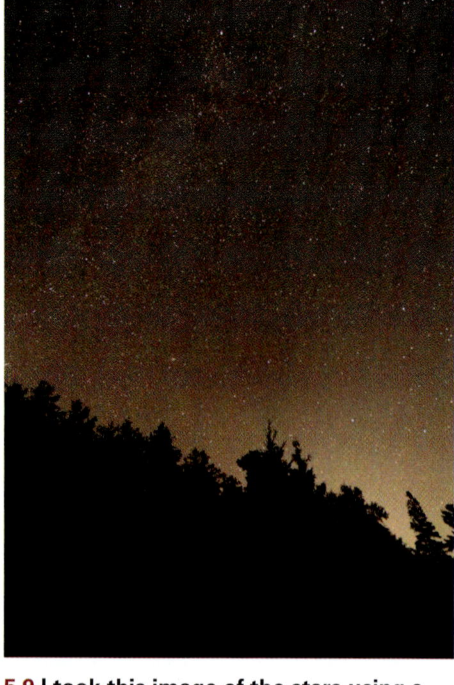

5.9 I took this image of the stars using a tripod and long exposure. Exposure: ISO 1600, f/5.6, 30 seconds, 12-24mm f/4.0 lens at 12mm, tripod.

NOTE The Canon RS-60E3 Remote Switch (cable release) fits the Canon T5i/700D remote control terminal.

CROSS REF For more information about Custom Functions, see Chapter 2.

Photographing stars is always a treat. In just a few minutes of exposure, you can create an image of stars moving across the sky. To see a lot of stars and movement, you need to get away from the city lights. It can take minutes to hours to get the desired image. Make sure that your camera is securely mounted to a tripod, and that the tripod is anchored. Any movement can cause blurring in the photo. When considering night scenes, look for colors, shapes, and patterns. Expect to take more than one photograph at multiple exposure settings.

Jeff White's Night Photography Tips

Jeff White is an urban night photographer. He enjoys shooting at night because he feels it gives him more flexibility, especially with shutter speed. He likes the option of creating an exposure at 1/30 second or several hours. In Jeff's opinion, night photography is more fun and offers more opportunities to create high-contrast images. He looks for opportunities to capture interesting light sources, such as moving lights that create streaks or reflections after a hard rain. The following are a few of Jeff's tips:

- **You need a tripod.** Consider attaching a weight bag to the tripod to help avoid camera movement on windy days.
- **Most of the time, you will use a wide-angle lens.** Photographers rarely use telephoto lenses for night photography, unless they are trying a specific creative technique, such as using a zoom lens to convey movement. This is achieved by zooming in or out during the exposure.
- **Bring extra lighting, such as an external flash, a flashlight, or a penlight.** Walk around the scene and highlight unique subjects to make your images more interesting.

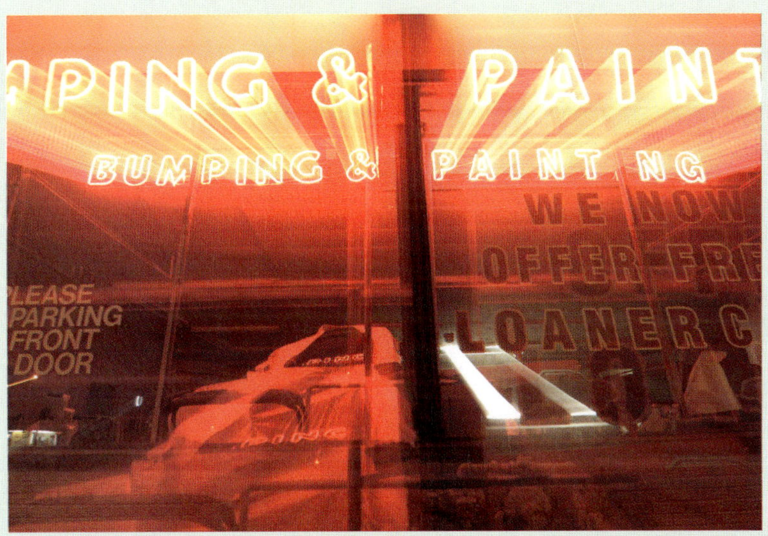

Image courtesy of Jeff White

Jeff White lives and works in Detroit, Michigan. Art directors and designers regularly purchase his work for marketing purposes, or simply to display on their walls. You can see more of his work at http://jwhitephoto.com.

Painting with light is a fun technique that requires a slow shutter speed and a tripod. It is best to do it in a dark room or outside at night. Try leaving the shutter open using the Bulb mode (**B**) or a long shutter speed, such as 30 seconds. Use a flashlight, match, or glow stick to write or draw a design in the air. If you are the subject, set the drive mode to Self-timer mode continuous (⏱c) so you can take up to 10 shots in a row without running back and forth to the camera.

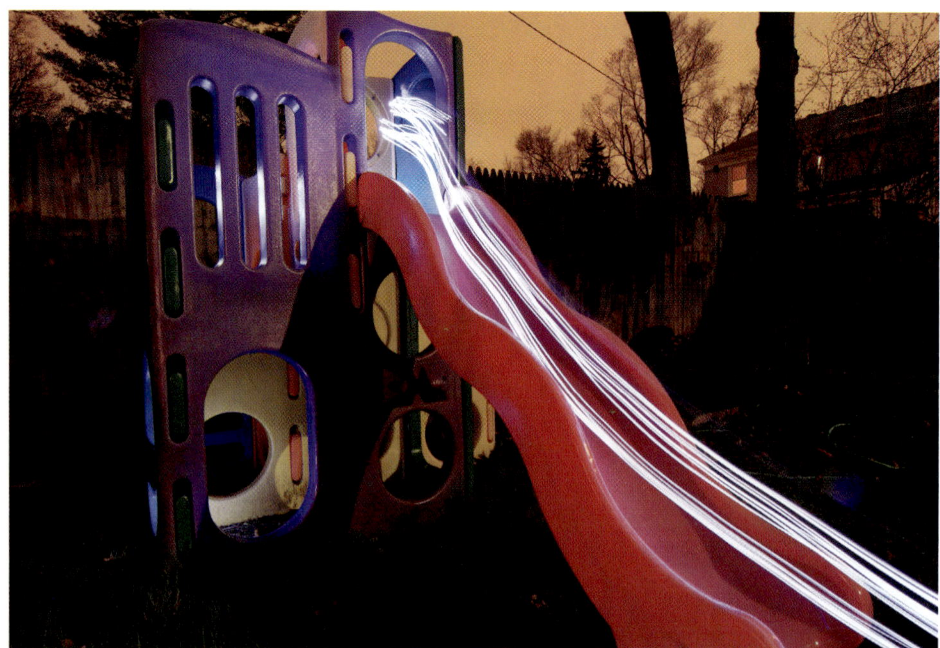

5.10 You can use a flashlight or LEDs to illuminate, draw in the air, or outline objects. To get this image, I ran around the playground and turned on the lights when I wanted to expose a section of the scene. Exposure: ISO 200, f/8.0, 16 seconds, 12-24mm f/4.0 lens at 12mm, tripod.

Setting the aperture

When you see a portrait with the background fading out of focus, or a beautiful landscape with the entire scene in focus, aperture played a role. Aperture is the opening inside the camera that lets in light. It is adjustable and represented by a number system that can be confusing. The larger the number, the smaller the opening. The smaller the number, the larger the opening. Most standard lenses have an aperture range of f/2.8 to f/22. Many of the better prime lenses have even larger aperture openings. Some standard lens apertures are f/2.8, f/4.0, f/5.6, f/8.0, f/11, f/16, f/22, and f/32.

NOTE If you don't have a lens attached to the camera, 00 is displayed as the aperture setting.

Think of *depth of field* as the area of focus around the subject. If there is a large area in focus surrounding the subject, then the photograph has a large depth of field (also known as *deep* depth of field), such as in landscape photography. If there is little focus around the main object of the photograph, then you have a shallow depth of field. For example, a portrait with a blurry background has a shallow depth of field. Unfortunately, you can't make the statement that f/8.0 has a depth of field of 8 feet in front of, and 16 feet behind, the subject. The combination of focal length and distance between the subject and the camera determines the total available depth of field. In other words, each focal length has a different effect on the depth of field around the subject at the same distance.

A 28mm lens at f/8.0 that is 10 feet from the camera doesn't have the same depth of field at the same distance as a 200mm lens. The 28mm lens spreads out the image and creates a larger depth of field, displaying everything in focus between 6 and 24 feet from the camera. The 200mm lens compresses the field of view, leaving little room for error with only 9.89 to 10.1 feet from the camera in focus. The Aperture-priority AE mode (**Av**) is good to use when depth of field is an important consideration. This mode lets you control the aperture, while the camera controls the shutter speed to create the proper exposure.

If the camera is in the Program AE mode (**P**), you can adjust the aperture by turning the Main dial (). Please note that if you increase the aperture, your shutter speed will be slower, and if you decrease the aperture, your shutter speed will be faster. Although the shutter and aperture numbers are moving up and down, the exposure stays the same because they are moving in proportion. If the shutter speed increases 1 stop, such as 1/60 to 1/125 second (which cuts the amount of light in half), and your aperture opens from f/8.0 to f/5.6 (doubling the amount of light), your exposure stays the same.

The following are some common situations in which you would use a deep or shallow depth of field:

- **A deep depth of field is excellent when shooting landscapes, or *environmental portraits* (that is, pictures of people posing in their environment).** Use a wide-angle lens to help increase the depth of field in your images. If you prefocus in anticipation of an important event, use a higher aperture to increase your depth of field. This increases the odds that your subject will be in focus, such as when trying to capture a runner crossing the finish line or a door opening as the guest of honor enters at a surprise party.

- **A shallow depth of field is commonly used in studio portraits, sports, and fashion photography because it separates the subject from the background.** A shallow depth of field adds a stylized look to your pictures. When you want a shallow depth of field, move in close to the subject. Use a lower aperture, such as f/2.8, to add a new dimension to your photographs. Not everything in a shallow depth-of-field image is in focus. When using this setting, decide on a *focal point* — the part of the subject on which you want the viewer to focus.

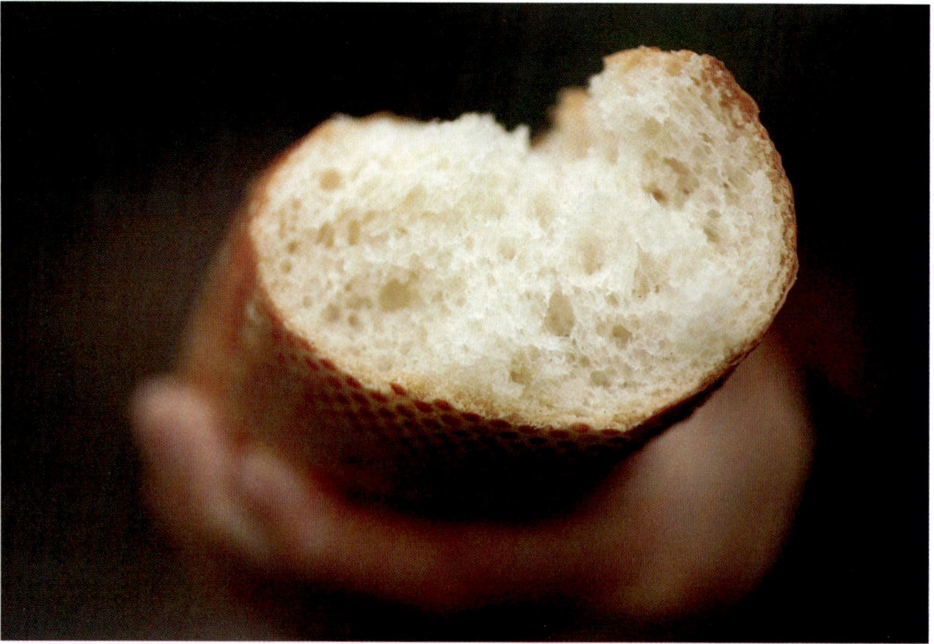

5.11 This image has a shallow depth of field; the background is out of focus and separate from the subject. Exposure: ISO 200, f/2.8, 1/250 second, 100mm f/2.8 lens.

Setting the ISO

The sensitivity of your camera's digital sensor is represented by its ISO (International Organization for Standardization) rating. The higher the number, the less light you need to take a photograph. The lower the number, the more light you need. For example, ISO 100 is perfect for a bright summer day while ISO 3200 is good for shooting in a school gymnasium. Each time you increase the ISO to the next level — from ISO 100 to ISO 200, for example — you double the camera sensor's light sensitivity. This allows you to reduce the aperture or increase the shutter speed 1 full stop.

You may be wondering why you wouldn't use a high ISO setting, like ISO 6400, all of the time. It's because high ISO settings create more digital noise than lower ones. *Digital noise* is similar to the grainy texture on film. Prints or enlargements of photos shot at ISO 6400 are not as crisp and clean as those shot at ISO 100. Your Canon Rebel T5i/700D is expandable to ISO 25600 using Custom Function 2. This is helpful when you need a faster shutter speed, aperture, or can't use a flash. However, ISO 25600 also has a lot more noise than the lower settings.

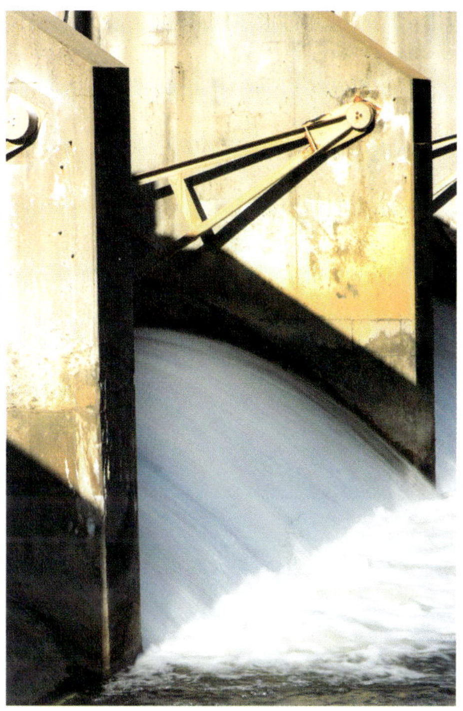

5.12 A low ISO setting was used for this image to create a silky look on the flowing water. Exposure: ISO 100, f/20, 1/15 second, 100mm f/2.8 lens.

A fast shutter speed is important for stop-action photography, such as sports, animals, or children on the move. If you don't have enough light to reach the desired shutter speed, then you need to adjust the ISO to a higher setting. Another advantage of a higher ISO setting is that the flash has a farther reach. If you are at an event, push the ISO higher to extend the reach of the flash across the room. How much noise can you handle? Your camera has the following eight ISO settings: 100, 200, 400, 800, 1600, 3200, 6400, 12800, and is expandable to 25,600 for still photography with the camera's Custom Function 2. When using ISO 3200 and above, the additional noise may be less than optimal depending on the type of photograph you want to create.

The following guide might be helpful when setting the ISO:

- **1SO 100-400.** This range is ideal for sunny days.
- **ISO 400-1600.** Use these settings when shooting with overcast skies or in the evening.
- **ISO 1600-6400.** This range is good for night photography or when shooting indoors in low light.
- **Custom Function 2.** Here, you can set the ISO to 25600 for use in low-light situations.

Fortunately, a few options on your Canon T5i/700D can help reduce the grain in your photos. Long exposure noise reduction is for exposures of more than 1 minute. If you are not concerned about noise reduction related to long exposures, leave this setting turned off. The function has an auto mode that detects if an image took more than 1 second to expose; it then automatically applies the function. You may also leave it in the *on* position, which applies noise reduction each time an exposure of more than 1 minute is created.

Another option when you use high ISOs is high-speed noise reduction. This option, found under Shooting menu 3 (📷), has the following four settings:

- **0: Standard**
- **1: Low**
- **2: Strong**
- **3: Disable**

NOTE If you activate a noise reduction function, you cannot take another photograph until the noise reduction process is complete.

The Multi-shot Noise Reduction option combines four consecutive images at high ISO settings to create low-noise images. This mode also optimizes to reduce subject blur, making night photography much easier. This option may not work if your shots are greatly misaligned. You can find this option with High ISO speed NR listed in Shooting menu 3 (📷). This option is not available when shooting in RAW (RAW) or Large RAW (LRAW). Both your Canon software and Adobe Raw have noise reduction filters. There are also plug-ins available for Photoshop that help reduce noise.

The ISO settings in the Basic Zone modes are between ISO 100 and ISO 3200 (except Portrait mode, which is fixed at ISO 100). The Creative Zone modes set the ISO between ISO 100 and ISO 6400. The automatic setting when shooting in Bulb mode (**B**) is ISO 400.

Using Exposure Compensation

You may not always agree with your camera's exposure suggestions for every scenario. Even with all the advanced technology in your camera, you may find that your photographs are regularly under- or overexposed in specific situations. You can correct these problems using exposure compensation.

If you photograph a white cat in the snow, the exposure may not turn out as you expect. You might need some help with all of the white light bouncing back to your camera, depending on the exposure mode you use. In this case, try overexposing the image to create a more accurate one.

Photographing a black horse in front of a dark background is another example of an extreme that might require exposure compensation. In this case, underexpose the photograph to bring out the detail of the horse better. When the main source of light is behind the subject, this is called *backlighting*. You can use exposure compensation to prevent unwanted silhouettes or the main subject from becoming too dark to see. This can happen if your subject is in front of a window or in bright sunlight.

TIP You have multiple options to use in backlit situations. Use the HDR Backlight mode (icon) to compensate for intense light behind your subject.

CROSS REF See Chapter 6 for more information about lighting.

If you are not sure of the exposure you want to use, you can play it safe and bracket. This option is only available when neither the subject nor the photographer is moving. *Bracketing* is taking multiple shots at different exposures. You can do this manually using the exposure compensation and taking one photograph at -1 (underexposed), another at normal exposure (or 0), and a third image at +1 (overexposed). This gives you three images with different exposure options.

Your camera is also equipped with Auto Exposure Bracketing (icon). AEB automatically takes three images — an underexposed image, a normal exposure, and an overexposed frame. You control the difference in the exposure range among the three images, up to 2 stops in 1/3-stop increments.

High Dynamic Range Photography

High Dynamic Range (HDR) is how photographers create colorful, high-contrast, fantasy-like images of landscapes, cityscapes, architecture, or even people. *HDR* photos are made by combining bracketed images to create a new hybrid image. Each image brings different exposure merits to the final one. Some images capture highlights while others capture the shadow detail. Combined, they do what a traditional single image cannot: expose for detail in both highlights and shadow at a high level of accuracy.

Sometimes photographers manipulate images to create a fantasy effect. This is a popular technique among landscape photographers. Not everyone likes the surreal quality of this photography style. Remember that HDR images also can be adjusted for a more natural look. Traditionally, HDR photographs require a steady camera on a tripod to get multiple images of the same scene at a variety of exposures. This is one reason why you rarely see true HDR photographs of people or moving objects. When you do see such images, chances are the photographer used a technique called tone mapping. The Canon T5i/700D has modes that can help you use the HDR technique. The nice thing about these modes is that you can handhold the camera while shooting, if you are steady.

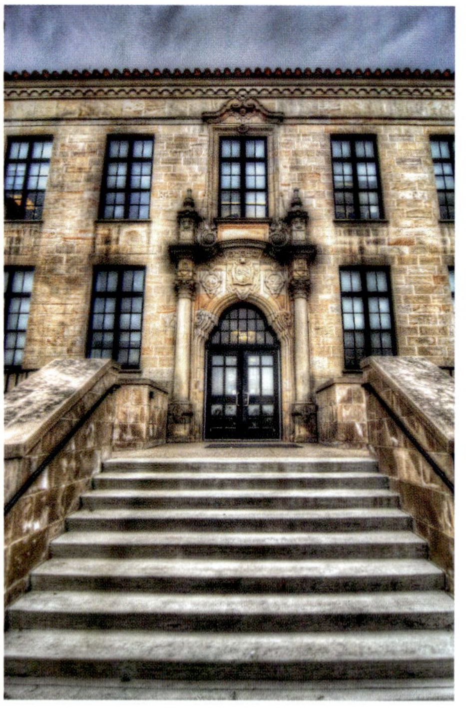

5.13 This HDR image is a combination of five exposures. Exposure: ISO 800, f/5.6, 1/160 second, 1/320 second, 1/640 second, 1/1300 second, 1/2700 second, 12-24mm f/4.0 lens at 12mm.

The Handheld Night Scene mode (), found in the Basic Zone under Special Scene (SCN), shoots and aligns four photographs while you handhold the T5i/700D. It then merges the four photos into one image that exposes for detail in the subject of your scene, while still allowing for ambient light.

The HDR Backlight control () is one of three modes found under Special Scene (SCN). It takes three consecutive shots at multiple exposures in a backlit setting, and then creates a well-exposed image. This function displays the detail from the bright light source, such as the sky, as well as the subject in the foreground. I recommend using a tripod when using this mode. The camera will not always line up the images correctly if the subject moves or if there is camera shake.

If you take individual brackets without using your camera's HDR Backlight control (), you need software to combine the images. Although you can do this in Photoshop, one of the more popular programs is Photomatix Pro. It gives you a good range of options to create both natural-looking and high-contrast, fantasy-style HDR images. It has a number of helpful features such as aligning the photos automatically. This is helpful if you don't use a tripod when bracketing the images. If you want to create the look of HDR and don't have a series of bracketed photographs, a Tone Mapping option is available for single frames.

Exposing for Video

A good place to start when exposing for video is Auto Exposure movie mode (). This works for most of your video needs, such as at family events. Auto Exposure movie mode () sets the ISO, shutter speed, and aperture. All you have to do is point and shoot.

The Manual exposure mode (**M**) is standard for advanced users, and it's a good option once you are comfortable with your camera. It prevents your camera from changing the exposure during the middle of a scene. When shooting a moving subject, shutter speeds from 1/30 second to 1/125 second are recommended. It is also worth noting that it is not a good idea to change your exposure while shooting. The change will distract the viewer and the video will not look professional.

NOTE Remember that you can't use exposure compensation when in the Manual Exposure mode (**M**).

You don't have as many options for exposure in Movie mode () as you do for still pictures, but there are a few. Exposure compensation () is available in the Auto Exposure movie mode (), and it is helpful when photographing light, dark, or back-lit subjects. To activate this option, press the Aperture/Exposure Compensation button (). Make your adjustments using the main dial () — they are viewable on the bottom of the LCD screen. You are limited to three stop adjustments in Movie mode () (for still photos, you can make up to five). The ISO can be set anywhere between ISO 100 and ISO 6400, and expanded to 12800 in Movie mode ().

You also have Picture Styles available in the Movie mode (). These are the same as those found in the still shooting modes. Picture Styles adjust color and tone based on the characteristic style or subject matter you are shooting.

CROSS REF For more information about Picture Styles, see Chapter 3.

5

Composition

Have you noticed that most of the photographs you appreciate don't have the main subject directly in the middle of the frame? This is because point-and-shoot photography (with the subject positioned in the middle of the frame) usually doesn't capture the scene as well as a planned-out and thoughtful composition. When it comes to composition, challenge yourself. Create variety in your photographs. Every scene or subject doesn't have to be shot in the same way.

While your camera does so much for you, the one thing it can't do is create your vision. The way that you see things is different from anyone else. The way that you frame an image is up to you, and that is what composition is all about. The Rule of Thirds and filling the frame are guidelines that can help you make good decisions when photographing the subjects in front of your lens. Another way to improve composition is to look for different points of view — not every photo has to be shot at eye level. Get down on your knees or climb up high (be careful!) to capture new angles. If you are photographing children, make sure that you get down on their level.

The lens you use plays a role in how you should frame an image. A long lens compresses a scene and brings the subject closer to you. A wide lens spreads out the scene, giving you more room to work when composing your photograph.

CROSS REF For more about lenses, see Chapter 4.

Sometimes, even though you may be following the rules, some compositions don't sit well with the viewer. Sometimes, it may be because part of the subject is cut off in an awkward position. There is nothing wrong with cropping your image later, but I don't recommend that you shoot with the mind-set that you can crop during editing. Work on getting your composition right the first time. Later, if you notice that the image could still use some adjustments, you can crop.

TIP When cropping images, make sure that you don't crop people at the knees or elbows — it looks awkward and uncomfortable to the viewer.

You have two ways to view a scene when developing a composition. You can use the viewfinder or Live View shooting mode (▣) to view the scene in front of the lens. Some photographers find the screen on the back of the camera easier to use. However, this is not always the case — in bright sunlight, looking through the viewfinder is often the better choice. The flexible, 180-degree LCD screen is also helpful when holding the camera high over crowds, when shooting down low from a ground view, or even for shooting around corners.

The Rule of Thirds

I'm a firm believer that you need to learn the rules before you can break them. After you learn them, you can use the rules as guides. When it comes to rules about composition, the Rule of Thirds is the most important.

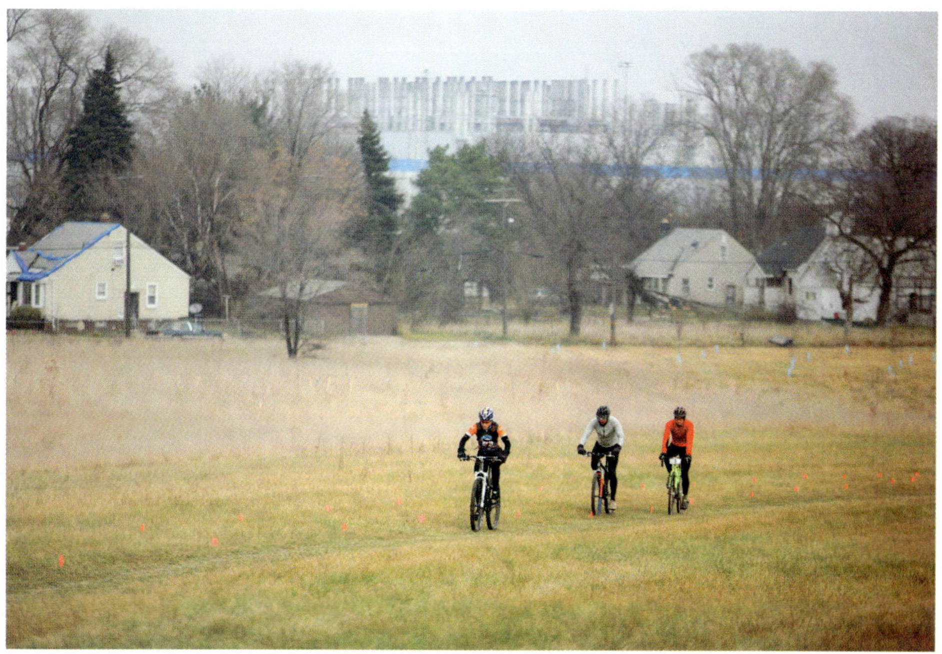

5.14 This image uses the composition technique Rule of Thirds because the subjects are not in the middle of the frame. Exposure: ISO 200, f/2.8, 1/800 second, 70-200mm f/2.8 lens at 200mm.

The idea is to divide the frame into thirds mentally, both horizontally and vertically. Combining the two creates what looks like a tic-tac-toe board, as shown in Figure 5.15. There are many ways to use this tic-tac-toe board on your camera. Consider the four cross sections in the frame as points at which you can place your subject. Another way to satisfy the Rule of Thirds is to mentally draw a diagonal line through the frame and photograph the main subject above or below that line. It's important to note, however, that sometimes you *do* want your subject in the middle of the frame. The Rule of Thirds encourages asymmetrical images, but that is not always the best result. In some circumstances, the best photograph is a symmetrical one, in which everything is balanced.

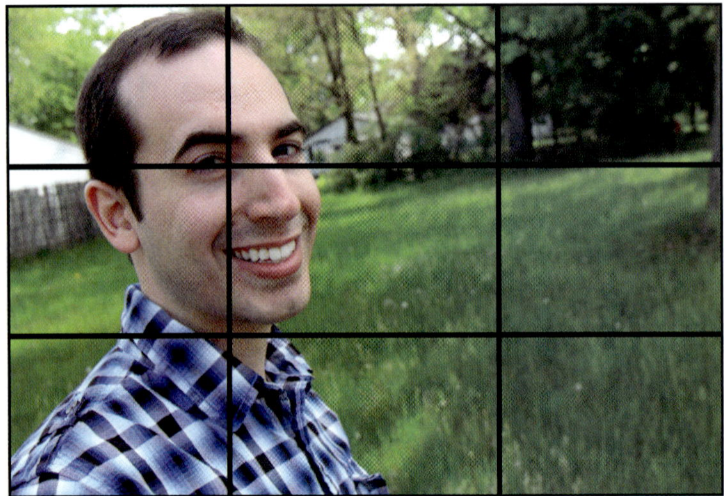

5.15 This grid demonstrates the Rule of Thirds. Exposure: ISO 200, f/8.0, 1/125 second, 12-24mm f/4.0 lens at 24mm.

Horizon lines should follow the Rule of Thirds. The horizon line between the earth and the sky should not be in the center of your frame. It also should not cut through the back of the subject's head. When photographing from a distance, the Rule of Thirds still applies. For example, a boat on the horizon should be placed anywhere but in the middle of the frame. Consider the direction in which the subject is moving, and then leave room in front of it to create a sense of motion by giving the subject a place to go. In the case of a runner, place him on the right side of the frame if he is moving to the left across the LCD screen.

Filling the frame

Don't be afraid of the edge of the frame — get closer. This is one of the best ways to satisfy the Rule of Thirds. In fact, get as close as the lens allows and don't worry if some parts are left out of the image. You will discover the closer you get to your subjects, the more interesting your photographs become. Take a step closer and look for details within your subject. Architecture is an excellent example. You don't need to show the entire building if the details tell the story. A close-up of a person's face creates an intimate image, which is often more powerful than a photograph of the entire body.

NOTE It is important to understand the limitations of lenses. Some only allow you to get so close before proper focus is unavailable.

TIP If you want to get really close to your subject, consider using a macro lens.

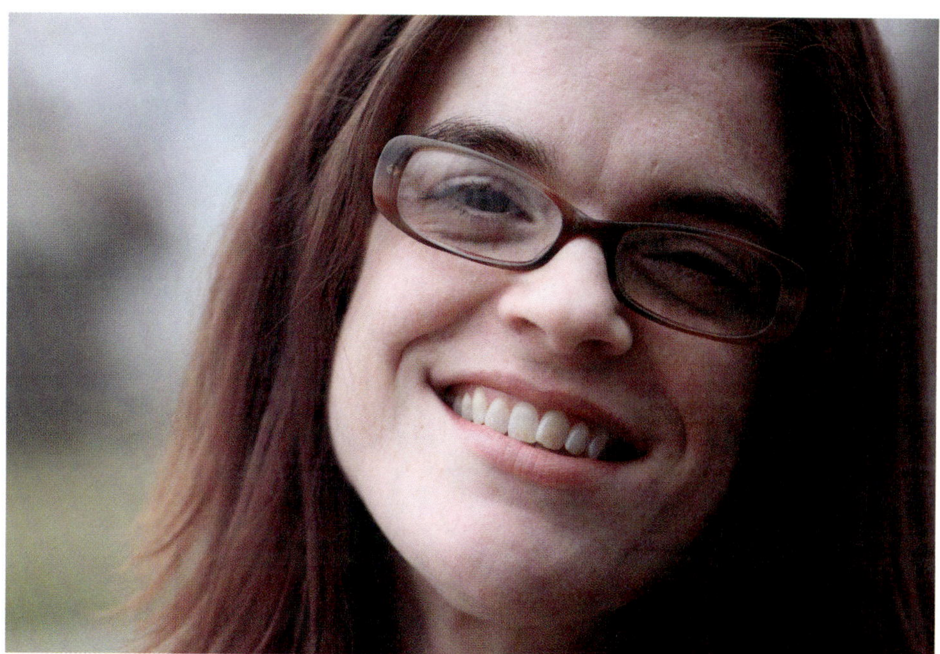

5.16 Filling the frame with your subject gives the image a more personal feel. Exposure: ISO 200, f/2.8, 1/400 second, with a 100mm f/2.8 lens.

Lines and shapes

One of the most important rules of composition is that you have a *focal point*, which is something to which the eye is automatically drawn, or a starting point at which to view the image. The eye then follows a pattern, shape, or lines through your image. Understanding this concept is helpful, whether you are developing high-level conceptual ideas or just photographing your kids at the playground.

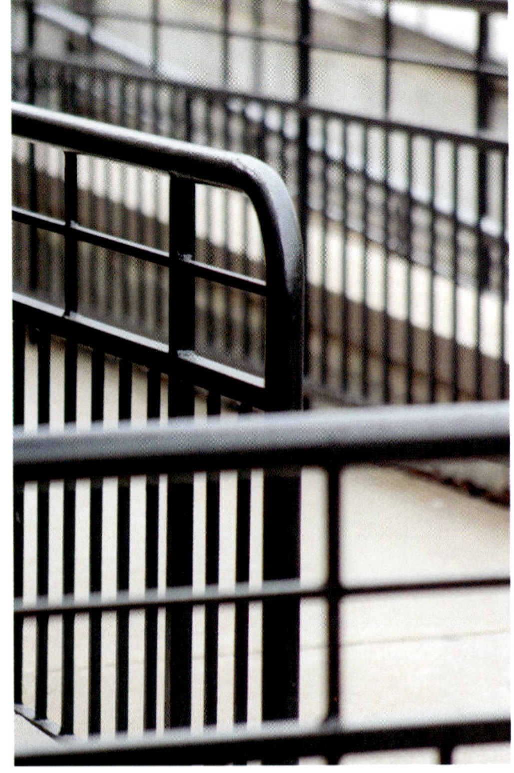

5.17 The layered lines in the fore- and background lead the viewer's eye through this image. Exposure: ISO 800, f/5.0, 1/200 second, 50mm f/1.4 lens.

One of the first things to which a viewer's eyes are drawn is the lightest object in the frame. Leading lines take the viewer's eye to the final destination of your image. S shapes are another nice compositional tool, and geometric shapes can be very powerful. The triangle is the most powerful shape in art. Start looking at your environment. You will be amazed at the patterns you find around you. Parking lines, columns of streetlights, rows of corn, and architectural details, such as windows, are all good examples of everyday patterns.

Challenge yourself to look for patterns, and see if you can incorporate them with your subjects. Use leading lines to guide the viewer's eyes where you want them to look. An S shape takes the viewer on a journey across the page. You can also lead your viewer's eyes into the distance with strong leading lines, or use them to create a vanishing point deep in the image.

Foreground and background

Most things do not happen on a single plane. You should consider the fore- and backgrounds as part of your composition. When you look at a scene, consider whether you should take a two- or three-dimensional photograph. If you keep everything on the same focal plane, such as a straight-on shot of a building, it creates a flat look. You can add dimension to your photographs by placing objects in the fore- or background, as shown in Figure 5.18. This technique is helpful in landscape and architectural photography.

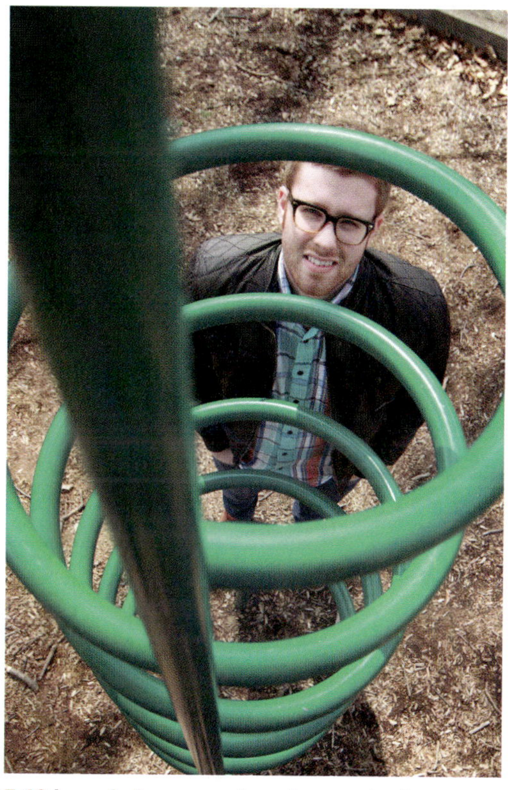

5.18 I used playground equipment in the foreground to add dimension to this photograph. Exposure: ISO 100, f/4.0, 1/250, 12-24mm f/4.0 lens at 24mm.

You can also play objects off the foreground. If you are shooting a mountain in the distance, look around to see if there is something of interest to use in the foreground, such as a flower or an interesting rock. Frame your subject with an interesting foreground object or shoot through a fence. Consider how you can use the background, such as clouds moving behind a mountain, as part of your composition.

Keeping it simple

Many of the best compositions are great because they are simple. The saying *less is more* holds true in photography. Every part of your photo should be there for a reason. *When in doubt, leave it out* is another good rule to live by. Make it easy for the viewer to understand what you are trying to show.

When you keep things simple, it is much easier to create an obvious focal point for the viewer, as shown in Figure 5.19.

As mentioned previously, a shallow depth of field is helpful because it sets the subject apart from the background. It also creates form and shape, rather than identifiable objects in the background. Sometimes colors, lights, shadows, or shapes can also be used as compositional balancing tools in an image.

In the beginning, composition is something you think about if you are trying to improve your photos. Fortunately, over time, composition becomes a habit, and you will automatically place subjects a little to the right or left, and fill the frame. It just takes time and practice.

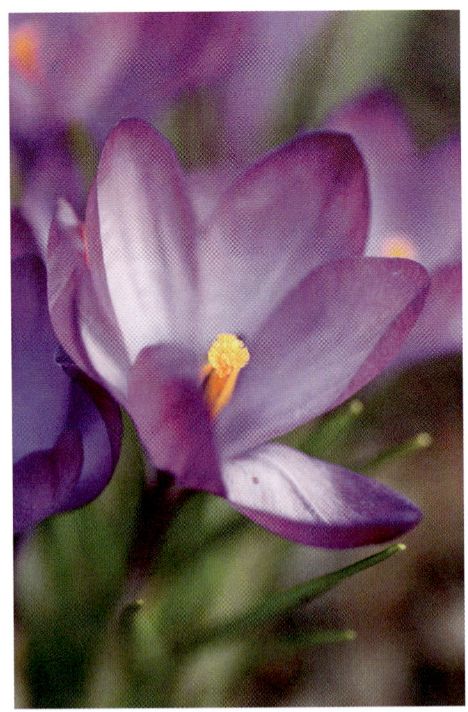

5.19 This flower fills the frame and a shallow depth of field makes it the sole focus. Exposure: ISO 100, f/2.8, 1/250 second, 100mm f/2.8 macro lens.

CHAPTER 6

Working with Lighting and Flash

Do you have enough light? Lighting is the most important element in photography. Fortunately, your camera's light meter serves as a guide. However, even if the light meter indicates that there is enough light in a scene to achieve a proper exposure, there is still a lot to consider before pressing the shutter button. No lighting situation is perfect for every subject. Some subjects look best with soft light, while others stand out in hard light. This chapter explores the lighting choices available to you when contemplating various types of scenes. Sometimes, natural light is the best choice, while other environments require flash to capture the subject. If you know how to use it to your advantage, proper lighting can make a good scene fantastic.

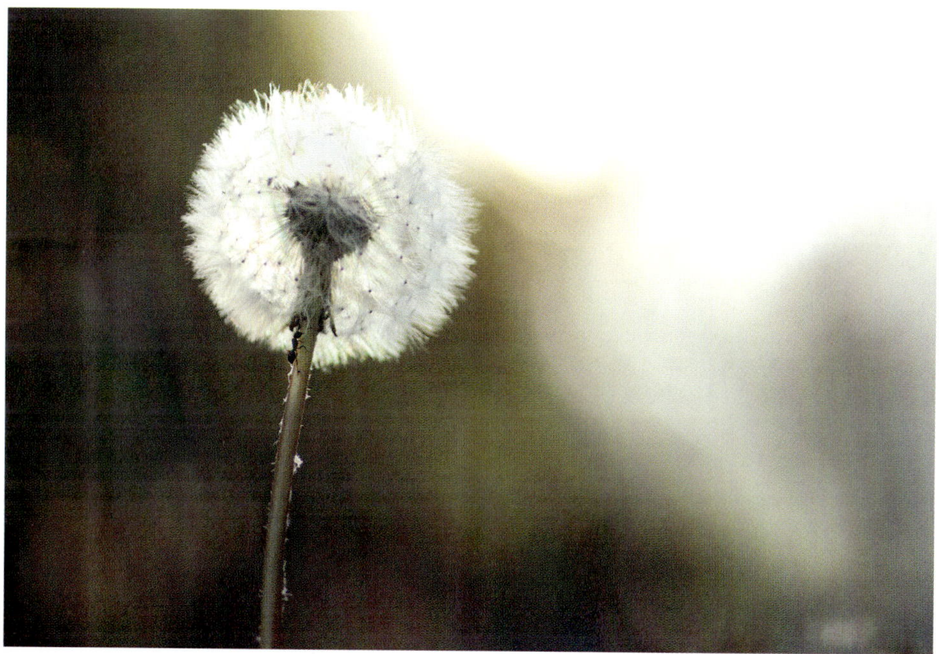

Understanding how to use light can greatly improve your images.

The Importance of Light and Shadow

The foundation of photography is light, and how you approach it separates the beginner from the more experienced photographer. Lighting doesn't have to be difficult, though. My best advice is to start with one light, and learn how the direction, quality, and color all play a role in creating good images. Using one main light source also helps you learn how to manage shadows. Once you feel more confident, you can add more lights. If you follow this basic rule, managing light will come more naturally over time.

The best way to improve your lighting skills is to practice. Look for images and scenes that inspire you and try to replicate them. Chances are that the lighting is playing a key role in these images. Try to figure out what decisions the photographer made to create the image. The rest of this chapter covers concepts, tips, and the Canon T5i/700D features that can help you create beautiful images.

A good way to approach light is by managing shadows. This doesn't mean that you should try to avoid or remove shadows from your photographs, but rather you should have an awareness of how they affect your subject or scene. Look for shadows that help balance your photograph. Some shadows can make the subject look mysterious or edgy. Observe patterns in shadows or think about how different shadow shapes may enhance your subject. Not all shadows need to be harsh or solid black — soft shadows can add dimension to a photo. In fact, a photograph without shadows is often flat or boring.

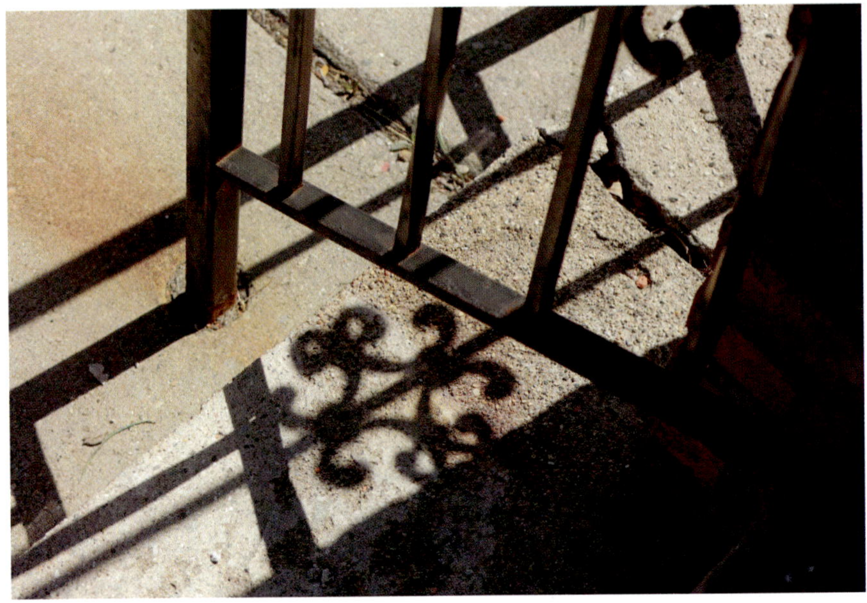

6.1 Look for shadows to add balance to your images. Exposure: ISO 100, f/5.6, 1/500 second, 28-70mm f/2.8 lens at 70mm.

6

The Direction of Light

The direction of light affects the mood of your photographs. When you use light well, it adds more depth to your images than straight-on lighting, which tends to flatten the subject. Always be aware of the location of the sun — it is more dramatic and colorful in the early morning or late evening than it is at midday. If you are using your camera's fixed-direction, pop-up flash, your options are limited. However, if you use an attached flash with swivel capabilities, you can bounce the flash in various directions to create different lighting effects. Using off-camera or multiple flashes opens up an unlimited world of opportunity because you are no longer dependent on the direction of the sun, as you can aim the flash anywhere.

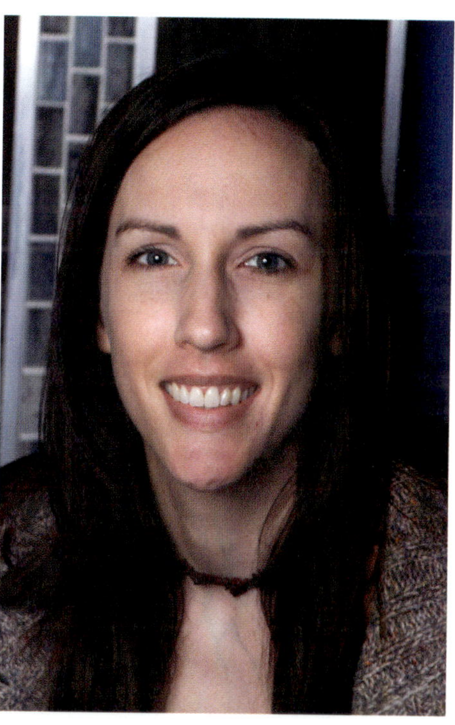

6.2 This example of frontlighting created with flash doesn't have as much depth when compared with portraits created using sidelighting. Exposure: ISO 100, f/6.3, 1/125 second, 100mm f/2.8 lens.

Frontlighting

Frontlight is generated from the sun behind you or an on-camera flash. When photographing nature or architecture, it is nice to have the sun at your back. If you are looking for a clean image with no shadows, frontlight does the trick. The downside of frontlighting is that you don't see the shadows that often add character to a photograph. Images with frontlighting from the sun or your flash appear flatter than images using sidelighting.

Sidelighting

Sidelighting is more dramatic than frontlighting, and adds depth to the subject, as shown in Figure 6.3. It is created when the light source is coming from the left or right of the subject. This casts the opposite side of the subject in shadow. The more intense the light source, the greater the contrast, and the darker the opposite side appears. Additional light sources or reflectors can be used to soften the harshness of sidelighting.

Look for sidelight when creating landscape photographs. Sidelight from the early-morning sun slanting through a stand of trees creates a dramatic shadow effect. In architectural photography, sidelighting brings out the texture of the building materials, such as wood or brick (both look much flatter with frontlighting). Keep an eye out for patterns or columns to which sidelighting can add interest and dimension. The earlier in the morning or later in the evening, the more dramatic the shadows.

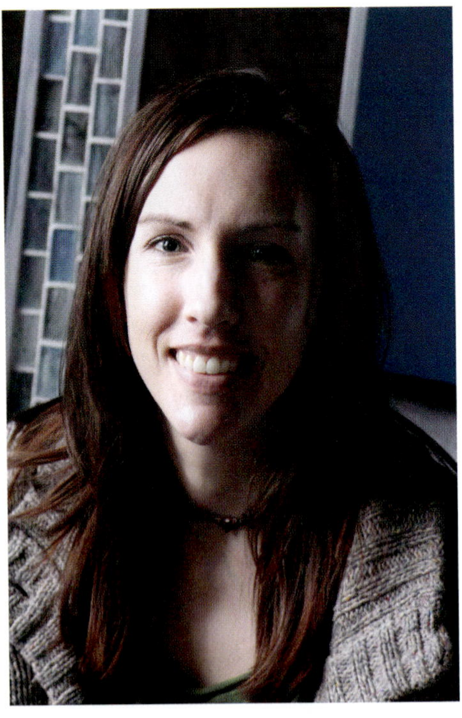

6.3 This image was shot with sidelighting to add some drama and character. Exposure: ISO 200, f/6.3, 1/80 second, 100mm f/2.8 lens.

There is more than one type of sidelighting. Any position between front- and backlighting could be considered a variation of sidelighting. Two of the most common types of sidelighting are short and broad lighting. Short lighting is created when the light is focused on the opposite side of the subject away from the camera. Broad lighting comes from the same side on which the camera is positioned and is a flattering form of lighting.

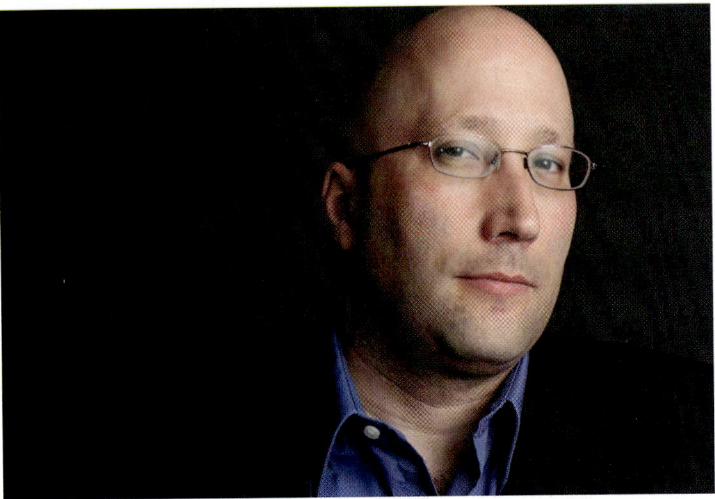

6.4 To create short light, place the light source on the far side of the face, as shown here. Exposure: ISO 200, f/3.2, 1/200 second, 100mm f/2.8 lens.

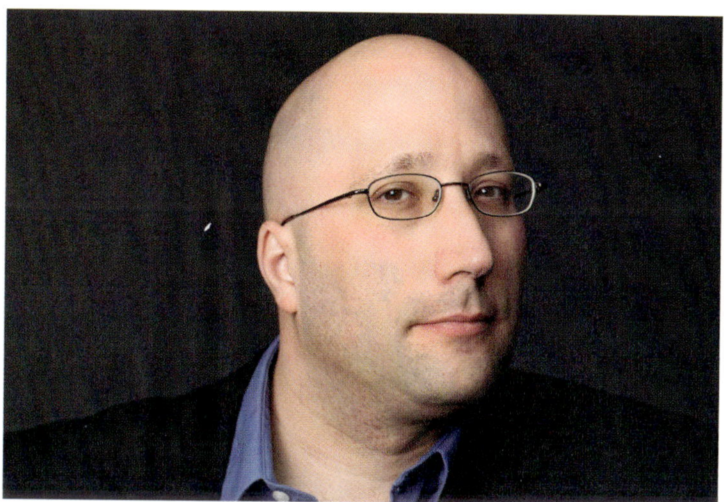

6.5 To create broad light, place the light source on the side of the face nearest the camera. Exposure: ISO 400, f/3.5, 1/160 second, 100mm f/2.8 lens.

Another popular form of sidelighting when photographing people is called *Rembrandt lighting*, after the master painter. This is achieved by positioning the light at a 45-degree angle at or above the top of the subject's head. You know you have achieved this type of lighting when you see an inverted triangle below the subject's eye on the opposite side from the light source. Sidelight adds dimension to your subjects and is good for portraits.

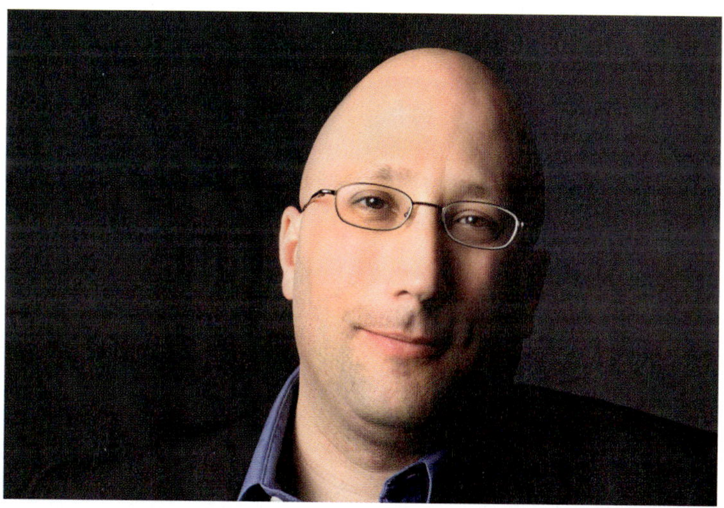

6.6 Rembrandt lighting is easy to spot due to the inverted triangle shape that appears below the subject's right eye. Exposure: ISO 400, f/3.5, 1/160 second, 100mm f/2.8 lens.

Overhead lighting

Overhead lighting is the result of artificial light found in ceilings, stage lights, or from the midday sun. This type of lighting is dramatic because it enhances the texture of some subjects. Generally, it's not flattering for photographing people because the subject's eyes are cast into dark shadows, as shown in Figure 6.7. Photographers who use overhead lighting also use additional lighting and reflectors to decrease the harsh effects.

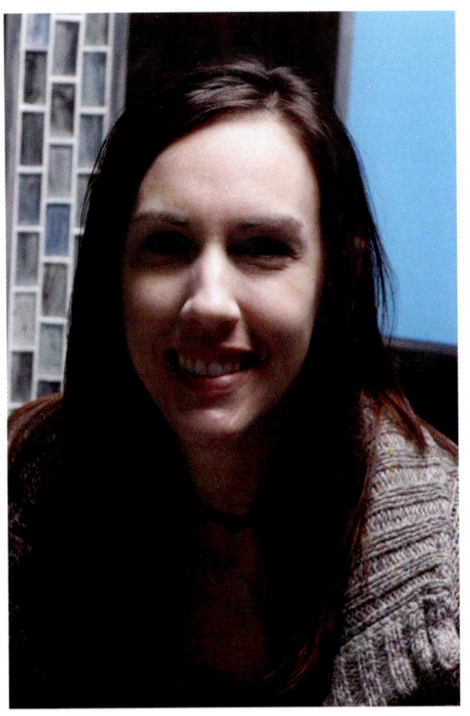

6.7 Overhead lighting casts unflattering shadows over the eyes. Exposure: ISO 200, f/6.3, 1/125 second, 100mm f/2.8 lens.

Backlighting

Photographers sometimes find *backlighting* difficult to master. It takes practice to achieve the best exposure to create the look you want. Backlighting offers two main possibilities. The first is the silhouette, as shown in Figure 6.8, which turns the subject into a solid black outline against the main light source (in this case, the sun). You can achieve this by metering off a bright light behind the main subject. If you meter off the subject with a strong light behind it, you get a form of *rim lighting*. This type of lighting blurs the edges of your subject with an outline of light. The strength of the light dictates the outcome. An overpowering light source will blow out the photograph background and overtake your subject.

Backlighting is a good choice when photographing translucent objects, such as leaves, flowers, or snow. Backlight is a popular advanced lighting technique when photographing people or subjects with interesting shapes. A hard, undiffused light (explained later in this chapter), such as direct sunlight, is recommended for displaying detail in a subject, as shown in Figure 6.9.

It is important to protect your eyes when pointing your lens toward the sun. If you have a lens hood, use it to help prevent undesired lens flare (unless the light is shining directed into your lens). Some photographers like to use lens flare as part of their composition. In such cases, use the LCD screen and Live View shooting mode (◘) to compose your image and prevent eye damage.

6.8 This silhouette was created by metering off the sky behind the subject. Exposure: ISO 100, f/5.0, 1/2000 second, 28-70mm f/2.8 lens at 55mm.

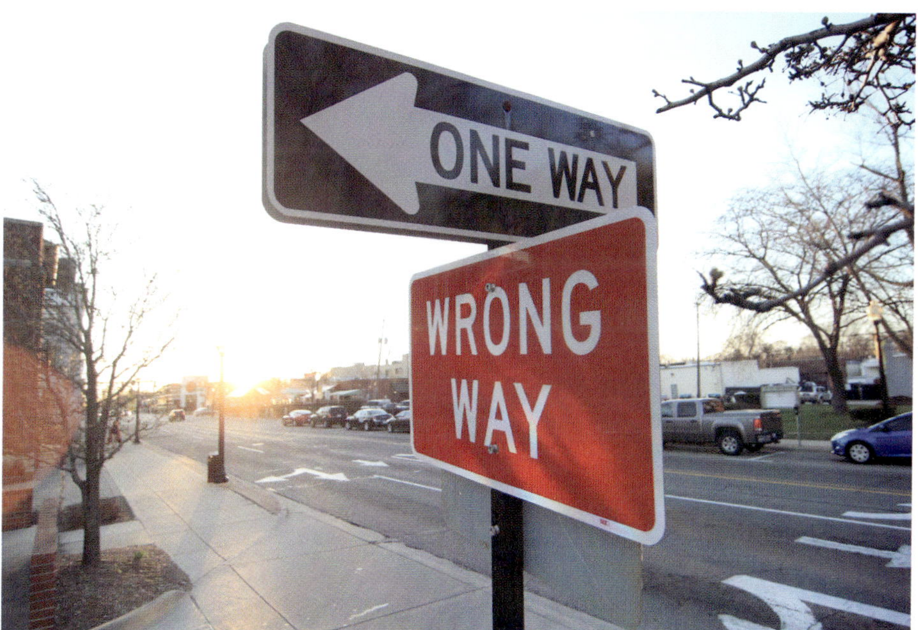

6.9 Here, the camera is pointing into the sun, backlighting the signs. Exposure: ISO 400, f/4.5, 1/250 second, 12-24mm f/4.0 lens at 12mm.

The Canon T5i/700D has an HDR Backlight mode (icon) designed to ensure that backlit subjects are not underexposed or made into an undesired silhouette. The camera combines three consecutive shots taken at different exposures (underexposed, correctly exposed, and overexposed). This creates a properly exposed final image with both good shadow and highlight detail. It is not a perfect system but it can be helpful in certain situations.

CAUTION Always use a tripod when shooting in HDR Backlight mode (icon). Otherwise, the three images may not align properly due to camera shake.

The Quality of Light

The mood of your images is greatly affected by the quality of the light. The *quality of light* refers to the light source, and how it affects the subject or scene. For example, a strong light at an extreme angle may add depth or texture to your subject. Contrast, color, and the textures revealed within an image all depend on the quality of the lighting.

Hard lighting

Direct light without diffusion is called *hard light* (see Figure 6.10). The rule is that the narrower the light source, the harder the light will be. This type of light generates high-contrast images with deep, dark shadows. Many photographers avoid this type of light in favor of softer light. However, hard light offers many opportunities to create exciting and intense images. It helps define the edges, curves, and angles of a subject. Photographers using hard light depend on good shadow management to create powerful images. Be aware of the depth, direction, and shape of the shadows in your scene. The summer sun or an unfiltered flash are good examples of direct light sources.

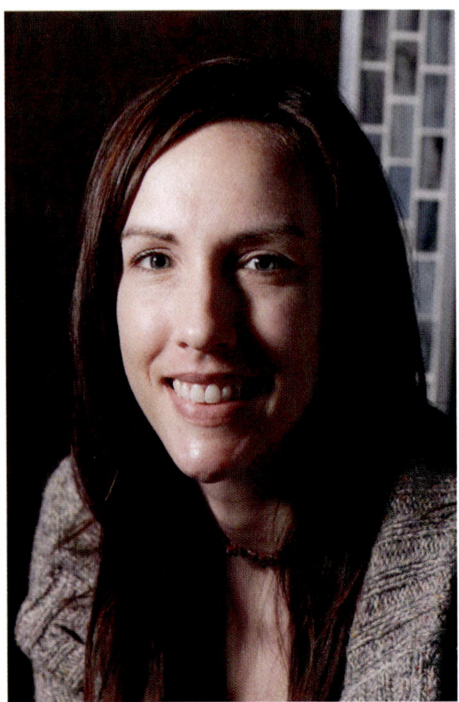

6.10 Hard light is unfiltered and produces strong shadows. Exposure: ISO 100, f/5.0, 1/125 second, 100mm f/2.8 lens.

You can create dramatic portraits using hard light because texture and details pop out, and shadows are strongly defined. Hard lighting can also bring out the detail in bricks on a building or highlight a fabric's texture. When used well, hard light can add drama and depth to your images.

TIP Hard light is an effective tool for creating contrast in black-and-white photographs.

Soft lighting

Diffused or reflected light produces what is called *soft light*. The rule is that the broader the light source is, the softer the light will be. Soft light is popular for portraits because it reduces the hardness of shadows. It doesn't show textures as well as hard light, but for many subjects this is positive because soft shadows make the skin look smoother. Placing translucent material, such as plastic, fabric, or a softbox, in front of the light source creates soft light. Soft light, as shown in Figure 6.12, can also be achieved by bouncing light off walls or reflective material, such as a photo umbrella. Nature offers its own soft light filters in the form of cloud cover, which diffuses harsh sunlight.

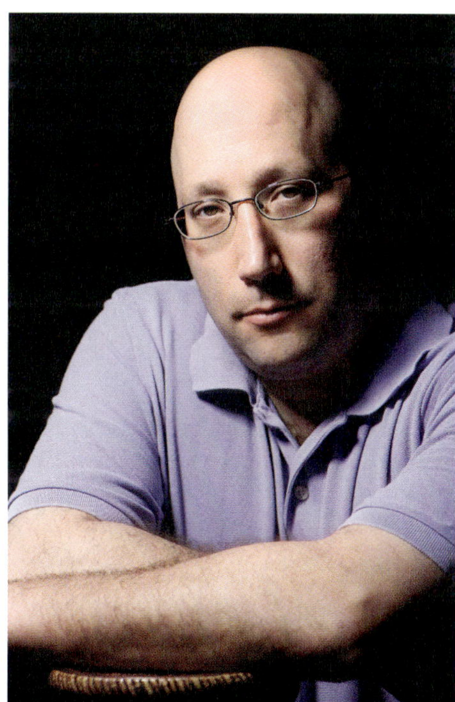

6.11 Textures and subject details are more visible and dramatic when you use hard lighting. Exposure: ISO 100, f/3.2, 1/200 second, 100mm f/2.8 lens.

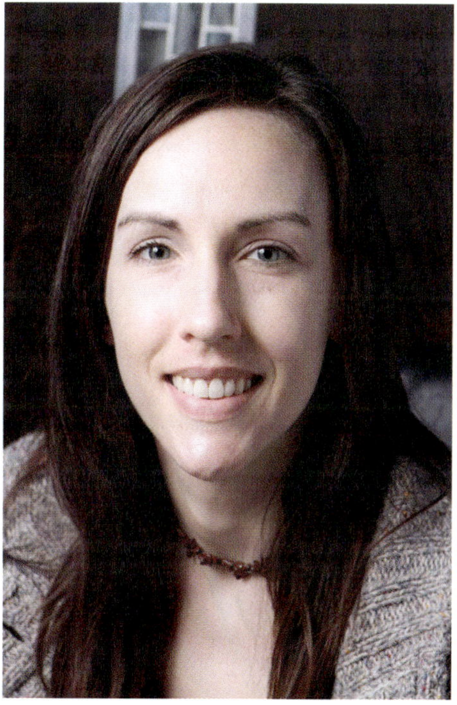

6.12 A photo umbrella and reflector softened the light for this portrait. Notice the soft shadows and catchlights in the subject's eyes. Exposure: ISO 100, f/5.0, 1/200 second, 100mm f/2.8 lens.

Soft light is ideal for subjects with multiple elements, such as a family or group photo. It limits the harshness of the shadows between complex elements that can detract from the image. Soft light is also popular when shooting video because it is easier to manage when following moving subjects. Harsh shadows move around as a subject moves, but soft light minimizes the need for heavy shadow management.

CAUTION Remember that when you bounce light off a wall or ceiling, the color of the surface bounces with it.

Types of Light

Sunlight, and flash and other artificial light (such as light bulbs) are the three main light sources used in photography. Many photographers have a favorite type that they use most often, but I like to use all three. You don't always have a choice of lighting options; flash may not be allowed at an event or the sun might be shining directly into your lens. It is a good idea to enhance your skillset so that you are prepared for any type of lighting situation. The ability to work with the light available to you is a valuable asset.

Natural light

The sun is the favorite light source of many photographers because it's readily available and free. Sunlight offers different lighting opportunities throughout the day. This is both a benefit and a curse because the photographer can't control the direction, quality, or color of the light. Fortunately, a well-planned shooting schedule allows you to create a variety of images as the day progresses. The three natural types of lighting are front-, side-, and backlighting. There is also midday, overhead light in the summer. The nice thing about sunlight, which may seem obvious, is that it always looks natural.

With that in mind, it is important to know which type of light you find at different times of day and during various weather conditions. The harsh or soft light on sunny or cloudy days affects contrast. The warmth or coolness of the light (depending on the time of day) sets the mood. Early-morning or evening shadows add dimension. All of these factors play a role in your photos.

Windows are an excellent source of natural light and can be used for indoor photography. You don't have to be satisfied with one light source — you can use reflectors to tone down harsh, direct light coming through a window. You can also use mirrors to redirect light. Beyond sunlight, there are other natural light sources. Using higher ISO settings, long exposures, and your tripod, you can capture images using light from the moon, the stars, or even an aurora borealis.

CROSS REF See Chapter 5 for more details about long exposures.

Continuous light

Artificial light (also known as a *hot light*) directs *continuous light* onto your subject. This type of light helps the photographer visualize what the photograph will look like in the final image. Some photographers mix continuous light with flash. Remember, flash light only extends so far and casts your background in darkness. Slowing your camera's shutter speed helps pick up the continuous ambient light in the background, adding dimension to the photograph.

There are many new types of continuous light sources available on the market. Light-emitting diodes (LEDs) are a popular lighting choice because they produce a flattering light that doesn't emit a lot of heat. This is valuable when photographing people. HMI (hydrargyrum medium-arc iodide) lights produce a powerful, consistent light, and are used to provide additional light inside, outside, or when competing with the sun. Continuous lights are also commonly used when shooting video. The light source may be attached to the camera or on a stand facing the subject. In most cases, a filter or softbox is used to diffuse light for video.

Flash

The flash produces a burst of white light. Many new photographers are unsure about using flash because they are often under the impression that flash photography is complicated. Fortunately, the Canon Evaluative Through-the-Lens (E-TTL) technology allows the camera and flash to communicate easily and create a proper exposure. This means that exploring new lighting techniques is low risk and a lot of fun.

The Canon Rebel T5i/700D has a maximum ISO rating of 12800, which is expandable to ISO 25600. This allows you to photograph using white balance filters in many indoor situations. You can use this technique in situations in which flash is not allowed or is inappropriate. When you photograph inside using *ambient* (available) light, you are dependent on the fixed placement and direction of the established lights.

Understanding how to use flash well opens a new world to photographers. Flash allows you to control the light on your subject, direct it where you want it, and adjust its color and quality. This is not the case with the sun or ambient light. You can also control the pop-up flash or the settings of an attached Canon speedlite (covered later in this chapter) via your camera's LCD screen.

Shutter speed and flash

You may set your shutter speed anywhere between 1/200 second and 30 seconds in the Shutter-priority AE mode (**Tv**). This means that you may select slower shutter speeds for different lighting and movement effects. This is helpful when you want to show more ambient light in the background. If you set your shutter speed too slow, and either you or the subject is moving, the camera creates a *ghosting* effect, as shown in Figure 6.13.

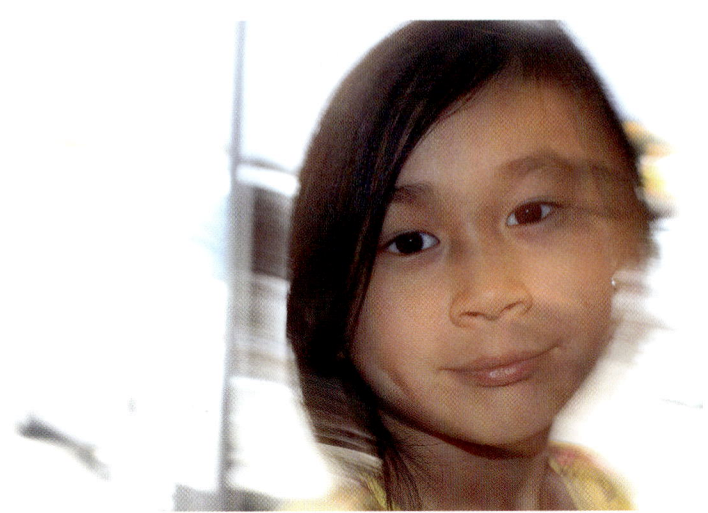

6.13 Ghosting is created by the combination of flash, slow shutter speed, and subject or camera movement. Exposure: ISO 100, f/11, 1/15 second, 40mm f/2.8 lens.

Your camera syncs up to 1/200 second with the built-in flash, which means that you cannot set your shutter speed above 1/200 second. If you do, only part of your picture will be exposed. This is why the camera automatically adjusts the shutter speed back to 1/200 second if you set it higher than the maximum sync. If you use a dedicated speedlite, you can engage its High-speed Sync mode and sync to the maximum shutter speed. When using the Canon Rebel T5i/700D, the maximum shutter speed is 1/4000 second.

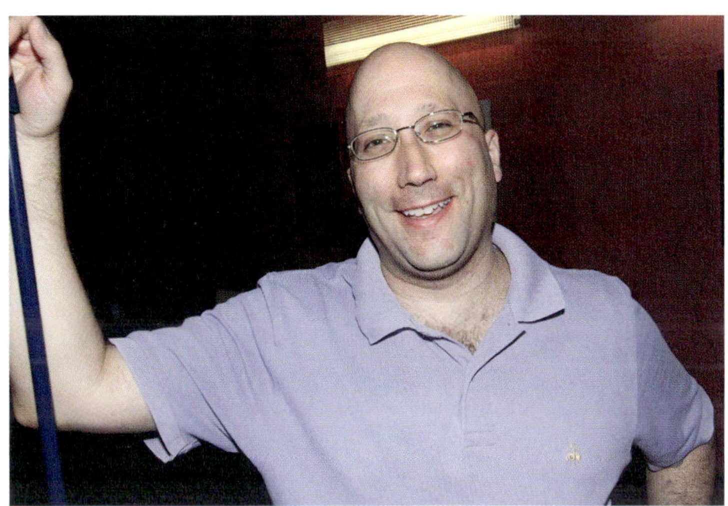

6.14 Flash and a fast shutter speed create a dark background in a low-light environment. Exposure: ISO 200, f/8.0, 1/160 second, 12-24mm f/4.0 lens at 24mm.

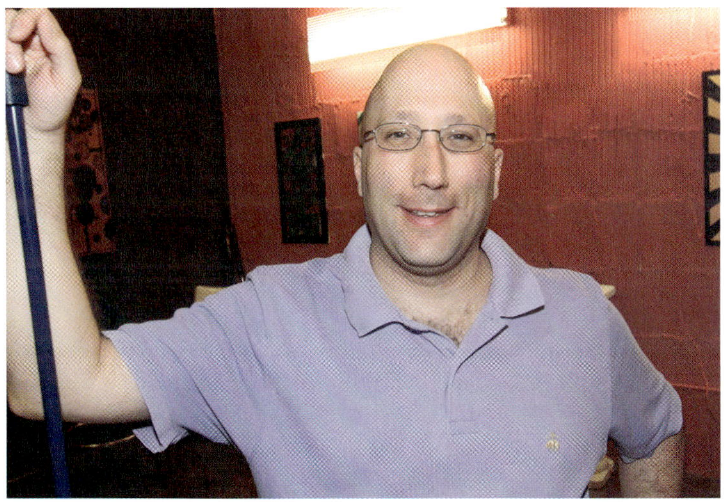

6.15 Even in a low–light environment, flash and a slow shutter speed can expose some background. Exposure: ISO 200, f/8.0, 1/8 second, 12-24mm f/4.0 lens at 24mm.

Aperture and flash

The Aperture-priority AE mode (**Av**) controls the amount of light that enters your camera. It also controls the *depth of field*, which is the area of focus around the subject. When using a larger aperture number, it takes more power for the flash to achieve the proper exposure. This wears down batteries faster and slows the recycle time, especially if you use a high aperture setting, such as f/16 or f/22. Family and wedding photographers often use an aperture range of f/5.6 to f/11 as all-purpose aperture settings. When I photograph events, I prefer to use f/8.0, as this allows a little room for error when focusing in a busy environment. However, that doesn't mean you can ignore the importance of focus.

Manual mode and flash

When photographing with flash, many professionals and advanced amateurs set their cameras on Manual mode (**M**) for full exposure control. As a general rule, the aperture controls the intensity of the flash, and the shutter controls the amount of ambient or background light visible. For example, if you use a fast shutter speed indoors, the background often goes dark or black. When you use a slow shutter speed, the ambient light brightens the background.

CROSS REF For more about shutter speed and depth of field, see Chapter 5.

Direct flash produced by the pop-up flash or an external model attached to your camera's hot shoe is convenient for everyday casual photography. Unfortunately, it doesn't always produce the most flattering light when compared with other options. To achieve more advanced results in your photography, it is important to learn about all of the opportunities flash photography offers.

Be aware, too, that ambient light from a ceiling fixture is not often flattering to your subject. It can be dull, flat, and does not enhance color as well as a direct light. Despite the criticisms of direct flash, its white light provides color that is more accurate and that can really pop the subject out of the background. If you have a Canon Speedlite 430EX II or equivalent that you can turn and adjust to bounce light off ceilings and walls, you have more options than straight-on flash. If you bounce your flash off the ceiling or wall, you achieve a softer light, and often produce a more natural-looking result. It's important to be aware of the color of the surface off of which you bounce light because that color will also bounce onto your subject. For example, if you bounce your flash toward a green wall, the light bouncing toward your subject will have a green tint.

NOTE Bouncing light off a high or dark ceiling is not very effective because the light is absorbed and doesn't bounce back onto your subject.

A diffuser is helpful when trying to soften the light produced from your flash. You may flip down the built-in diffuser available on many Canon flashes. Another option is to cover your flash with a translucent fabric or other material. There is a large selection of flash diffusion and bounce accessories available at your local camera store or online. One such accessory is an *umbrella*. You can use umbrellas to bounce light from inside back to the subject. Some umbrellas are so thin that they are translucent or they convert to a translucent material, allowing the photographer to use them as a flash diffuser.

Different materials create different results. A gold umbrella bounces warm light toward the subject. Metallic silver creates more contrast and *specularity* (the brightness or metallic feel in reflective highlights) when compared to the softness of a white, pearl-colored reflector. A light fabric disperses the light differently than a plastic cover. Both may be good options, but it is good to test multiple options and styles of bounce flash and diffusion accessories to find the right one for you. Flash is also helpful outdoors. It can be used as *fill light* (support or secondary light) to help minimize shadows from harsh, direct sunlight. Outdoor flash is also helpful for separating the subject from the background.

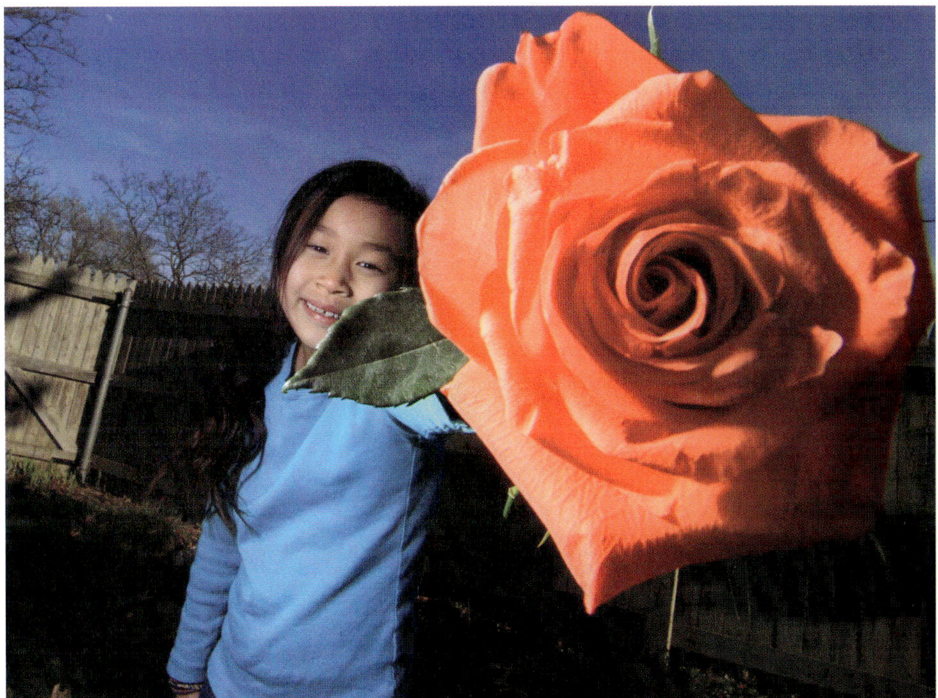

6.16 This photograph was taken in the evening using a filtered, off-camera flash under the shade of a large tree. Exposure: ISO 400, f/22, 1/200 second, 12-24mm f/4.0 lens at 12mm.

For more advanced results, remove the flash from your camera. Canon makes E-TTL off-camera shoe cords (such as the Canon D OC-E3) that attach between the camera's hot shoe and the flash. This gives you the flexibility to move the flash around and create customized lighting. You can also use one or multiple flashes off-camera with Canon's wireless system, which allows you to fire multiple flashes at once. However, before you start using multiple flashes, make sure that you know how to use one flash well.

The Color of Light

Whether you use warm, cool, or unnatural-looking colors in your photography depends on the mood and style you are trying to create. The color of the light is measured by its *Kelvin temperature*. For example, white light is measured as 5500K. Light with a temperature below 5500 degrees displaying reds, oranges, and yellows is considered warmer, even though its temperature in degrees Kelvin is lower. Light with a temperature above 5500 degrees that displays more blue tones is considered cooler, but it is actually hotter when measured in degrees Kelvin.

NOTE The color of the light alters the appearance of the objects in the scene.

Many new artificial lights, such as modern white fluorescents and LEDs, create daylight colors. Other options, such as older fluorescents, create an unpleasant green cast. Older tungsten light bulbs give off a familiar yellow cast. Photographers adjust their cameras and use external gels to manipulate the color of light sources. For example, the Fluorescent white balance setting (), which you can activate by pressing the White Balance button (**WB**), neutralizes the green cast from fluorescent lights.

TIP You can mix different types of artificial light, such as LED, tungsten, fluorescent, or neon to create colorful images.

Images don't have to be neutral or balanced to white light. Photographers have the following choices:

- **Warm light.** The early morning and late day sun produces reds, oranges, and yellows, providing the opportunity to create beautiful and inviting images. This light is excellent for landscapes and outdoor portraits. Near cities and high-pollution areas, sunsets tend to be warmer than sunrises. This is because the particles from daytime pollution increase the amount of scattered light.

- **Cool light.** Cool colors have a blue tint to them, representing cold or winter weather. Dark or sad moods are also connected with cool lighting. Winter is a good time to capture cool light landscapes. Snow reflects the blue sky, increasing the visual feeling of cold weather.

Combining warm with cool lighting can create a dramatic effect. A warm foreground with a cool background is a creative option. Lighting one side of a subject with warm light and the opposite side with cool can create an interesting contrast. One way to create this effect is to place a warm filter over your flash on a cool, overcast day. The subject close to your camera is lit with the warm light from the flash and the background is cooler or bluer from the natural light.

White balance options

The term *white balance* means adjusting the camera to see the existing light as natural or white light. The technology in your camera makes this easier than trying to change the light source with filters. White or natural light is not always available, so the existing light needs to be corrected to give the scene a more natural look. Even sunlight changes color temperature throughout the day. To adjust for the changes in light or different color light sources, your Canon T5i/700D has seven white balancing options beyond the Auto white balance (AWB). If one of the seven settings doesn't satisfy your needs, you can set your own white balance, which is helpful in mixed-light situations. White balance saves time when color-correcting your images on the computer. Use the white square on the color chart in Appendix C to create a custom white balance under the actual light source.

Your camera has a White Balance Auto Bracketing mode (WB) that is like exposure bracketing (explained in Chapter 5). The camera takes three consecutive shots, and adjusts between blue and amber, or magenta and green. This feature also gives you white balance options you can decide on later when you edit your photos on your computer. If you use the camera's RAW setting (RAW), you can make white balance adjustments without degrading image quality.

CROSS REF For a full list of the available white balance settings on your Canon T5i/700D, see Chapter 3.

Using Picture Styles

Picture Styles (☰) are a convenient way to photograph scenes or subjects based on preset or custom settings. These settings are like the past practice of selecting different types of film. Each style adjusts the color, saturation, contrast, and sharpness commonly preferred in such images. For example, you may want softer images with higher color saturations for portraits rather than what you get in standard shooting modes. The Portrait Picture Style setting () is a preset that provides just that.

CROSS REF The Canon Rebel T5i/700D has the eight preset Picture Styles () from which you can choose. The full list is available in Chapter 3.

The Picture Style Editor

Canon offers a Picture Style Editor on the DVD that comes with your camera. Designed for advanced users, this method is more precise than using the LCD screen to create custom Picture Style adjustments. To do this, open a RAW image in the Picture Style Editor. Apply a Picture Style to the image, and then make adjustments with the multiple color adjustment options. Once you make your custom changes using the editor, save your changes as a Picture Style file (PF2). Use the EOS utility program (also found on the Canon DVD) to register the file in the camera so you can apply it to future photographs.

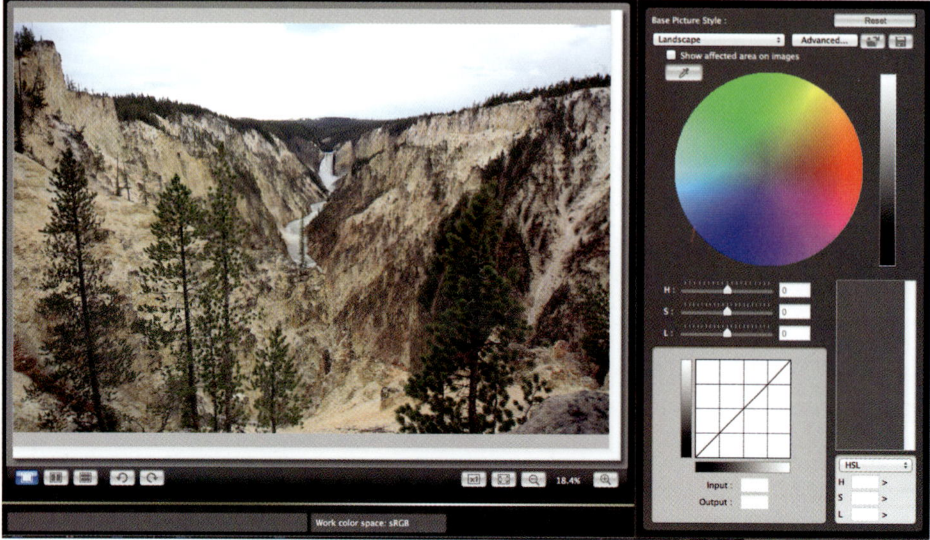

6.17 The Picture Style Editor allows you to customize hue, saturation, and lightness settings. You may save your custom Picture Style settings for future use in your camera by registering them as a PF2 file.

NOTE To upload a PF2 file to your camera, it must be connected to your computer via a USB cable.

Ambience Effects

When photographing in the automatic modes, you can set Ambience Effects to enhance your images. These are similar to Picture Styles for automatic settings. You can check the ambience effect on the screen by pressing the Live View button (▣) on the back of your camera. If you want to enhance your images, select from the following effects:

- **Standard.** The camera does not adjust your photograph.
- **Vivid.** Adds color saturation, and increases contrast and sharpness.
- **Soft.** Decreases the sharpness for a soft-focus look.
- **Warm.** Adds warm tones, such as reds and oranges, and softens the image.
- **Intense.** Increases color saturation and contrast beyond the Vivid setting.
- **Cool.** Adds cool blue tones to your image.
- **Brighter.** Lightens the photograph.
- **Darker.** Darkens the photograph.
- **Monochrome.** Creates black-and-white photos with color tint options similar to Picture Styles.

NOTE Ambience effects are not available in the Scene Intelligent Auto (A+), No Flash (⚡̸), or HDR backlight (▣) modes.

Choosing a color space

A common dilemma among photographers is deciding which color space to use. The available options — Adobe RGB or sRGB — are found under Shooting menu 2 (📷). Adobe RGB is the standard choice for photographers who regularly print their images. This is because Adobe RGB has a larger color gamut (that is, more colors to work with). As more images are shared on the Internet, many photographers have switched to sRGB because it displays colors better for e-mail and web use.

Color Calibration

Everyone's monitor is different. When you view your photograph on the LCD screen on your camera, it looks different from your computer's display. This is because different manufacturers and styles of screens use different technologies. In addition, all screens shift color over time. When you e-mail your photos or post them to a website or social media platform, each viewer sees it (at least slightly) differently. Even the lighting in the room in which they are sitting affects the way people view images.

This is why it is important to calibrate or profile your computer monitor with a color management system (CMS). A CMS helps your monitor display the best possible colors. The goal is to keep the color as consistent and true as possible among all of your devices (camera, monitor, printer, and so on). There are various brands and price ranges. If you are looking for the most accurate color, a good CMS is worth the investment. Check with your monitor manufacturer for suggestions and recommendations.

Measuring Light

What is a correct exposure? The answer depends on your goal for the photograph. Consider which part of your subject or scene you want to see or highlight. The direction of the light and how much of it is illuminating your main subject helps you determine which metering mode to use.

When you press your shutter button halfway, the camera combines four distinct elements to calculate the proper exposure of a scene: the intensity of the light (source), the size of the opening allowing light into the camera (aperture), how long the camera lets light in (shutter), and the light sensitivity of the material capturing the image (ISO). With dSLRs, photographers have a large latitude of digital sensitivity settings.

Choosing the proper exposure

The first step is to consider the scene. Everything has detail, and it is important to show as much as possible in a properly exposed photograph. *Highlight detail* is found in the light or white areas of your photograph. If your subject is wearing a white shirt, you should be able to see the fabric details. If there is no texture in the whites, the detail is considered *blown out*.

Shadow detail is the fine points found in the shadows or blacks. If your subject is wearing a black shirt, the detail in the shirt should be visible. You also want your photographs to have a nice balance of contrast. Too much contrast leaves your photos with little or no highlight and shadow detail. Low contrast leaves your images flat and lifeless. Often in high-contrast scenes, it is difficult to successfully capture the entire highlight and shadow detail. In this case, the photographer must decide which of the details is more important and adjust the exposure as needed.

CROSS REF The Canon T5i/700D offers multiple exposure mode options. A full list and explanations are found in Chapter 3.

When evaluating your exposure, consider the histogram — an often feared and misunderstood, yet valuable tool for the digital photographer. The *histogram* is a graph that charts the brightness levels in an image from darks to lights in a range from 0 to 255. In the center is medium gray. The darker areas are on the left and the lighter on the right, as shown in Figure 6.18.

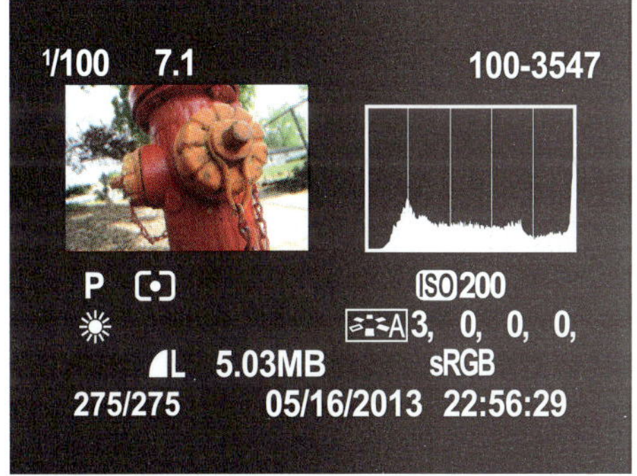

6.18 This histogram shows some overexposed highlights from the background and sidewalk.

A brightness histogram gives you a sense of the distribution of the lights and darks in your image. Generally, a good histogram spreads across the entire screen, but this is not always the case. If you photograph a white cat in the snow, chances are the histogram will not break anywhere near the left side. It is worth noting that if your histogram bumps up to either edge of the graph with many pixels, you may be losing some important shadow or highlight detail. If your histogram is bunched up in the middle of the graph, you may find you have a rather flat image.

CROSS REF To view your image's histogram, press the Playback button (▶), select the image you want to view, and then press the Info button (**INFO.**).

A color or RGB histogram displays how the brightness levels of all three colors (Red, Green, and Blue) are distributed in the image. Colors on the left side of the graph are more prominent than the brighter or less intense colors on the right. If a color is bumping up against the left side of the graph, it may be oversaturated and not displaying much detail. If the color histogram channel is bumping against the right side, it may be completely lacking in the scene. Ultimately, a histogram is a guide, not a pattern you must obey.

Metering modes

Your camera has four metering modes from which you can choose. Each mode calculates the scene exposure using different parts of the scene or subject.

Evaluative metering mode

This is Canon's all-purpose metering system. The camera divides the viewfinder into zones from which to work when calculating the proper exposure of a scene. In the Evaluative metering mode ([⊙]), the camera software selects multiple points and applies different weight to any of the active nine focus points seen through the viewfinder. The Evaluative metering mode ([⊙]) is the default metering system for the camera's automatic modes. It is also a good default setting to leave your camera in for everyday photography. When you face a backlit subject, Evaluative metering mode ([⊙]) is recommended.

Center-weighted average metering mode

The Center-weighted average metering mode ([ ]) averages the light in the entire frame, but assumes that the subject is in the center, giving more weight to those points of exposure. The advantage of this metering system is that it is not overly influenced by bright edges or spots of light within the scene. It is the default setting for many photographers because the exposure is more predictable than the Evaluative metering mode ([⊙]), which uses complex calculations to determine the best exposure. As long as the subject is in the center, this is a good standard exposure setting.

Spot metering mode

The Spot metering mode ([·]) focuses on approximately 4 percent of the frame to calculate the best exposure. A circle in the middle of the viewfinder represents it, as shown in Figure 6.19.

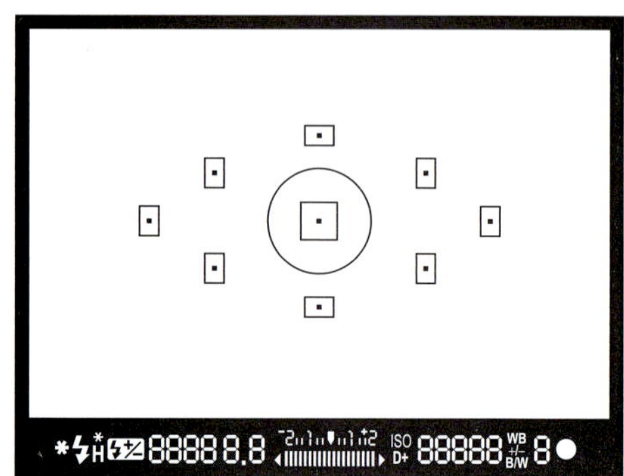

6.19 The circle in the middle of the frame represents the Spot meter's coverage.

If you need a precise meter measurement, this setting gives you more control over the exposure. You can also use this mode if you need the best exposure for only part of a scene. This setting is helpful when there is a lot of light behind your subject or if it is in the shade.

NOTE If you find that your favorite metering mode regularly under- or overexposes your images, consider using exposure compensation.

If you set your camera to the Spot metering mode ([•]) and point it at bright light behind your subject, you create a silhouette. If you don't want to create a silhouette, use the Spot metering mode ([•]) and focus on your subject. The spot meter calculates the proper exposure based on approximately 4 percent of the frame pointed at your subject.

If you are concerned about your exposure, consider using Auto Exposure Bracketing (AEB), which is explained in Chapter 3. This feature takes three consecutive images at different exposures. This gives you a choice of exposures when you are ready to edit or print your images. Another recommendation is to photograph using the RAW setting (RAW). This allows you to readjust your exposure while editing your images.

Partial metering mode

The Partial metering mode ([○]) is similar to the Spot metering mode ([•]), except that it takes into account about double the area of the center of the frame when calculating the proper exposure. This mode is good for exposing small or distant objects.

The Canon Flash System

The Canon flash system consists of multiple flash models, called speedlites, which are available for the Canon Rebel T5i/700D. The Speedlite 270EX II is a compact flash that is a step above your camera's pop-up flash. The 270EX II is fine for casual use when photographing subjects within a range of less than 12 feet. It is also a good choice for use as a trigger flash for multiple-flash photography, which is covered later in this chapter. The Speedlite 430EX II is a good all-purpose flash with a swivel head, bounce, and enough power to cover most of your needs. If you need a durable, high-performance flash, the Speedlite 600EX-RT is a good choice. The 600EX-RT is a wireless, multiple-flash system that uses radio wave communication for up to five groups of flashes.

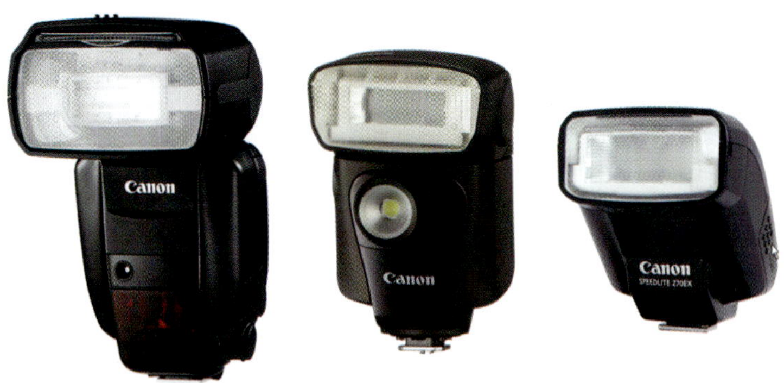

Image courtesy of Canon.

6.20 From left to right, Canon Speedlite 600EX-RT, 320EX, and 270EX.

The pop-up flash

The pop-up or built-in flash, shown in Figure 6.21, is on top of your camera. It is good for casual photography of subjects that are within a 12-foot range. Make sure that you are not using a lens hood because it may obstruct the flash and create unwanted shadows. If you are serious about flash photography, I recommend that you consider purchasing an external flash. You will have more flexibility, features, and power with most external flashes, especially Canon Speedlites.

To turn on the built-in flash, press the Flash button (⚡) on the front of the camera just above the Lens Release button. You must press this button to turn on the flash in the Program AE (**P**), Shutter-priority AE (**Tv**), Aperture-priority AE (**Av**), Manual (**M**), and Bulb (**B**) exposure modes. In the automatic exposure modes, such as Sports () and Landscape (), the camera automatically pops up the flash when required.

While the flash is charging or recycling, a Busy (**buSY**) icon is displayed in the viewfinder. When the flash is ready, the icon (⚡) is displayed in the bottom left of the viewfinder. Your pop-up flash has a convenient Red-eye Reduction mode. To enable this option, go into Shooting menu 1 (), select Redeye reduc., and then select Enable. Red-eye Reduction works in every mode except Flash Off (), Landscape (), Sports (), and Movie ().

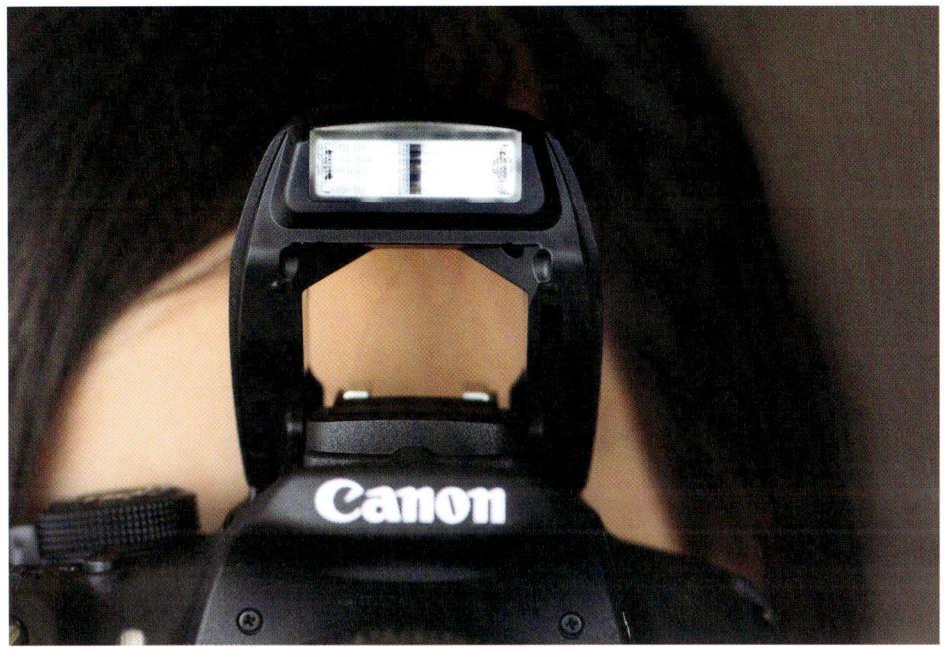

6.21 The Canon Rebel T5i/700D pop-up flash ready to fire.

NOTE The Red-Eye Reduction mode is not foolproof. It works better when there is more light in the environment.

The pop-up flash also works with the camera's self-timer, which is helpful when shooting family pictures. Your camera has two options for this: Self-timer 2 seconds (⏲2) and Self-timer 10 seconds (⏲10). You can also select up to 10 additional continuous shots so that you don't have to keep running back and forth to the camera.

Using an external flash

On top of your camera is a hot shoe for external flashes. This is where you can attach a Canon Speedlite flash directly to the camera. You may also use an off-camera shoe cord and hold the flash in your hand or attach it to a bracket. Just because external speedlites are larger and more powerful does not mean that they are more difficult to use. The Canon Speedlite's E-TTL II technology makes it easy for the flash to talk to the camera. As a result, well-exposed flash photographs are as easy as attaching the flash to the camera hot shoe, turning on the flash, and pressing the shutter button.

An external flash is generally optimal for subjects in the range of 8 to 50 feet away, depending on the flash model and ISO setting. The maximum range is limited when you bounce the flash, which is good for softening the light. Some flashes can reach more than 150 feet, but the intensity of the flash diminishes the farther your subject is from the camera.

All Canon Speedlites, including the T5i/700D pop-up flash, have a Flash Exposure Lock button (ϟ*). If you focus on your subject and press the Flash Exposure Lock button (ϟ*), the flash emits a pulse of light to calculate the proper exposure, and then stores it in memory. Press the AE Lock button (✱) and recompose your image. Once your photograph is composed and you press the shutter button all the way, the flash-locking system uses the flash exposure settings stored in memory.

NOTE The Flash Exposure Lock button (ϟ*) doesn't work in the Live View shooting mode (◘).

When you don't agree with results of your flash photography, consider using Flash Exposure Compensation (FEC) (ϟ±). You can quickly access it by pressing the Quick Control/Print button (Q) on the back of your camera.

CAUTION You can set Flash Exposure Compensation directly on your speedlite, but it will override any flash setting on your camera.

Flash Exposure Compensation is commonly used in fill-flash situations when the subject is in front of a bright light source, such as the sun or a window. More advanced photographers use Flash Exposure Compensation with exposure compensation. Flash Exposure Compensation is used to control the flash exposure, and exposure compensation is used to adjust the ambient light. It's like adjusting two exposures in one photograph. If you are using the flash on your camera, I recommend purchasing a bounce reflector, a softbox, or a filter designed to soften its light.

Using multiple flashes

Removing the flash from your camera is a great way to quickly improve the quality of your photography. Whether you use one or multiple flashes, you can spend a lifetime learning new skills related to off-camera flash photography.

The Canon flash system includes a remote system that allows the use of multiple flashes at one time. There are many ways you can approach using multiple flashes. You can use your camera's external or pop-up flash to trigger external Canon Speedlite flashes in Slave mode (SLAVE). Another excellent option is to use Canon's Speedlite radio transmitter to trigger up to 15 individual flashes at one time. Radio transmitters have an advantage over optical triggers. Optical triggers depend on light from other flashes to be triggered, whereas radio transmitters are not affected by the direction of another flash or obstructions between multiple flashes. Be sure to use a radio transmitter when shooting around other photographers, so their flashes do not trigger your equipment.

You should always have one main light source. When using multiple light sources, consider assigning one of your flashes as the main light at a higher power level. The rest of the flashes can then be used as support lights. How you approach multiple light sources depends on your photographic goals.

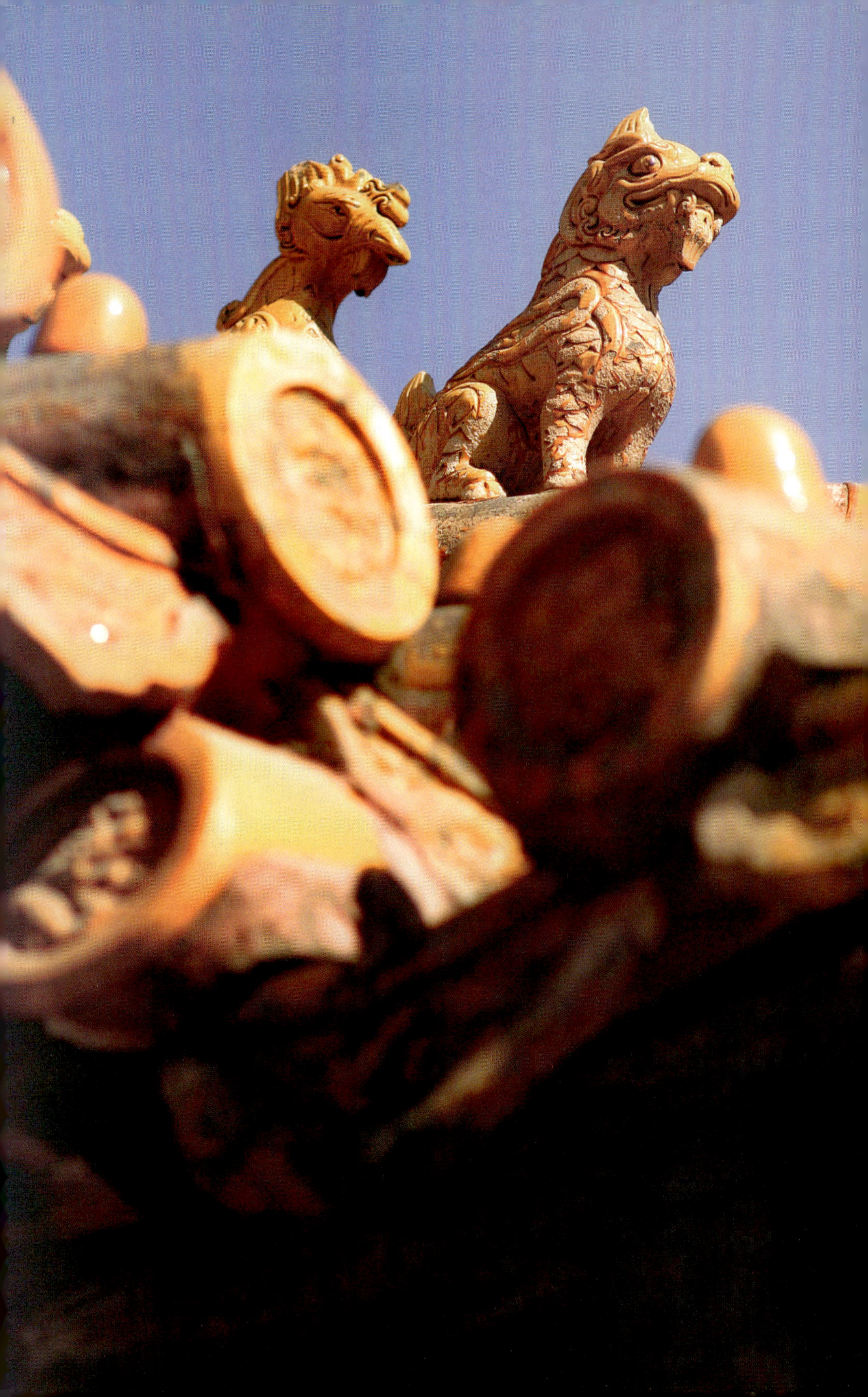

CHAPTER 7

Shooting Photos

To create beautiful photographs, you first must understand how to use your camera. The T5i/700D has many useful features that make creating images easier. Camera control modes, such as Shutter-priority AE (**Tv**) and Aperture-priority AE (**Av**), also known as the Creative Zone modes, give you flexibility and control over your photographs. The automatic modes, such as Landscape (), give you options best suited for various subjects. It takes practice and experience to take high-quality photographs.

This chapter explores different types of photography and includes tips for improving your images. It includes information about composition, lighting, equipment, and the best practices for advancing your skills. The best part of this chapter, in my opinion, are the tips from photographers who have years of experience with various photographic disciplines. The more information you have, the better decisions you will make before clicking the shutter button.

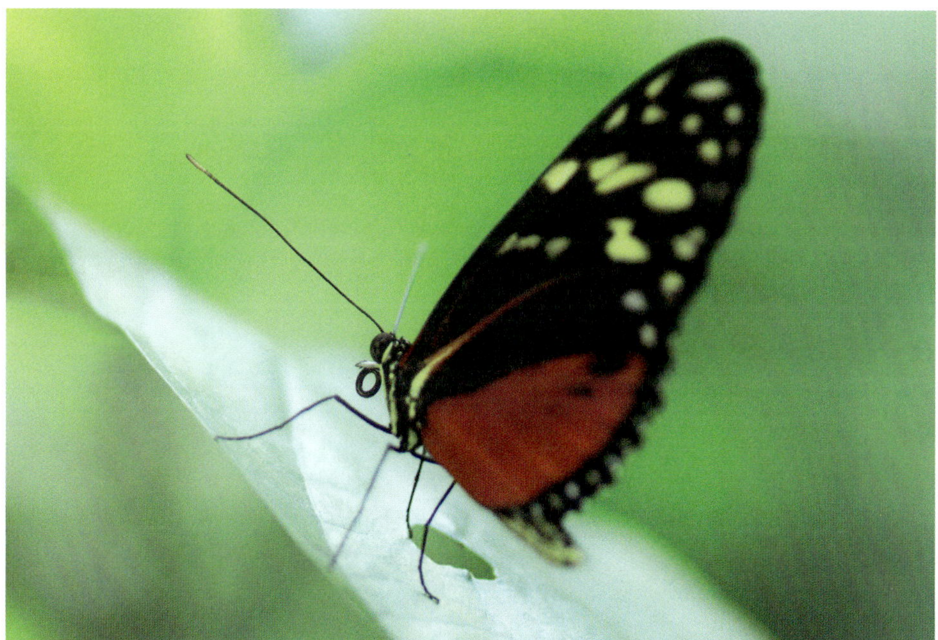

Wildlife is a favorite subject for photographers, and you don't have to travel too far to find great photography opportunities.

Portrait Photography

Creating portraits is an art, and developing your style takes time. A good way to begin a portrait session is to ask how the picture will be used. Is the photograph for professional use or family memories? There are many reasons why people want a portrait. Images of family and friends are in demand, whether in print or for online sharing. You never know which photographs you create will become a treasured family memory. Develop a plan before you start shooting, and think about who will view the photos.

There are two main types of portraits: Studio and environmental. Although taken in different environments, both are controlled by the photographer. A *studio portrait* is created in a photographer's studio or a portable one that is used on location. An *environmental portrait* is taken in the subject's environment, outside the traditional studio. The idea behind this type of portrait is to tell the subject's story with the support of her surroundings. These types of photos are common in documentary photography and photojournalism. In a *candid portrait*, the subject is unaware of or ignoring the camera.

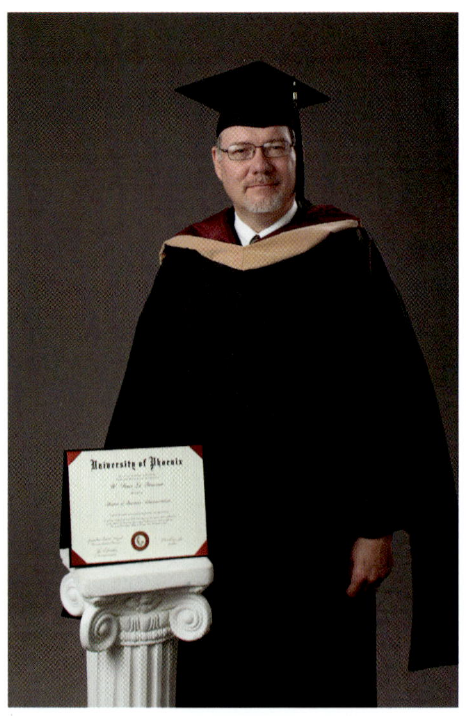

7.1 This graduation portrait was shot in a studio. Exposure: ISO 200, f/5.6, 1/200 second, 28-70 2.8 USM lens.

Equipment

Most studio portrait photographers use lenses over 70mm because they don't want a wide-angle lens to distort their subjects. The preferred range is 70mm to 135mm. Lenses that are 200mm or larger also take great portraits, but they can be intimidating. To add a formal look to your photographs, consider purchasing a background. Photographers often use a longer lens to create candid-style photographs. Longer lenses are nice when you want to stay out of your subject's personal space. Use a wide-angle lens, such as a 20mm, to create a portrait that shows the environment and tells the subject's story.

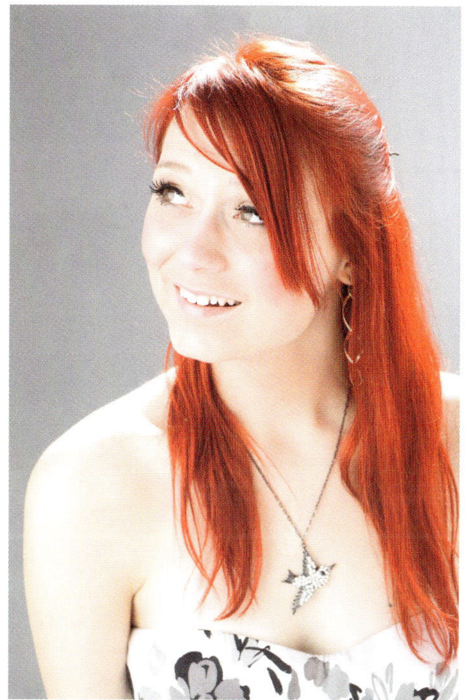

7.2 A studio portrait shot using a softbox. Exposure: ISO 100, f/5.6, 1/160 second, 100mm f/2.8 lens.

Lighting is an important part of creating a portrait. Most portrait photographers prefer to use a soft light to minimize the harshness of shadows. A softbox, umbrella, or using a soft filter on the flash is highly recommended. When photographing groups, a soft light is even more important because it minimizes harsh shadows created when people stand close together. Consider using window light for your portraits — the soft light or warm glow of a sunset through a window adds a nice dimension to your pictures. If one side of your subject's face is too dark, use a reflector, white board, or bounce a flash off the opposite wall to add fill light.

The *self-portrait* is a popular form of photography. If you don't have a wide enough lens (or long enough arms), I recommend using a tripod along with your camera's self-timer to take a portrait. One nice feature of the continuous self-timer option is that you can take multiple images without having to run back and forth to your camera to reset it. If you handhold your camera, an ultrawide-angle lens is helpful. Use the Live View mode (◘) and turn the LCD screen to face the same direction as your lens so that you can see what is in the frame.

It's helpful to carry tools in your bag to make the experience of creating a portrait more pleasant for your subjects. Include little things, such as small toys, that might grab a child's attention. Keep a mirror handy for your subjects to check their hair and makeup. Small clips are useful to hold back loose clothing. Often, these extras can make the difference between an average image and a great portrait. Another thing that professionals do is carry a booklet of sample poses on which you and your subject can collaborate. This tool also breaks the ice and can give nervous subjects a bit more confidence.

Best practices

Most formal portraits are photographed with a long lens (over 70mm) while holding the camera vertically. However, this does not mean that all portraits *must* be shot vertically — horizontal studio portraits are interesting, too. Studio portraits are usually best when photographed using a shallow depth of field, as shown in Figure 7.3. Use the lowest aperture number possible on your lens (I prefer f/2.8 to f/4.5). The Portrait mode (portrait icon) on your camera does this automatically.

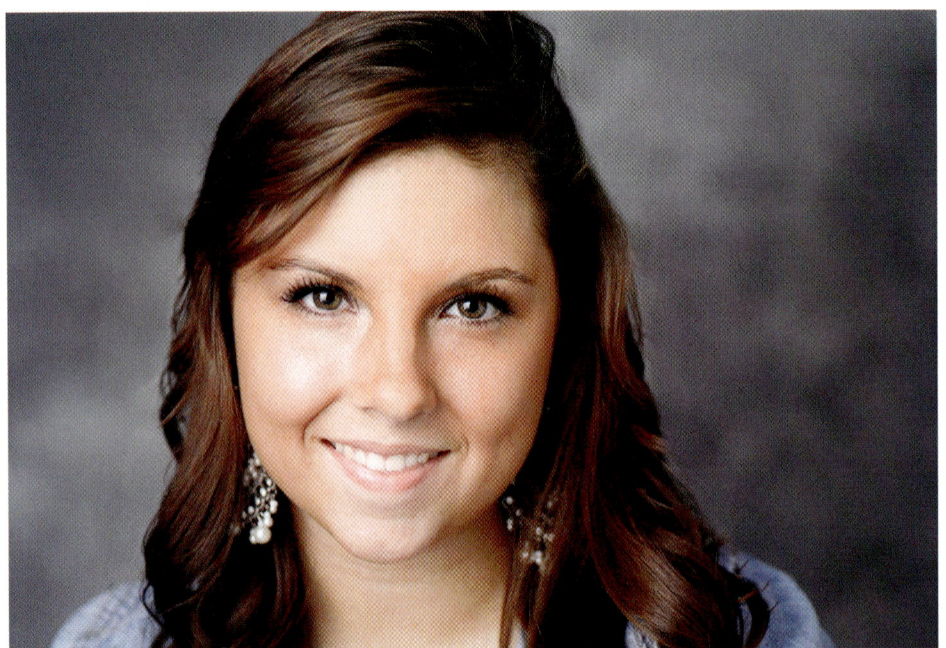

7.3 It is normally best to shoot portraits with a shallow depth of field. Exposure: ISO 125, f/3.5, 1/125 second, 100mm f/2.8 lens.

> **TIP** When using a shallow depth of field for portraits, pay close attention to your focus, especially around the subject's eyes.

Environmental portraits tend to be horizontal, wide-angle photos. Sometimes, though, the best choice is to use a longer lens (70mm or more) vertically, as shown in Figure 7.4. The objective of environmental portraiture is to see the subject's environment, so creating a large depth of field by using a large aperture number (which is a smaller opening), such as f/16, is recommended.

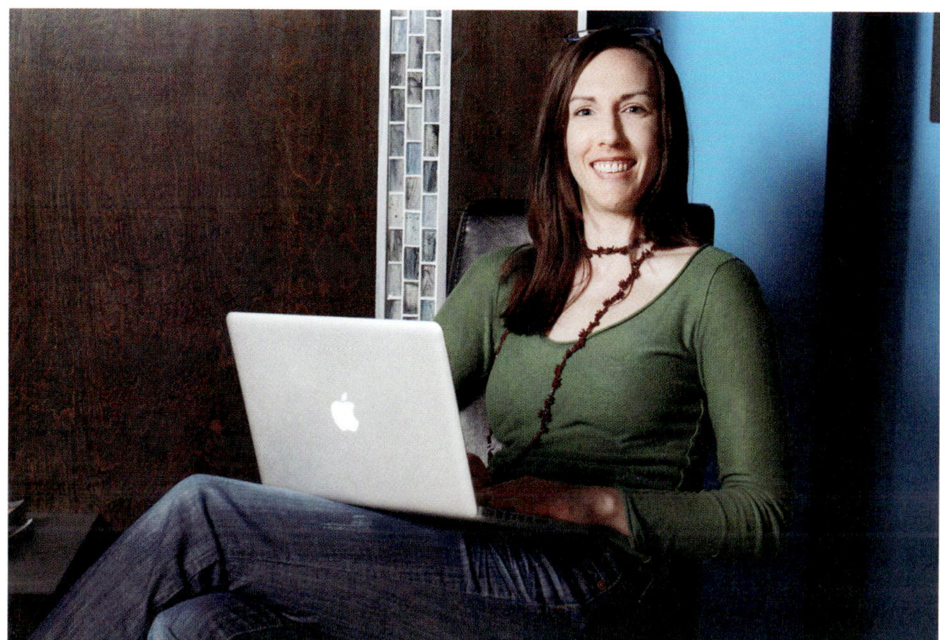

7.4 **Environmental portraits can show the subject either sitting or standing. Some may feature props, while others rely on the environment to tell the story. Exposure: ISO 125, f/6.3, 1/200 second, 50mm f/1.4 lens.**

When photographing a group, make sure that heads are not aligned — that is, directly above one another. It's better to stagger people so that they are at different heights. It is also important to make sure that all of your subjects are in focus. Make sure that you have enough depth of field by using an aperture of at least f/5.6. After you take a group shot, double-check it by pressing the Playback button (▶), and then zooming in on each individual to make sure everyone is in focus. You can zoom in by pressing the Magnify button (🔍), or by spreading your index finger and thumb across the LCD touchscreen.

No matter which portrait style you choose, your main goal is to keep your subject's eyes in focus. If the eyes are not in focus, it is hard for the viewer to relate to the person in the photograph. This can be tough when using a shallow depth of field, especially at apertures of f/2.8 or lower. Take the time to review a few of your portraits to make sure you are on target. Press the Playback button (▶) and you see an instant preview of your last image. Also, keep your subject away from walls. Depending on the lens and depth of field you are using, you may capture distracting details on a wall behind your subject. Pulling people away from the wall allows the shallow depth of field to do its job and blur any distracting elements in the background. Walls are not all bad, but only use them as a backdrop if you think it will enhance the photograph.

Try different compositional techniques, such as the Rule of Thirds and new perspectives. Not every portrait needs to be shot at eye level. Take advantage of your camera's Live View shooting mode (◘), hold the camera higher or lower, and use different lenses. Look for objects that compete with your subject, and if you see distracting elements try a new angle. Make sure that the background is free of poles and other intrusive objects that might appear to be coming out of your subject's head or body.

In a *candid portrait,* the subject ignores, or is unaware of, the camera. The goal is to be patient enough to wait for peak moments when people are laughing, gesturing, or smiling. This takes practice, a little stealth, and luck. The photographer must be ready to press the shutter button at any moment. Many photographers do not consider these portraits, but a good candid image captures a moment in time and tells a story. Children are excellent candid subjects, especially because they usually don't like to sit in one spot for very long. However, pointing the camera down at a child does not effectively capture his world and point of view. Make sure that you get down on their level. Interact and play with them for a few minutes before you start shooting. Just let kids be kids and you will capture some great shots.

You rarely get the best photo on the first shot (although, it can happen), so take a lot of pictures. A slight movement, smile, or shift of the eye can change the entire mood of an image, turning a nice shot into a great portrait. The more photos you take, the greater your chance of capturing the right moment.

Tips

Use your camera in the Live View mode (◘) to allow interaction between you and your subject while you shoot. People come in all shapes, sizes, and colors, and knowing how to approach a subject makes for a better photograph. For example, people with long noses should be photographed straight on to minimize the size, rather than allowing the nose to detract from other facial features. Ask older people to look up at you to smooth out any wrinkles in their necks and faces. Overexpose photos of people with darker skin by 1 stop or, better yet, add more light so you can see facial details.

It's not unusual for portrait subjects to stiffen when the camera is pointed their way. Remember to have fun — portraits don't have to be such serious business. I'm not very good at telling jokes, but I try to relate to my subjects in any way that I can to make them feel comfortable and get them to smile. Sometimes, subjects may think they are smiling when they are not. Show them a few of your photographs so that they can make adjustments and understand what you are doing. A trick I learned a long time ago from an opera singer was to ask your subjects to look down and count to three. On three, ask them to look up with a big smile. Another idea is to ask your subjects to pretend that they just ran into an old friend they haven't seen in years.

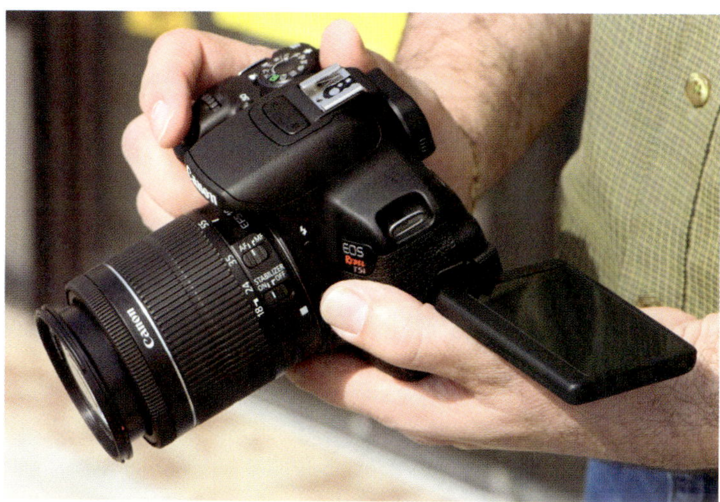

7.5 Use the LCD screen in the Live View shooting mode to check your composition. When shooting portraits, this also allows you to interact with your subject.

Try different backdrops or locations behind your subject. Sometimes, just turning the other direction makes a big difference. It's amazing how different background objects can improve your photograph. Always look for light, colors, or interesting textures that you can use as part of your composition. Don't be afraid to use props in your images. Include things that relate to the subject, such as a teddy bear if you're photographing a child. Have someone hold a photograph of a grandparent at a younger age, or pose him with his favorite piece of sporting equipment. Let the props help tell the story.

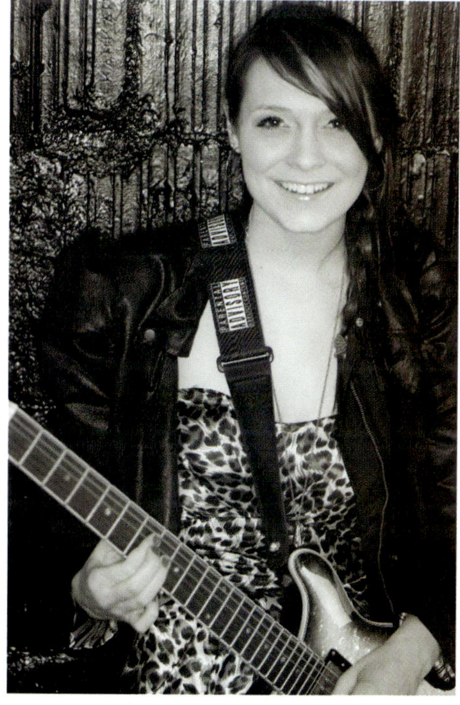

7.6 Black-and-white photographs can be more dramatic. Exposure: ISO 160, f/3.2, 1/160 second, 100mm f/2.8 lens.

You can also use the Monochrome Picture Style (M) on your camera to create black-and-white portraits. In some cases, you might want to wait until postproduction to change your photos to black and white. This is especially true if you are shooting JPEG files because you cannot later convert them back to color. If you generally don't do a lot of post-processing, take a few color and black-and-white shots for variety. Try using the Portrait mode (🯅) and see if it enhances your photos to your satisfaction. If you don't like the results of the preset modes in your camera, you can create up to three of your own Picture Styles.

Regardless of whether photography is your hobby or career, it is always good to remember that interesting subjects make the most interesting photos. This may seem obvious, but it is a fact that is often overlooked. Look for interesting (not just beautiful) people to photograph — people with character in their faces, or interesting clothing, hairstyles, and body art.

Try photographing parts of the body, such as the hands or legs, as part of an environmental portrait. The face does not have to be in every shot, especially if the photo is one in a series of images. Creating a series can be a lot of fun. It can be composed of the subject in different poses, making faces, or in different environments. Usually a series is grouped in odd numbers such as three, five, or seven photographs. Use your imagination — you will be surprised at the interesting combinations you can envision.

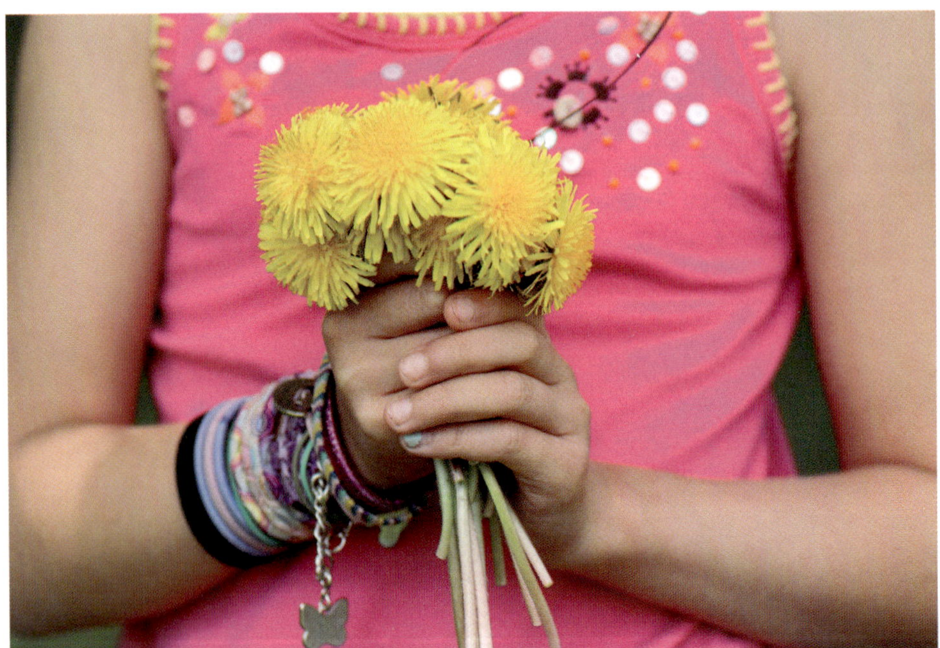

7.7 Here, a person's body is used to display the subject. Exposure: ISO 400, f/3.5, 1/1000 second, 100mm f/2.8 lens.

If you want to create a softer, cleaner look, experiment with overexposing your portraits. It's not right for every subject, but a quick test never hurts. Try playing with movement. Sometimes, blurring your subject in the foreground adds interest. This technique doesn't work well for formal portraits, but it's a nice addition to a series. Another idea is to ask your subject to stand still, and then use a slow shutter speed to show the motion of people or traffic in the background. You should also always keep model release forms on hand. You never know how you might want to use your photographs in the future. If you have signed model releases for all of your portraits, you're good to go.

Portrait Photography Tips

Geoffrey Creighton, a photographer based in Halifax, Nova Scotia, believes that a strong interaction between the photographer and the subject is the key to creating a successful portrait. Good rapport is an important part of capturing the personality of a subject, which, in turn, helps create a connection between the subject and the viewer. Here, Geoffrey shares some tips for taking portraits with your Canon Rebel T5i/700D:

- **Use the Creative Zone modes — specifically Aperture-priority AE (Av).**
- **Use the lowest aperture possible, such as f/2.8.**
- **Experiment with the main light behind the subject (backlight).** This is a more advanced technique that can produce exciting results.
- **Don't photograph your subject straight on.** Shooting at different angles can add depth and make your subject more interesting.
- **Ask people to shake their hips to loosen up before you shoot.**
- **Take a range of shots from *no smile* to *insanity,* and then back to *no smile.*** You will find your hero shot at some point during the process.
- **Use reflectors and fill flash.** These tools will help improve the quality of your images.

Geoffrey Creighton specializes in actor headshots and portraits. You can view his work at: www.geoffreycreighton.com.

Family Photography

Family portraits are one of the most common types of photography. For most people, it is an integral way to remember the milestones in our lives. When shooting family portraits, it is important to take a variety of photographs. Don't position everyone against a wall for every shot. Take some candid images, and use different lenses and techniques to help tell the family's story. Let personalities shine — don't do too much directing. If a child is holding her favorite toy, let her keep it. The more natural family photographs are, the better the memories will be.

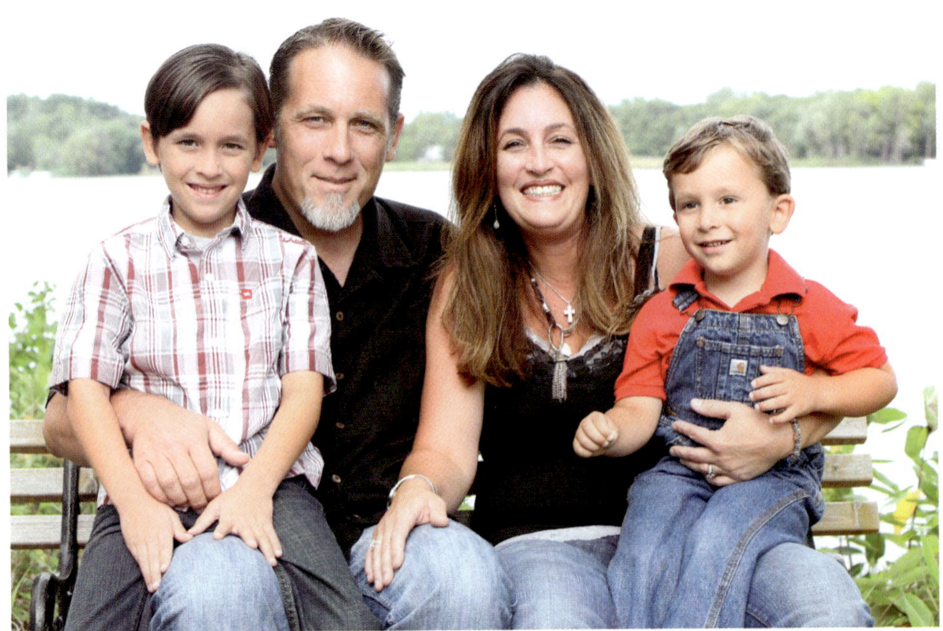

7.8 Casual family photographs can capture fun memories. Exposure: ISO 400, f/5.6, 1/250 second, 50mm f/1.4 lens.

Equipment

I recommend using zoom lenses for family photo opportunities because you never know what will happen at family gatherings. The ability to use a wide-angle lens one moment and a telephoto the next can mean the difference between capturing a memorable image or not.

Don't forget about yourself. Use a tripod to set up your camera for formal and casual photographs that include you. You can also use a remote to take photographs from a distance in both group and random photographs.

Best practices

If you plan to take formal family portraits, setting them outdoors tends to yield the best results. Coordinate clothing, if possible, to help create unity. Suggest that no one wear loud colors, patterns, or extreme styles. Of course, how you approach this topic depends on your family dynamic. When photographing groups, use soft light or shade to avoid unwanted shadows.

Try to plan family photo shoots when kids are likely to be in a good mood. This is most important for younger children who take naps. Inquire and plan ahead if more than one family is involved. Don't forget about four-legged family members — they are also an important part of a family's story, so make sure to get some shots with and without pets. Take individual portraits of each of the animals, too.

Tips

Use a wide aperture for group shots and a small aperture for individuals. Take many pictures, especially if there is more than one person in a photograph. It can take many frames before you successfully capture an image in which everyone looks their best.

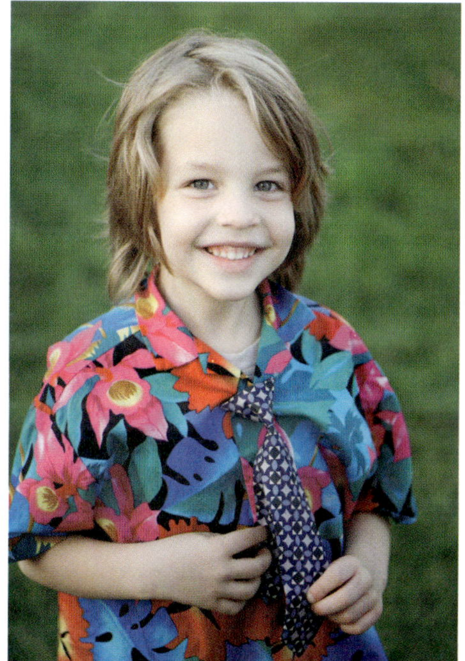

7.9 Let kids be kids to preserve their personalities in your photographs. Exposure: ISO 400, f/2.8, 1/400 second, 100mm f/2.8 lens.

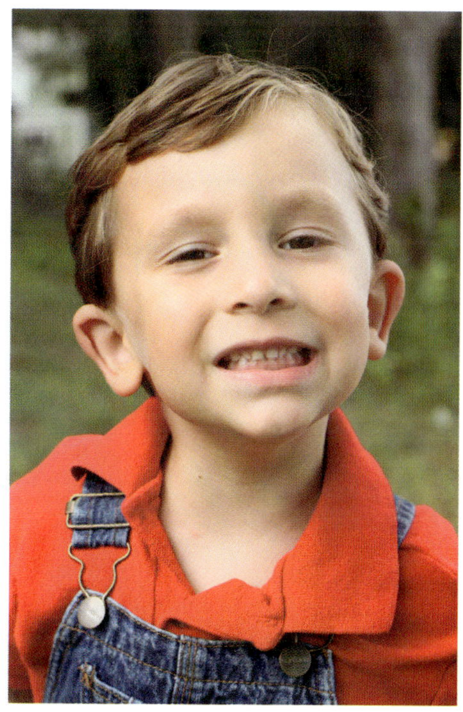

7.10 I took this casual portrait between formal shots. Exposure: ISO 400, f/5.6, 1/320 second, 50mm f/1.4 lens.

Family Photography Tips

Todd Muskopf, a professional family and senior portrait photographer, believes the first thing an aspiring photographer should learn is how to use light. Fill-flash and reflectors are a good place to start. In Muskopf's opinion, the most important thing to do then is shoot a ton of images. The following are Todd's eight tips for photographing friends and family:

- **Never ask people to look directly into the sun.**
- **Consider the angles at which you photograph people.** Make sure the result is desirable. For example, you might want to photograph heavier people at a higher angle rather than straight on.
- **When posing people, remember, *if it bends — bend it.*** This prevents portraits from looking stiff.
- **Use a longer lens for portraits.** An 85mm f/1.2 or 70-200mm f/2.8 lens is ideal.
- **Use a shallow depth of field for a single person and a larger depth of field for multiple subjects.**
- **Purchase an external flash.** It improves the quality of photographs without adding a lot of cost.
- **Bounce flash indoors.** Point your flash at walls and ceilings, rather than directly at your subject. Bounce flash softens the shadows on your subject.
- **Always keep backup batteries and memory cards with you.** You don't want your camera to run out of power or space on the memory card before your session is complete.

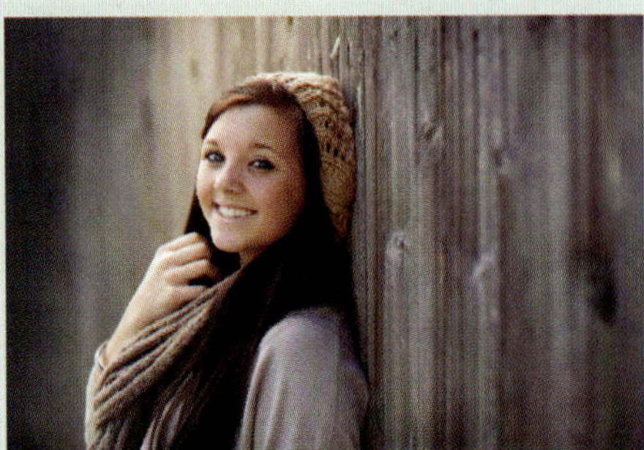

Image courtesy of Todd Muskopf

Todd Muskopf is based in Beavercreek, Ohio. He has photographed professionally for over 10 years, and has sold his images in over 16 countries. You can see more of his work at his website: http://www.muskopf.org.

After your photo session ends, you can identify the people in the photograph in the metadata. *Metadata* is information stored in your image files. You can access and add to the photograph's metadata under File Info in most photo-editing software. Be aware that some Internet websites, including many social media platforms, strip the metadata from photographs, so don't depend on these locations for archival storage. Frame your memories and pick a special place in your home to display family photos. These become conversation pieces and serve as reminders to take more photos.

Action and Sports Photography

Action photography takes a lot of practice. When it comes to sports photography, it is helpful to understand the sport you are shooting. The goal for most action photographers is to capture the *peak moment*, also known as the *decisive moment*. It takes patience and timing (and many frames) to capture it right.

Equipment

Most sports photographers use a long, fast (f/2.8 is ideal) lens to photograph their subjects. Setting the camera at a higher ISO, such as 800 or 1600, helps get the shutter speed as high as possible. Your Canon T5i/700D has a Sports mode (🏃) designed to photograph fast action.

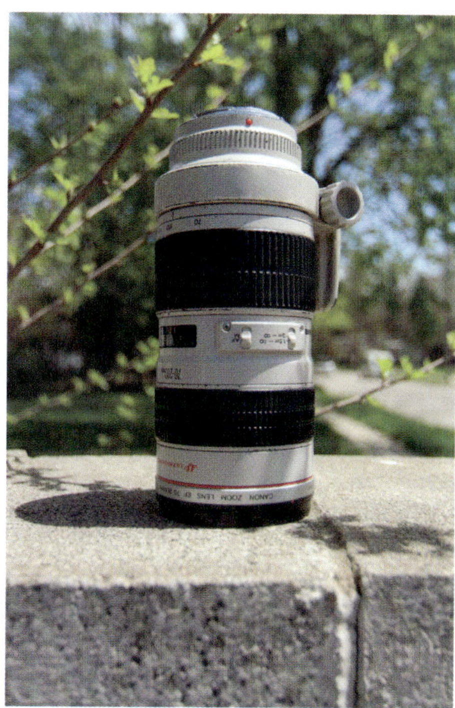

7.11 The Canon 70-200mm f/2.8 is a good all-around sports lens.

Photographers at professional sporting events can create stunning and clear images because the buildings and locations they work in usually have bright lights for television. In some cases, they even have flashes mounted in the ceiling. I'm not suggesting this is the only reason they capture such great images, but it is an advantage most don't have at the local school gymnasium. Local gyms tend to have low light that requires high ISO settings and fast lenses. Fortunately, your camera has an ISO range to help keep your shutter speed as high as possible with an f/2.8 lens.

If you are in the middle of the action and a full tripod is not practical to prevent camera shake, use a monopod (which is like a tripod, but only has one leg) to stabilize your camera.

You are going to take many photographs if you're shooting action, so I recommend that you shoot in the JPEG format rather than RAW. The RAW format is nice for making corrections later, but RAW-format images quickly fill up your camera's buffer. The last thing you need is your camera to stop shooting during peak action because it is processing your images. Your camera shoots 5 frames per second (fps), which is helpful, but it does not replace good timing on your part. Don't rely on the fast frame advance to capture the action. I recommend that you use your instincts and press the shutter button at the peak moment. Leave your finger on the shutter button to continue shooting and capture the rest of the action.

Best practices

If you want stop action, you have to get your shutter speed over 1/500 second. In some cases, if the subject is moving toward or away from you, a lower shutter speed does the trick. If the action is moving from side to side, the higher your shutter speed is, the better. Keep your camera in the AI Servo focusing mode (**AI SERVO**) to follow focus your subject so that when you are ready to press the shutter button, the camera is already focused.

Be prepared — great action shots can happen at any moment. Don't put your camera down, even if you think the play or action is complete. Watch for emotions and accidents, which often happen before and after a play. If you are on the slopes, follow the action as the skier or snowboarder does his tricks. Follow him until you see the reaction or emotion on his face after a successful run. One thing you learn over time when shooting action is how to compose quickly. Just because something happens fast is no excuse for a lack of composition or background that plays off your subject.

Go where the players are or be patient for the action to come to you. Photos taken from across a field (unless you have a very large, expensive lens) are useless. This is especially true when shooting football, soccer, or any game played on a large field. If you have to photograph subjects from farther away, shoot horizontally, and when they get close switch to vertical. Try to fill the frame with the action. When shooting sports, it is important to capture the faces of the players and the ball, if possible. The backs of heads and players running away from the camera rarely make for successful sports images.

Once you know that you have some good shots, try different techniques, such as *panning* or *ghosting*. Panning is using a slower shutter speed and following the subject. Ghosting is a similar process, except it's done while using a flash. In the resulting image, the subject is in focus and the background is blurred. This is a good technique when shooting cars, bikes, or other moving objects. If you know where the action ends (such as at a finish line or home plate), I recommend that you pre-focus on that area and prepare for the runner or player to appear in the frame.

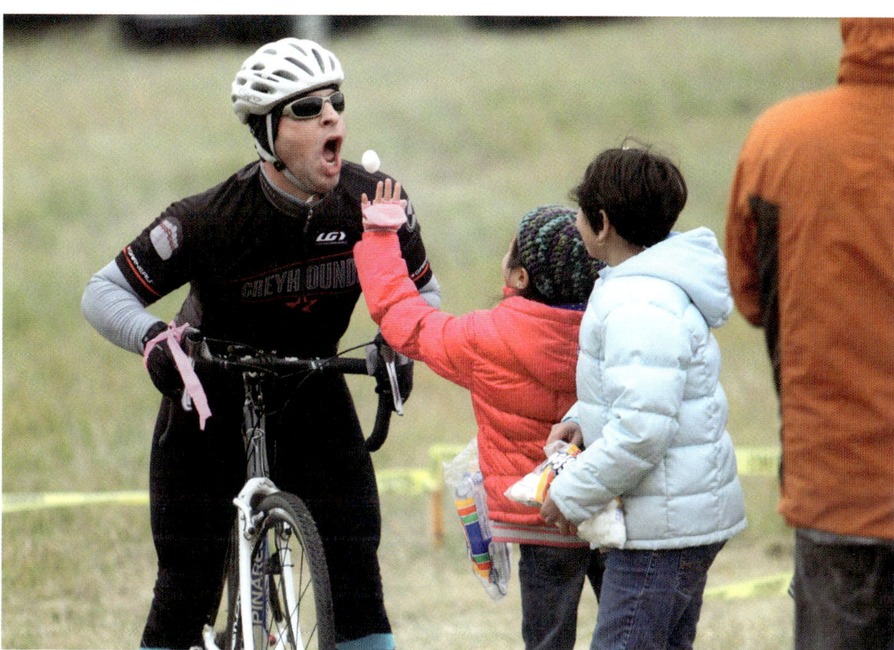

7.12 This image from a cycle cross race was caught at the peak moment. Exposure: ISO 400, f/4.5, 1/1000 second, 70-200mm f/2.8 lens at 190mm.

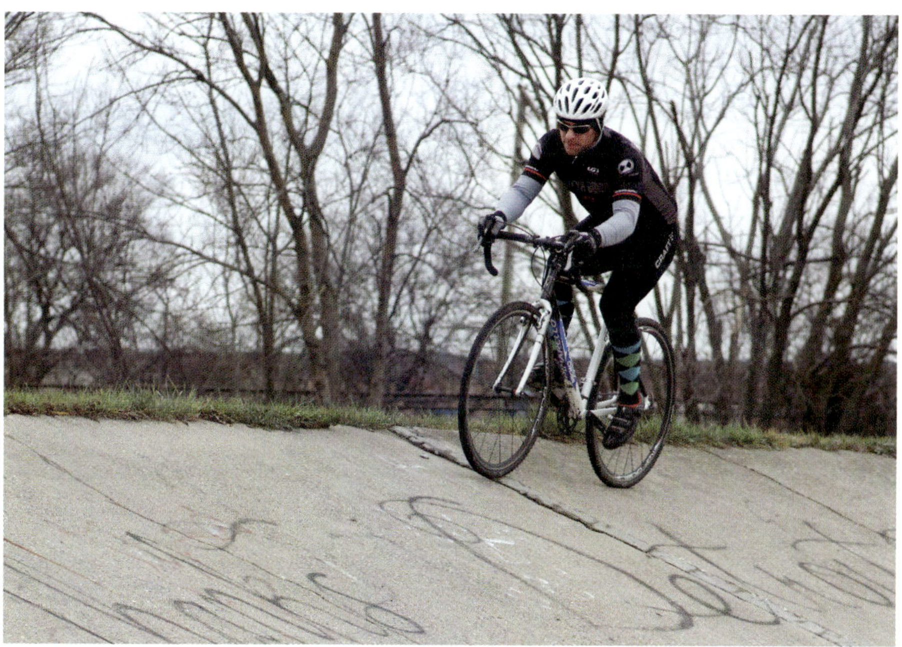

7.13 For this shot, I pre-focused on the track and waited for the cyclist to reach that spot. Exposure: ISO 800, f/4.5, 1/1600 second, 100mm f/2.8 lens.

CROSS REF See Chapter 5 for more information about panning and ghosting.

Try to tell the story of the game through your images. The action may be on the field, slope, or raceway, but coaches, teammates, and fans are all part of it, too, and make great photographic subjects. Use your imagination and try to shoot images you've never seen before. Don't be intimidated by photographers who have larger lenses. Remember, the size of a lens doesn't automatically mean its owner is a good photographer. Learn how to use the equipment you do have to the best of your ability.

Usually, a little post-processing is required for action and sports photographs. Some images may need sharpening, lightening, darkening, or color correction. The biggest alteration that might be necessary in postproduction is cropping images to fill the frame with the action.

Tips

If you are going to be photographing a sport, learn about it. This includes Little League, school teams, and pickup games. Sometimes, the rules are adjusted at different levels, and knowing what to expect helps ease the learning curve. By understanding what should happen next, you can anticipate photo opportunities. Always keep extra memory cards and batteries with you. When you notice that your memory card is getting full, pull it during a break in the action before it gets full. This way, you won't run out of space at a peak moment.

Keep business cards with you. Even if you are photographing family and friends at a local ball field, people often ask for copies. Have a plan in place about how you will handle that request. You should also be prepared for all types of weather. Make sure that you have a way to protect your valuable equipment in case it rains or snows. Also, be prepared for the action to come a little too close. Through my years of photographing sports, balls have hit me, hockey pucks flying at dizzying speeds have just missed my head, and I have been run over by large players. Always be aware of what is going on around you.

Event Photography

Event photography is one of the more popular forms of photography. Most photographers enjoy capturing these moments for family, friends, and themselves to document memories. Once people know that you have a good camera and like to take photographs, you will most likely be asked to shoot events.

When photographing an event, it's important to plan ahead. Set expectations about what you are going to do, including how long you will shoot, how many images you plan to take, and the amount of postproduction you want to do. Postproduction takes a long time if you plan to correct and adjust every image. Plan in advance where and how you will share the photos. Make sure that you understand what the event is about, who the key people are, and if there are any special restrictions regarding photography. For example, some churches and historical locations do not allow flash photography.

Equipment

Using a zoom lens, such as an EF 28-135mm f3.5-5.6 IS USM, is a good idea for events because you might be asked to photograph a group one moment and an intimate exchange the next. A zoom lens helps you adjust quickly. Keep a flash handy to illuminate subjects in a dark room and use as fill flash when you have to photograph in front of bright windows.

TIP If you plan to shoot video at an event, make sure that you have a tripod and an external microphone with you. This will keep your camera steady and the sound will be high quality.

CROSS REF For more information about shooting video, see Chapter 8.

Make sure that you have extras of everything, including batteries and memory cards. An event is generally not something that can be re-created. If any piece of your equipment breaks or runs out of power, it is important to have a backup.

Best practices

When photographing an event, I use what I call the triangle method of photographing. The idea is to create a variety of images, rather than shooting the same style or composition repeatedly. The triangle method forces you to think about and take a variety of shots. Begin with a wide shot to set the scene. Next, shoot medium-distance shots that help tell the story. Try to capture images featuring one to three people, either posed or candid. Finally, take some close-up shots that highlight details. For example, photograph the food, the floral centerpiece, or details on the cake. Look for decorations on the wall, signs, or focus on someone's hands.

Challenge yourself to take a variety of images using different angles, lighting methods, and compositions. Employ the same three-part method of wide, medium, and close-up shots. When you are done, you will have a great collection of images that tell a story.

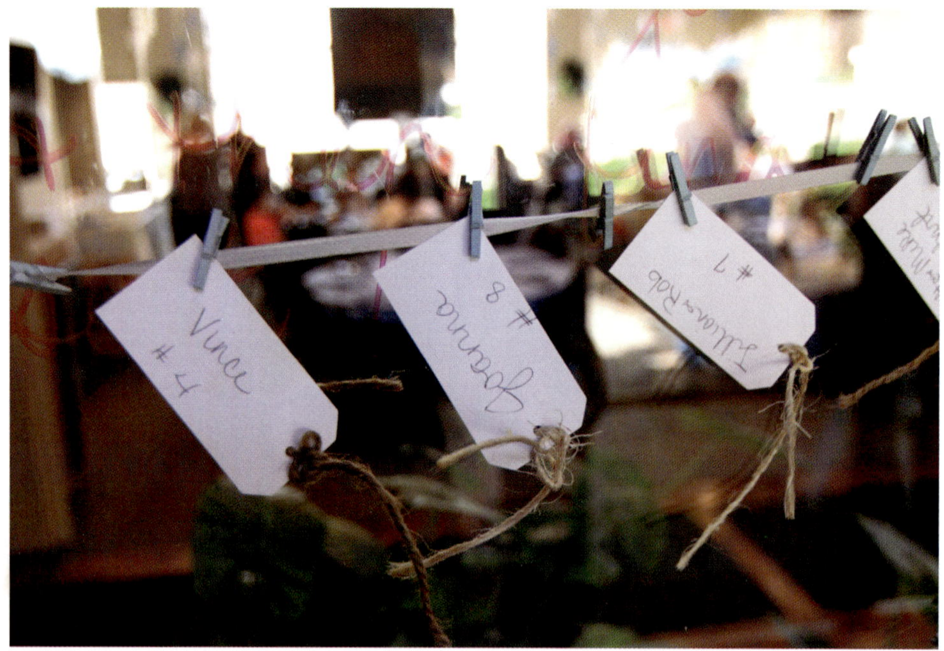

7.14 This establishing shot sets the scene at a communion celebration. Exposure: ISO 800, f/4.0, 1/80 second, 12-24mm f/4.0 lens at 24mm.

Avoid using flash whenever you can so it is not flashing in people's eyes while they are having a good time. If you must use one, consider using a flash filter to soften the light. A slower shutter speed also helps capture the ambient light in the room. Ambient light adds depth to an image and prevents the room from looking like a black curtain behind your subject. If you don't use a flash, chances are that you will get better candid shots that include emotion and laughter. The best compliment an event photographer can receive is that people didn't even know she was there.

Tips

When using an external flash, keep it off the camera to avoid red eye. Use a cord to hold your flash off-camera or a bracket in a fixed position for convenience. Try not to interrupt people by asking them to pose for photos. If you need to get a group shot, try to capture a few good candids first. Using your camera's Live View shooting mode (▣), hold the camera up high to capture crowd shots and new angles.

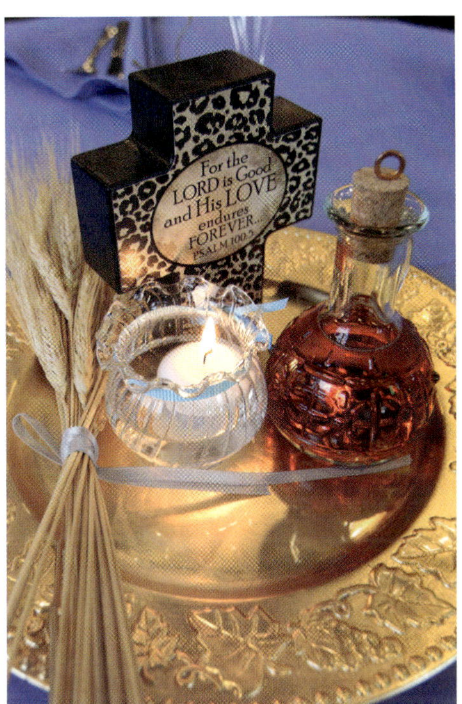

7.15 This detail shot was captured using the triangle method to capture the spirit of the event. Exposure: ISO 100, f/1.8, 1/200 second, 50mm f/1.4 lens.

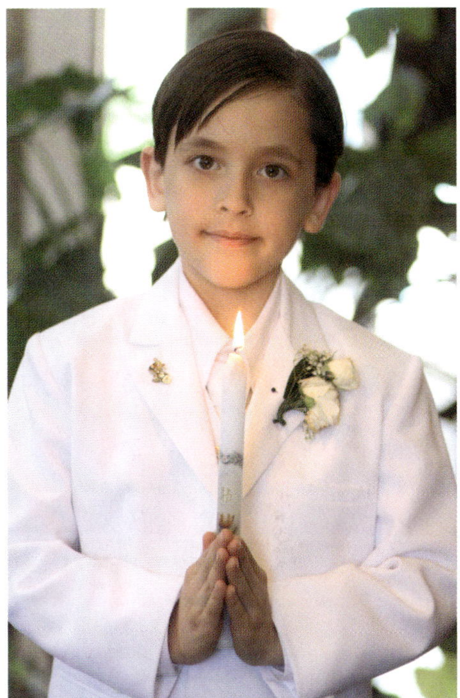

7.16 When using the triangle method, a medium shot (in this case a portrait) should tell the whole story of an event. Exposure: ISO 800, f/2.8, 1/100 second, 100mm f/2.8 lens.

When photographing an event at which someone is speaking, make sure that you photograph the speaker before and after he leaves the podium. Many of the best photographs in those situations are captured before someone starts speaking. Pay attention to the speaker's hand movements, and try to capture any interesting gestures. Look away from the podium occasionally — there are often great subjects to capture in the audience.

Avoid photographing people during a meal. It may seem like a good idea at the time, but people don't look very good when they are eating and if you ask them to stop, they generally are not very happy about it. This is especially true if you ask them to stand up and move around the table for a better shot. It is better to get group shots after everyone is done eating and away from the dirty plates.

Five Event Photography Tips

As a photojournalist and independent photographer, I've shot many events. The following five tips can help you capture any type of occasion:

- **Use the triangle method to capture a variety of images.** Shoot a wide overall shot to set the scene, medium-range shots to help tell the story, and close-ups to capture the details of an event.
- **Use a 100mm or 135mm f/2.8 lens to photograph candid shots.** These lenses are light and long enough to get close without intruding on your subject's space.
- **Tell a story.** Every event has one, and it's your job to convey it through your images.
- **Occasionally look away from the podium or stage.** There is often action or interesting photo opportunities in the audience or among the guests.
- **Always carry backup equipment and supplies, such as extra batteries and memory cards.**

Landscape and Nature Photography

Wildlife, landscape, and nature are some of the most enjoyable and rewarding types of photography. The adventure and discovery of new locations and subjects is exciting. Every trip outdoors becomes a mission to bring back quality photos. Remember that what makes an enjoyable photograph is up to you. Everyone has his own vision or way he approaches certain subjects. Many photographers simply want to capture memories with family in the beautiful outdoors. Others are on a quest for breathtaking scenery, elusive wildlife, or rare flowers.

Equipment

Landscape photographers use a wide lens to capture as much of the scene as possible. Wildlife photographers require a long lens to get close to animals that don't want to be anywhere near humans. Some forms of nature photography require all types of lenses. Macro lenses are common for photographing insects, plants, and rocks found in the field.

A strong and lightweight (carbon fiber) tripod is helpful, especially for keeping long and macro lenses steady in the field. I also prefer backpacks designed for camera equipment because it's easier to carry items in the organized compartments when hiking. Make sure that you are always prepared for changing weather — both extreme heat and cold can be dangerous. Always carry backup equipment, such as extra memory cards and batteries.

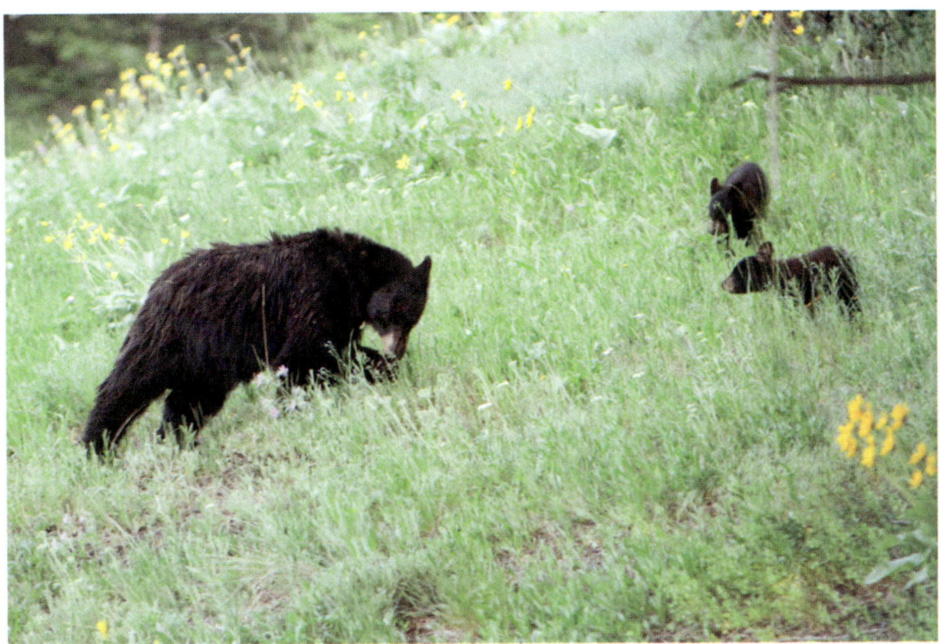

7.17 For some photographers, successfully capturing wildlife is what makes photography enjoyable. Exposure: ISO 1250, f/2.8, 1/160 second, 135mm f/2.8 lens.

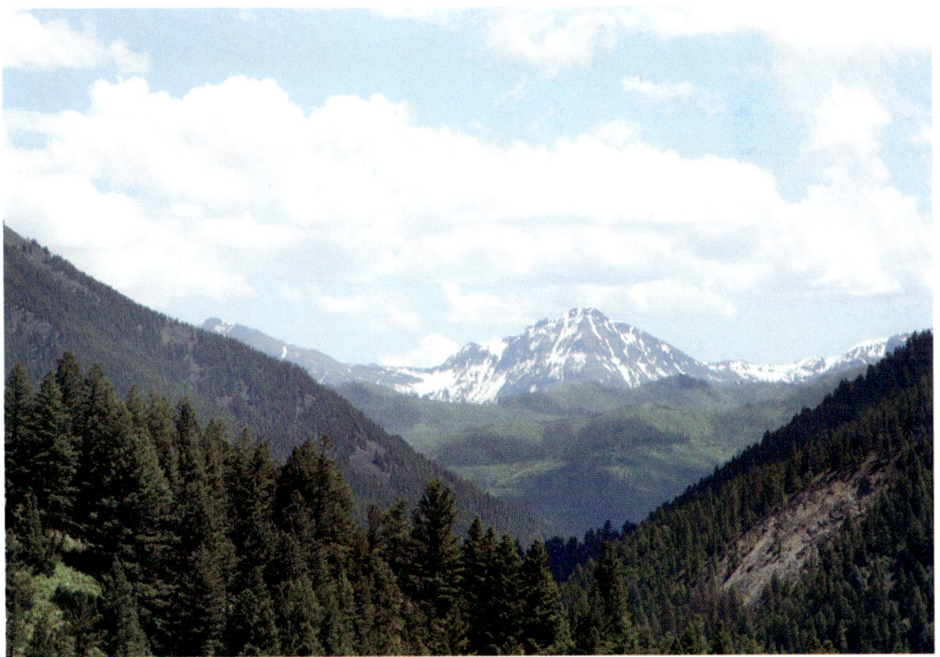

7.18 Landscape photography should capture as much of a scene as possible. Exposure: ISO 800, f/8.0, 1/1600 second, 135mm f/2.8 lens.

Best practices

Quality imagery is expected of outdoor photography. You want to use the best practices, such as lower ISO settings and photographing in the RAW format, to create the best photographs you possibly can. Lower ISO settings produce less noise in your images so you can enlarge them. Shooting in the RAW file format allows greater latitude when you adjust your images in postproduction.

Most landscape photographs require a large depth of field so the viewer can see all of the details in the scene. Your wide-angle lens makes this easier, but a tripod is also helpful during the twilight hours because you must use a slower shutter speed in dwindling light. Remember the Rule of Thirds, and keep your horizon lines above or below the middle of the frame, depending on what you want to highlight in your scene. The best landscape photographers understand that it's not always the land that makes the shot, but the weather. Keep an eye on the weather— especially clouds, and how they play off the landscape and sunlight.

When photographing landscapes, make sure that you have a *focal point* (where you want the viewer's eye to go) in your image. Use the fore- and background to balance each other. For example, you can balance the composition of a flower with a cloud. Look for interesting rocks to balance with the peak of a mountain in the distance.

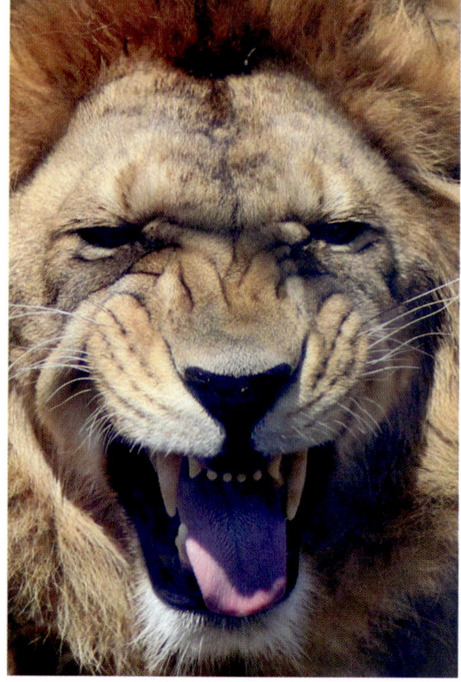

7.19 This intimidating subject was not photographed in the wild, but this is a good example of how patience and preparation can pay off. Exposure: ISO 400 f/2.8, 1/4000 second, 100mm f/2.8 lens.

Look for patterns and lines. As covered previously, lines lead the eye into the distance or toward your main subject. Patterns add interest to a photograph, such as rows of corn or trees. The S-curve of a stream can lead the viewer's eye through a beautiful valley or to the base of a mountain. Look for contrasts in nature, and play the soft and beautiful off the strong and hard.

Wildlife photography, like so many other types, takes patience. Just as it is with people, it's important to capture the eyes and faces of your subjects. Filling the frame can sometimes be difficult, but it is a necessity if you want it to be considered a successful image by many viewers. Always keep the focus on your subject — you never know when an animal might do something interesting. It is helpful to study the animals you expect to encounter ahead of time, but perseverance provides the biggest reward.

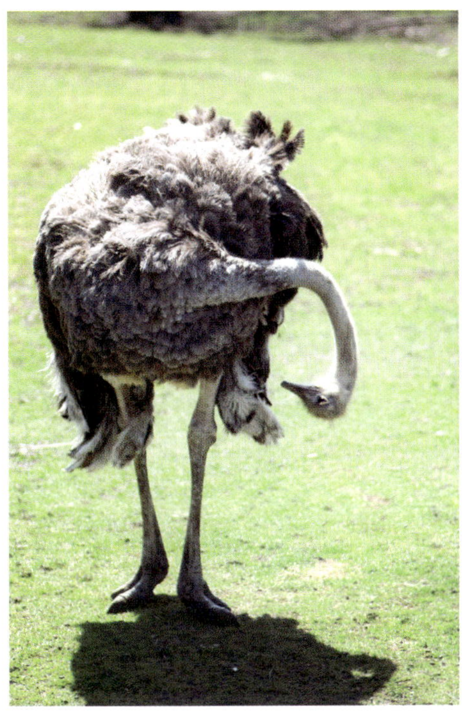

7.20 **You can practice wildlife photography at the local zoo; be prepared to capture interesting moments, like this one. Exposure: ISO 100, f/2.8, 1/800 second, 100mm f/2.8 lens.**

Try to keep your photographs simple — too much information can be overwhelming and hard for viewers to digest. Break your scene down into different photographic opportunities rather than trying to get everything in one shot. Nature photography also requires planning. For example, flowers bloom at different times of the year. If you are in a mountain region, the same flower may bloom at different times at various elevations.

For many, nature photography is a peaceful search for the small things you may never notice if you walk too fast. Others look for the grand scenes that nature has to offer. Whether you are looking for large or small subjects, good light improves the quality of them all. Plan to shoot around the Golden Hours of sunrise or sunset. These times of day add beautiful color and dramatic shadows to your images. In addition, just being outdoors and away from the city with your camera offers great rewards.

Tips

When photographing sunsets, look behind you. The clouds or landscape reflecting the fading light may be more dramatic than the sunset itself. You can practice your wildlife photography at a local zoo. You will gain patience as you realize that animals rarely do what you want them to do. When it comes to nature, you might be surprised at the number of interesting photographs you can find in your own backyard, especially with a macro lens.

It is best to travel with other people when you leave the main roads of civilization. If you go alone, always tell people where you are going and when you plan to be back. Be prepared and always dress properly for the conditions.

Macro Photography

Exploring the world of small objects is fun with macro photography. This type of photography requires at least 1X magnification. This means that the subject is projected onto the sensor by the lens at life size. For small creatures, such as bees, this takes a good macro lens and patience. One of the great things about Macro photography is that you don't have to go far to find new subjects and interesting opportunities. Small objects and unseen worlds are all around you. In fact, your backyard is a great place to start. Use the Close-up mode (🌷) to increase your chances of success when photographing with a macro lens.

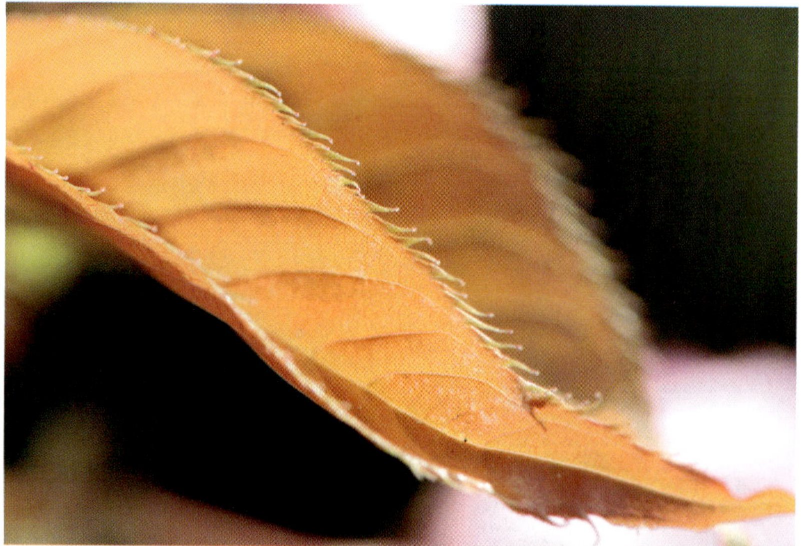

7.21 Macro photography allows you to see details like the edges of this leaf. Exposure: ISO 400, f/5.6, 1/100 second, 100mm f/2.8 macro lens.

Equipment

Macro photographers use different types of equipment for photographing small objects. A macro lens is a good start, but you can also use extension tubes (also known as extension rings) that fit between your camera and lens. These move the lens farther from the image plain so the lens can focus more closely on the subject. Magnifying filters can be the less expensive option. They fit on the front of the lens and increase magnification for macro photography.

NOTE Kenko (www.kenkoglobal.com) is a popular brand of extension tubes worth considering if you want to pursue Macro photography.

Macro lenses produce a very shallow depth of field. It is worth using a tripod and setting your camera at a larger aperture number to get as much depth of field as possible. Even at f/11, the depth of field will be shallow because your subject is so close to the lens.

Consider using a flash when shooting macro — a ring flash or twin light flash holders are beneficial. These provide additional, even light on small subjects. Try using back- and sidelighting for macro photographs, especially when photographing an object with a lot of detail, such as a bee. This makes the details of the subject stand out. The backlight can come from the sun or your own external flash. Keep a reflector handy; a simple index card or piece of paper often does the trick. You can also use reflectors to either reflect light onto your subject or block unwanted light from the scene. To reflect light, place the index card opposite the source light. This reflects the light onto the darker side of the subject. To block light, place the card in front of the light source. These items can also create a clean background or block the wind. Macro photography and wind do not mix well — every movement pushes your subject out of focus.

Best practices

Sometimes photographers forget about composition when shooting macro. They are so excited to get such a small subject in focus, they sometimes forget that the same rules of composition apply in the small world. When shooting macro, balance your subjects off each other. Use your fore- and backgrounds effectively, and keep your images simple by filling the frame as much as possible.

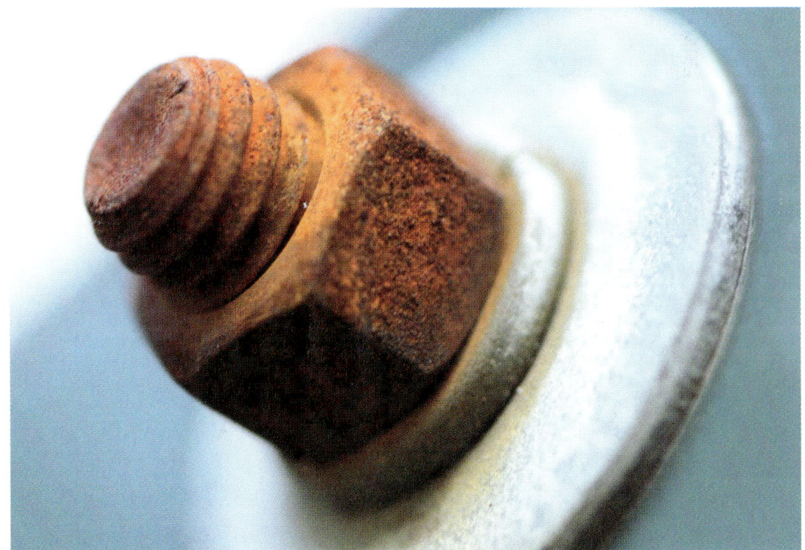

7.22 Objects you may ignore in everyday life can become more interesting with a macro lens. Exposure: ISO 800, f/3.2, 1/160 second, 100mm f/2.8 macro lens.

Manual focus is highly recommended with macro photography. Your camera focuses close up using a macro lens. Unfortunately, considering the depth of field is so shallow, you may not want to depend on where the camera decides to focus. One millimeter off in focus can make the difference between a great or unusable photo.

Tips

When you photograph insects, try to get them in action. For example, photograph bees just before they land on, or after they leave, a flower. This is much easier said than done. As in wildlife photography, it takes patience. Also, just like any type of photography, viewers want to see the face of your subject, not the back end.

Don't let your tripod keep you trapped in one location. Try different angles, and look for patterns and textures. Consider the time of day. The Golden Hours of the morning and evening have the same quality effect on small objects that they do on larger ones. Don't forget that there are many subjects to photograph — Macro photography is more than just insects and flowers. Consider shooting the imperfect, old, and strange items around your yard or city. I like to look around older buildings for little details. Old cars also make interesting subjects for Macro photography.

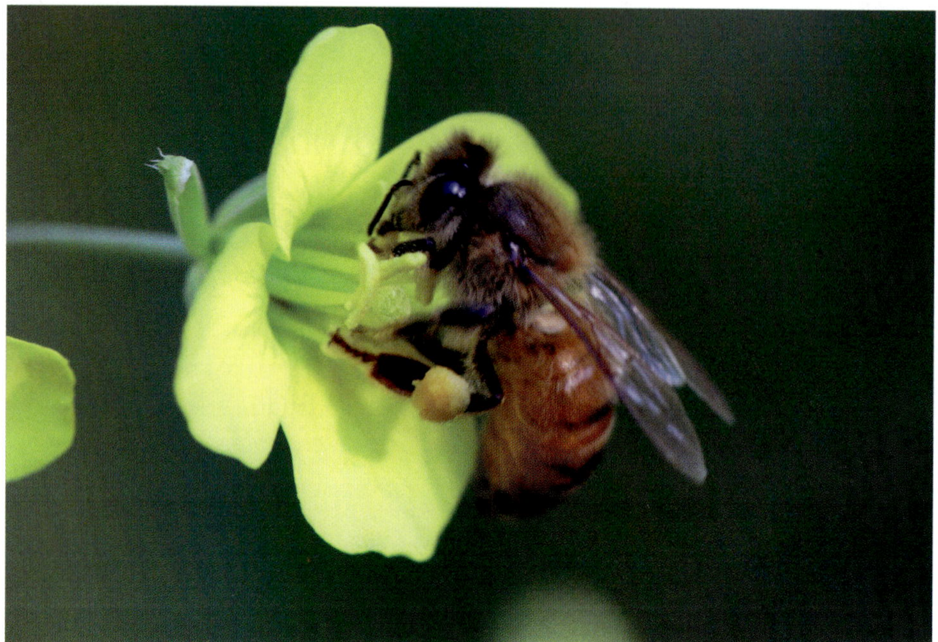

7.23 Your backyard can provide some great subjects for Macro photography, like this bee I caught in my garden. Exposure: ISO 640, f/5.6, 1/160 second, 100mm f/2.8 macro lens.

Night and Low-Light Photography

You may not think of nighttime as the optimal time to take photos. However, although you don't have the sun to work with, the night is full of light. In a city, you find neon signs, and street and car lights; in the country, you have the moon and stars. Many wonderful images can be taken at night, but because the light is not as powerful, a longer exposure is required. This means that moving lights (like headlights) create action in your photographs. If you plan it right, these movements around your scene can enhance your image. The movement of water, clouds, and lights can also add great points of interest to your photos. Like all of the other types, night and low-light photography takes practice and experimentation. Experience plays a big role in your success — the more you practice, the better you will get.

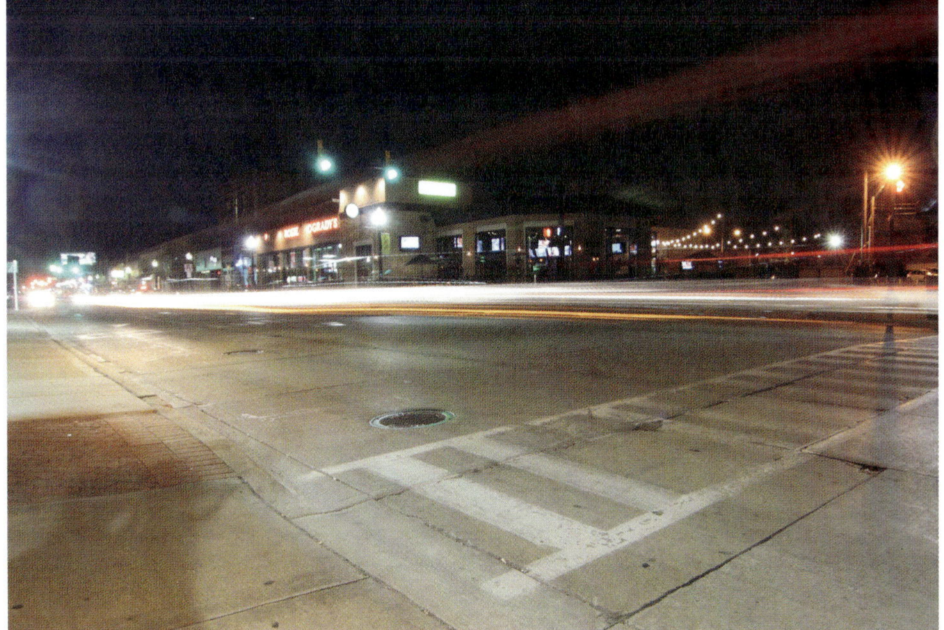

7.24 I took this night shot on a busy street using a tripod. Exposure: ISO 200, f/9.0, 4 seconds, 12-24mm f/4.0 lens at 12mm.

Equipment

A tripod is a necessity for night photography. Your camera also has a number of features to help you when you are shooting in very little light. The Long exp. noise reduction setting, found in Shooting menu 3 (📷) helps reduce noise in long-exposure photographs. For really long exposures, the combination of a tripod and remote makes for much more successful photos.

Time-lapse photography has become more popular in the last decade. If this is something that interests you, consider purchasing an *intervalometer* to make the process easier. An intervalometer takes photographs after set periods of time, such as every 2 minutes. It works like a remote and plugs in to your camera in the same location as the Canon remote. Like the remote, you can leave the shutter open for long periods of time on the Bulb setting (**B**) using an intervalometer. The big difference compared to a standard remote is that you can program an intervalometer to take multiple photographs over a specific period of time. When you import it into a video or slide show editing program, you can then create a time-lapse photography video. You can find intervalometers, such as the Vello ShutterBoss, online or at your favorite camera store.

Best practices

Night photography is all about testing. The camera's light meter will be useless in most cases because there is not enough light for your average meter reading — especially if you are going to add light to the scene with a flashlight or glow stick. Photograph in the RAW format, so that you can make adjustments later. Use a wide lens and manually set the focus to infinity so that everything is in focus. It may be tempting to use a higher ISO setting, but you have time on your side, so keep your ISO setting as low as you can. This will give you better quality images with less noise.

Light painting is another technique that is a lot of fun. To do it, you use an artificial light to draw shapes, words, or images in the air in a completely dark environment. You can use any light source — a flashlight, a candle, a glow stick, the backlight of a cell phone — to create interesting effects. To light paint, set up a tripod in a low-light or dark environment, and then move the light source around to create different patterns. Consider using multiple types of light to capture different shapes and colors. Some lights have a dimmer switch that enables you to control the light. Like all other types of low-light photography, you should use a tripod, a remote, and Custom Function 5 to lock the mirror up when light painting.

NOTE To lock the camera's mirror up, go to Setup menu 4 (🔧) and select Custom Function 5.

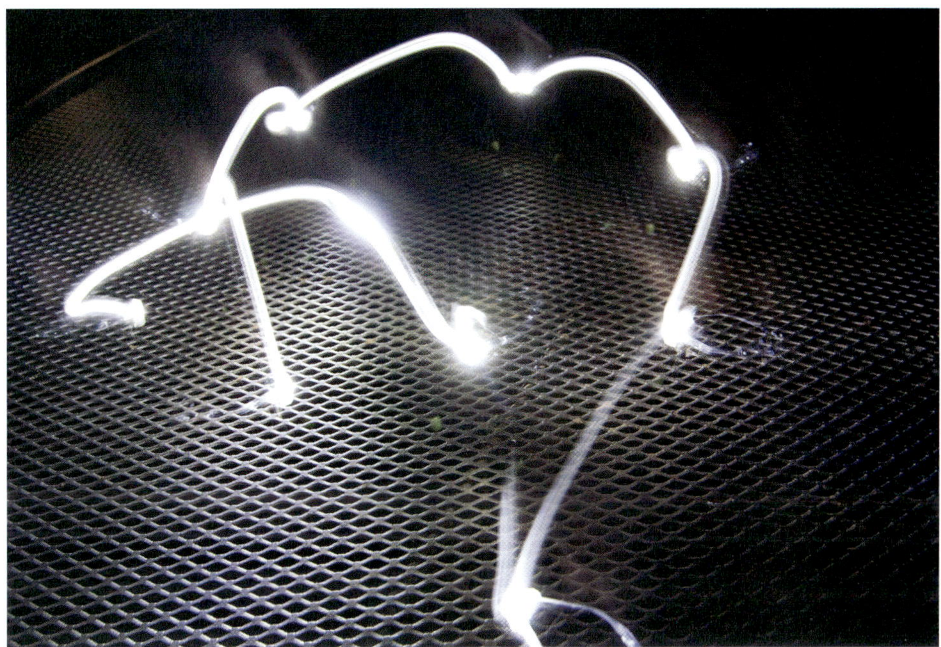

7.25 I created this image by moving a bug-shaped LED around on a table. Exposure: ISO 400, f/8.0, 16 seconds, 12-24mm f/4.0 lens at 20mm, tripod.

Tips

If you want to photograph lightning, point your camera in the direction of the storm. Place your camera on a tripod and use the remote and Bulb setting (**B**) to keep the shutter open. Eventually, a flash of lightning will streak across the sky and expose your image. Take a few test shots to find the right exposure. Don't let a few sprinkles hold you back — reflections in the rain can be an interesting addition to a night shoot. However, weather can also quickly turn on you, so always be cautious, and have a planned escape route. Keep a flashlight with you in case you need to check your equipment, light up the foreground of a photograph, or find your way back to your car.

When shooting at night, you should also consider the environment. By combining the movement of the stars with trees or other fixed structures, you can add scale to your photographs. Take note of when meteor showers are happening so you can plan to catch the streaks across the sky. If you just want stars to appear as pinpoints in the sky, you have to use an exposure of less than 20 seconds for most wide-angle lenses. Record your exposure times so you have a reference point to work from in the future. Use prime lenses because they have fewer elements, thereby decreasing the chance of unwanted lens flare.

If you are going to photograph fireworks, bring a black card to use as a handheld shutter. When the fireworks start, place your camera on a steady tripod pointed toward the sky. Set the camera to the Bulb setting (**B**) and leave the shutter open using your remote. Place the black card in front of the lens and, when you see interesting fireworks, remove it. When you think you have enough fireworks for one image, advance to the next frame and repeat the process.

Travel Photography

Creating photographs of your travel adventures may be why you purchased your Canon T5i/700D. Photography is a great way to keep the memories alive. Prepare for travel photography opportunities in advance by researching your destination before you leave. Think about the people, the history, and the story of your location. You should also think about how you are going to use the photographs — documenting personal memories, stock shots, or a serious outdoor adventure publication. Think about the type of photography on which you plan to focus, such as people, landscapes, or food. Whatever your intention, make sure you bring the right equipment for the job.

Equipment

A zoom lens is helpful for travel photography because you don't have to carry as much equipment. The goal is to keep it light: your camera, one or two lenses, a flash, backup batteries, and extra memory cards should be the foundation of your travel photography kit. A large tripod is not practical when traveling, but there are numerous mini-tripods available on the market that can keep your camera steady in low-light situations.

If you have a laptop computer, make sure that you download your images on a regular basis. Bring extra CDs or flash drives to back up your images. You can even mail a CD home as a backup. If you have reasonable Internet access while traveling, consider uploading some of your best images to a cloud storage service, such as Dropbox (www.dropbox.com).

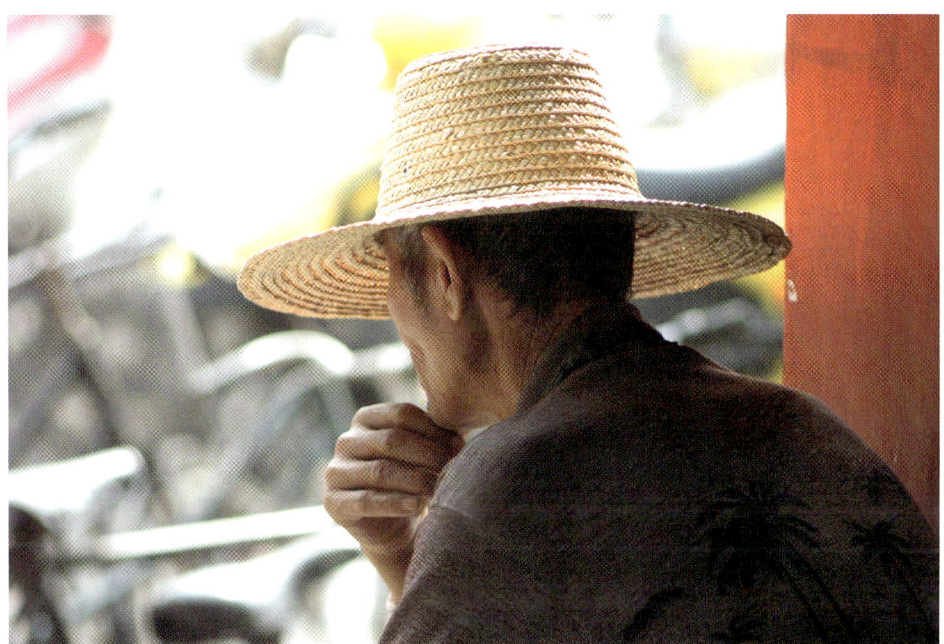

7.26 Travel photos, like this one taken in China, should tell the story of your trip. Exposure: ISO 400, f/2.8, 1/750 second, 135mm f/2.8 lens.

Best practices

Most travel is relatively safe, but remember that you have expensive equipment with you, so always be aware of your surroundings. Consider using small, nondescript bags and unbranded camera straps. Be respectful of the local people; not everyone wants his picture taken. Don't be intimidated, though — photos of the locals are an important part of your trip. Just be courteous and ask people if you can take their picture — you will be surprised at how friendly most are to visitors.

When you first arrive at a new location, look around before you start shooting. Look for colors, contrast, and textures. Notice the little things in your environment. What do you smell or hear? What is the weather like? Can you photograph any of these things? Using your camera to answer these types of questions helps you tell the story of your travels and create lasting memories.

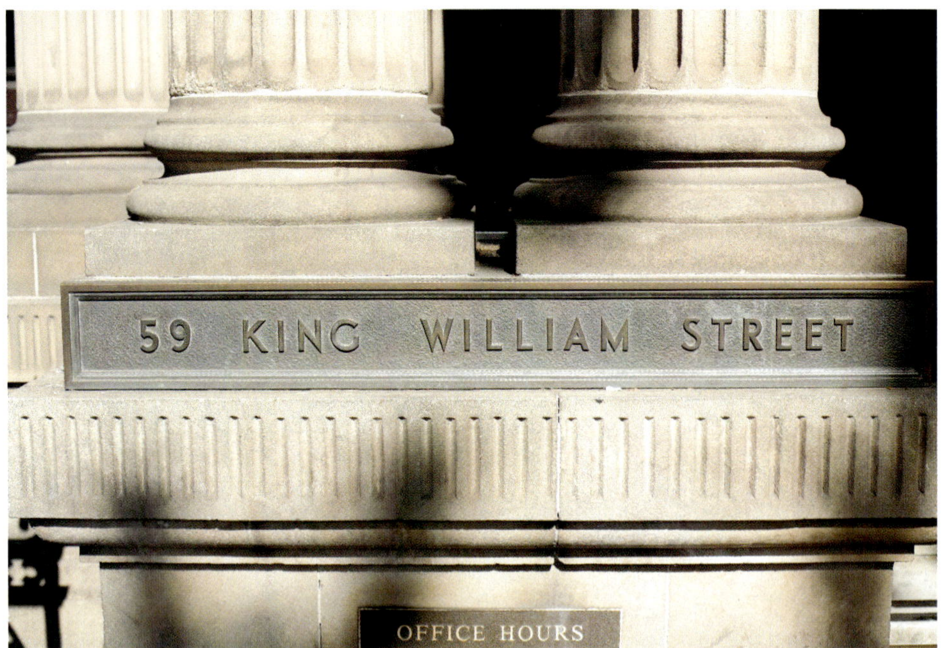

7.27 Using your camera to tell the story of a location creates lasting memories. This street marker reminds me of the places I've been in Australia. Exposure: ISO 200, f/5.6, 1/400 second, 50mm f/1.4 lens.

After photographing the well-known sites, visit the non-touristy areas. These locations may not be instantly recognizable, but there are just as many (and in some cases, more) interesting subjects off the beaten path. Use the triangle method: shoot wide-angle establishing shots, medium shots to tell the story, and close-ups to get the details.

Food is as much a part of a culture as the clothing the local people wear. Look for interesting signs that help tell the story of the environment and the people who live there. Consider what a day in the life of a local person might be like, and what elements represent the native people and culture.

Learn to work with the available light. If it's not working in your favor, try creative techniques, such as creating a silhouette. A *silhouette* is the black outline of a subject with a bright light behind it. Use the camera meter to expose for the light behind your subject. If you have a tripod, use the HDR Backlight mode (▣) for a better exposure when shooting subjects that are backlit. You can use this mode without a tripod, but you must remain very steady as the camera takes three rapid exposures. Experiment and use the different functions on your camera to see if they improve your photos.

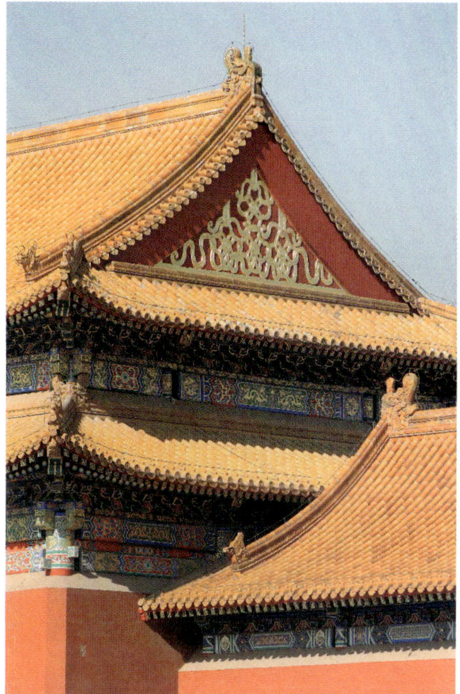

7.28 Architectural details, like those on this building in Beijing, China, can make an interesting theme for your travels. Exposure: ISO 200, f/4.5, 1/1500 second, 135mm f/2.8 lens.

Tips

Take notes about your trip. Keep a journal, notebook, or use a digital recorder so you will remember what you photographed on your journey. This is especially helpful when trying to remember names and places. If you're in an historic building or museum, don't shoot through glass with a flash because it will reflect into your photograph. Increase the ISO and consider buying a polarizing filter for your camera to remove the glare from glass.

Pick a different theme each day to keep things interesting. One day, it could be architecture, and the next people or food. This exercise helps you study more facets of the environment in which you are traveling. Some people put themselves in every photo, and that is fine. Unfortunately, others go through an entire vacation without one shot of themselves. Make sure that you are in at least *some* of the photos.

Be ready at all times to take a photograph. Don't edit in the field — you might miss a great photo opportunity. Try to find an angle or composition that is different from what everyone else is taking, especially at tourist locations. Take the time to see the world with your eyes, as well as through the lens — after all, you want to experience the location as well as photograph it.

Travel Photography Tips

Here are a few tips for getting better travel shots from travel and landscape photographer, James Brandon:

- **Bring a tripod.** Even a small one will enhance your images. Some tripods even come with a case you can carry on your back while traveling.
- **Put your photo gear in a backpack rather than a rolling travel case.** This is particularly helpful if you plan to use multiple types of transportation, such as airplanes and trains.
- **Get up early or plan time in the evening to photograph during sunrise and sunset.** The warm light and long shadows create stronger photographs than those taken in the midday sun.
- **Photograph the details.** Photographers often forget to do this, but it's the little things that support the story of your travels and often make your images more memorable.
- **Be respectful.** Ask people for their permission before you take their photograph.
- **Explore the camera's Creative Zone modes.** Don't leave your camera on automatic. Taking control of the settings provides more opportunities to capture your creative vision.
- **Shoot what makes you happy, not what you think other people want to see.** You don't have to spend your time shooting famous landmarks — focus on the people or the food if that is what you enjoy.

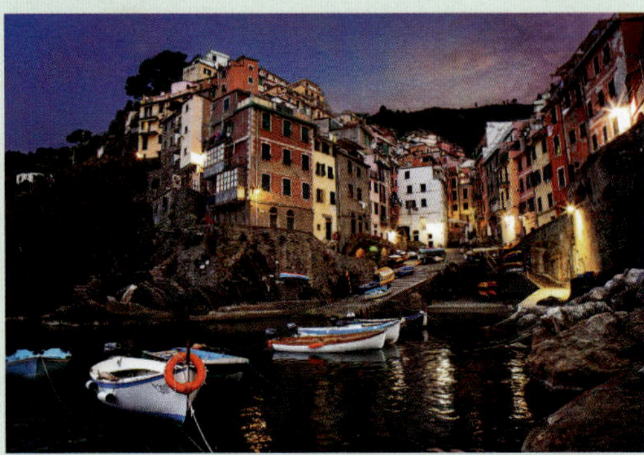

Image courtesy of James Brandon

James Brandon is based in Fort Worth, Texas. He has been a professional corporate photographer since 2009, and regularly teaches and speaks about photography. You can see more of his work at his website: http://james-brandon.com/.

CHAPTER 8

Shooting in the Live View and Movie Modes

Video is a fun way to preserve memories, and creating them with a dSLR camera has become popular due to the advantages of price, ease of use, and the lenses that are available. Your Canon Rebel T5i/700D is a powerful video tool. Perhaps you have seen a beautiful video created by a photographer using a dSLR camera and wondered if you could do the same thing. The answer is yes, if you follow the standard production rules. The goal is consistency — it doesn't matter if you are creating a family video, a school project, or the next great documentary. It is important to plan ahead, especially if you are going to edit your video. You don't have as many postproduction options with video as you do with still photography, so it isn't as easy to fix problems later.

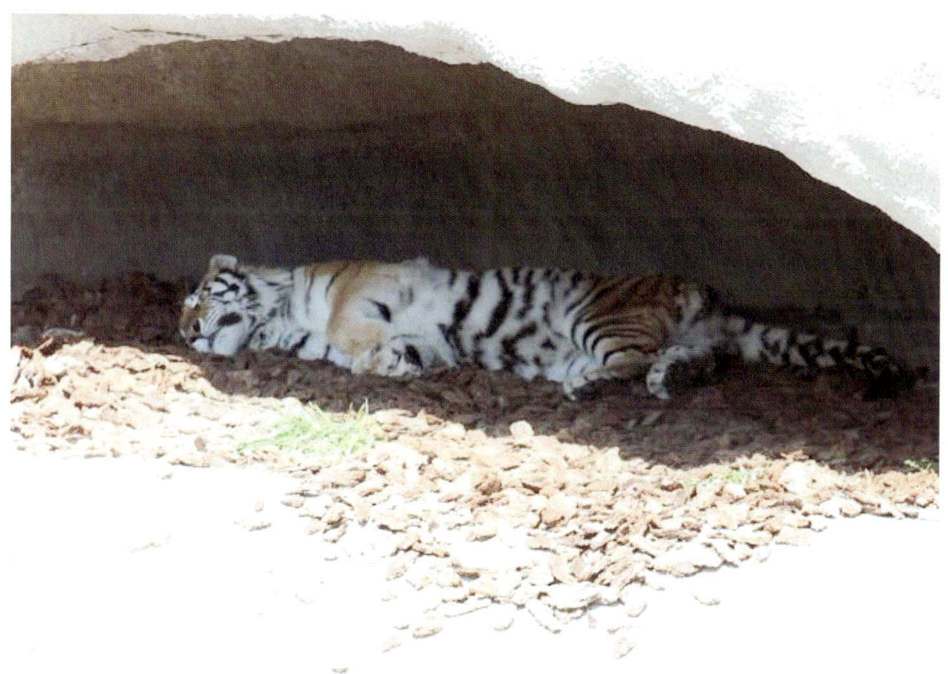

An outtake frame from a video shot with the Canon Rebel T5i/700D.

Using the Live View Shooting Mode

Live View shooting mode () is helpful for creating both still photographs and videos. The large, 3-inch touchscreen makes it easier to view and follow subjects in real time. The Canon Rebel T5i/700D has a vari-angle LCD screen that swings out 175 degrees. This allows you to place the camera at unique angles, or hold it above your head or down low while following your subject. You can flip the screen 180 degrees so you can protect it against the back of the camera, view it on the back of the camera, or extend it out to view it from the front of the camera.

A helpful feature in the Live View shooting mode () is the Magnify option (). This feature magnifies the scene in front of you up to 10 times. The Magnify button () is in the lower-right corner of the LCD screen. You can also use the Magnify button () on the back of your camera. Use the four arrows along each side of the frame to view different parts of the scene. This option is helpful when focusing on subjects at a distance. When you press the Live View shooting mode button () to record a movie, the camera returns to 1X magnification.

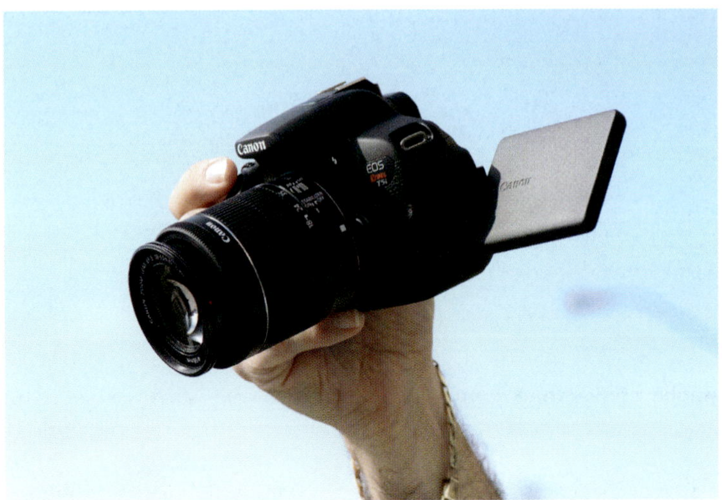

8.1 You can hold your camera high or low and use the vari-angle LCD screen to capture new angles.

CAUTION If you use the Live View shooting mode () for an extended period of time, it can raise the camera's internal temperature, which can affect image quality. Make sure that you turn off the Live View shooting mode () when it's not in use.

To turn on the Live View shooting mode, press the Live View button to the right of the eyepiece. You should note that the Live View and Movie shooting modes, while similar, have different menus and features. When you turn on Live View shooting mode, you see an information display on the LCD screen. Most of this information is related to exposure settings. The exposure information display has four variations that you can access when you press the Info button (**INFO.**), including exposure mode, an automatically adjusting histogram, and Picture Styles. The last option clears the screen of all information.

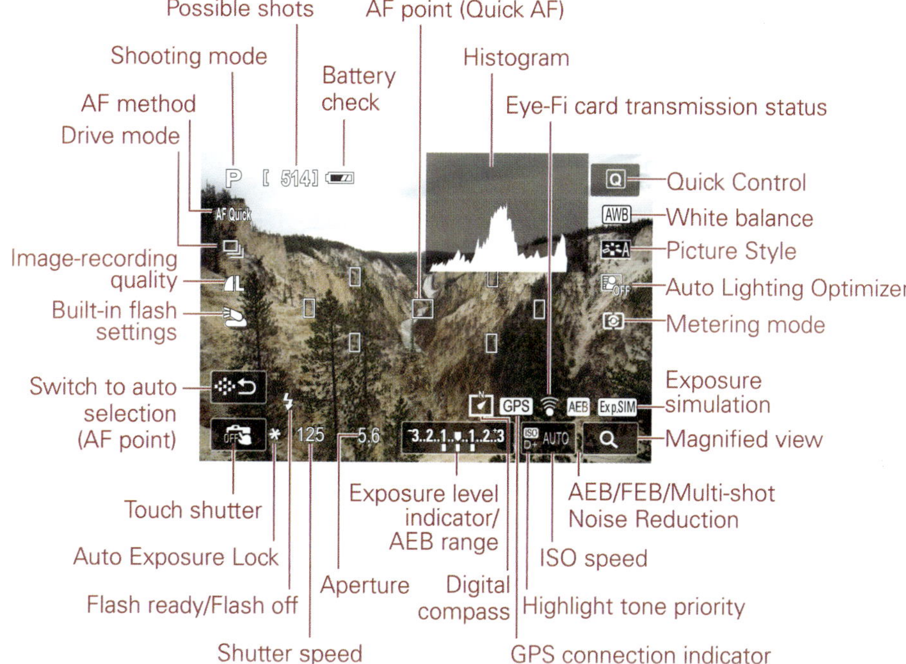

8.2 This graphic shows the information available via your camera's Info button.

NOTE If you don't see the information display on the screen after pressing the Live View button, press the Info (**INFO.**) button.

The Live View information display offers four options — one is clear, and the other three have different combinations of the following options:

- **Shooting mode.** The exposure mode to which your camera is set, such as Program AE (**P**) or Portrait.

- **Possible shots.** This the estimated number of available shots left on the memory card.
- **Battery check (🔋).** This icon shows how much battery power is left in your camera.
- **AF point (Quick AF).** This is one of the nine autofocus points available for focusing in Quick mode (AFQuick).
- **Histogram.** This is a live, continuously adjusting graphical representation of the shades of white to black in your scene.
- **Auto Lighting Optimizer ().** This adjusts your photograph to the optimal brightness and contrast when using the Basic Zone modes.
- **Quick Control (Q).** Press this for quick access to your shooting functions. Each individual mode displays different options.
- **White balance.** Internal adjustments naturalize the light found in the shooting environment. This icon indicates which white balance setting is in use.
- **Picture Style.** Displays the Picture Style your camera is currently using.
- **Metering mode.** This shows you which of the four metering modes your camera is using: Evaluative (), Partial (), Spot (), or Center-weighted ().
- **Eye-Fi card transmission status.** Indicates that the Eye-Fi card is active.
- **Exposure simulation.** Your camera displays real-time exposure (how your photo looks at the current exposure settings).
- **Magnified view.** This option allows you to magnify the scene, which is helpful for checking focus.
- **AEB/FEB/Multi-shot Noise Reduction.** Displays the Auto Exposure Bracketing setting, Flash Exposure Bracketing setting, and Multi-shot Noise Reduction (which reduces noise at all ISO settings).
- **ISO speed.** Indicates the ISO setting of your camera.
- **Highlight tone priority (D+).** This indicates that this feature is active. It is designed to improve the highlight detail in your scene.
- **GPS connection indicator.** This shows that the Global Positioning System is active (a GPS receiver is required).

- **Digital compass.** This indicates the direction in which your camera is pointing when used in combination with a GPS receiver.
- **Exposure level indicator/AEB range.** This displays how under- or overexposed the camera setting is. It also indicates the set range of the Auto Exposure Bracketing feature.
- **Aperture.** This displays at what aperture your camera is set.
- **Flash exposure compensation.** You can adjust your flash exposure by up to 2 stops in 1/3-stop increments.
- **Shutter speed.** This displays at what shutter speed your camera is set.
- **Flash ready (ϟ)/Flash off (⚡).** This indicates whether the flash is on or off.
- **Auto Exposure Lock (✱).** This reminds you that the Auto Exposure Lock is engaged.
- **Touch shutter.** This turns the LCD screen touch shutter on and off. This option allows the photographer to trigger the shutter from the LCD touchscreen.
- **Switch to auto selection (AF point).** Turns auto selection on or off. Auto selection selects the best autofocus point. If the subject moves, the camera switches to AI Servo AF (**AI SERVO**) and follow focuses on the subject.
- **Built-in flash settings.** This lets you know that the pop-up flash is active.
- **Image-recording quality.** This represents the quality and size of the image file.
- **Drive mode.** This indicates which of the following drive modes is engaged: Single shooting (□), Continuous shooting (⧉), or one of the three Self-timer options (⏲).
- **AF method.** This shows which focusing method is being using when the Live View shooting mode (▣) is on. The options are Face tracking (AF☺), FlexiZone-multi (AF( )), FlexiZone-single (AF□), and Quick mode (AFQuick).

To get to the Live View menu, press the Menu button (**MENU**), and then select the Live View shooting mode (▣). The menu has seven options to consider, such as focusing, grid display, and aspect ratio.

CROSS REF See Chapter 2 for a full explanation of menu options.

8

The Quick Control/Print button

The Quick Control/Print button (Q) or the Quick Control icon (Q) in the upper-right corner of the Live View screen enables you to make changes to many key functions, depending on the mode you are using. When you are photographing in a Basic Zone mode, Live View gives you access to the AF method, image-recording quality, and drive mode. If you are shooting in one of the Creative Zone modes — Program AE (**P**), Shutter-priority AE (**Tv**), Aperture–priority AE (**Av**), or Manual (**M**) — you have access to the same options that you do in the Basic Zone modes, plus the built-in flash options, white balance, Picture Style, Auto Lighting Optimizer, and Metering modes.

Shooting stills

You have two options to trigger the shutter button while using the Live View shooting mode (◘). You can use the shutter button the same as you would when looking through the viewfinder, or you can enable the touch shutter by pressing the Touch Shutter disabled button (OFF) in the lower-left corner of the LCD screen. To disable the touch shutter, press the Touch Shutter enabled button (). You can also enable this option under Live View shooting menu 1 (◘). I find it easier to use the LCD touch-screen when the camera is mounted on a tripod rather than when handholding it.

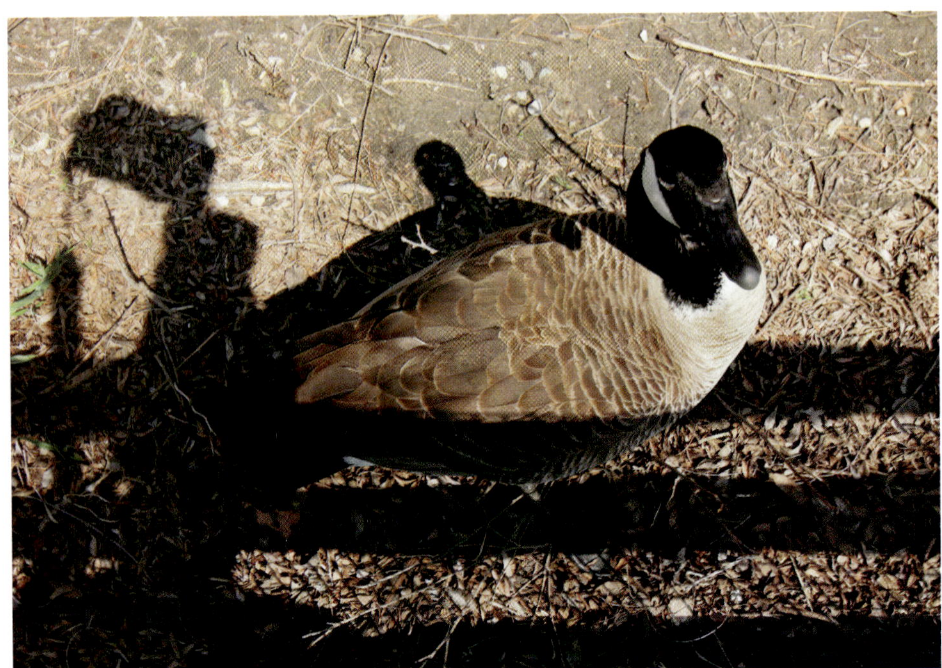

8.3 This photo was shot handheld and composed using the Live View shooting mode. Exposure: ISO 200, f/8.0, 1/800 second, 12-24mm f/4.0 lens at 24mm.

CAUTION The Live View shooting mode () drains the battery much faster than the viewfinder, so be sure to turn it off when it's not in use.

The camera's sensor, viewfinder, and LCD screen all have a standard aspect ratio of 3:2. When shooting in Live View mode (), you have three additional options beyond standard: 4:3, 16:9, and 1:1. When you turn on the 4:3, 16:9, or 1:1 ratio, a black mask outlines the new screen proportions. If you shoot in the RAW file format (RAW), the images save as 3:2 with the information stored and appended to the RAW file. If you photograph in the JPEG file format, the ratios are saved permanently. If you are unsure, use 3:2 and crop your images later.

Focus modes

The default focus mode for Live View shooting () is Continuous focus. This means that the camera follows your subject to keep it in focus. You can disable Continuous focus in the Live View shooting menu (). When you do so, the camera switches to One-shot focusing mode (**ONE SHOT**). This means that the camera focuses once and stays that way until you lift your finger from the shutter button. You can designate a new focus point by touching the LCD screen, but you need to press the shutter button for the camera to refocus.

You have four autofocus (AF) methods available in Live View shooting mode () and three when shooting video (which is covered later in this chapter). In Face Tracking mode (AF face), the camera detects a face and follows it until you take the photo. If you have multiple faces in your scene, the camera selects one. You can change the focus target by touching the subject's face on the LCD screen. FlexiZone-multi (AF multi) uses up to 31 autofocus points to focus on your scene. When you press the Setting button (SET) or touch the LCD screen, this AF option divides your screen into nine focus zones. To revert to the larger AF focus area, press the Setting button (SET) again.

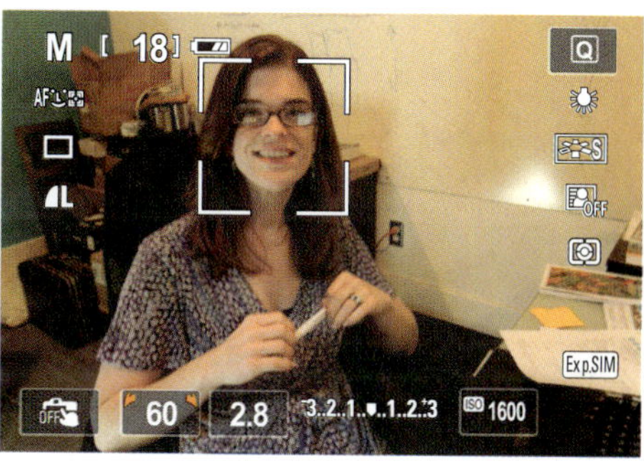

8.4 The Face Tracking technology follows your subject anywhere in the frame.

NOTE If your subject is far away from the camera and his face is too small in the frame, Face Tracking mode (AF) may not work.

FlexiZone-single (AF) uses the 31 autofocus points individually. Press any point on the LCD screen and the focus point lights up where your finger is placed. You can also press the Setting button (SET) and Cross keys (✣) to make autofocus adjustments. The last focus option is the Quick mode (AFQuick), which is the fastest of the four focus options. It drops the mirror, the LCD screen goes dark, and the camera uses the nine traditional focus points to focus. This option is not available in the Movie shooting mode ('Ṝ).

If you prefer, you can use Manual focus (**MF**) in Live View shooting mode (▣). While the large LCD screen is helpful for manually focusing, consider using the Magnify button (🔍) to get in close on your subject for fine focusing. To help line up horizon lines and elements in your scene, you have the Grid display option found under the Live View shooting menu (▣). You can also check the depth of field in the Live View shooting mode (▣) by pressing the Depth-of-Field Preview button on the right side of the front of your camera.

Live View and video

When you set your camera to Movie mode ('Ṝ), the viewfinder turns black. To view the scene, use Live View shooting mode (▣) on the LCD screen so you can watch the environment. This allows you to prepare for a subject coming into the frame from any direction. For even better viewing, attach your camera to a larger screen, such as an external monitor or TV. Live View shooting mode (▣) has four information display options: autofocus, histograms, drive mode, and movie size. There is also an option to clear the information. Press the Info button (**INFO.**) to access each of the display options.

Here are some tips to help you when shooting video:

- **Use a tripod.** Because video is shot in the Live View shooting mode (▣), you cannot brace the camera in the same way that you do when holding it to your eye to shoot still photos. Camera shake is also very noticeable in video, so you need a tripod to avoid it. If you do decide to handhold your camera, or if the subject is moving, take advantage of the camera's Movie servo AF mode (SERVO AF) to help keep your subject in focus.

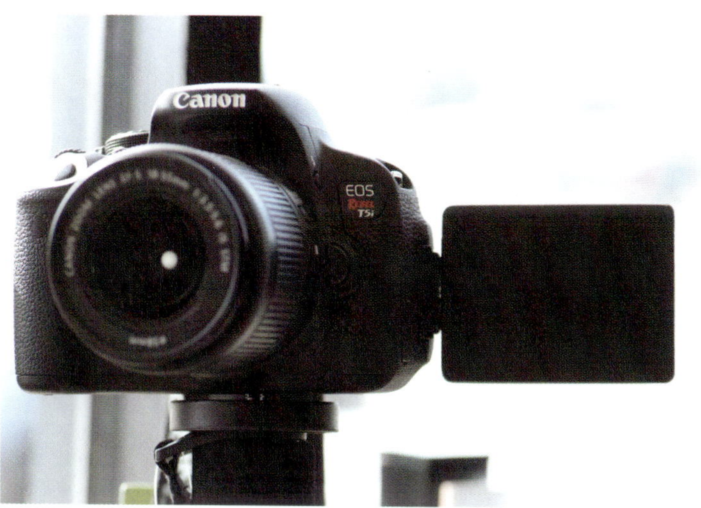

8.5 Use a tripod whenever possible to create professional-looking videos.

- **Use Quick Control (Q).** There is a slightly different setup on the LCD screen for this option in the Live View shooting mode (◘) when you are shooting video. You have additional options, such as Movie recording quality and frame rate (the flash control option is not available because you cannot use flash while shooting video). The Creative Zone modes have a few more options than the Basic Zone modes, such as white balance and Picture Style.

Shooting Video

A great advance in dSLR camera technology is the option to shoot video, and your Canon T5i/700D is no exception. It has high-definition (HD) capabilities that give you the power to create high-quality videos. However, it is important to understand both the limitations and the advantages of shooting video with a dSLR camera. One thing to consider is that a dSLR is not designed to be a movie camera.

If you are serious about creating video with your camera, you might want to consider investing in accessories that will help you operate the T5i at peak performance, such as a screen loupe, external microphones, lights, and steady support brackets to prevent camera shake. Don't forget the necessary ingredients of a good video: Steady images, quality sound, well-thought-out scene development, and editing. All of these are necessary to create quality productions. The same applies to home productions of events with family and friends.

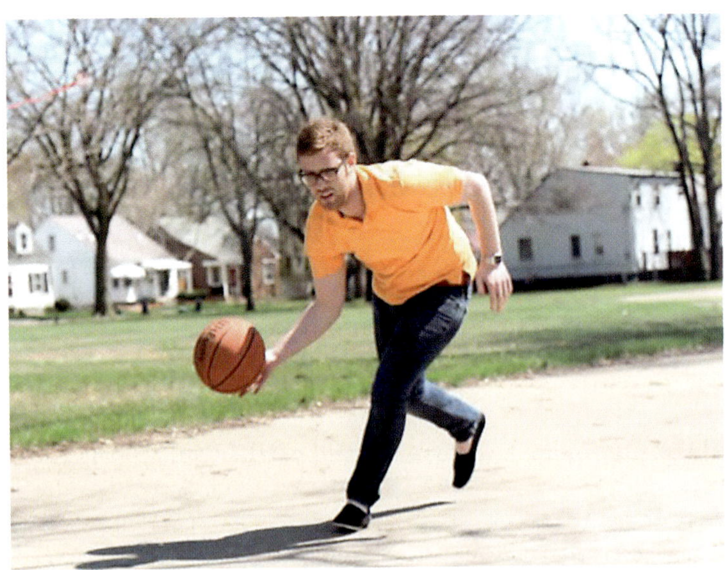

8.6 A frame from a video shot with the Canon Rebel T5i/700D. Exposure: ISO 400, f/5.6, 1/1000 second, 50mm f/1.4 lens.

One of the biggest advantages of using a dSLR rather than a traditional video camera is the lower cost. Additionally, many dSLRs offer higher-quality results, with higher sensitivity and less noise. One of my favorite advantages is the ability to change the lens. The traditional consumer video camera may have a zoom lens, but you are stuck with the one that is attached. A Canon dSLR can use any Canon E-series lens. The option to attach a lens, like a 50mm f/1.4, which creates a cinematic style with a shallow depth of field, is popular with still photographers. The ability to add a macro or tilt-shift lens is a wonderful advantage to traditional video cameras.

CROSS REF For more information about lenses, see Chapter 4.

Shooting video requires a different mind-set from creating still photographs. When you photograph stills, your goal is to capture the decisive moment. When you shoot video, you are capturing multiple moments, and all of these should tell a story with a beginning, a middle, and an end. Most experts recommend that you avoid the automatic settings when creating a video. Manual settings allow you to maintain control over your equipment and the look of your video. Automatic modes and settings that adjust in the middle of a scene distract the viewer, and make your video look unprofessional.

Your camera's video shooting feature is great for everyday shooting. If your goal is to create a longer, edited video, make sure that you have lots of extra footage before and after each scene. In other words, don't shoot video clips less than 10 seconds long unless you have a good reason. Make sure that you take at least 15 to 20 seconds of video before and after a scene to give yourself room for editing.

The two microphones built into your camera are very basic. They pick up camera noise because they are part of the camera body. They are not bad for a quick family-and-friends clip. If, however, you plan to shoot a lot of video, buy an external microphone. You can even use a completely external recording device, such as a digital audio recorder, to replace your camera's sound. I recommend keeping the internal microphones on if you use an external microphone and recording device because this makes it much easier to match the sound during editing. The more you can do while shooting to make your editing easier, the happier you will be in the end. Preparation and planning in advance the style of video you want to create is very important — even for family videos.

If you like to shoot with autofocus, you might want to consider Canon's STM lenses. They are designed to be quiet while continuously focusing in Movie Servo AF mode (SERVO AF). Whatever lens you use, remember that shooting video, just like shooting still photos, requires good-quality lenses.

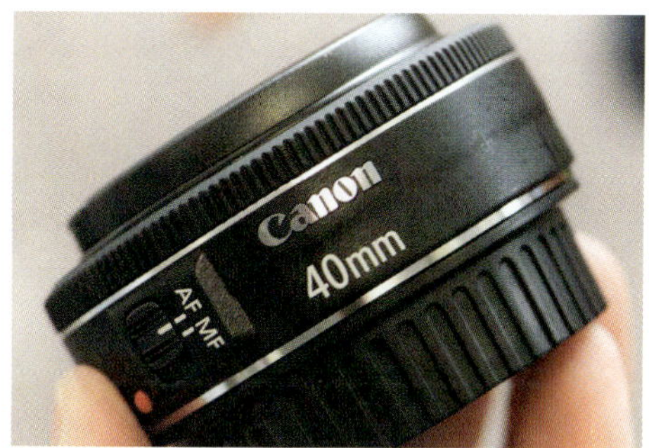

Image courtesy of Canon

8.7 The Canon 40mm STM lens is designed to shoot video.

Setting up for a video shoot

Preparation is an important part of shooting successful video. Take the time to plan, even if it is just a few moments before you press the record movie button (which is the Live View shooting button). Think about your goal and what you want to accomplish. Are you documenting family memories? Are you telling the story of a company or recording a testimonial video for the Web? Remember that planning makes the editing process easier.

What type of scene are you shooting? This is a good question to ask when making setup decisions, such as selecting the aperture. You have a wonderful advantage with a dSLR because you have a selection of multiple lenses, some of which generate a very shallow depth of field and offer a cinematic effect, as covered earlier. If your scene involves a person, shallow depth of field is the perfect choice. If you are panning over a beautiful landscape, a large depth of field is considered the better option.

You must also decide what size file you want to use. I recommend you use the largest one available. You can always downsize later, but you cannot increase the size of your movie files without losing quality. To select the video recording size, look in the Movie shooting menu 2 (). Two of the three options (1920 and 1280) are high definition (HD) and shoot in a 16:9 aspect ratio. The smallest of the three is shot at 4:3. You also have the options of shutter speed and film rate, which are discussed later in this chapter. Are you going to use the manual modes, as many professionals recommend? Do you plan to rely on the incredible technology your camera has to offer, such as the Scene Intelligent Auto () and Movie Servo AF () modes, and the AF tracking methods?

Picture Styles work for videos, too. If you keep the Picture Style () on auto, the camera picks the best style to suit the scene. All Picture Styles apply the same sharpness, contrast, saturation, and color-tone effects when shooting video that they do for still images. Standard () is a general style that is good for most scenes, while Portrait () is ideal for accurately capturing skin tones and softening a scene. Landscape () creates sharp images with vivid blues and greens. Neutral (), as its name suggests, keeps images natural looking. Faithful () offers accurate color of images captured under light that is less than 5200K. Monochromatic () is for black-and-white photography. Your user-defined Picture Styles (those that you create) also work when shooting video.

There is more to video than shooting visuals. You must also consider how you are going to record the audio and if you plan to edit it. By the time you finish this chapter, you'll have a better understanding of how to handle the audio and editing portions of video production.

The frame rate

You're not alone if you are a little confused about frame rate or fps (frames per second) compared to shutter speed. The *frame rate* is the number of frames captured per second by the camera. The *shutter speed* is how long that frame is exposed to light. Your camera has two options under Setup menu 2 () for frames per second: PAL and NTSC standards. PAL is the standard for Europe, while NTSC is the standard in North America. The default setting for your camera is NTSC. You have three further options under each standard. Under NTSC, your options are 24, 30, and 60 fps. PAL options are 24, 25, and 50 fps. All are progressive (or noninterlaced) scanning for both standards. This means that each line of the movie is displayed in order or sequence, rather than every other line, as it is with interlaced scanning.

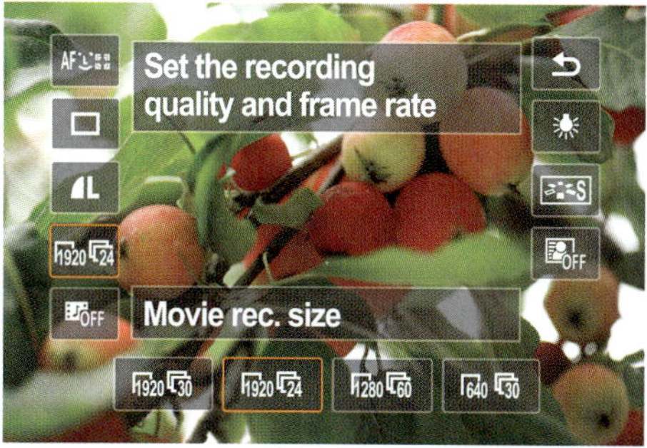

8.8 The recording quality and frame rate options are based on the NTSC standard. You can choose the standard under Setup menu 2.

The following list includes the different frame rates and the types of video recordings for which each is best suited:

- **24 fps 1/50 second.** This is the combination used to achieve a classic film look.
- **30 fps 1/60 second.** This combination makes your video resemble 35mm film, which is a middle point between classic cinema style and the video look produced using faster shutter speeds.
- **60 fps 1/125 second.** If you shoot action or sports, this setting gives you a sharp video. It is especially useful if you plan to use slow motion as part of your video presentation.

Blur is not a bad thing when it comes to video. In fact, blur can give your footage a more natural feel. Faster shutter speeds result in less subject blur from frame to frame. No matter the fps, the shutter speed should be double the frame rate based on what is called the *180-degree rule*. Your camera uses a *rolling shutter*, which means that it doesn't capture the entire image at the same time. Unfortunately, the result of this type of shutter is the *Jell-O effect*, which means the video is wobbly or skewed. This effect is the result of quick movement or panning your camera from side to side. The best way to avoid this is to limit fast movements, use a tripod with a smooth head, and pan slowly whenever possible.

When you set the ISO to automatic, the camera chooses the right option for the best exposure. Unfortunately, maximum ISO is not available for video. If you want to expand the ISO to 12800, use Custom Function 2. However, this option is very grainy and not recommended. If Custom Function 3 — Highlight tone priority (D+) — is set, the range is ISO 200 to ISO 6400.

The shutter speed

The shutter speed when shooting video is how long each frame is exposed to light. Slower shutter speeds show more motion through image blur, as shown in

Figure 8.9, which lends a more natural feel to your video. Faster shutters speeds are much less fluid, as shown in Figure 8.10, but are valuable for action, such as sports shooting.

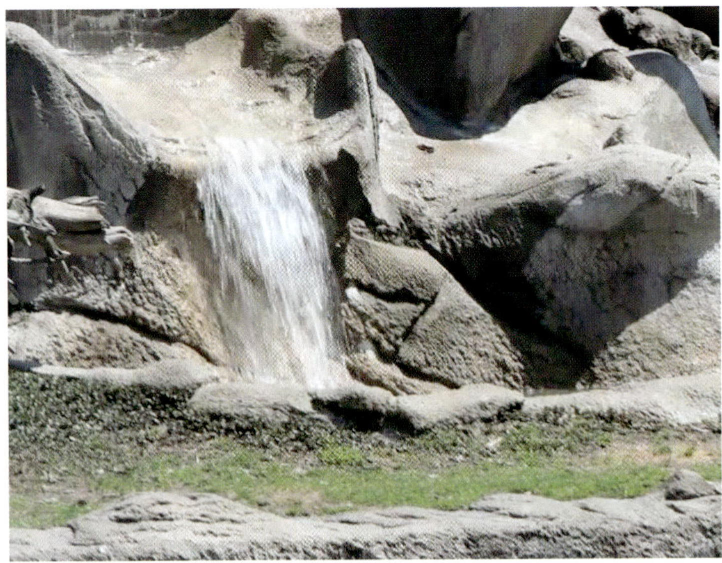

8.9 In this video frame, you can see the motion of the water. Exposure: ISO 100, f/16, 1/30 second, 100 mm f/2.8 lens.

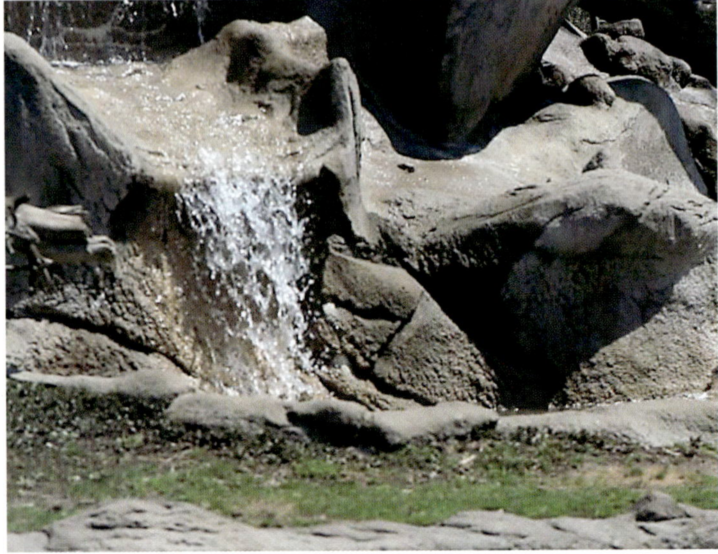

8.10 You can see the spray and droplets of the water in this video frame, which was captured at a faster shutter speed. Exposure: ISO 100, f/5.0, 1/500 second, 100 mm f/2.8 lens.

If you plan to use slow motion in your video, a faster shutter speed gives you a crisper image for each frame. To achieve a shallow depth of field, you sometimes have to set a faster shutter speed or lower the ISO to set a lower aperture. Your camera does not let you go below the designated shutter speed set with your frame rate. It's worth experimenting to find which shutter speed is best for the type of video you are creating.

The combination of shutter speed, aperture, and ISO gives you the proper exposure for your video. You have a lot of latitude with higher ISO options. Although your camera allows up to ISO 6400 for stills and ISO 12800 in Movie mode ('), this doesn't mean that you should use it. Avoid using the higher ISOs if possible because graininess is not as forgiving in video as it is in still photography. The lower the ISO, the better the video.

Lighting

Like still photography, video needs proper lighting to work well. However, the approach is a bit different with video. You cannot use the flash to light your subject, so a continuous source of light is the solution. The most common approach is to keep the light flat and even so that unexpected shadows don't develop while you are shooting your video. If you use more dramatic light, you need to plan for changes in the light as your subject moves or the scene changes, which is a lot of work.

You can use many types of lighting for video. The sun is a good choice, but it can be harsh. Without a diffuser, strong shadows are cast on the opposite side of your subject. Try shooting on a cloudy day for a softer, more even light. When shooting indoors, consider bringing your own light sources rather than depending on the light available in the room.

If you leave your camera on Auto white balance (AWB), it should adjust to the light in your environment or the light that you provide. Auto white balance is not perfect; you may want to consider using a Custom white balance setting (). For example, you may not be satisfied with the color tint, such as a yellowish cast, that you see in the overall environment. To fix this, make sure that you have a white piece of paper to photograph (fill the frame) in the environment in which you are shooting. Next, in Shooting menu 2 (), select Custom white balance (). Select the photograph of the white piece of paper, and then press the Setting button (SET). This step ensures that your custom white balance is not based on the light in the room or environment.

CROSS REF For more information on other white balance options, see Chapter 3.

When you are indoors, some of the first considerations should be from where the light is coming and if you have enough light to use lower or higher ISO settings. Bringing your own light source is a good option. You can use almost any light source, such as tungsten, if you balance it using your camera's Custom white balance setting (▲). LEDs have become popular on- and off-camera — some even attach directly to your camera's hot shoe. Fluorescent lights come in a variety of Kelvin temperatures and are often used with softboxes. When you need high or powerful light output, HMI lights are a good choice.

CROSS REF For more information on lighting, see Chapter 6.

CAUTION When bouncing flash, remember that the color of paint on a wall will also bounce onto your subject. Therefore, a green wall may not be the most flattering one to use.

Sound

It is often said that the most important part of video is the audio. Viewers will suffer through visual glitches, but bad audio will lose their attention fast. The built-in microphones are on top of the camera, as shown in Figure 8.11. The external microphone terminal is on the left side of your Canon Rebel T5i/700D. The internal microphones pick up all of the noise around you, including camera noise. This is why you should consider using an external microphone when shooting video.

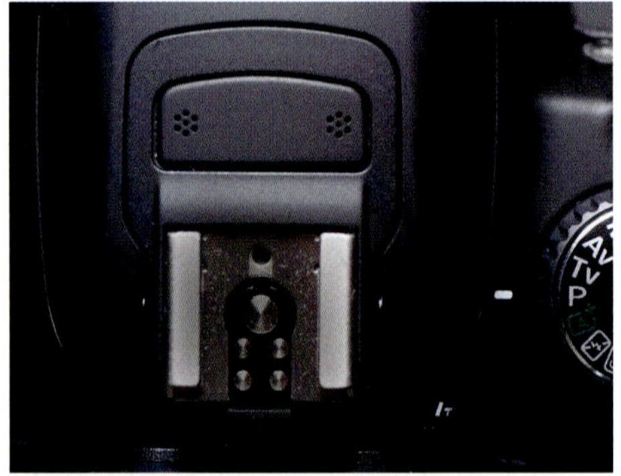

8.11 The microphones on top of your camera are good for casual use.

There are different types of microphones, such as booms, shotguns, and lavaliers, and each is available in various levels of quality and designed for a different use. Price is often an indicator of quality, but it is worth testing a few microphone brands before you decide on one. I recommend purchasing at least one that attaches to the camera's hot shoe. Microphones that work with your Canon T5i/700D have a 3.5mm-diameter plug.

NOTE You can purchase a converter to enable some microphones to fit your camera.

The following are the different types of microphones you should consider using with your camera:

- **Boom.** This is a direct microphone (unidirectional) attached to a *boom*, which is a pole. A boom mic is often handheld and extended over the subject.
- **Omnidirectional.** This all-purpose microphone gathers a wide range of sounds from different directions. The microphones built into your camera are omnidirectional.
- **Unidirectional.** This is the type of microphone you use when you want to focus on a single sound and minimize ambient noise.
- **Handheld.** Most often, you see these used by reporters interviewing someone on the street or a person singing onstage. These microphones are either omnidirectional or unidirectional. Unidirectional is best for interviews.
- **Shotgun.** This is also known as a boom mic because it is often held in the air by a boom. They are good for focused recording (unidirectional).
- **Lavalier.** You see these small microphones clipped to the clothing of people being interviewed. Also sometimes called lapel microphones, these are good for capturing clean audio from a single source.

Sound is a complex subject with many solutions. Your camera offers a few options for the internal microphones. In the Movie shooting menu 2 (▣), press the Sound recording option. Notice that the Disable level meter at the bottom of the LCD screen reacts to the sound around you.

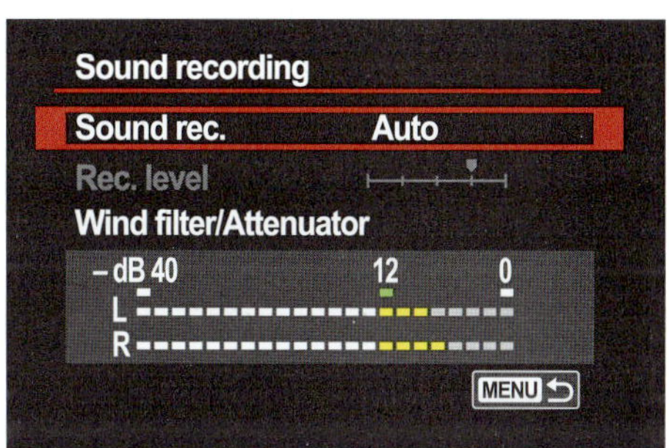

8.12 This is what the Sound recording menu looks like under Movie shooting menu 2.

On this screen, if you are in one of the Basic Zone modes, you can select sound On or Off. If you are in one of the Creative Zone modes, you have the following sound options:

- **Sound rec.** You have three options under this selection: Auto, Manual, and Disable. Auto adjusts the sound recording level automatically. Manual turns on the next option, Rec level. Disable turns off the camera's audio recording ability.
- **Rec level.** Advanced users select the Manual recording option to set the recording to one of 64 levels.

- **Wind filter/Attenuator.** The wind filter reduces wind noise; it is only available for the internal microphones. The attenuator is recommended if there are very loud sounds in your recording. It works in both Auto and Manual audio settings.

NOTE The sound level balance between the right and left built-in microphones cannot be adjusted.

You can add music to your slide shows and videos. To do so, register the music using the EOS utility that comes with your camera. To use this option, the utility must be installed on your computer and your camera must be connected to your computer via USB. Follow these steps:

1. **With your camera turned off, connect your computer and camera via USB.**
2. **Launch your EOS utility and turn on your camera.**
3. **Click Register Background Music.**
4. **After registration is complete, disconnect your camera from the computer.** The next time that you play a slide show or video, you can turn on the music option, and your selections will be available.

To play your background music for a video, press the Setting button (SET), press the Background music button (♫ON) in the lower-right corner of the LCD screen, and then select your music. To play your background music for a slide show, select the slide show option in Playback menu 2 (▶). Music options are in the Setup menu (🔧) under the Background music option.

NOTE In the EOS utility, you are limited to WAV files of up to 29 minutes and 59 seconds. When you register a new list of music, it overwrites the old list.

Choosing a focus mode

Your camera automatically defaults to Movie servo AF mode (SERVO AF) when placed in the Movie shooting mode ('🎥). This means that it continuously focuses until it finds something to focus on, and then it continues to adjust and follows your subject to maintain focus. If you are not using an external microphone, your camera picks up the sound of the lens focusing. Canon offers the STM series of lenses to minimize this problem. You can disable Movie servo AF mode (SERVO AF) in the Movie shooting menu 1 (🎥). When Movie servo AF mode (SERVO AF) is turned off, your camera reverts to the One-shot autofocus mode (**ONE SHOT**). Press the shutter button halfway to focus. Once the focus is locked, it stays fixed until you lift your finger and refocus.

NOTE You can temporarily stop Movie servo AF mode (SERVO AF) by pressing the Auto Exposure Lock button (✱) or tapping the AI Servo button (**AI SERVO**) on the lower-left side of the LCD screen.

You have three autofocus options available when shooting video. To access the three AF methods, press the Quick Control/Print button (Q), and then press the top icon on the left side of the LCD touchscreen. Look for the three AF methods of focus displayed at the bottom of the frame. The first option is Face Tracking (AF), which means that your camera detects faces, and then tracks them to keep your subject in focus while you shoot. If you have more than one face in the frame, the camera selects one. If you want to switch to a different subject, touch it on the LCD screen with your finger. You also can use the Setting button (SET) to reset the focus to the center of the LCD screen.

The FlexiZone-multi focusing mode (AF( )) uses your camera's 31 autofocus points to focus on the scene. If you press the Setting button (SET) or touch the LCD screen, this AF option divides your screen into nine focus zones. To revert to the larger AF focus area, press the Setting button (SET) again.

The FlexiZone-single focusing mode (AF □) uses the 31 autofocus points individually. In other words, you can select any one of the 31 points to focus on your subject. To do this, press any point on the LCD screen or press the Setting button (SET). You can press other points of focus or use the Cross keys (✣▴▾◂▸) to move the focus point.

Even with all of this wonderful technology inside your camera, professionals still recommend using Manual Focus mode (**MF**). For everyday shooting, the other options are useful, especially if you are using Canon's STM lens system. If you purchased a kit lens with your Canon T5i/700D, it is an STM lens. However, when you want more professional-looking videos, Manual Focus mode (**MF**) is still a good choice. To switch to Manual Focus mode (**MF**), look on the left side of your lens and flip the switch to Manual.

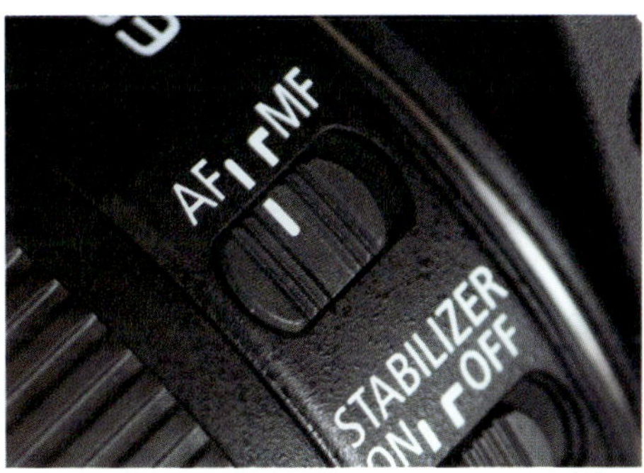

8.13 Flip the switch on your lens to change the focus mode from Autofocus to Manual.

NOTE When in Manual Focus mode (**MF**), you can use the Magnify button (🔍) to help you focus. However, you cannot magnify while recording.

NOTE If your lens is in Manual Focus mode (**MF**), the LCD touchscreen does not react to your touch for focus-point adjustments.

Turn on the grid display found in the Live View shooting menu (▣) to help balance the composition of your scene. You have two grid display options. One looks like a tic-tac-toe board (nine sections) and the other divides the frame into 24 sections.

Recording video

To turn on the video option, dial the power switch to Movie mode ('🎥). When you're ready to start recording, press the Live View shooting mode button (▣) on the back of your camera. If you are shooting family or casual events, handholding your camera and using the built-in microphones is fine (although an external mic is better). Try not to move your camera around too much. Fast movement and swings lead to what is called the *Jell-O effect*, which is unnatural-looking movement, or wobbly scenes or subjects. Also, too much movement tends to make your viewer seasick. When you are recording, you should always keep your camera horizontal because that is the orientation of televisions and monitors.

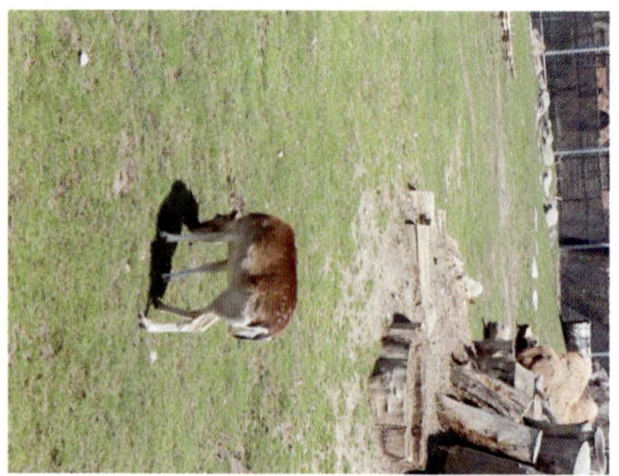

8.14 As you can see from this outtake, this video doesn't work because it was shot at a vertical orientation. Video should always be shot horizontally to match the orientation of TVs and monitors.

The Canon Rebel T5i/700D has some recording limitations. For example, once the file size hits 4GB, the camera automatically creates a new file. The camera also has a video shooting time limit of 29 minutes and 59 seconds, and it stops recording once you reach this limit. Don't panic — just press the Record button (▣), and the camera begins recording again, creating a new file. I recommend that you look for a good break in the action at about the 20-minute mark so you can restart your recording. It's much better than having the camera stop automatically during a peak moment.

NOTE A 16GB memory card can easily hold a full 29 minutes and 59 seconds of recording time.

In the Creative Zone modes, both Aperture-priority AE (**Av**) and Shutter-priority AE (**Tv**) work the same as the Program AE mode (**P**). Manual mode (**M**) gives you control over the shutter speed, aperture, and ISO settings. All Basic Zone modes use the Scene Intelligent Auto mode (). In the Creative Zone modes, you can use the Auto Exposure Lock button (*) to lock your exposures. This is helpful to fix your exposure during recording. When shooting, use the Basic Zone exposure setting. An icon appears in the upper-left corner of your screen representing the exposure mode it is using.

When you are not recording, you can press the Quick Control/Print button () to change standard features, such as the frame rate, AF method, image quality, and so on, but you cannot use it while recording. You can make a few adjustments (depending on the mode you are using), such as turning Movie servo AF () on or off, or adjusting the shutter speed, aperture, and ISO settings via the touch controls at the bottom of the LCD screen. If you don't see the options, press the Info button (**INFO.**). Maintaining consistency is important while you are recording. Make sure that you leave room for editing, keep your movements slow and smooth, and avoid making adjustments during recording. Professionals recommend that you use the Manual settings; changing options while shooting distracts the viewer and makes your video look inconsistent and unprofessional.

While shooting video, you can still take photographs by pressing the shutter button. It is important to note that if you are using your camera's internal microphones, camera noise will be picked up. When you take a photograph, the Live View shooting mode () is turned off and the video is delayed or interrupted for up to 1 second. Once you see the Live View screen again, the camera has resumed shooting video. The video and photo are saved as separate files. When it comes to focusing during a video shoot, it is important to check and recheck. This is especially true when you shoot in Manual mode (**M**) or with a shallow depth of field because you never know if your subject is moving out of your focal range.

Creating video snapshots

Your camera has the ability to capture short video clips for 2-, 4-, and 8-second sessions, and then place them in a video snapshot album. Ultimately, all of the clips you record are combined into one longer clip (a single movie file). When you play the album, the

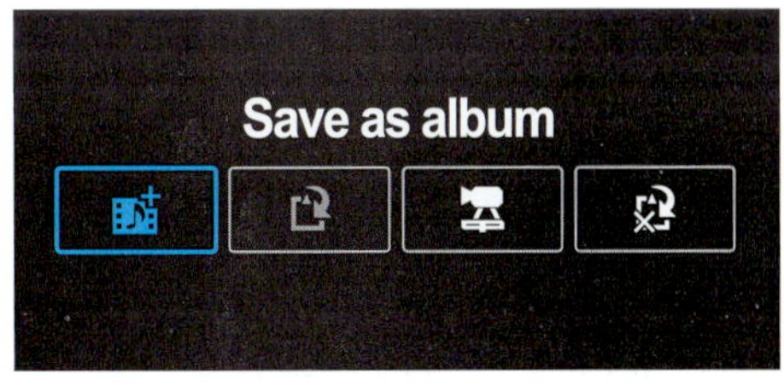

8.15 The Video snapshot Save options.

clips play in the order of creation. This is a nice option when you are photographing events. You should note, however, that there are a number of limitations when using this option. For example, you can only combine video clips of the same length. If you turn off your camera, a new file is created and starts a new album, so plan accordingly. You can review a clip before deciding to keep it or delete it from your album.

To create an album while in Movie shooting mode (', look in Movie shooting menu 2 () and select Enable. You then have two additional options: Use the current album file, or create a new one. The next option is to determine how long you want your clips to be. Once you engage this option, all of the videos you shoot are limited to the time selected. A blue bar appears on the LCD screen, and it counts down how many seconds you have left while shooting your movie. When you finish using this mode, disable it to return to the standard recording functions. Press the Playback button (▶) to view your movie.

NOTE Once you create a video snapshot album, you cannot add new video clips to previous albums in the camera.

Equipment

Support equipment is important to turn your dSLR into a serious video camera. Lights, lenses, microphones, a good tripod, and focusing aides help make your videos appear more professional. The following is a list of equipment you should consider purchasing if you plan to shoot serious video:

- **Color meter.** This is a useful tool when you are shooting different scenes in various lighting conditions. It measures the Kelvin temperature of the light in your scene so that you can accurately correct the white balance. It also helps flow each scene together by preventing obvious color shifts that may distract the viewer.
- **Microphone.** As covered earlier in this chapter, microphones are an important investment when it comes to video. The type that you purchase depends on your needs. An omnidirectional microphone captures the sound all around it, while a unidirectional mic focuses where it picks up sound.
- **Neutral density (ND) filters.** If you want to take advantage of slow shutter speeds and shallow depth of field, you can achieve this with neutral density (ND) filters. They limit the amount of light coming into your camera without altering color, which helps maintain the desired exposure in bright environments that would otherwise require faster shutter speeds and larger aperture settings.

- **Lenses.** If you are interested in lenses designed specifically for video, Canon offers the STM series. They are quieter than traditional lenses, reducing the amount of camera noise picked up by the internal microphones. Lenses with stabilization features are also worth your consideration because they can add a shutter speed the equivalent of up to 4 stops faster and prevent any unwanted camera shake.
- **Lights.** LEDs are popular with dSLR photographers shooting at close range. Daylight-balanced fluorescents are also a good, all-purpose solution. HMI lights are ideal when you need powerful lights.
- **Loupe.** This can help you check the camera's focus, and it is important that you continuously do so, especially if you are using the Manual Focus option (**MF**). A full LCD screen cover loupe or viewfinder is also helpful outdoors because bright sunlight often makes it tough to see the LCD screen clearly. You can also press the Magnify button () to see details of your scene or image without a loupe.
- **Audio recorder.** A secondary audio recorder is highly recommended if you need high-quality sound. Make sure that you have a good set of headphones, too.
- **Support.** When you handhold your camera, keeping it steady is important. Many companies make different types of brackets or support rigs that attach to you to keep the camera steady, even while you are moving.
- **Tripod.** A good tripod is one of the most important pieces of equipment you can buy for your camera — especially for shooting video. The head should be fluid and move the camera without jerking it.
- **Bag.** Consider purchasing a good utility bag or belt to keep everything handy when you are on the move.

The Movie mode () uses a lot of power and drains batteries more quickly than still photography, so make sure that you always carry extras. Video also takes up a lot of space on memory cards. I recommend that you always have a few backups, and purchase at least one fast (at least class 6), high-quality 16GB memory card.

Types of video

There are many ways to approach shooting a video. Before you do anything, think about the type of video that you are going to create and where you are going to use it. Some videos, like a family event, are simple because you can keep all of the camera's settings on automatic. If you plan to share your video only online, you might want to consider a smaller movie size. As you become more comfortable and begin shooting more complex videos, you may decide that manual settings are the right option.

The following is a list of a few types of videos you can shoot:

- **Testimonials.** Let your clients do the talking. Businesses upload videos of their clients singing their praises to YouTube or Vimeo to share on their website or social media. These videos are rarely more than 2 minutes long, and, in most cases, less than a minute is ideal. Make sure that you use a tripod and flattering lighting. You don't want to make your good client look bad. Ask your clients to share who they are and why they like working with you. Record the testimonial a few times until you are both satisfied with the results.
- **Business videos.** In general, these videos tell a company's story. You need to let people know what the business is and why they should use it. A person standing in front of the camera talking for 15 minutes doesn't accomplish this very well. Show people what the person is talking about. This involves capturing and editing in some b-roll detail segments of the company. *B-roll* is additional video that supports the main video with details, behind-the-scenes footage, or examples of what the subject is talking about. Successful business videos are often entertaining and funny.
- **Demonstrations.** Sometimes, it's easier to show people how to do something rather than tell them. Video is a great way to share your knowledge and expertise.

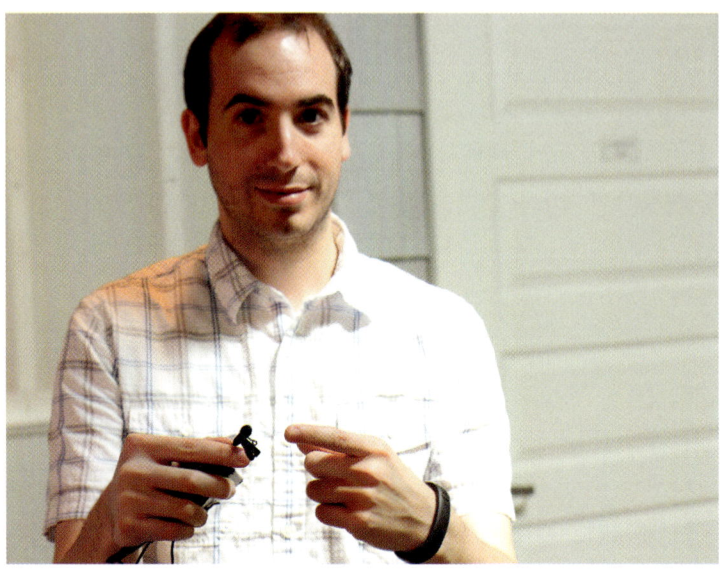

8.16 A sample frame from a demonstration video created with the Canon Rebel T5i/700D. Exposure: ISO 400, f/4.5, 1/50 second, 50mm f/1.4 lens.

- **Sports and action videos.** This type of photography requires longer lenses, faster shutter speeds (over 1/125 second), a great eye, and timing. You must anticipate what is going to happen, which requires a deep understanding of your subject.
- **Documentaries.** This type of moviemaking has been helped greatly by dSLRs with video. It has made recording video available to people of all skill levels, giving many a voice to tell a story. Some are personal, and others are related to a cause they want to share with the world. When creating your documentary, it is important to follow the professional rules of good moviemaking. Use the manual settings, and make sure that your camera is steady and that you have good audio.

Tips for Shooting Video

Pascal Depuhl, who has travelled as far as Afghanistan for his video projects, has a few tips to help you create better videos:

- **Think about movement.** Consider all the things that can move during the video-shooting process, such as your camera's position, the subject, and the focus. Think about how you can synchronize with your subject and the choreography of the scene in front of you.
- **Use a good tripod.** Avoiding camera shake is an important part of creating good video. If your video is too bouncy, it can make your viewers sick. Your tripod should have a fluid, movable head to help avoid jerky motions.
- **Use lenses with Image Stabilization.** This is helpful to keep your images sharp when handholding your camera.
- **Pay attention to sound.** Half of the story you are telling is in the sound. People will accept poor video quality if the audio is good but not vice versa.
- **Shoot from multiple angles.** Don't shoot an entire video from a static location — move around. You will appreciate the variety in the editing process.
- **Touch the camera as little as possible.** You can use a video rig, to keep the camera steady, and build your equipment around it.

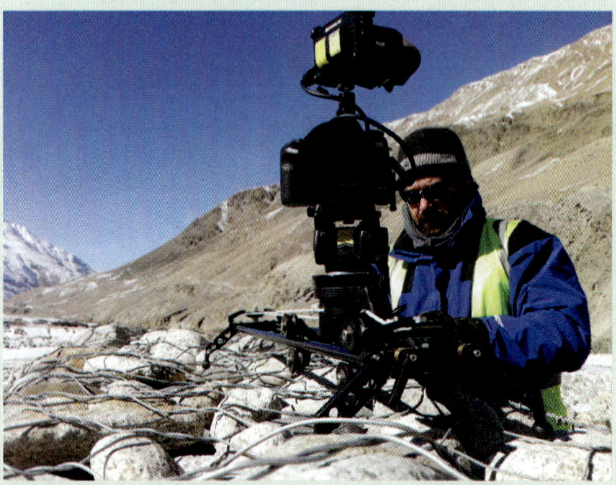

Image courtesy of Pascal Depuhl

Pascal Depuhl is a still photographer and videographer from Florida. His most recent film work is the acclaimed documentary, On Wings of Hope. *You can view Pascal's photography work at: http://blog.depuhl.com, and his recent video projects at: http://movies.depuhl.com.*

CHAPTER 9

Viewing, Editing, and Sharing Your Content

Once you fill a memory card with images, it's time to review and edit them. Postproduction editing with computer software can sometimes be complex. Portrait touch-up, for example, is an art unto itself. If you only want to make a few minor adjustments to your photographs or movies, you can do so on your camera.

The T5i has some helpful options, including a series of creative filters, an image lock, and a photo rating system. This chapter covers the options available for reviewing your content, making simple edits, and sharing your images with family and friends.

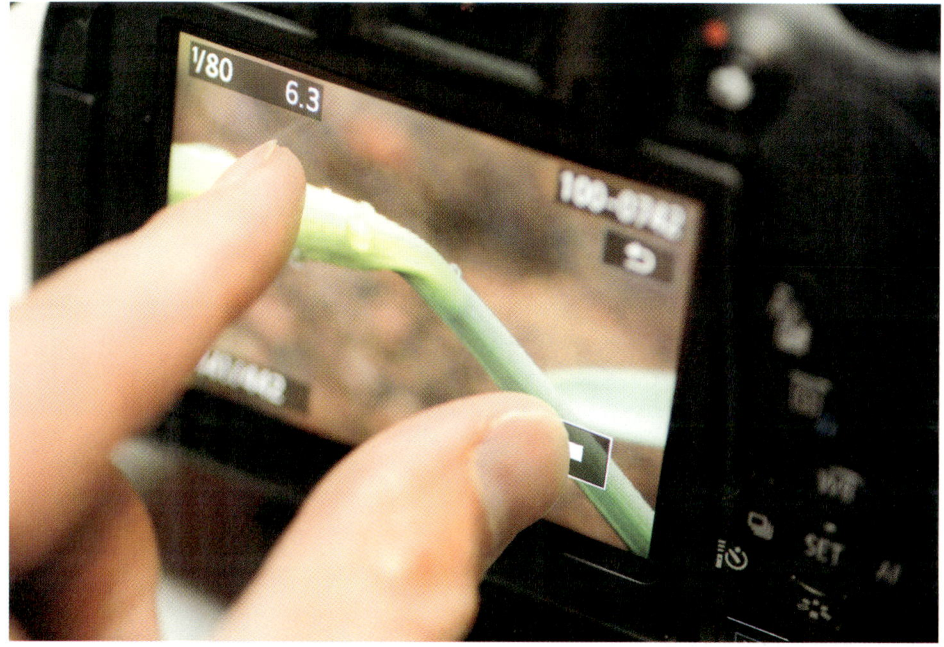

You can use your fingers to zoom in on the details of your photograph.

Viewing Content

As soon as you shoot images, you want to view them, and the LCD touchscreen on the back of your camera makes this easy. There are multiple ways that you can review your images beyond the LCD screen, but it's a good starting point.

Viewing content on the camera

In most cases, the first place that you see your photographs and videos is on the LCD screen on the back of your camera. I highly recommend that you protect the LCD screen from scratches by closing it when it's not in use. To close the screen, turn it around to face the camera. The LCD touchscreen is a helpful feature on the Canon T5i/700D. It's fun, easy to use, and adds a new dimension to viewing pictures. I'm sure that it's soon to become a standard feature on Canon cameras.

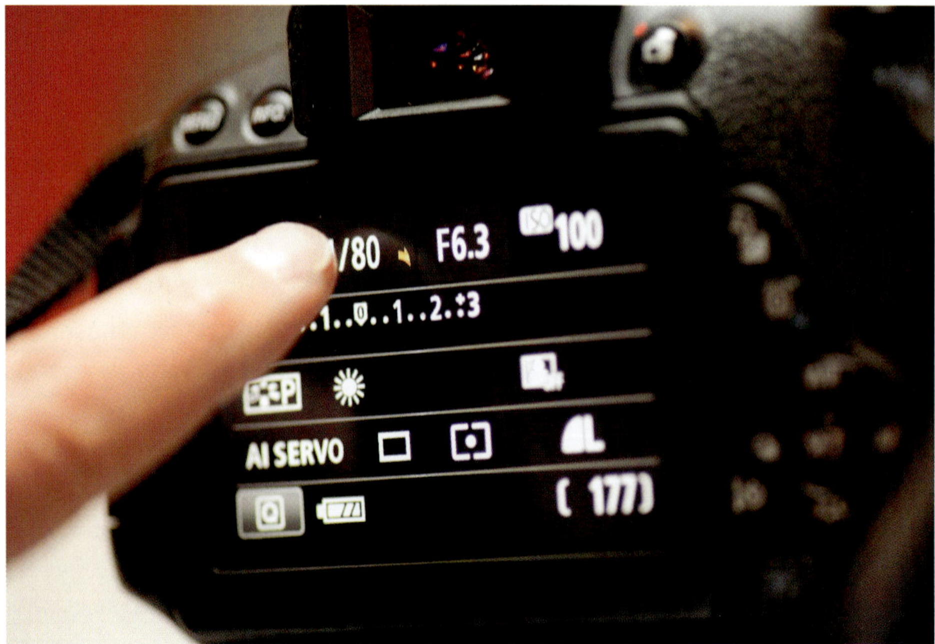

9.1 The LCD touchscreen on the back of the camera.

Playback

To review your photos or videos, press the Playback button (▶). To scroll through your images, use the Cross keys (✣) or swipe your finger across the LCD screen. To magnify an image, place two fingers (generally the thumb and index finger) on the

LCD screen and spread them apart in a swiping motion across the LCD screen. To zoom out, create a pinching motion, bringing your fingers together across the LCD screen. If the image on your screen is a video, you see a large Playback icon (▶) in the middle of the screen; press it to start the video. To stop a video, tap the LCD screen with your finger or press the Setting button (SET). If you see the Movie Set icon (SET) in the upper-left side of the LCD screen, this means that the video is part of a video snapshot album.

CROSS REF For more information about video snapshot albums, see Chapter 8.

To control a video, use the other icons along the bottom of the screen. The Slow motion playback button (I▶) is next to the Playback button (▶). Use the Cross keys (✥) to change the playback speed rate. The next icon, First Frame playback mode (I◀◀), takes you back to the first frame. Next to that are the Previous Frame playback (◀II) and the Next Frame playback (II▶) buttons.

On the far right is the Last Frame playback button (▶▶I), and then the very last icon turns music on or off. Above the music icon is the Edit mode button (✂). You also can use the Magnify (🔍) and Reduce (▦·🔍) buttons on the upper-right side of your camera to zoom in or out on a video or image. Press the Delete button (🗑) to erase the image you are viewing.

If you want to hear the sound of your recording, the speaker is on the back of the camera. I recommend downloading the video to your computer and listening to it with a good set of headphones.

The Quick Control/Print and Info buttons

There are additional viewing and editing options available via the Quick Control/Print button (Q). In the left corner of the LCD screen, you see the following list of helpful features:

- **Protect images (O-π).** This option protects important images from being accidentally deleted. Once protected, locked images cannot be erased until you unlock them or clear all information by formatting the memory card.
- **Rotate image (⟳).** You can rotate images 90 degrees to the left or right, or rotate them to be horizontal. If you need to flip or turn your photograph upside down, you have to do so in photo-editing software.
- **Rating (RATE).** For better organization of your photographs, you can rate them based on how much you like each one using a 1–5 star rating system.

- **Creative filters.** You can add creative filters to your photographs in-camera. You have the following options: Grainy B/W, Soft focus, Fish-eye Effect, Art Bold Effect, Water Painting Effect, Toy Camera Effect, and Miniature Effect. All options are saved as a new file on your memory card.
- **Resize.** If you want to save your file as a smaller size, use this option. You can resize an image to any size smaller than its current one. For example, you can resize a Large fine image (◢L) to the Small 3 size (S3). You cannot increase the size of any image. Once you resize an image, it is saved as a new file. RAW and Small 3 image files cannot be resized.

When you press the Info button (**INFO.**), you get one of four display options in which you can review image data, such as the aperture, shutter speed, and ISO settings. Other options let you review histogram data, including brightness and RGB.

Viewing content on a TV or smart device

Sometimes, you may want to view your images on a larger screen. The following list includes additional options for viewing and sharing your photos and videos:

- **Viewing images on a standard TV.** Connecting your camera to a non-HDTV requires a stereo AV cable (the AVC DC400ST is available from Canon). Insert the plug into the AV Out terminal on the left side of your camera. Connect the three split connects to the TV's right audio (red), left audio (white), and video (yellow) ports. Turn on the TV and select the TV's video input option. Turn on your camera and press the Playback button (▶). You should then see the camera screen on your TV.
- **Viewing images on an HDMI HDTV.** To connect your camera to a high-definition TV (HDTV), you need an HDMI cable (HTC-100) compatible with the HDMI terminal on the left side of your camera. Connect the cable to your camera's HDMI Out port and the other end to the TV's In port. Turn on the camera and press the Playback button (▶). The image only appears on your camera's LCD screen — you must press the Info button (**INFO.**) to change the view settings.
- **Viewing images on a smart device.** You can connect your camera to some smart devices using downloadable apps. Some require that you connect to a Wi-Fi-enabled computer first or use an Eye-Fi card with workarounds, which I do not recommend. Workarounds can get complicated and even void your device warrantee. Apple has an iPad camera connection kit available that allows you to connect your device via a USB cable to view photos and video. This area is continually evolving, so it's worth searching the Internet occasionally to check out the latest updates.

Downloading and Storing Your Images

There are three main methods of downloading images to your computer. You can connect your camera to your computer via a USB cord. If your computer is equipped, you can insert the memory card into a built-in reader, or you can take the memory card out of the camera and use an external memory card reader. If you prefer to use software programs such as iPhoto, Image Browser EX (which came with your camera), or Lightroom, you can easily import your photos.

Another option is to use an Eye-Fi card, which transfers your photos wirelessly. The downside to transferring your images wirelessly is that it can take longer than a direct connection. Your camera has Eye-Fi card settings in Setup menu 1 (🔧). Once you are connected to (or after you have transferred your photographs to) your computer, you can open them in your favorite editing program. I recommend that you tweak and adjust your photographs before sharing them. I cover how to use your Digital Photo Professional software later in this chapter.

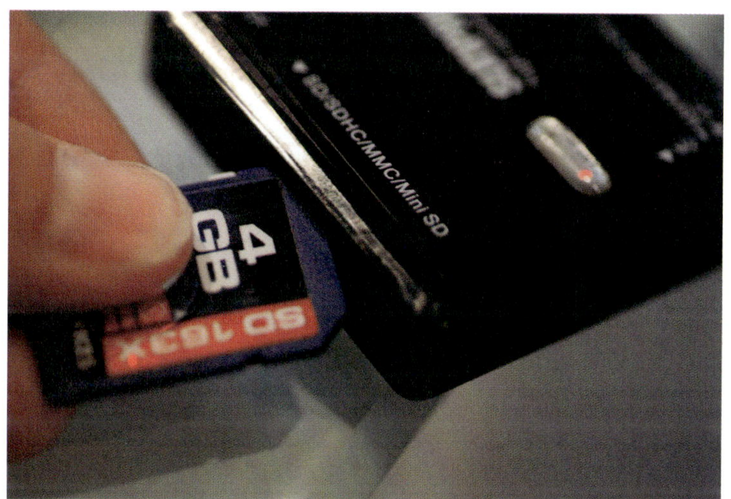

9.2 Some photographers prefer to use an external memory card reader to download their images.

Storage

Storage is an often overlooked and important part of the photography process. You don't want to lose your digital files. You have many choices when it comes to storing your photographs. Many casual photographers just leave photos on memory cards, and buy new ones or erase old images on them when they run out of room. If this is your method of storage, I recommend that you consider using one of the following options instead. Your computer hard drive is a good starting point. If you take a lot of photos and videos, your computer's hard drive will fill up fast. Consider purchasing an external hard drive on which to store all of your photos and videos.

Optical storage options, such as CDs, DVDs, and Blu-ray discs, are another storage option. Optical storage uses light (such as lasers) to read and record data. They are easy to use and are a good short-term option or for use as part of an overall storage plan. I don't recommend optical storage for the long-term, though, because they can degrade over time if not stored in a cool, dry location.

If you are concerned about backup and generate many images, consider purchasing something like a RAID (redundant array of independent disks) system or Drobo hard drive. These are designed to be redundant and prevent data from being lost by using multiple hard drives. If one drive crashes, it can be replaced without the worry of losing information, like your photographs.

The cloud is another storage option to consider. Storing your images on *the cloud* means that your photos are saved on a company server via the Internet — such as Google, Amazon, or Dropbox. So, consider the cloud as one more place that can keep your files safe. There are many locations online that give you even more storage space for a price, so make sure that you compare costs. I wouldn't recommend storing all of your photographs online because it can get expensive very quickly, especially if you shoot video. It also takes a lot of time to upload an entire vacation's worth of photos and videos. However, consider storing at least some of your prize photographs, such as important memories and portfolio-worthy images, online.

You should definitely take the time to organize your photographs. Give them filenames that make it easy for you to find them later. You have a numbering system available on your camera in the Setup menu 1 (🔧). There are three options: Continuous, Auto reset, and Manual reset. Continuous keeps the name of your files in order from 0001 to 9999, and then resets. Auto reset restores the file number to 0001 each time the memory card is replaced or when you create a new folder. Manual reset lets you reset the numbers at any point in time.

Photograph files start with IMG_ and video files begin with MVI_. This may not be the best way to store your files for the long term. Creating folders with descriptive names is a good way to store your images. A better way is to use software, such as Lightroom or Digital Photo Professional Batch, to rename your images so that they can easily be found through the search function. I explain this in more detail later in this chapter.

The 3-2-1 rule

When storing your photographs, it is important to follow the 3-2-1 rule. My friend Peter Krogh, who is an expert in digital asset management, taught me this rule. He suggests having three copies of your photographs on two types of media, including one off-site. Saving three copies of all of your files could mean putting them on different hard drives, DVDs, or Blu-ray discs. The idea is that you don't keep all of your images in one location where you could lose everything in a matter of seconds — this includes storing all of your photographs on your camera.

The rule to save your files on two different media forms is a safety net in the event that one type fails or becomes obsolete. Remember Zip drives and floppy disks? If you had data saved on any of those mediums, you would have trouble retrieving it. Storage methods are changing all of the time and you should be prepared. It has been said that a CD will last 100 years, and some might, but I'm sure many CDs from just 10 years ago are not being stored at their optimal temperature and humidity levels. Many people have lost data that they thought was secure on CDs and DVDs. Make sure that you increase the odds in your favor by using multiple technologies.

Finally, make sure that one of your storage devices is off-site. This could be at your office, in a safety deposit box, or on the cloud. The bottom line is if all of your data is stored in the same place, and that place burns in a fire or is swept away by a flood, it really doesn't matter if you kept your files on three different devices.

Editing and Adjusting Content on the Camera

Deleting unwanted images is the most common form of in-camera editing; however, it is the one that I least recommend. You never know which images you might want to share later. Additionally — with the possible exception of obviously out-of-focus images — your camera's lower-resolution LCD screen is not the best way to judge the quality of an image. Sometimes, though, you may have to delete images to make room on the memory card. This is why having backup memory cards is important — it prevents you from having to delete images on-camera.

Other editing options in your camera include resizing and creative filters, all of which are found under Playback menu 1 (▶). Resizing allows you to decrease your images to sizes smaller than the originals. The creative filters give you seven options to enhance or experiment with your photographs. The options include Grainy B/W, Soft focus, Fish-eye Effect, Art Bold Effect, Water Painting Effect, Toy Camera Effect, and Miniature Effect.

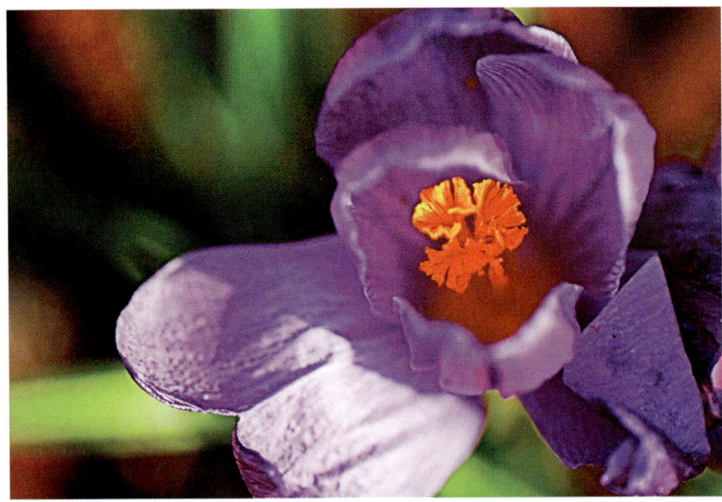

9.3 The Canon T5i/700D has creative filters, such as the Art Bold Effect, which can enhance your photos. Exposure: ISO 100, f/2.8,1/320 second, 100mm f/2.8 macro lens.

You can also use the Picture Style Editor to adjust photographs on your camera. If you don't like the results of the auto or Picture Style setting you chose before shooting, you can adjust or change it. You can also customize a RAW (RAW) photo with a custom style using the available tools (sharpness, contrast, color saturation, and color tone) under the advanced menu in the Picture Style Editor. Use the Side-by-side windows option to compare your adjustments to the original image.

If you like the Picture Style you have created using this utility, you can save it to your camera as one of the user-defined options. To do this, click the File menu in the Picture Style Editor and save the style as a Picture Style file. If you don't want anyone to make additional adjustments to your file, select the Disable subsequent editing check box. If you do this,

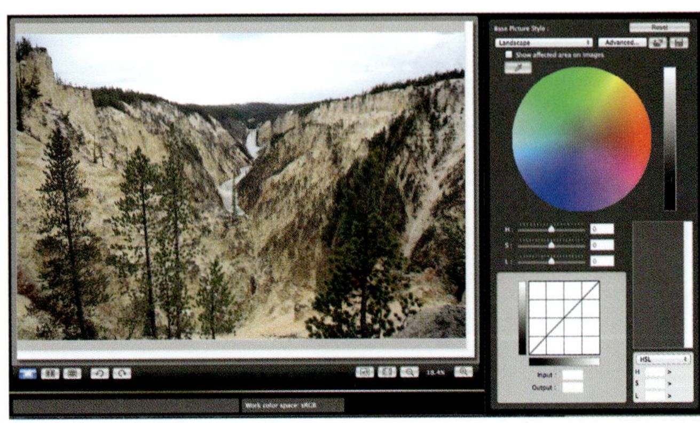

9.4 The Picture Style Editor with one of my RAW images loaded, displaying standard and advanced options.

though, note that you can't reload the file in the Picture Style Editor for use or additional adjustments.

To load your Picture Style onto your camera, connect the camera to your computer and launch the EOS Utility. Click on Camera settings/Remote shooting, and then click the red camera icon in the middle of the screen. Next, select Register User Defined style. To the right of the current listed Picture Style is an open folder icon that opens a browser to your computer files so that you can search for your Picture Style file (called a PF2 file). Select the file, and then click OK, and the computer and camera do the rest. Now you can use your Picture Style with the remote utility and on your camera.

You can also perform some basic video-editing functions on the camera. Press the Edit mode button (✂) to go to the Editing screen. You can delete the first or last 1 second of your video at a time. This option is not available for video clips in albums. You do have the option to save your edited video as a new file or overwrite the old file.

> **TIP** You can download additional Picture Styles from Canon here: http://web.canon.jp/imaging/picturestyle/file/index.html.

Sharing Photos and Videos

The Internet and social media make it easier to share photos with friends and family. I enjoy the instant feedback I receive from people I know around the world. This section covers how to share your images using the latest technology.

9

E-mailing images

You can use the Image Browser EX software that came with your camera to e-mail your photos. The e-mail option is under the Share menu, and it downsizes the file for you before launching your e-mail program. You can also download and attach an image in your e-mail program. If you need to downsize your image for e-mailing purposes, it can be done on your camera. Press the Playback button (▶) and use the Cross keys (✣▲▼◀▶) to find the image you want. Then, press the Quick Control/Print button (Q) and select the Resize option. You can also select Resize in the Playback 1 menu (▶). Small 2 (**S2**) or Small 3 (S3) are good file sizes for e-mail.

Printing images

Your Canon Rebel T5i/700D supports Pictbridge, the industry standard for printing directly from a camera to a printer without a computer. The options that appear on the camera's LCD screen differ depending on the printer. Some of the most common options include brightness adjustment, contrast, histogram distribution, cropping, frame rotation, and image title correction.

To print from the camera, turn it off and connect it to your printer via the provided USB cable. Set up your printer to communicate with your camera (you may have to consult your printer manual to do this). Turn on the printer — it may beep to let you know that it is connected to the camera. Next, press the Playback button (▶) and use the Cross keys (✣▲▼◀▶) to find the image you want to print. Press the Setting button (SET), and then follow the directions on the back of your camera.

Your camera has multiple options and adjustments you can make before you print your image. For example, you need to decide if you want the date or file number imprinted on your image and how many copies you want.

If your camera and printer are not compatible, you can try placing your memory card directly into the printer, if that option is available. You can also use the Image Browser EX software to print your images from your computer.

Uploading content to a website

When you upload a photograph to a website or a blog, you don't want to upload the original file because it's too big. In most cases, website images only need to be less than 800 pixels wide (often, they are even smaller than that). Your camera's RAW and large files produce 51.3MB images with more than 5000 pixels, which are too large and take too long to upload. This means that you need to reduce the size of your images in editing software. If your original file is still on the memory card in your camera, you can downsize your photos on-camera. This option is found under Playback menu 1 (▶).

The following are just a few of the many ways in which you can upload images to the Internet:

- **FTP (File Transfer Protocol).** If you need to upload your photos to a website or for storage on the web, this is generally the way to do it. There are many FTP programs, such as Filezilla (http://filezilla-project.org/), available for Windows users. Some cloud storage websites have their own FTP sites available for customers to transfer files. I use the FTP client Transmit on my Mac (http://panic.com/transmit/). It has two windows: One displays my computer files and the other is where they are uploaded or downloaded. I like this program because you can easily drag and drop files onto the server folder.

- **WordPress.** A blog is a good way to share your images with friends and family. WordPress is a popular blogging platform. It certainly isn't the only one, but if you know how to use WordPress, the others will be easier to navigate. Under the title box on your post or page, there is an icon that looks like a camera. This is a common icon in social media, and when you click it, it opens a new window with multiple options. Select an image from your computer using a browser window, or drag and drop it. There is also an option for sharing an image via a URL, which is a link to a photograph that is already posted on the Internet. The final option is to use images already uploaded and stored in the WordPress gallery.

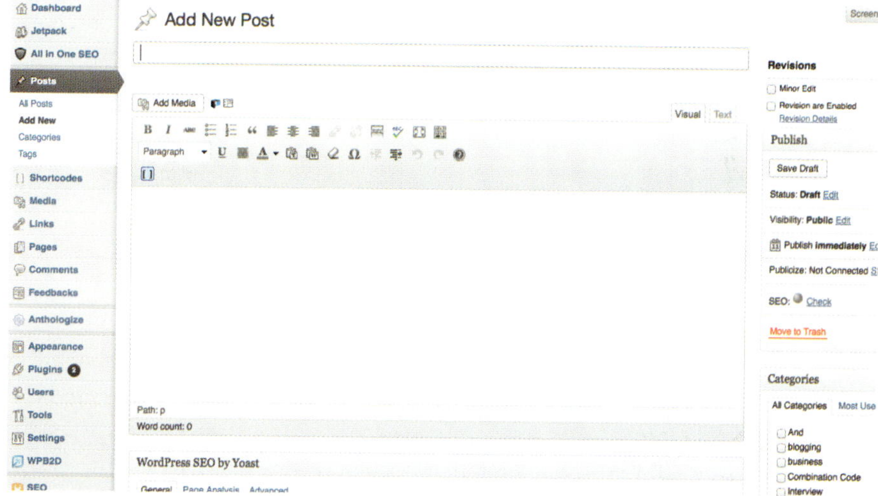

9.5 To upload images to WordPress, press the Add Media button above the main post window, and then select upload files.

Sharing content via social media

Social media is a great way to share your story with friends, family, and associates around the world. Your photos and videos tell your story and keep you connected. Websites such as Google+ and Facebook have nice gallery options to display your photos in groups. Although you can store many photographs online through these services, I would not recommend using them as permanent archival locations.

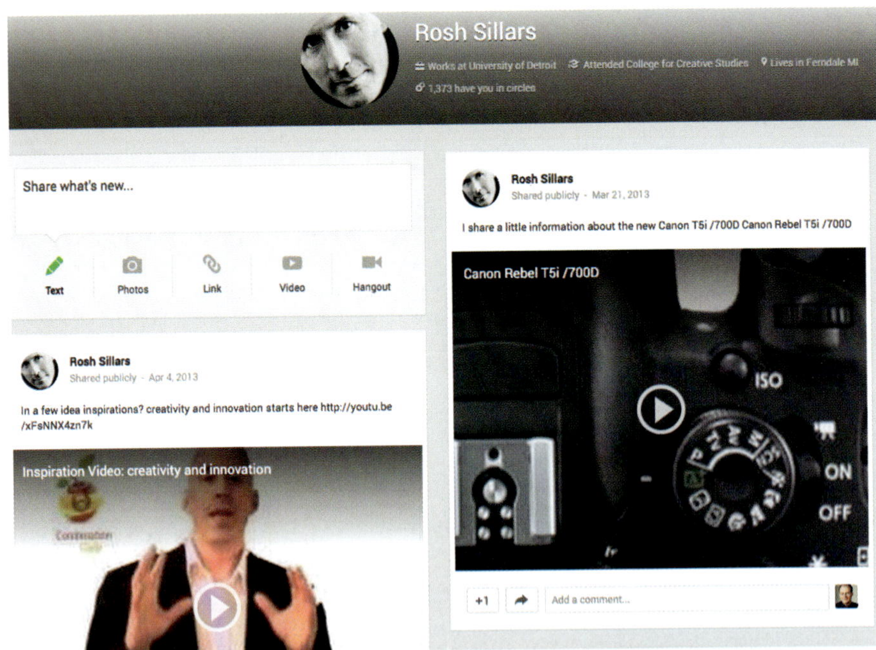

9.6 Google+ is just one of the many online options available for sharing photos.

The following are a few of the social media websites on which you can share your photos and videos:

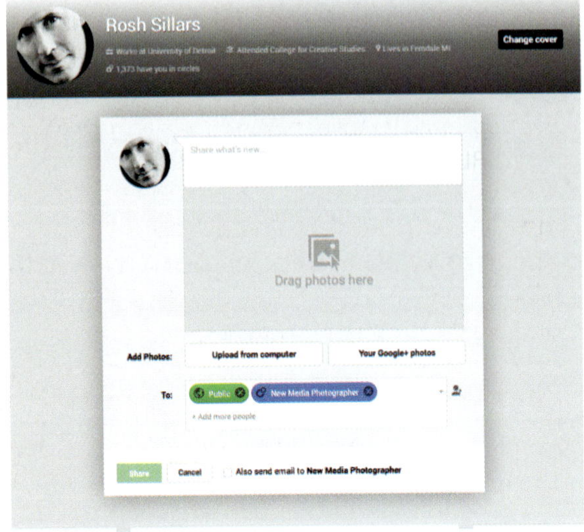

9.7 On Google+, you can upload images, or drag and drop them from your computer or your Google+ photo album.

- **Google+.** Adding a photograph to Google+ is easy. All you need to do is click the camera icon below the status update icon. You are then given two upload choices: Upload from your computer or add from your Google+ photos. There is also a drag and drop option. Next to the Link icon, you'll see the video icon, which allows you to upload a video from your computer.

- **Facebook.** To attach a photograph to your Facebook status update, click the Add Photos/Video button above where you place status updates at the top of the page. Two options appear: Upload photo/video, and Create photo album. Click Upload Photo/Video to select a video from your computer.
- **Twitter.** To add a photograph to Twitter, click the camera icon in the lower-left corner of the Tweet message box. The browser screen appears so you can search your computer and upload your image.
- **Pinterest.** To upload a photograph to Pinterest, click the Add button (+) inside a board and a new screen appears with two Add a Pin options: Choose File and Find pins. The first option is for uploading photos from your computer and the second allows you to find a Pin via a web address (URL).

When sharing your images on social websites, always read the terms of service, and make sure you understand how they apply to your content. Many terms of service for websites indicate that the owners of the website have the legal right to do anything they

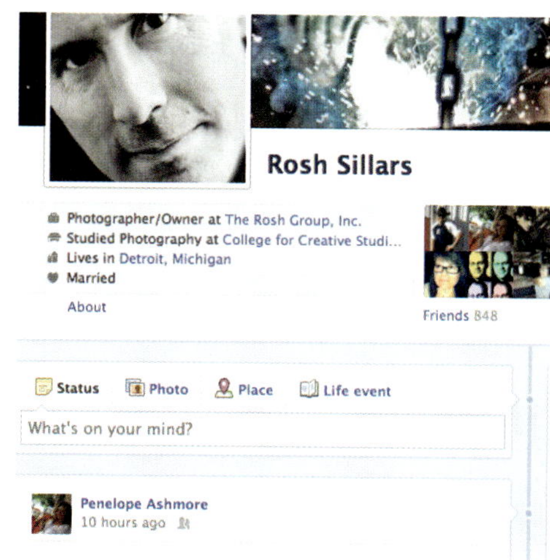

9.8 Click the Photo button above the status bar to share your images with friends on Facebook.

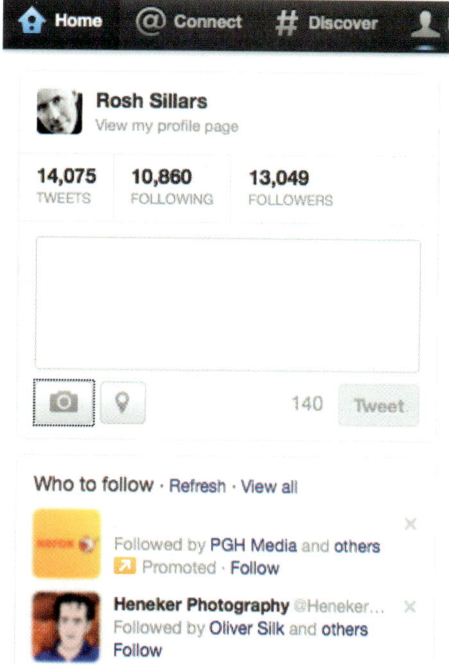

9.9 Click the camera icon to upload a photo to Twitter.

9

want with your files. If you are concerned about losing control of a specific photograph, don't upload it to any Internet website.

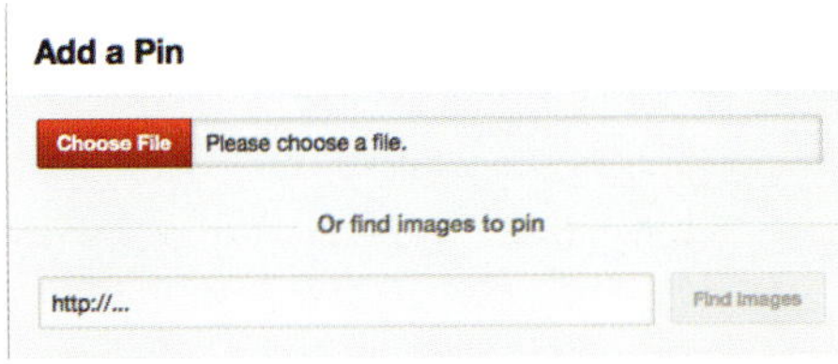

9.10 Click the Add button (+) on the front page of Pinterest, and then click Choose File to share photos from your computer.

The following are seven social media tips for the photographer:

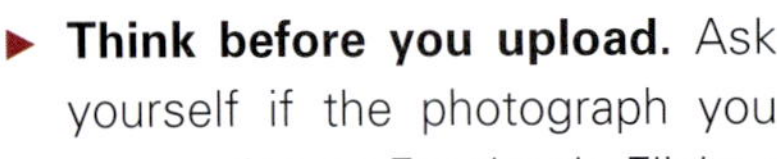

- **Think before you upload.** Ask yourself if the photograph you are posting on Facebook, Flickr, or Instagram is one you will regret sharing later.
- **Consider adding a watermark to your photographs.** Your name or website, year the photograph was taken, and the copyright symbol are good standards. This information can usually be added in any software that allows you to place text on your images.

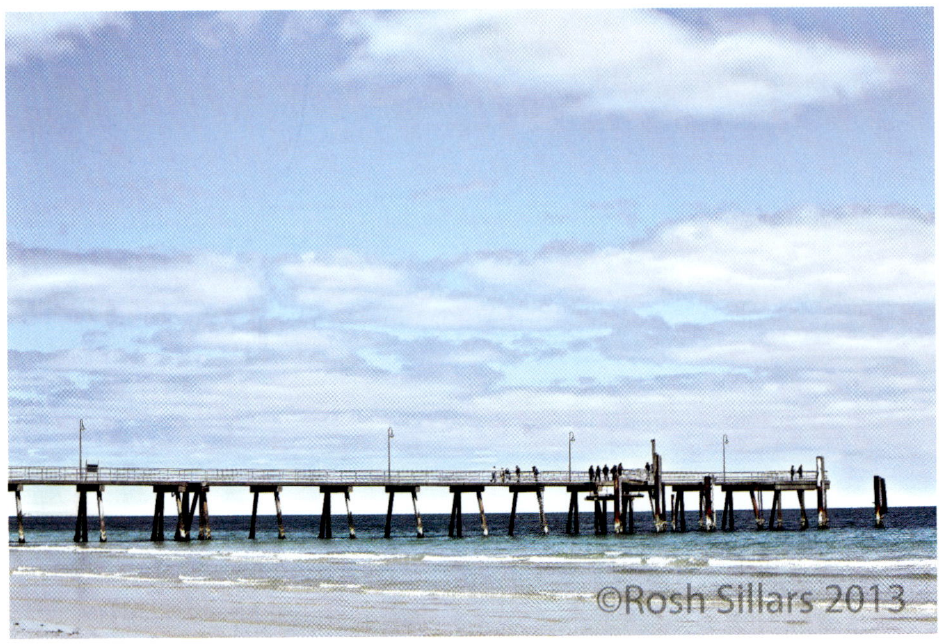

9.11 This photo has a watermark with the copyright symbol, my name, and the year. Exposure: ISO 200, f/7.1, 1/1000 second, 50mm f/1.4 lens.

- **Link to your work.** If you post an image to a blog or website, attach a link to more of your photos or your portfolio.
- **Let criticism roll off your back.** When you post your work for the world to see, don't expect everyone to like all of your images. Of course, you shouldn't tolerate

abusive behavior, but just be open to opinions. I've found constructive criticism from my social media community helpful for improving my work.

- **Learn online.** Most photographers like to help other photographers via social media. Tips, tricks, and tutorials are all available on the Web. Ask pros any questions you may have about lighting, Photoshop, and so on.
- **Use interesting titles.** Often, people see the title of a photo post before they see the image, so make your titles interesting. Asking a question is a good way to encourage people to click.
- **Explore new photography-sharing websites.** It seems like there is a new way to share photographs every week. Test new sites and applications to stay on top of the latest technology.

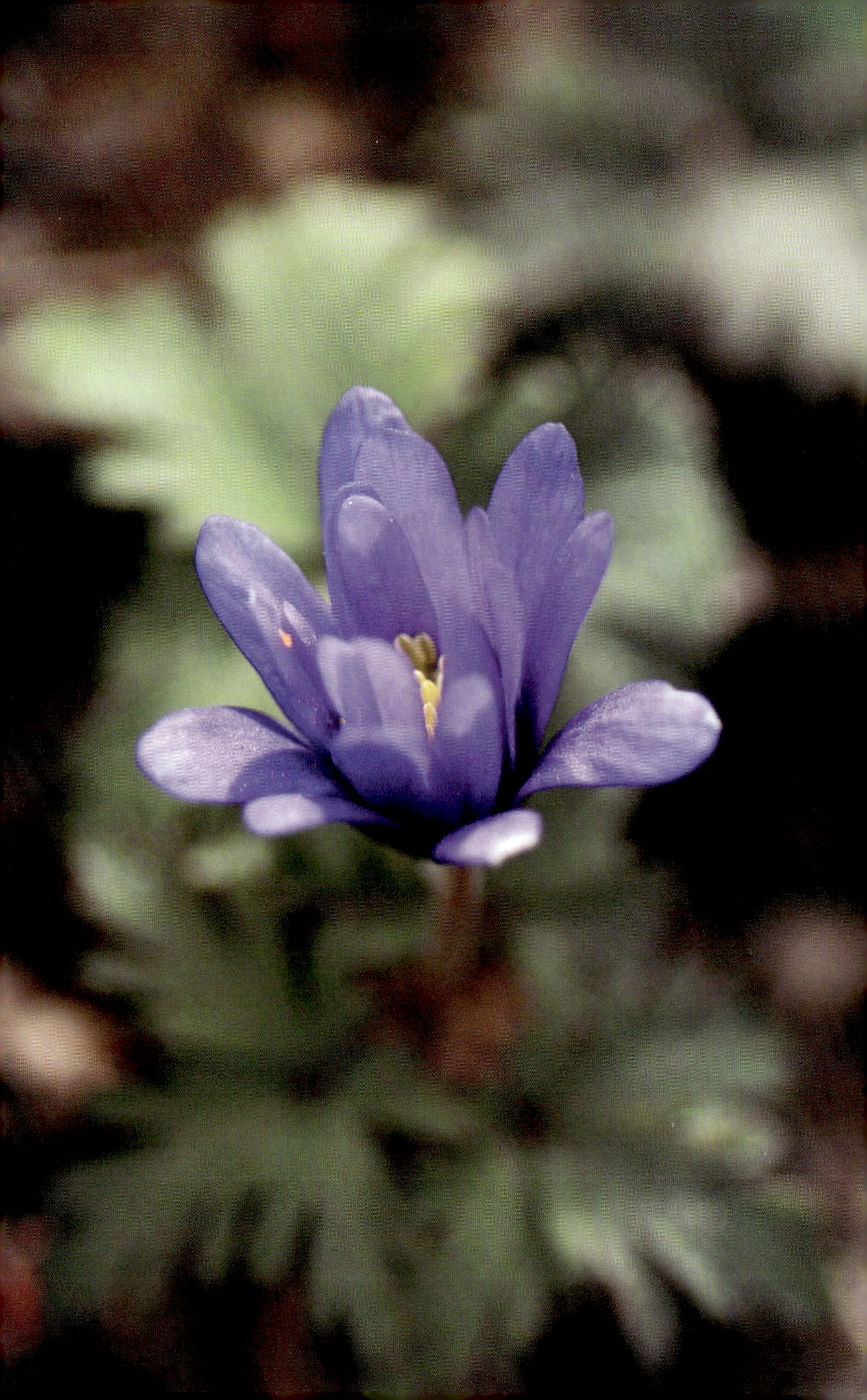

Postproduction

After you press the shutter button to create a photograph or capture a video, you're only halfway done. Next, you need to download, store, and edit the photos you want to share. Chances are you will make some adjustments to improve the sharpness, color, and contrast of the images you select. If you need to upload photographs to a social media site or send them via e-mail, you may want to resize or crop the images. Other times, you many want to print or create a work of art.

To create a successful video, postproduction is an important part of the creative process. After shooting a video, you combine the best clips to tell a story. Entire books have been written about image editing and image-editing software, so I recommend that you refer to those for more detailed information. However, this appendix will give you a brief introduction.

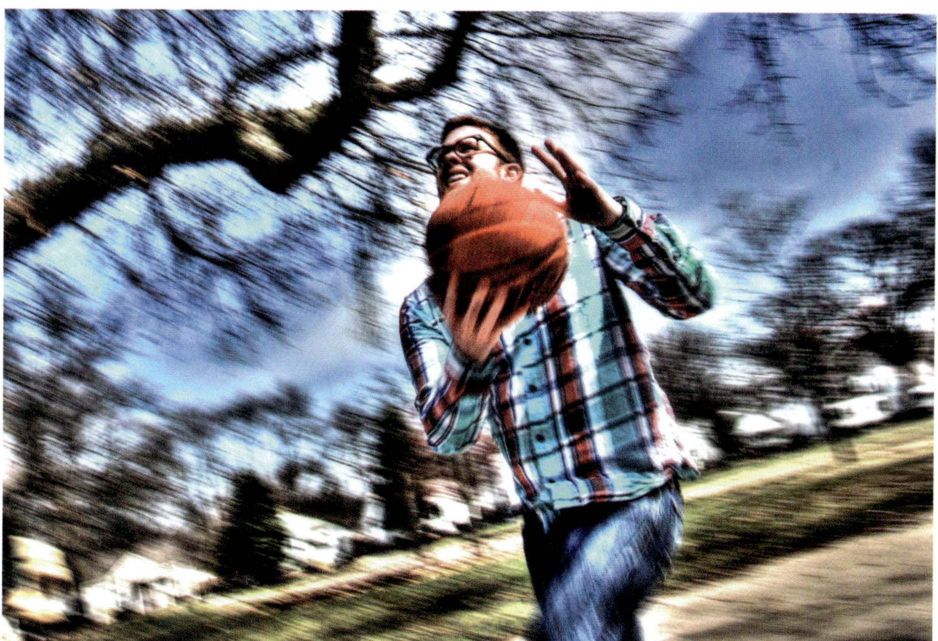

AA.1 I used a slow shutter speed and panning technique to capture this image. In postproduction, I applied a high-contrast style. Exposure: ISO 100, f/18, 1/50 second, 12-24mm f/4.0 lens at 24mm.

Photo-Editing Software

Selecting the best versions of a batch of images is an important, and often, time-consuming task. Most photographers put a lot of emotional energy into choosing their best images. However, they often select images to share for the wrong reasons. For example, perhaps the photographer is emotionally linked to the backstory of how a photograph was created. Unfortunately, the backstory is often not apparent to the viewer. Sometimes, you might capture an image just in time or overcome an obstacle to get a shot, but the result isn't as great as the experience. It takes practice to pick your best photographs, and both aesthetic and technical considerations are part of the process. Some considerations are the exposure of the image, composition, subject matter, and focus. You have multiple editing options available on your camera while shooting, such as adding filters, resizing, and applying Pictures Styles.

Once you make your selections, you need to apply additional adjustments. When you are reviewing the images on your computer, there are numerous photo-editing programs that can help you enhance them, and I cover these later in this appendix. If you don't have photo-editing software on your computer, use the Canon Digital Photo Professional software that came with your camera.

You will find basic functions, such as color correction, cropping, and sharpening, in most photo-editing programs, but each program handles the tools a bit differently. I cover the additional features specific to each program later in this appendix. The following are some of the standard options found in most photo-editing software:

- **Color balance.** Sometimes your photographs look too red, too green, or too blue (among other possible shades) and need to be corrected. Often, the goal is to neutralize a color that is tinting your entire photograph away from the natural color. Color balance is generally presented in the form of a slider or curves tool (a grid with a diagonal line). A curves tool is designed to be more precise than a slider, although sliders are easier to use.
- **Cropping.** If you don't like all of the elements in your image, you can cut them out with a cropping tool. Some tools allow you to crop any way that you want, others offer ratio guides so that you don't crop at odd dimensions, and some offer both. If your final crop is not in line with a standard ratio, it makes it difficult to print using traditional paper sizes.
- **Dodge and burn.** If you want to lighten an area of a photograph, select the dodge tool. When you want to darken an area, pick the burn tool.
- **Exposure.** This option makes your photograph either lighter or darker.
- **Fill light.** The idea behind this tool is to lighten your subject as a fill flash would so that you can see more detail in the shadow areas.

- **Filter effects.** Each program has its own suite of filter tools. These effects can range from turning a color shot into a black and white, to softening or posterizing (that is, changing the entire color scheme).
- **Red-eye correction.** When you use flash in a dark environment, the subject's eyes can reflect light back to the camera lens, making them appear red. This is called red-eye, and these tools make adjustments to minimize the effect.
- **Resize.** Sometimes you need a large image resized for the web or e-mail. Although you can accomplish this in your camera, it may not be necessary at the time. There are free photo-resizing tools available online, such as www.picresize.com or www.webresizer.com.
- **Rotate.** When you want to turn your image to the left or right, use the rotate option.
- **Saturation.** When you want to intensify the colors in your image, use this option. A little saturation is helpful for most images, but too much makes the photographs look unnatural.
- **Sharpening.** Sometimes, your image may not be as sharp as you want. Sharpening tools are helpful, but don't expect miracles, especially from online editing software. Higher-end programs, such as Photoshop, do a good job depending on the degree of blur. There is a point, however, at which sharpening tools cannot save your photos, such as subject motion blur.
- **Touching-up/healing.** These tools are good for small imperfections in the photograph, such as dust or blemishes on skin. They do a good job in most cases. The larger the area, the more effort it will take to correct it.

There are many photo-editing software programs available. Some are available on your computer when you buy it, such as Apple's iPhoto or Photo Gallery for Windows. Others, like GIMP, are open source and can be downloaded from the Internet. If you want to take your photographs to a professional level, you can purchase premium software with deep features and more control.

The following sections offer an introduction to some of the available photo-editing options. The secret to using editing software is to avoid overdoing it. Although heavy effects, such as high-contrast and saturation filters, are popular, it is good to start small and work your way up. Not every technique or filter works for every image. Don't use more than one or two effects on an image unless you have a well-thought-out plan. Too many styles in one photograph usually do not work. As I tell my students, if the first thing people think when they see your image is that you used Photoshop, you need to rethink your process.

Digital Photo Professional

I cover this program more extensively than the others because it comes with your camera. If you don't have a software option available to you, such as an updated version of Lightroom, this program works with Canon T5i/700D RAW images. You may also work with your TIFF and JPEG files in this software.

When you launch Digital Photo Professional, the main options, such as Edit image window, Tool palette, and Batch process, appear at the top of the program screen. To find the photographs you want to process, select the Folder view button located on the menu bar. This will open a selection window on the left side of the software where you can locate your images. You can also save collections of images for future processing or viewing. To view an image larger than the provided thumbnail, highlight it, and then double-click it.

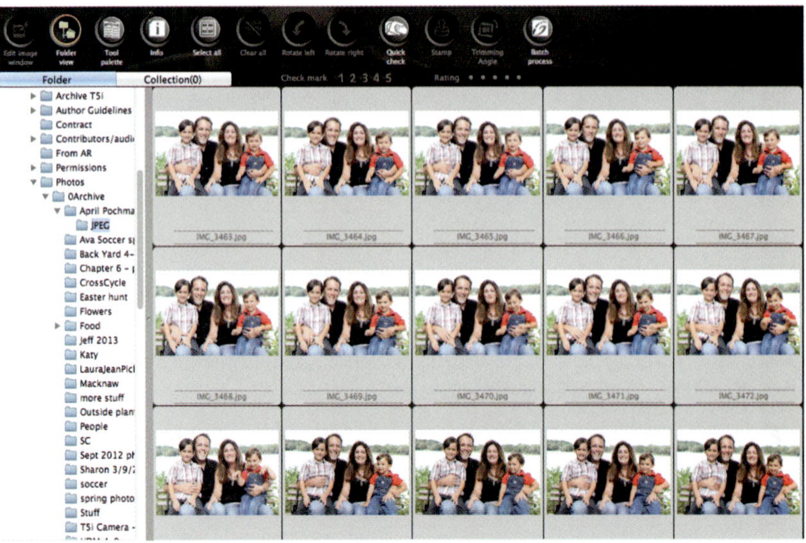

AA.2 The main window of the Digital Photo Professional software that comes with your camera.

After you select the image(s) you wish to edit in the Main window, you can select from the following tools available in the toolbar of the Digital Photo Professional software:

- **Edit image window.** After you highlight the photos you want to work on, click the Edit image window button. This takes you to the editing window where you can work on your images.

- **Folder view.** To select images to work on, you need to see the folders on your computer. This option lets you display or hide the window showing your files.
- **Tool palette.** You can use this palette to make color corrections with curves, or to sharpen, increase saturation, or adjust contrast and brightness on both RAW and JPEG files. The palette contains a section under the first tab to adjust RAW files. In this section, you can adjust brightness and white balance, and add or change Picture Styles. You can also adjust contrast, highlight and shadow detail, color tone, saturation, and sharpness.
- **Info.** To see the photograph's shooting information, select this option to view items such as shutter speed, aperture, ISO, and image size.
- **Select all.** Use this option to select all of the images available in the Main window. Selecting all images allows you to apply the same action or adjustment (such as rotate or batch processing) to all of them.

NOTE When all images are selected, you cannot make exposure adjustments to your files with the RGB adjustments in the Tool palette.

- **Clear all.** To deselect all selected images, click this button.
- **Rotate left/Rotate right.** Use these buttons to rotate your photos left or right.
- **Quick check.** This option is good for a quick review of metadata. You can also rate or rotate your images. A nice feature is the ability to see which focal points were used to create the image.
- **Stamp.** This tool can replace part of your image with a similar section to repair it. If you are using the Dust data collection option, found in Shooting menu 3 (📷) on your camera, you can also process it in this window.
- **Trimming Angle.** This cropping tool allows you to make crop adjustments by rotating your image up to 45 degrees in either direction.
- **Batch process.** Use this option when you need to resize or rename multiple files.

NOTE A stand-alone batch process program called Digital Photo Professional Batch also comes with your camera.

When you click the Edit image window button, a new screen appears with a different set of icons. Some of these are the same as those in the Main window, such as Tool palette, Info, and Batch process. If your photograph needs a lot of work, this is the window you want. You also have access to the Tool menu at the top of the screen.

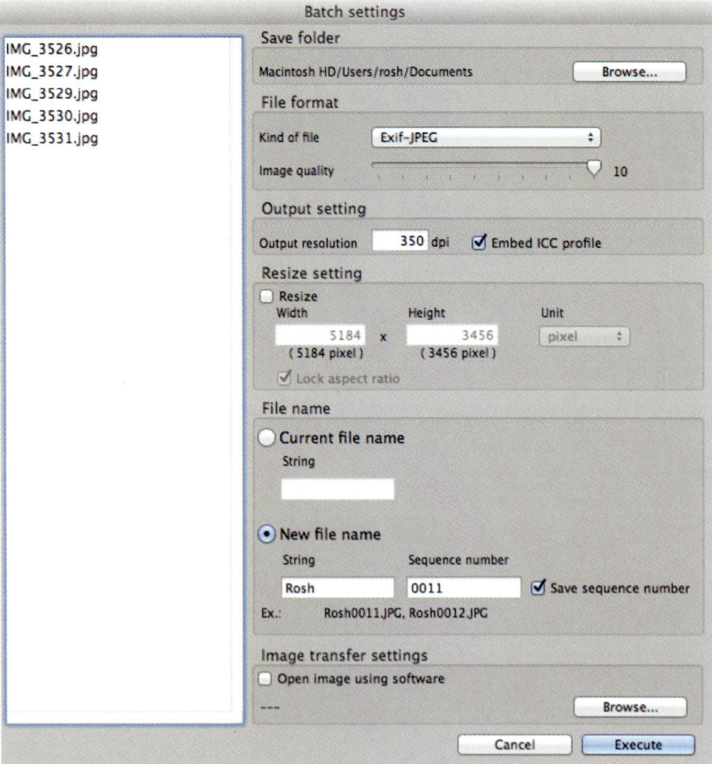

AA.3 You can batch process to resize or rename multiple photographs in Digital Photo Professional.

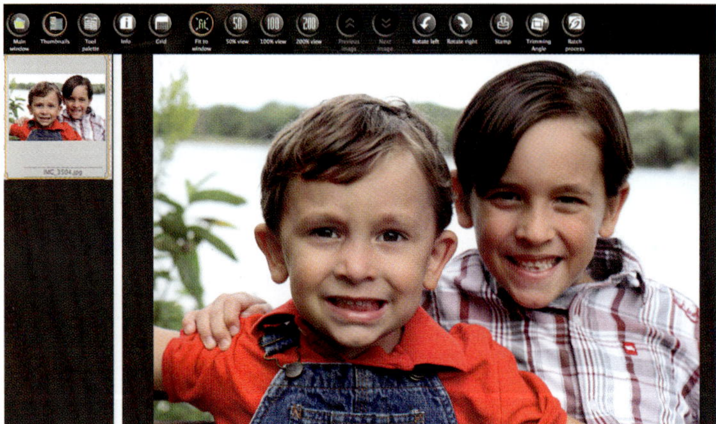

AA.4 The Edit image window of the Digital Photo Professional software. The options are at the top of the screen.

After you select Edit image, the following options are available:

- **Main window.** This option returns you to the Main window.
- **Thumbnails.** This displays the images selected in the Main window as thumbnails.
- **Tool palette.** This is the same palette found in the Main widow. You can use it to adjust curves, sharpen, increase saturation, or adjust contrast and brightness in both RAW and JPEG files.
- **Info.** Click this button to review shooting info and metadata.
- **Grid.** Clicking this places a grid across the image. Use this option when you want to confirm that the image lines are straight. The size of the grid can be adjusted (grid pitch 8-256 pixels) in Preferences under the View settings tab.
- **Fit to window.** If you magnify or reduce your photograph, use this to resize it to the original viewing size that fits the screen.
- **50%, 100%, and 200% view.** These buttons magnify or reduce your images for viewing purposes.
- **Previous image/Next image.** These buttons take you to the next or previous photograph within your selected group.
- **Rotate left/Rotate right.** Use these buttons to rotate your photos to the left or right.
- **Stamp.** This same tool appears in the Main window. You can use it to replace part of an image with a similar-looking section to repair it. If you are using the Dust data collection option found in Shooting menu 3 (📷) on your camera, you apply that information and process it here.
- **Trimming Angle.** This same tool appears in the Main window. You can use it to crop your photos by rotating them.
- **Batch process.** This is the same option as that in the Main window. Use it when you want to resize or rename multiple files.

You can use the NR/ALO option at the top of the Tool palette to reduce noise in RAW or JPEG images. You can adjust the NR (noise reduction) sliders as needed. Use the ALO (Auto Lighting Optimizer) setting to lighten images and increase contrast.

Image Browser EX

The CD included with your camera also contains a photography management program called Image Browser EX. This software can be used for quick browsing, importing, and managing your photos and videos. Image Browser EX is also useful for importing the content from your camera to review on your computer. You have three review options: Thumbnails, Preview, and Full screen. The software opens a new window specific to each adjustment. I find the pop-up window awkward, but the adjustments are easy to access.

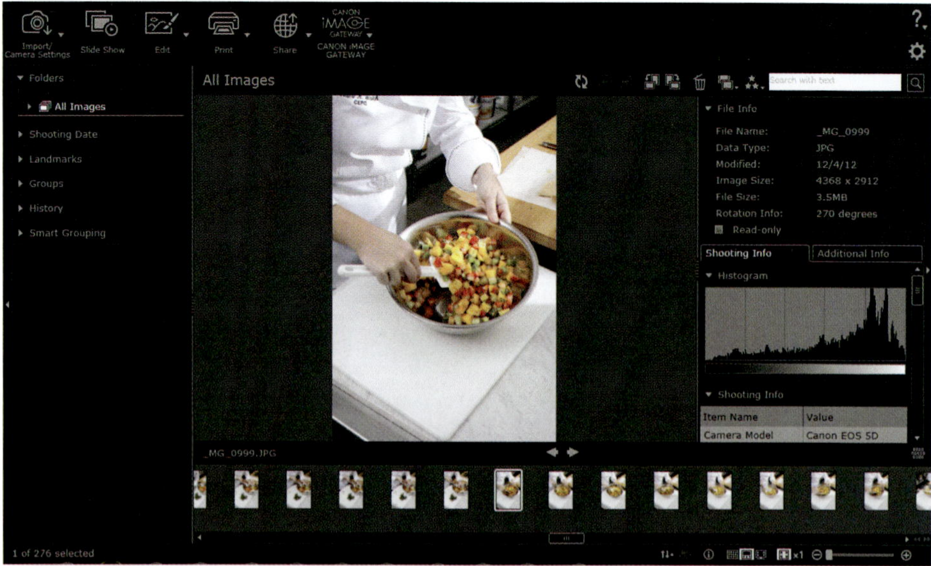

AA.5 The main screen of Image Browser EX.

The following features are available in Image Browser EX:

- **Correct Red Eye.** This reduces or eliminates the red-eye effect from a subject's eyes. You have both automatic and manual removal options.
- **Auto Correct.** Use this option to correct image color and brightness automatically.
- **Adjust color and brightness.** This option allows you to adjust color, saturation, and brightness manually.
- **Increase sharpness.** Use this option to improve the sharpness of your photos.
- **Crop image.** Basic image-cropping options are available here, as well as a few advanced features.
- **Insert text.** Use this option to add text to your photograph. You can choose the text color, size, and font.
- **Correct levels.** Correct your photo's brightness, contrast, and color levels.
- **Correct tone curves.** Correct your photo's brightness, contrast, and color curves.

- **Stitch photos.** This option allows you to merge multiple photos into one image. The images can be displayed in four arrangements: Horizontal, vertical, matrix, and 360 degrees.
- **Process Raw Images.** Image Browser EX opens Digital Photo Professional to process RAW images.
- **Edit Movie.** Edit your movies with effects, such as transitions, text, and audio effects.
- **Extract multiple images from movie**. Use this tool to extract still images from your movies.
- **Edit EOS video snapshot.** Here, you can edit your short 2-, 4-, or 8-second video snapshots.

While Image Browser EX can be helpful for organization and making minor adjustments, if you have a lot of editing to do, I recommend that you use your favorite editing software or Digital Photo Professional.

Lightroom

Lightroom is a photo-management and editing software package made by Adobe, the same company that owns Photoshop. It makes it much easier to work with many photos because you can make the same adjustments, such as sharpening, contrast, color, and saturation, to multiple images. When you have major enhancement or repair work to do on a photograph, you can also switch to Photoshop (if you own it) to complete that task. If you don't own Photoshop, you can use Digital Photo Professional or your favorite photo-editing software. Like Photoshop, you can create and download Presets in Lightroom. A *Preset* is a recorded series of commands that create a specific effect and can be applied to other images.

Lightroom features the following seven modules to help you manage and share your photos:

- **Library.** The Library module helps you organize your photography. Here, you can import, export, rank, and review images. You can also add keywords, apply presets (programs that adjust or add specific settings to your images), or publish your photographs to Facebook and Flickr.
- **Develop.** You adjust your photographs in this module. All of the basic options, such as cropping, exposure, contrast, and color correction, are available. Presets are also available under this module. Presets are like actions — they allow you to run a series of adjustments on a photograph at the click of a button.

- **Map.** If you geotag your photographs, this map displays the location at which the image was shot. You can also add location information to your photos in this module.
- **Book.** This module allows you to lay out a photo book that can be uploaded to the book-publishing service Blurb (a Blurb account is required). You can also create a PDF or JPEG version of your book.
- **Slideshow.** In this module, you can create a slide show of your favorite images. It features useful options, such as adding text, sound, background images, and transitions. You can also export your slide show as a PDF or movie.
- **Print.** Use the Print module to send your files to a selected printer.
- **Web.** This option helps you create a website gallery to display your images online. It is also helpful as a preview site creator for friends or clients. You can save your gallery to your desktop, or upload it to your server or website-hosting service.

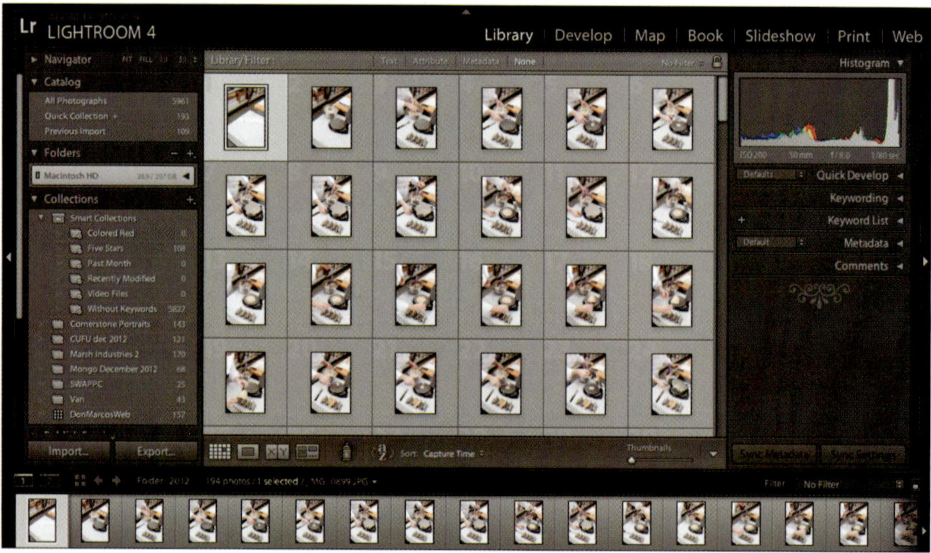

AA.6 Adobe Lightroom is a powerful photography management tool.

iPhoto

This software is available for Mac users. It comes preloaded on Apple computers, and it can be upgraded as part of Apple's iLife software package. It is more of a photo-management tool than editing software. It does have basic adjustments available, such as lighten, darken, saturation, and creative filters. I often use iPhoto for slide shows and presentations.

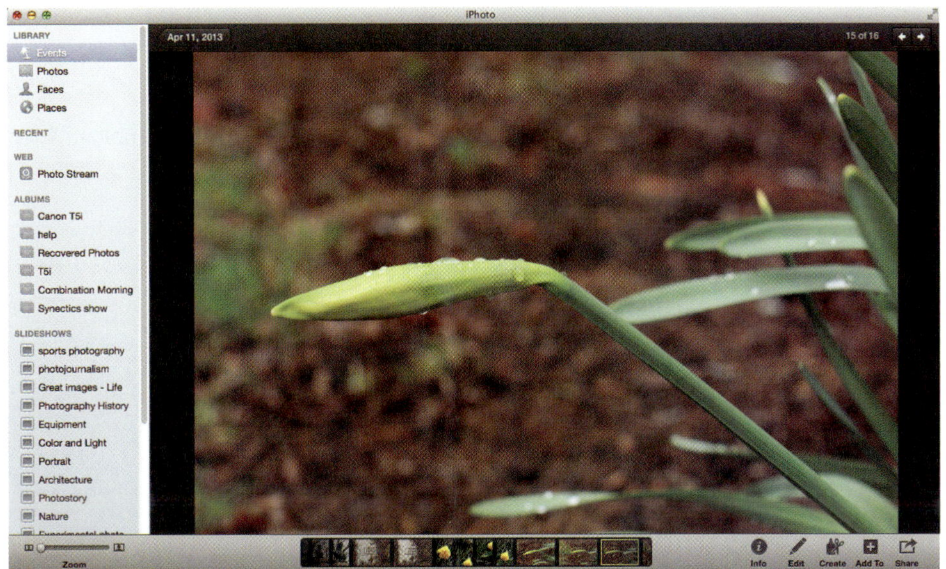

AA.7 iPhoto is a good photo-management tool for the Mac platform.

iPhoto has a few options worth noting. You have three tool sections found under the Edit button called Quick Fixes, Effects, and Adjust. Quick Fixes is convenient when you have a few minor adjustments. Here, you can Rotate, Enhance (increases saturation), Fix Red-Eye, Straighten, Crop, and Retouch. Effects includes the following exposure adjustments: Lighten, Darken, Contrast, Warmer, Cooler, and Saturate. Effects also has nine style options, including B&W, sepia, and vignette. Adjust gives you more manual control with the use of sliders to change image exposure and color.

Photoshop

If you have heavy-duty work to do on your images, Photoshop is the software you need. Most photographers consider this program the standard for professional photo editing, touchups, and manipulation. In my opinion, the layers feature is better than that of any other program. It has powerful filters, such as Liquify, sharpening, and the blurring options. Additionally, it includes the Content-Aware Patch, which allows you to move subjects from one area to another within an image, and the Adaptive Wide Angle tool, which corrects camera distortion. Even with so much potential at your fingertips, it's important to learn the basics first.

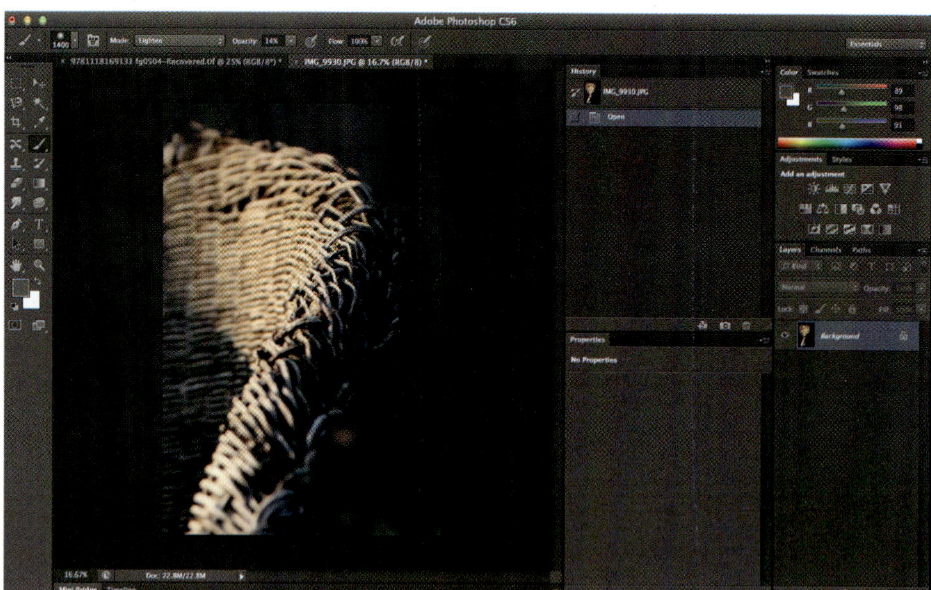

AA.8 Advanced amateurs and professionals often use Photoshop for heavy-duty editing projects.

The following list covers some of the tools available in Photoshop:

- **Actions.** This feature helps you complete a series of tasks at the click of a button. If you regularly perform the same adjustments on multiple photographs, create an *action* (a mini program) rather than performing repetitive clicks. To create an action, open a photograph, and then click the Actions tab (next to History). Use the Record, Stop, and Play buttons at the bottom of the window as you would any recorder. The next time that you need to apply the same steps, click Play, and the action adjusts one image or a folder full of them.
- **Burn tool.** There are many uses for both the Dodge (lighten) and Burn (darken) tools, and you should learn to use both well. One common use is to darken distracting backgrounds or create a vignette around the edges of your photograph.
- **Color dodge.** Try using the Color dodge option in combination with the Brush tool to lighten an area of your photograph rather than the standard Dodge tool. Select the Brush tool, click the Mode menu, and then select Color dodge. Use the Eyedropper tool to select the color you want to use as part of the dodge function. Make sure that you use this option at a low opacity (15–25 percent). I apply this technique to create a sunlight effect on the front of a building or to add a glow of light through a window.
- **Erase.** This tool's use may seem simple and obvious, but it's also an excellent blending tool when used with layers. If you erase portions of an upper layer, you

see the layer below it. In some cases, the best option is to set the eraser at a lower opacity, and then gradually erase the top layer until the front and back layers are blended to your satisfaction. Click the eye icons next to the layers to review what sections have been erased.

- **History Brush tool.** Use this tool to revert sections of your image back to their original state (that is, when the file was first opened).
- **Layers.** Learn to use *layers* (multiple images stacked on top of each other) well. They are helpful when making adjustments, adding effects, or blending objects and scenes.
- **Liquify.** This tool is so much fun to use, it's easy to overdo it. Liquify (found under the Filter menu) allows you to push, pull, and move sections of your image as if it were liquid. It is common to use this option to exaggerate your subject's features. A more practical use is to make small adjustments to your scene or subject. For example, photographers use Liquify to make their subjects look thinner.
- **Patch tool.** This freehand healing tool (my personal favorite) blends areas of any shape, making it easy to remove scratches, blemishes, or dents from your subject. The Content Aware Patch tool allows you to remove or move a subject from one part of the image to another.
- **Transform.** These options are found under the Edit menu. Select a portion of or an entire image to apply one of the Transform options. I often use Transform to straighten lines in scenes or buildings. Other useful options under Transform are Scale (use this to increase or decrease the size of a layer image, an object, or the entire image), rotate, distort, adjust perspective, and warp.

Experiment with each of these options to find the ones that suit your needs. One tip is not to use every tool at 100 percent — a little goes a long way, and that includes filters. Learn to use the basic tools, such as Crop, Healing, Eyedropper, Paintbrush, Dodge, and Burn to develop your own style. There are excellent books on the topic of Photoshop that can guide you through this feature-rich program. If you don't want to invest in the full version of Photoshop, Adobe offers a stripped-down, but still powerful version called Photoshop Elements.

Video-Editing Software

Your goal when editing a video is to tell a story. Unlike still photography, the story is not told in one moment of time, but in moments of time. Editing takes a lot of work, and organization is one of the editor's best friends. If your video has a lot of sections, take the time to plan the result. When shooting your video, think about what you might need during editing, such as *b-roll* (that is, extra video elements and details), ambient sound recordings, and extra footage before or after a scene. In other words, don't be too quick on the trigger — keep the camera rolling a little longer. In this section on video editing, I introduce different types of software you can use for video editing.

The following are some of the basic features found in most of these software packages:

- **Edit clips.** To tell your story, you need to trim and combine different video clips.
- **Sound.** Sound is a very important part of your video. Some editors have multiple tracks so you can add or replace the sound on your video.
- **Timeline.** This displays your video and audio in chronological order within the software. Some programs also call it a storyboard.
- **Track.** A track contains video media data within different points of the video timeline. Editors like to have a lot of tracks for complex videos. Some editing programs limit the number of tracks available.
- **Transitions.** Rather than having hard cuts between clips, you have the option of adding transitions. These make the ending of one clip and the beginning of another more natural, exciting, or dynamic. Professionals use transitions, but tend to keep them simple. Some transitions dissolve, some swirl, and others fade between clips. Also, once you select a transition, use the same one throughout the movie to keep your presentation looking professional rather than gimmicky.
- **Text.** Usually, you will want to add text as an introduction or title for your video. You may also want to display information, such as an introduction to the story, the name of your subject, or list credits at the end of your video.
- **User Interface.** If a program is difficult to navigate, or you can't figure out where some features are or how to use them, you are not going to be able to create the best possible video. Don't settle for the first editor that you try. Download and test free trials to see which option works best for you.

Windows Movie Maker and iMovie for Mac are two of the better free choices available. Image Browser EX comes with your camera and is a good alternative if the other options are not available. It is easy to use and should fit well with your workflow, especially if you use Digital Photo Professional and the other Canon software that comes with your camera. If you want to create higher production videos, consider some of the more professional software, such as Final Cut Pro X and Adobe Premiere Pro CC.

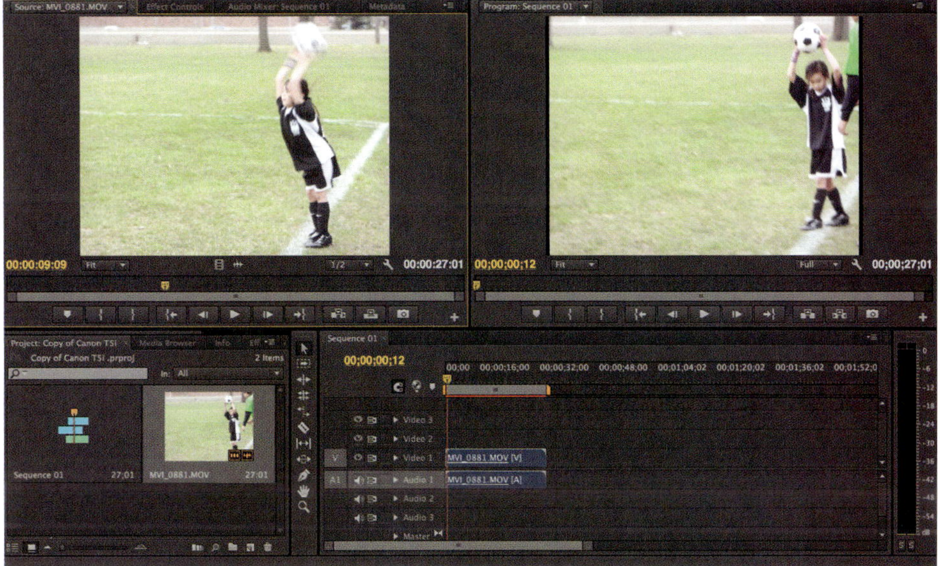

AA.9 Adobe Premiere Pro is used by advanced amateurs and professionals for video editing.

Image Browser EX

This browser comes with your camera. It is relatively easy to use and has some basic editing features, such as Transitions, Filter effects, and Text. You can also add external audio. I find the Image Extraction tool very useful. If you want to use a single frame as a still image for another use, this tool makes it easy to do. The browser also has a basic tool for editing video snapshot albums created in your camera.

To add videos to the Edit module, highlight the file in the main photo window in your Browser EX software. Under Edit, select Edit Movie to open a new pop-up window containing the video(s) you selected and the available editing options. The Edit module has four tabs: Arrange, Effect, Audio, and Save. Click Arrange to combine clips by dragging and dropping them into the desired timeline position. Effect contains the transitions, text, and filter effects. You can add seven transitions and 15 text options to your video here. Filter Effects has three options: RGB adjustment, Sepia, and Monochrome. RGB adjustment is helpful for correcting color when your video scene environment colors do not match. Audio allows you to add audio files from external recorders or music from your computer. Save gives you export options, such as File size, Type of file, and Sound quality.

iMovie

If it's not already installed on your Mac, this software is available in the Apple App Store. It is easy to use and can handle most basic editing. I often use it to edit basic videos for the Web, such as how-to or testimonial videos. It interacts with iPhoto and iTunes, so you can easily add music and still photos. It includes basic features, such as transitions, and adding text and fun video effects. iMovie also gives you the option of exporting your movies to online platforms, such as Facebook, YouTube, and Vimeo.

Editing is as simple as highlighting your desired scene, and then copying and pasting it into your timeline. You don't have to highlight an entire scene; you can select portions of a file down to a fraction of a second. You can rearrange the timeline by dragging and dropping scene files. Transition times can be adjusted, and audio levels are raised and lowered by highlighting the audio section found below the video file. Once you complete your video, you can upload it to YouTube, Vimeo, or render it to your computer.

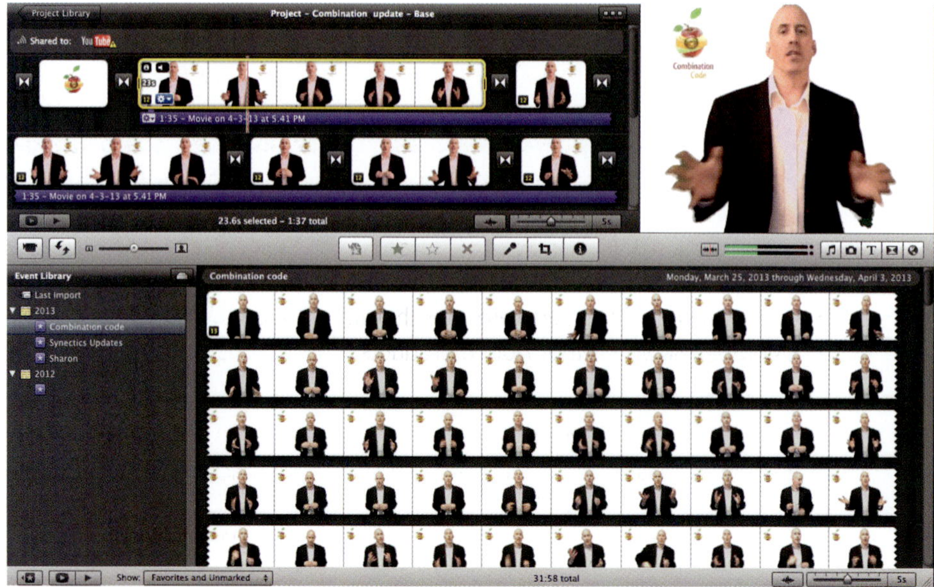

AA.10 iMovie is a good basic editor that comes with Mac computers.

Windows Live Movie Maker

Microsoft offers free editing software for those using Windows Vista, Windows 7, or Windows 8. It is bundled with Windows Live Essential. You can download it at the Microsoft Windows website in the Downloads section. It is similar in design to iMovie but has fewer windows. It has standard features, such as Titles, Transitions, and Auto track. It also has nonstandard features, such as animated titles. Editing is easy: First, import your video and photos by browsing your hard drive or dragging and dropping them to your storyboard window. You can rearrange your files as desired. If you click the Auto Movie button, the software adds titles, transitions, and zoom and panning effects for you. You will be asked to add an audio file from your computer during the process.

The auto feature is most effective for slide show presentations. If you don't like the results of the Auto Movie feature, you can always tweak it. It's a good tool to help you quickly create movies. You can also share your movies directly to Facebook and YouTube. When you save videos to your desktop, the files are saved with the .wmv (Windows Media Video) file extension. If you have a version of Windows before Vista, you can use Windows Movie Maker.

Other video-editing software

The following programs are powerful video-editing tools, and have features most amateur and semi-professional filmmakers and video producers need:

- **Adobe Premiere Pro.** This is a professional-based video-editing tool. It gives you more flexibility for the finer details of editing. Available plug-ins and applying options from Adobe After Effects make this level of editing very deep. It has multicamera editing, adjustment layers, and a nice stabilizing feature for shaky clips. Even the layout allows you to customize available buttons and options. Good transitions (21 available) and filters, such as colorize, give you options you don't have in basic editing software. Another advantage this software offers is that it is compatible with other Adobe products.
- **Final Cut Pro X.** This video-editing software is created by Apple and is the preferred platform of many advanced amateurs and professionals. It's well organized, similar to iMovie, has a good drag-and-drop editing interface, and has become faster with recent upgrades. Final Cut has all of the basic editing features you would expect, including a large number of transitions and effects, plus third-party plug-ins to expand its capabilities. If you find that iMovie is not giving you the flexibility or advanced edits that you need, consider upgrading to this program.

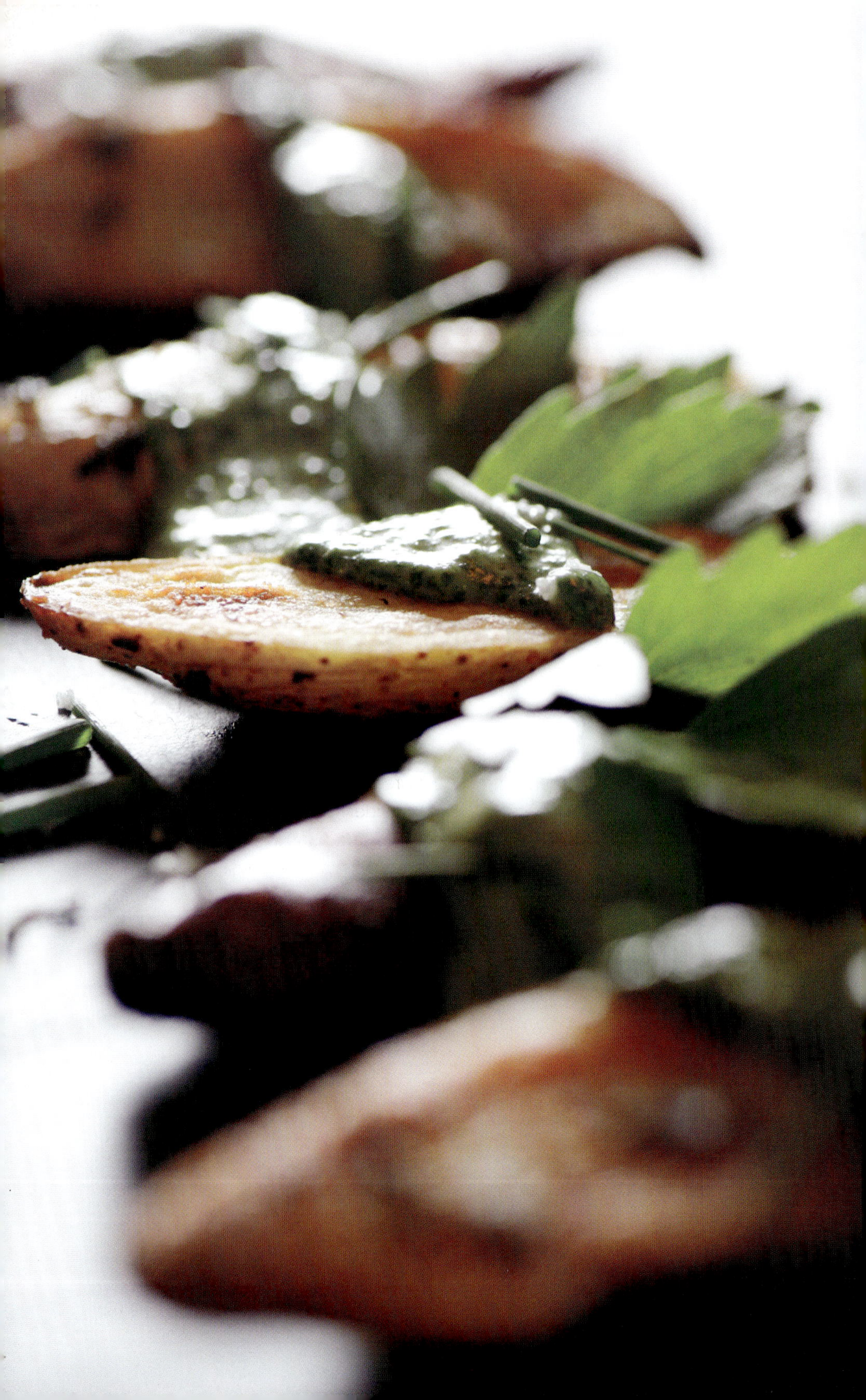

APPENDIX B

Accessories

The Canon Rebel T5i/700D body is just a starting point. The list of accessories available for your camera is long and can get expensive quickly. It is important to think through your purchase decisions. The accessories you choose have a lot to do with the type of photography you want to pursue. For example, food photography requires different accessories than landscape work does. The best place to start is investing in quality lenses. A tripod is also a smart purchase for both still photography and video. If you plan to create serious videos, you will need support accessories, lights, and microphones. I like to purchase grips for my cameras because it makes them feel more solid, and they also hold two batteries for a longer shooting time. Finally, don't forget that you need a camera bag to hold your equipment and keep it safe.

Grips and Remotes

A grip fits on the bottom of your camera and stores two batteries. It also adds weight to your camera, which some photographers consider a benefit because it makes it easier to balance. Remotes give you the ability to take long exposures (beyond the 30-second limit) with your camera. An intervalometer is a more advanced remote control that can be programmed to take multiple photographs over specific periods of time.

The Canon grip for your T5i/700D is the BG-E8. It is useful for several reasons. First, you can shoot more comfortably holding the camera vertically. The grip also holds two batteries, giving you longer battery power in the field. It also offers additional balance when handling your camera. To install a grip, you need to remove the battery door cover, as shown in Figure AB.1. Because the grip holds two batteries, you may want to purchase an additional LP-E8 battery pack.

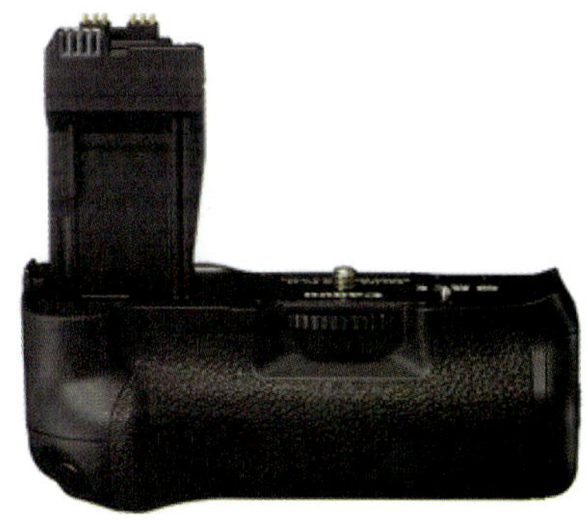

Image courtesy of Canon

AB.1 This is the BG-E8 grip designed for the Canon Rebel T series cameras.

NOTE You can also use the BG-E8 grip on the Canon T2i, T3i, and T4i.

You can't set an exposure time longer than 30 seconds on the Canon Rebel T5i/700D. The Bulb setting (**B**) requires you to hold down the shutter manually as long as necessary. In some situations, such as when shooting the night sky, you can use your camera's timer to take up to 10 images in a row, and then combine them later in a program like Adobe Photoshop.

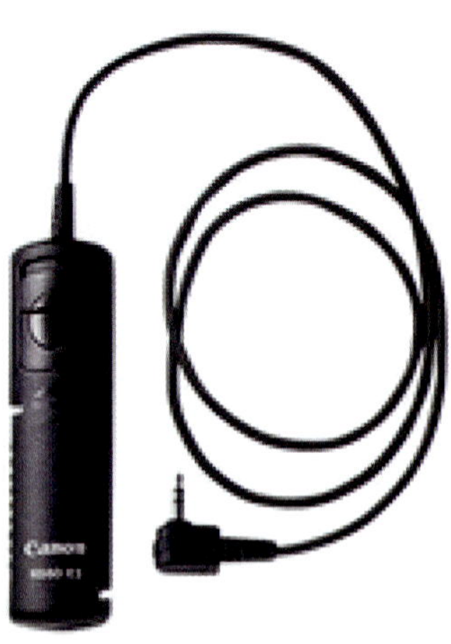

Image courtesy of Canon

AB.2 Use the RS-60E3 remote to keep the shutter open for long exposures.

Remotes make the process of shooting long exposures easier. The Canon RS-60E3 remote connects directly to the remote port on the left side of your camera. This is like having an external shutter button. Remotes — also known as cable releases — are also helpful for macro and night photography because they prevent camera shake when taking long exposures.

The RC-6 is a small, infrared wireless remote used to avoid camera shake when shooting long exposures. Another benefit is that you can be in the photograph and wait until everyone in the group is ready before you take the picture. You have the choice of a 2-second delay, a 10-second delay, or taking the photo instantly. The delay gives you time to prepare yourself or quickly put the remote in a pocket. You can also easily stand up to 15 feet away from your camera to take a photograph. It's a nice, inexpensive accessory to have in your bag.

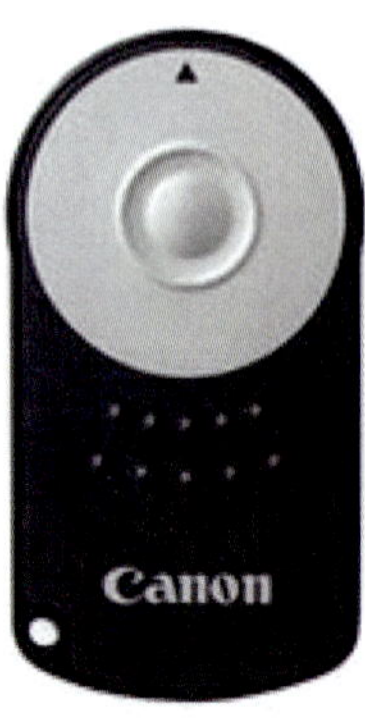

Image courtesy of Canon

AB.3 The RC-6 is a small, infrared wireless remote for Canon cameras.

Video Accessories

Video accessories make creating movies easier and, in many cases, can make your video look more professional. The following list of accessories can help you create better videos:

- **A steady camera.** Keeping your camera steady is one of the tricks of creating good video. Begin with a tripod. When you need to be on the move, there are many options to handhold your camera. Some of these options, such as the Merlin 2 Steadicam, shown in Figure AB.4, are simple, handheld devices. Others require two hands, or that you rest your shoulders or your body. There are also rigs with monitor holders.

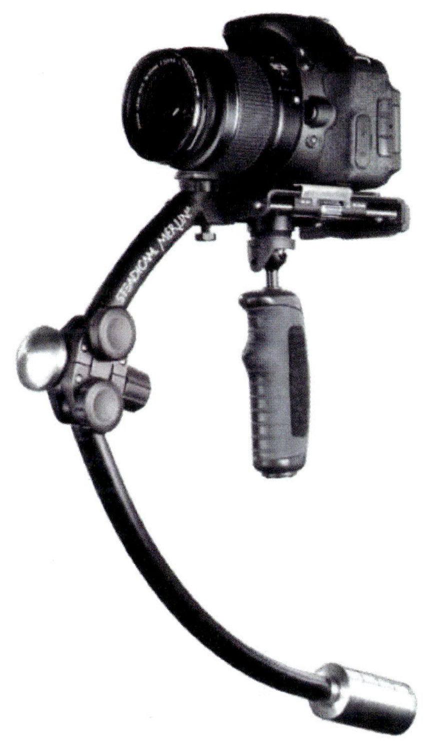

Image courtesy of Tiffen

AB.4 Tiffen's Merlin 2 Steadicam is designed to be handheld for the photographer on the move.

- **A loupe.** A loupe magnifies the image on the camera's LCD screen. Some of the more sophisticated models are found with viewing hoods, and the best have a diopter to help you see more clearly. A few companies that make loupes are Kalt, Peak, and Schneider.
- **Lights.** Good lighting accessories can drastically improve your videos. You have many choices, such as LEDs (light-emitting diodes), fluorescents, and HMIs (Hydrargyrum medium-arc iodide), to name a few. LEDs, like the Manfrotto 24 LED with a color temperature of 5600K, are good for short distances. They are a popular light source and usually fit in your camera's hot shoe. LED kits often come with filters to match different lighting situations. HMI lights are much more powerful than LEDs, and are commonly used in movie and video production. However, if you like to use light boxes and umbrellas, I recommend using a fluorescent lighting kit.

CROSS REF For more detailed information about lighting, see Chapter 6.

- **An LCD screen hood/shade.** The LCD screen on the T5i is great until it meets bright sunlight, and then it disappears. If you are shooting stills, you can use the camera's viewfinder to overcome this problem. If you are shooting video, however, you need a way to turn the back of your camera into a viewfinder so you can see your screen clearly. A screen hood blocks the sunlight so you can clearly see the camera's LCD screen.

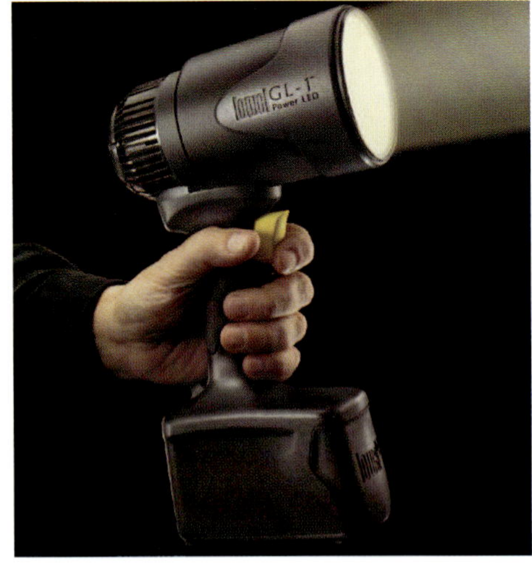

Image courtesy of Lowel

AB.5 The Lowel GL-1 Handheld LED can be used for video or still photography.

Microphones

For the casual user, your camera's built-in microphone might do the trick. However, as mentioned previously, one of the most important elements of good video is good audio. I recommend that you invest in an external microphone. In-camera microphones traditionally don't deliver the high-quality sound necessary for professional video production. While the T5i's microphone and software are better than others, and you can make some adjustments in-camera, if you need high-quality video sound, an external microphone is the answer.

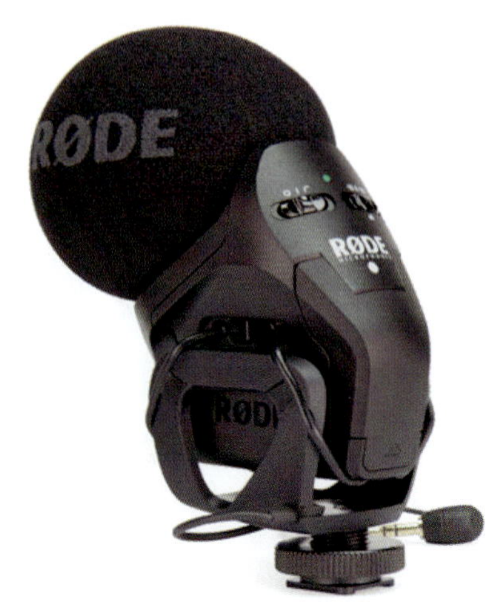

Image courtesy of Rode

AB.6 Rode makes a series of microphones, some of which are designed to fit in your camera's hot shoe.

There are a number of models on the market, and most fall under one of the following three categories: Omnidirectional, bidirectional, or unidirectional.

Each type has its advantages, depending on your needs. *Omnidirectional microphones* capture sound from all directions. This type of microphone also easily records ambient noise in the background (wanted or unwanted). A *bidirectional microphone* captures sound from two directions, and the *unidirectional microphone* records sound from one direction. Unidirectional mics come in multiple styles and are used for different purposes, each covering different angles or focus areas of sound capture.

A *shotgun microphone* is a common, all-purpose unidirectional microphone for subjects that are relatively close to the front of your camera. Many companies make shotgun microphones that connect to your camera's hot shoe. For interviews, a handheld microphone is a good option for the photographer on the move. A *lavalier microphone* clips to the subject's clothing and is often used for more static or formal interviews.

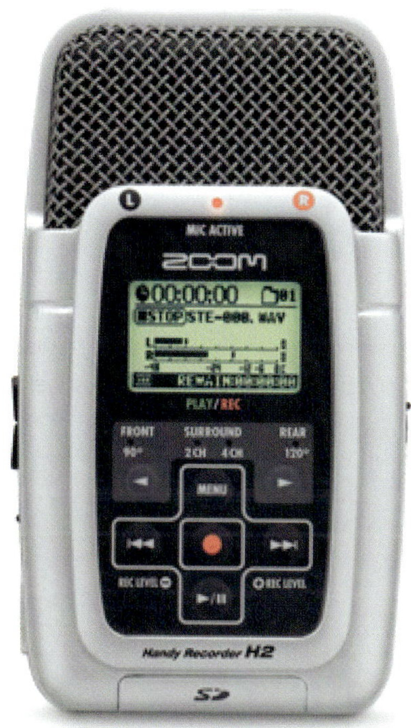

Image courtesy of Zoom

AB.7 The Zoom H2 digital recorder is small and easy to use.

If you want to achieve the best audio possible, consider using an external recording device in addition to a microphone. The combination of microphones and recording devices necessary depends on your goal. The downside of using an external recording device is that you must align the sound and video in the editing process. This is why you see clappers being used on movie sets — they help match the sound with the scene in editing. Many audio recorder manufacturers, like Zoom, make it easy to attach microphones to dSLR cameras.

Tripods

Tripods come in many sizes and shapes. A good tripod keeps your camera steady, while still offering the flexibility of smooth motion for actions like *panning* (following a moving object). The type of tripod you purchase depends on the type of images you like to create. Heavy tripods are good for the studio and long exposures. Lighter and portable tripods are helpful when you are on the move, such as when hiking or traveling.

How high your tripod should be is also an important consideration. All of this depends on what you plan to photograph. The heavier the tripod is, the steadier it will keep your camera. Heavy tripods and those made of higher-quality materials, such as carbon fiber, tend to cost more money, though. Less expensive tripods are usually made of aluminum, come in one piece, and have a tilt-and-pan-style head. These heads are not as flexible as the more versatile ball heads found on higher-quality tripods.

Usually, tripod companies require you to select a head separately. When selecting a head, make sure it has all of the features that you need. Some things to consider include smooth movement, ease of adjustment, and a quality plate that is easy to connect to your camera and tripod head. If you are a photographer on the go, such as a sports photographer, consider using a monopod. A *monopod* has only one leg, and allows you to be mobile while offering the support necessary for long lenses.

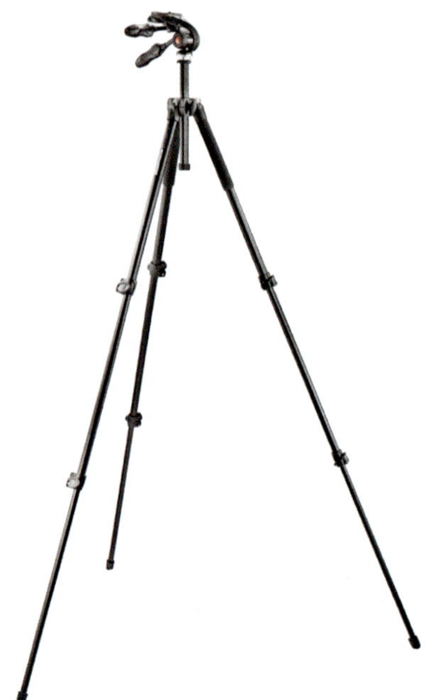

Image courtesy of Manfrotto

AB.8 This series 290 Manfrotto Tripod kit is fine for casual use.

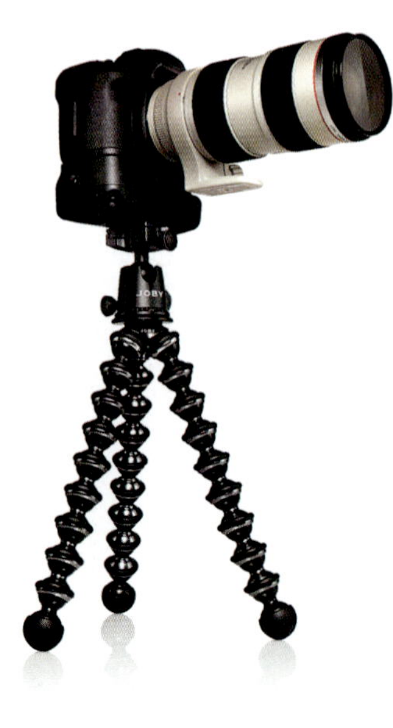

Image courtesy of Joby

AB.9 Gorillapods are light, flexible, and ideal when you don't want to carry a lot of equipment.

Occasionally, you may not have a tripod available. In these situations, a handbag, backpack, or clothing can support your camera on top of a wall, fence, or a rock. A small, flexible tripod, like the Gorillapod shown in Figure AB.9, is good to keep in your bag for when you don't have a full-size tripod available. I have had many tripods throughout my career, and those that I invested some money in are still in great working order.

Bags

Make sure that you have a good bag, pack, or case to protect and carry your gear. It is nice to have many pockets, but my biggest concern is ease of use. How easily and quickly can you grab equipment when you need it? Also, consider whether the bag is weatherproof and durable. Is it designed for the type of photography you are going to be doing? A photojournalist needs a different bag than a commercial photographer working in the studio does.

Commerical photographers often use hard cases to protect their equipment in storage and transit. Standard shoulder bags have a lot of pockets and are good for the photographer on the move who needs multiple lenses, filters, and small support tools. Messenger bags, like the one shown in Figure AB.10, with their simple design and ease of use, are popular with photographers. If you are a travel, nature, or wildlife photographer, you might want to consider a backpack-style bag.

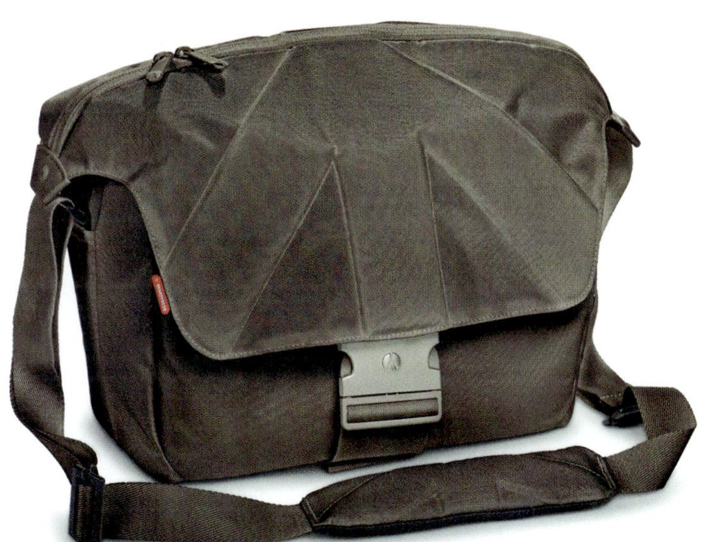

Image courtesy of Manfrotto

AB.10 Messenger-style bags are preferred by many travel and wildlife photographers.

Reflectors are handy as an extra source of light to fill in shadows. Some reflectors are designed to turn into light modifiers and they fit on a flash, hotlight, or external strobe. Here, my focus is on handheld and collapsible reflectors. They come in many sizes and reflective colors. The color of a reflector is the color that reflects back onto your subject. For example, soft white reflects softer light onto your subject, while light from a gold reflector is warmer. Often, reflectors have different colors on each side, such as silver and gold, as shown in Figure AB.11. Some reflectors are also light diffusors, which are convenient for softening sunlight on bright summer days — I find them particularly handy when shooting on location.

Additional accessories you might consider are light modifiers to focus light, colored gels, or backdrops to create formal portraits. Extra stands are useful for rigging external lighting and holding accessories. I like to keep some extra heavy-duty clamps, like those shown in Figure AB.12, in my bag at all times because they have many uses, including holding reflectors to stands and pinning clothing in place.

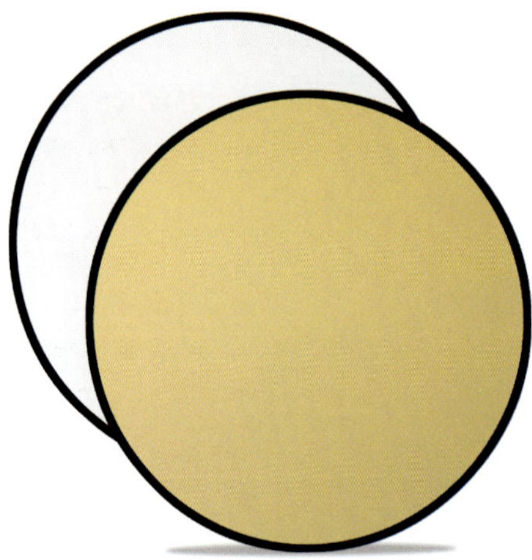

Image courtesy of Westcott

AB.11 This reflector is collapsible, and is gold on one side and silver on the other.

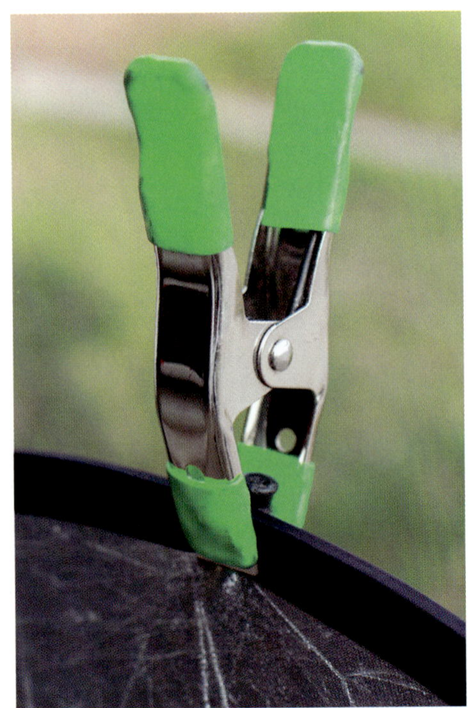

AB.12 You can find clamps like these at most hardware stores.

APPENDIX C

How to Use the Gray Card and Color Checker

Have you ever wondered how some photographers are able to consistently produce photos with such accurate color and exposure? It's often because they use gray cards and color checkers. Knowing how to use these tools helps you take some of the guesswork out of capturing photos with great color and correct exposures every time.

The Gray Card

Because the color of light changes depending on the light source, what you might decide is neutral in your photograph isn't neutral at all. This is where a gray card comes in very handy. A gray card is designed to reflect the color spectrum neutrally in all sorts of lighting conditions, providing a standard from which to measure for later color corrections or to set a custom white balance.

By taking a test shot that includes the gray card, you guarantee that you have a neutral item to adjust colors against later if you need to. Make sure that the card is placed in the same light that the subject is for the first photo, and then remove the gray card and continue shooting.

TIP When taking a photo of a gray card, unfocus the lens a little; this ensures that you capture a more even color.

Because many software programs enable you to address color correction issues by choosing something that should be white or neutral in an image, having the gray card in the first of a series of photos allows you to select the gray card as the neutral point. Your software resets red, green, and blue to be the same value, creating a neutral midtone. Depending on the capabilities of your software, you might be able to save the adjustment you've made and apply it to all other photos shot in the same series.

If you prefer to make adjustments on the spot and if the lighting conditions will remain mostly consistent while you shoot a large number of images, it is advisable to use the gray card to set a custom white balance in your camera. You can do this by taking a photo of the gray card, filling as much of the frame as possible. Then, use that photo to set the custom white balance.

The Color Checker

A color checker contains 24 swatches that represent colors found in everyday scenes, including skin tones, sky, foliage, etc. It also contains red, green, blue, cyan, magenta, and yellow, which are used in all printing devices. Finally, and perhaps most importantly, it has six shades of gray.

Using a color checker is a process very similar to using a gray card. You place it in the scene so that it is illuminated in the same way as the subject. Photograph the scene once with the reference in place, and then remove it and continue shooting. You should create a reference photo each time you shoot in a new lighting environment.

Later on, in software, open the image containing the color checker. Measure the values of the gray, black, and white swatches. The red, green, and blue values in the gray swatch should each measure around 128, in the black swatch around 10, and in the white swatch around 245. If your camera's white balance was set correctly for the scene, your measurements should fall into the range (and deviate by no more than 7 either way), and you can rest easy knowing your colors are true.

If your readings are more than 7 points out of range either way, use software to correct them. However, now you also have black-and-white reference points to help. Use the levels adjustment tool to bring the known values back to where they should be measuring (gray around 128, black around 10, and white around 245).

If your camera offers any kind of custom styles, you can also use the color checker to set or adjust any of the custom styles by taking a sample photo and evaluating it using the on-screen histogram, preferably the RGB histogram if your camera offers one. You can then choose that custom style for your shoot, perhaps even adjusting that custom style to better match your expectations for color.

G

Glossary

Adobe RGB A large color space focusing on Cyan and Greens. It is a common option for photographers shooting for print.

AI Servo focusing mode A focusing mode that follows the subject's movement until the shutter button is pressed completely to expose the image.

ambient light Available natural or existing light that is not provided by the photographer.

angle of view The amount of area seen through the viewfinder and measured in degrees. For example, telephoto lenses have a narrow angle of view.

aperture The opening in the lens that allows light into the camera. See also *diaphragm*.

Aperture-priority AE An exposure mode in which the photographer controls the aperture and the camera controls the shutter speed to create a proper exposure based on the information provided by the camera's metering system.

archive Long-term storage of data. In the case of photography, your image files are the data that is stored on a hard drive, DVD, or on the Cloud.

artificial light Light from a manmade source, such as a light bulb or flash.

aspect ratio The proportional relationship of a shape's width compared to its height.

Autofocus (AF) Focusing mode in which the camera focuses on the subject using select points.

Automatic Exposure (AE) The camera selects all of the elements for proper exposure or the photographer selects some of them, and the camera selects the rest. For example, in Shutter-priority AE mode, the photographer selects the shutter speed and the camera selects the aperture.

Automatic Exposure Lock A button on the camera that locks the exposure setting so that the photographer can recompose the image, or point the camera in a different direction using the locked exposure.

Automatic White Balance (AWB): A process in which the camera detects and applies the necessary adjustments to make the color of light in a scene appear natural.

backlighting A type of lighting in which the subject stands between a light source and the camera lens. Depending on where the photographer meters, the exposure might blow out the background or create a silhouette.

barrel distortion Distortion created by wide-angle and fisheye lenses in which straight lines are bowed.

bounce light Reflected light that is bounced off a wall, ceiling, or reflector, or any light that does not come directly from the original source.

bokeh The out-of-focus, aesthetic quality of blurred shapes (often circles) created by lights in the fore- or background of an image.

bracketing Taking a series of images, some of which are under-, over-, and correctly exposed. This technique is often used when photographers are unsure of the proper exposure or want backup options.

brightness The lightness of an image.

broad light Lighting that illuminates the side of the subject that is facing the camera.

buffer A temporary storage location for digital data. Your camera uses a buffer to store bursts of generated images before they are written to the memory card.

built-in flash A flash hardwired into the camera. It is usually located on top of the camera above the viewfinder.

Bulb An exposure mode that allows the shutter to remain open as long as the shutter button is pressed or the cable release (remote) is engaged.

cable release A tool used to manually trigger or keep the shutter of a camera open without the photographer touching the camera.

calibration Adjusting the color of one device to match that of another, or a predetermined standard.

camera shake A condition caused by the movement of a handheld camera, usually while using a slower shutter speed, which results in blurry photographs.

candid A photograph taken when the subject is ignoring or unaware of the camera.

card reader A device that transfers data from a memory card to a computer.

Center-weighted metering A metering system that emphasizes and gives more weight to the center of a scene when calculating the correct exposure.

chromatic aberration Light rays of different wavelengths coming into focus at different distances and causing color fringing. See also *color fringing*.

close-up A tight photograph often taken within just a few feet of the subject.

CMOS (Complementary Metal-Oxide Semiconductor) The type of imaging sensor used by the Canon T5i/700D (and many other cameras) to capture photos.

color balance How the camera reproduces colors in comparison to the original scene.

color fringing A chromatic lens aberration that creates a color (such as purple) outline or halo around parts or all of a subject. See also *chromatic aberration*.

color space A model in which colors are represented, such as RGB or CMYK. Different color spaces have large and small ranges of colors.

color temperature The representation of light based on Kelvin temperature. See also *Kelvin*.

composition How and where subjects and objects are placed within the visual frame of an image.

compression The process that reduces the size of a file. Unless lossless compression is used, some of the file information may be permanently lost. For example, a JPEG file compresses file data, making the file smaller. See also *JPEG*.

contrast The range between light and dark. The fewer shades there are, the more contrast there will be. The more shades there are, the less contrast.

crop Removing or only printing a section of an image. This is done when the photographer does not want part of the frame to be in the final image presentation.

CRW The RAW file format used by Canon digital cameras.

daylight balance A white balance adjustment designed to correct light to equal the color temperature of the midday sun.

dedicated flash A flash designed for a particular camera brand.

depth of field The amount of focus in front of and behind the subject of a photo.

diaphragm The adjustable opening (aperture) inside the lens that works like the iris of the eye, allowing more or less light to hit the camera sensor. See also *aperture*.

diffused light Indirect light that is usually shot through a material that disperses it, making it softer.

download Transferring image and video files from a camera to a computer.

DPI (**dots per inch**) The number of dots printed per inch by output sources, such as printers.

dynamic range The difference (measured in f-stops) between the darkest and lightest values in a photographic scene.

exposure The result of the combination of the amount of light reaching light-sensitive material, the sensitivity of that material, and the length of time the light strikes the light-sensitive material.

E-TTL II (Evaluative Through–the-Lens) Exposure system created by Canon. It uses a brief preflash before the main flash to calculate the proper exposure.

fill flash Using flash, often outdoors, to fill in deep shadows caused by the sun or a strong light source.

filter A material (often glass) usually placed on the front of a camera lens to change the way the camera sees the scene. dSLR cameras have digital filters programmed into them.

flare An effect that occurs in an image when direct light shines into the camera lens and hits the digital sensor. It is often created when a light (such as the sun) is behind the subject. It is sometimes a desirable effect.

flat A low-contrast photograph predominantly comprised of middle tones. Flat photographs tend to lack dimension and detail.

f-number The number that indicates the size of the opening in the lens aperture. A smaller f-number equates to larger openings, allowing more light to hit the digital sensor. Larger numbers equate to smaller openings, allowing less light into the camera.

focal length The length of the camera lens represented in millimeters from the focal plane. A larger number indicates a longer focal length, such as a telephoto lens, while a lower number indicates a shorter focal length, such as a wide-angle lens.

frame The boundaries containing the subject of a photograph.

frames per second (fps) The number of frames produced by a video camera within a second.

frontlighting Light shining in the same direction that the camera is facing.

f-stop See *f-number.*

ghosting A ghost-like look created by the combination of flash, movement, and a slow shutter speed.

gray card A card that is made up of middle 18 percent gray and used with a reflective light meter to find a proper exposure.

grayscale A scale that shows the progression between black and white.

highlights The bright areas of a photograph that are often white.

histogram A graphical representation of the tone distribution in a photo between white and black, or the Red, Green, and Blue channels.

hot shoe The location where the flash is attached to an SLR camera.

hue The pure color of an object.

infinity The maximum distance of focus on your camera.

ISO (International Organization for Standardization) A setting that represents a camera's sensitivity to light.

intervalometer A function of a camera remote to create interval recordings of images or time-lapse photography. See also *time-lapse photography.*

JPEG (Joint Photographic Experts Group) An image file type that uses lossy compression. It is one of the most common digital image file types. See also *compression.*

Kelvin A scale that helps determine the color and origin of light. See also *color temperature.*

LCD (liquid crystal display) Commonly used for flat screen televisions, computer monitors, and the back panel of cameras.

lens One or more pieces of optical glass designed to focus and create an image within a camera body at the focal plane. An image is created by the light coming through the lens and reaching the photo sensor in a camera.

lossless A compression method that allows the exact original data to be reconstructed from the compressed data.

macro lens A lens designed to take extreme 1:1 or closer photographs. A 1:1 ratio means the subject is captured at life size on the camera sensor.

Manual exposure An exposure setting in which the photographer sets both the shutter speed and aperture to expose an image.

megapixel 1 million pixels. See also *pixel*.

memory card The electronic card used to record photographs in a dSLR camera.

metadata Information about a file stored or embedded within it.

midtone The point between white and black.

monochromatic An image that uses different shades, tones, and tints of the same color.

noise Visible artifacts (similar to grain in film) found in underexposed images, or images taken with high ISO settings or long exposures.

overexposed An image that receives too much light.

panning An exposure created while following a moving subject with the camera, resulting in an image in which the subject is in focus and the background is blurry.

pincushion distortion Type of image distortion in which lines in a photograph bow inward toward the center of the frame when longer lenses are used This is the opposite of the barrel distortion found in wide lenses.

pixel The smallest picture element that can be manipulated to change tone and color. See also *megapixel*.

polarizing filter A filter designed to minimize reflections and glare, while increasing color saturation and contrast.

Program AE An exposure mode in which the camera is in full control of the aperture and shutter speed.

RAW An image file that has not been run through compression software and can be adjusted without loss of information.

reflective light meter A light meter that bases exposure on the light reflected off a subject or object.

reflector Anything used to reflect light back on the subject. Photographers often use white, gold, and silver surfaces to reflect light onto their subjects.

RGB Red, Green, and Blue color channels. The mixing or adding of these three colors combines to create a given color. This additive color model is used in televisions and computer monitors.

self-timer A device used to set and count down the seconds before it releases the camera shutter.

sharp The point at which an image is well-defined or considered in focus.

shutter A curtain or moving cover that opens and closes to let light into the camera in a matter of seconds, or fractions of seconds.

sidelighting Light hitting the subject from the side.

slave Flash unit that is triggered by another flash unit.

spot-metering mode A metering mode in which the camera uses a small segment (1 to 5 percent) of the frame area or scene to calculate exposure.

sRGB A color space best used for images meant to be displayed on computer monitors and the Internet.

telephoto A long lens that makes the subject appear closer.

Through-the-Lens (TTL) A type of flash metering system that reads the information from the camera sensor to make exposure calculations. This is the type of flash metering used on most dSLR cameras.

TIFF (Tagged Image File Format) A high-quality and commonly used image file format that uses lossless compression.

time-lapse photography Capturing images at a slow frame rate over time so that, when shown at normal speed, it appears that time is moving faster. See also *intervalometer*.

tonal range The range of light to dark within a photograph.

tungsten light Type of light that often comes from incandescent bulbs. It produces light that is low on the Kelvin scale and often produces a yellow cast.

underexposed An image that did not receive enough light.

viewfinder What the photographer looks through to see the scene in front of the lens.

vignetting A darkening of the edges of a photograph. It is considered a sign of a poor or defective lens, although it can also be used for creative photographic enhancement.

white balance Adjustments made in the camera or image-editing software to establish neutral color based on white light or daylight.

wide-angle lens A short focal-length lens, such as a 20mm, that offers a wide range of view.

I

Index

NUMERICS

180-degree rule, 203
3-2-1 rule, 223

A

Access Lamp, 21
accessories. *See also* equipment
  AVC DC400ST (AV cable), 220
  backdrops and colored gels, 258
  bags and hard cases, 257
  BG-E8 (battery grip), 10, 15, 251
  Canon GP-E2 (GPS device), 46
  Canon Speedlites, 151–155
  hood/shade (LCD touchscreen), 254
  HTC-100 (HDMI cable), 220
  LED lights, 253–254
  lens extenders, 88
  Loupe (magnifier), 253
  LP-E8 (battery pack), 15, 251
  Merlin 2 Steadicam (Tiffen), 253
  microphones, 254–255
  RC-6 (wireless remote), 17, 252
  reflectors and light modifiers, 258
  rigging stands and clamps, 258
  RS-60E3 Remote Switch (cable release), 112, 252
  tripods, 255–257
action photography. *See* sports photography
Adobe Lightroom, 66, 79, 221–222, 236, 241–242
Adobe Photoshop, 66, 78–79, 91, 118, 120, 231, 235, 241, 243–245, 252
Adobe Premiere Pro CC, 246–247, 249
Adobe RGB, 36, 147, 261. *See also* RGB color model
AI Focus, 7–8, 21
AI Servo, 7–8, 21, 50, 57–60, 170, 195, 261
ambience effects, lighting, 147
aperture, defined/described, 89–90, 261
Aperture/Exposure Compensation
  about the functions, 5–6
  overcoming under-/over-exposure, 151
  selecting the options, 19–20, 35
  set-up options, 46–47
  shooting HDR photos, 119–120
  shooting video, 81, 121
  viewfinder display, 26
Aperture-priority AE (exposure mode), 4–5, 56, 261
Apple Final Cut Pro X, 246, 249
Apple iMovie, 248
Apple iPhoto, 221, 235, 242–243
architectural photography, 99, 108, 119, 127, 131–132
archive, 261. *See also* downloading and storage
artificial light, 261. *See also* light/lighting
aspect ratio, 38, 261
aspheric lens, 86
Auto Exposure Bracketing, 26, 35, 119, 151, 194–195
Auto Flash, 71
Auto rotate. *See* rotating images
auto sensor cleaning. *See* dust removal
Autofocus (AF). *See also* Scene Intelligent Auto Shooting
  accessing the menu, 7–8
  AF point select button, 5
  defined/described, 261
  dioptric adjustment and, 19
  displaying movie information, 29
  flash control and, 33
  Live View options/display, 38, 194–197
  Movie shooting options, 39–40, 82
  Movie/Video shooting options, 198–201, 208–210
  selecting focus options, 7, 21, 24–25, 57–61
  set-up options, 47
  using the Cross Keys, 6
  viewfinder display, 26
Automatic Exposure (AE), 261
Automatic Exposure Lock (button), 261
Automatic White Balance. *See* White Balance
A/V Output, 23–24, 220

B

background, composition, 127
background music, 208
backlighting, 56, 58, 73, 119, 132, 134–138, 181, 261. *See also* HDR backlight control

backup, files and images. *See* downloading and storage
barrel distortion, 262, 265
Basic Zone. *See also* Creative Zone
about setting the Mode dial, 4–5
advantages of selecting, 49
comparison to Creative Zone, 28–29, 199
Drive modes, 65
exposure controls, 102–105
exposure modes, 14, 50–57
flash controls, 33–35, 71–75
focusing options, 57–60
ISO setting, 76
lighting control, 194
Live View Shooting mode, 28–29, 37–39, 61, 196
long exposure settings, 39–40
menu options, 17–22
movie shooting mode, 39–40
setting aperture and depth of field, 114–116
setting ISO, 116–118
setting shutter speed, 105–111
Setup menus, 43
shooting menu 1, 32–33
shooting menu 2, 35–36
shooting menu 3, 37
shooting video, 81–82, 210–211
sound options, 207
battery grip (BG-E8), 10, 15, 251–252
battery pack (LP-E8), 15, 251
battery/battery compartment, 2, 15, 194, 197
blurred images, 102, 105–112, 134, 165, 170, 203, 235, 243, 262. *See also* Image Stabilization
bounce light, 131, 138, 142–143, 154, 159, 168, 206, 262
bracketing
auto exposure, 26, 35, 151, 194–195
defined/described, 262
exposure compensation, 119
flash exposure, 27
HDR photography, 119–121
white balance, 36, 70, 145
brightness, 262. *See also* light/lighting
broad light, 133, 262
buffer, 170, 262
built-in diffuser, 143
built-in flash, 9, 27, 34–35, 51, 73, 111, 195, 262. *See also* pop-up flash
built-in microphone, 206, 208, 210, 254
Bulb (exposure mode)
defined/described, 262
exposure time, 103, 252
extra-long exposures, 110, 114
ISO setting, 76, 118
time-lapse photography, 184
using flash, 152

C

cable release, 103, 112, 262
calibration, 148, 262
camera resolution, 78, 223
camera shake, 12, 34, 50–51, 90, 103, 120, 170, 199–200, 252, 262
camera specifications, 46
candid portrait, 158, 162, 262
Canon Speedlites, 151–155
card reader, 221, 262
Center-weighted metering, 36, 150, 194, 262
Certification Logo Display, 46
chromatic aberration, 86, 262–263
Clear (images/settings), 35, 47, 77, 198, 219, 237
clearing the memory card, 27, 41, 77. *See also* deleting images and files; erasing images
close-up photography, 4, 14, 51, 97, 105, 262. *See also* fill the frame; macro photography
cloud storage, 186, 222, 261
CMOS, 262
color balance, 36, 69, 234, 262
color calibration, 147–148
color checker, 260
color fringing, 33, 263
color saturation, 64, 145–147, 235, 237, 239–243
color space, 36, 147, 261, 263, 266
color temperature, 36, 145, 253, 263
composition, photo
considerations for, 122–123
defined/described, 263
filling the frame, 9, 125, 178–179
foreground and background, 127
less is more (keep it simple), 127–128
lines and shapes, 126
Rule of Thirds, 123–124, 162, 178
compression, 78–80, 263
contrast. *See* sharpness and contrast
copyright information, 47, 230
Creative Auto (exposure mode), 4, 50–51
Creative Zone. *See also* Basic Zone
about setting the Mode dial, 4–5
aperture and exposure compensation, 19–20
comparison to Basic Zone, 28–29, 49, 102, 199
comparison to Creative Zone, 49
exposure controls, 102–105
exposure modes, 14, 55–56, 211
flash controls, 17, 60, 73–74
focusing options, 21, 57
Live View Shooting mode, 28–29, 37–39, 61, 196
long exposure settings, 39–40
setting aspect ratio, 38
setting ISO, 75–76, 118
Setup menus, 43
shooting menus, 32–37
shooting video, 81–82, 210–211
sound options, 207–208
white balance adjustment, 22
crop (images), 37, 39–40, 122, 197, 234, 240, 245, 263
crop factor, 84, 86–87, 93
Cross keys
about the functions, 5–6
adjusting exposure compensation, 35
Autofocus button, 21

Drive mode button, 21
Picture Style button, 21
selecting images, 19
selecting My Menu settings, 48
setting autofocus method, 197–198
setting focus mode, 197–198, 208–209
setting tracking mode, 60–61
viewing images and videos, 5, 9, 28–29, 218–219
White Balance button, 22
CRW (RAW file format), 263
Current, Trevor (photographer), 10
Curtain sync (flash mode), 72–73
Custom Functions (Setup), 46–47
Custom White Balance. *See* White Balance
customized settings. *See* My Menu

D

Date/Time/Time zone, 45
daylight balance, 213, 263
Delete button, 6, 20
deleting images and files, 43–44, 47, 212, 223. *See also* clearing the memory card; erasing images; protecting images
depth-of-field, 16–17, 89–90, 198, 263
diaphragm, 89, 263
digital noise, 4, 75, 81–82, 106, 112, 117. *See also* noise
Digital Photo Professional, 8, 222, 236–239
Digital Photography Café (podcast), 10
Dioptric Adjustment dial, 5, 19
Display Off sensor, 19
distance scale, 24–25
downloading and storage
camera firmware, 47
defined/described, 263
images, 186, 221–223, 233
photo-editing software, 235, 241, 246, 248–249
videos, 219
dpi (dots per inch), 6–7, 263
Drive mode
about the feature, 21
accessing the menu, 6
selecting the options, 21
using the functions, 65
viewfinder display, 195
Dropbox (cloud storage), 186
dust removal, 37, 46, 235, 237, 239
dynamic range, 47, 119–121, 263

E

editing images. *See* photo-editing
e-mailing images, 225
environmental photography, 99, 115, 158–161, 164
equipment. *See also* accessories
action and sports photography, 169–170
event photography, 173
family photography, 166
landscape photography, 176
macro photography, 180
night and low-light photography, 183–184
portrait photography, 158–159
rental resources, 92
travel photography, 186
video support, 212–213
erasing images, 6, 41–42, 219, 221–222, 244–245. *See also* clearing the memory card; deleting images and files
E-TTL/E-TTL II technology, 8, 33–34, 36, 47, 139–140, 144, 153, 263, 266
event photography, 96, 172–176
exposure, 14, 263. *See also* Aperture/Exposure Compensation; Main dial; *specific modes*
Eye-Fi card/setting, 21, 43, 44, 194, 220–221

F

Face Tracking, 195–198, 209. *See also* tracking modes
Facebook, photo sharing, 227–231
family photography, 37, 85, 99, 104, 138, 142, 166–169
favorite settings. *See* My Menu
file formats and numbering, 43–44, 78–80
Filezilla (FTP client), 226
Fill flash (flash mode), 73, 168, 263
fill light, 234
fill the frame, 9, 125, 178–179
filters/filter effects
creative options, 42
defined/described, 263
filter factor, 103
magnifying filters, 180
photo-editing software, 235, 245, 247
polarizing filter, 189, 265
vignetting, 91
Final Cut Pro X, 246, 249
firmware, camera, 47
flash
about the use of, 4, 8–10
control options, 33–35
exposure modes, 71–75
Flash off mode, 50
lighting techniques, 139–144
Flash Exposure Compensation, 74–75, 154, 195
Flash Exposure Lock, 5, 20, 27, 153–154
Flash systems, 151–155
focal length, 86–90, 95–96, 108, 115, 264
focus mode. *See also* Autofocus; Manual focus mode; One-shot autofocus mode
about focusing options, 57–61
Continuous focus, 197
Movie shooting options, 208–210
selecting the options, 7–8
viewfinder display, 26
focus ring, 24
food photography, 51, 99, 173, 251

foreground, composition, 120, 127, 145, 165
frame/frames per second (fps), 21, 40, 52, 65, 170, 202–203, 264
frontlighting, 131–132, 264
f-stop/f-number, 263, 264
FTP (File Transfer Protocol), 226–227

G

getting started
  battery, installing and charging, 2
  choosing the shooting mode, 2
  controls on the back of the camera, 5–6
  controls on the top of the camera, 4–5
  memory card, installing and formatting, 2
  preparing for a "photo shoot," 10
  reviewing images and videos, 9
  selecting image-quality options, 6–7
  selecting the focus mode, 7–8
  shooting videos, 3
  tips for taking better photos, 9–10
  using the flash, 8
ghosting, 34, 52, 72, 106, 111, 140, 170, 264
GIMP (photo editing software), 235
Google+, photo sharing, 227–231
GPS (accessories/connectors), 46, 194
gray card/grayscale, 259–260, 264
grid display, 9, 37–40, 124, 198, 210, 239
grips. *See* battery grip (BG-E8)

H

Handheld Night Scene photography, 4, 53–54, 105, 108, 120
hard lighting, 129, 136–137
HDMI, 22–24, 43, 220
HDR backlight control, 4, 13, 32–33, 43, 51, 71, 105. *See also* backlighting
HDR Backlight photography, 54–55
High Dynamic Range photography (HDR), 47, 119–121, 263
highlight and shadow, 26, 36, 47, 54, 119, 136, 143, 148–149, 194, 264
High-speed sync, 27, 111, 141
histogram display. *See also* RGB color model
  comparing color checker to, 260
  defined/described, 264
  display options, 19
  evaluating exposure using, 149–150
  Live View Shooting mode, 198
  playback menu 2 option, 42
  viewfinder display, 193–194
hot shoe, 13, 264

I

Image Browser EX, 221, 225–226, 239–241, 246–247
image size and quality, 6–7, 78–80, 82
Image Stabilization (IS), 24, 88, 90–91, 95, 108, 216
iMovie, 248
Index button, 5, 20
Info button
  about the functions, 5
  choosing display options, 19
  display exposure and shooting info, 32, 193, 198
  display movie and recording info, 211
  display the photo histogram, 42, 149
  in photo editing software, 237–239
  power conserving options, 47
  reviewing and editing images, 219–220
  reviewing images and videos, 9
  selecting the display options, 28
intervalometer, 184, 264
iPhoto, 221, 235, 242–243
ISO button/settings, 4, 12, 26, 75–77, 264

J

JPEG (file format)
  aspect ratio, 197
  defined/described, 264
  dust removal, 37
  editing software, 234–245
  file compression, 263
  image size and quality, 6–7, 79–80
  lighting correction, 36
  monochrome conversion, 62, 163–164
  resizing images, 42

K

Kelvin (temperature scale), 62, 66, 144, 206, 212, 264. *See also* color temperature
Kenko (extension tubes), 180

L

landscape photography, 4, 51, 56, 62, 99, 105, 115, 127, 132, 144, 176–179, 190
Language, Setup options, 45
LCD touchscreen
  about the feature, 6, 17, 22
  accessing the camera controls, 3, 51
  focus point and tracking mode, 60–61
  magnifying and zooming, 161
  reviewing images and videos, 9, 218–219
  Setup options, 44–45
  Shooting menu functions, 32
  touch controls, 28, 38, 46, 60, 195–197, 209–211
  use in Live View mode, 27–29, 37–39, 192–195
  using Manual mode, 210
  using Special Scene modes, 105
lenses. *See also* accessories
  about the importance, 83
  aperture and depth of field, 89–90
  attaching/removing, 17, 84
  autofocus systems, 89
  barrel distortion, 262

control features, 24–25
correcting aberration, 33, 86
crop factor, 84, 86–87, 93
defined/described, 265
determining quality, 84–86
focal length, 86
Image Stabilization (IS), 89–90
pincushion distortion, 265
prime and zoom lenses, 95–96
specialty lenses, 96–98
types and uses, 87–88, 92–95
vignetting, 33, 86, 90, 266
less is more, photo composition, 127–128
light, painting with, 111–114
light meter, 10, 26, 56, 129, 184, 265
light/lighting. *See also* accessories; flash; Kelvin; sharpness and contrast; White Balance
about the importance, 129–130
ambience effects, 147
color calibration, 147–148
color of, 144–145
effects from direction of, 131–136
measuring and metering, 148–151
quality of, 136–138
tips for taking better photos, 9–10
types and uses, 138–144
using Picture Style Editor, 146–147
using Picture Styles, 145–146
Lightroom, 66, 79, 221–222, 236, 241–242
lines and shapes, 126
Live View Shooting (button/mode). *See also* Movie; Shooting menus
about the functions, 5, 27–29
accessing the menu, 18, 37
focus modes, 197–198
information display options, 193–195
Quick Control/Print button, 196
shooting menu options, 37–39
shooting stills, 196–197
tips for taking better photos, 9
using the mode, 192–193
lossless (compression method), 265
low-light photography. *See* night and low-light photography

M

macro photography, 97–98, 176, 180–182, 252, 265. *See also* close-up photography
Magnify button
about the button functions, 5
adjusting autofocus, 7
checking focus, 161, 194, 213
Live View Shooting mode, 19–20, 192, 198
reviewing images and videos, 218–219
using Manual focus mode, 210
magnifying filters, 180
Main dial (Mode dial)
about the dial functions, 4–5
about the exposure modes, 2–4
aperture and shutter speed, 19–20, 115–116
focusing options, 7–8, 60
image/video viewing options, 21, 29, 121
selecting the MENU options, 13–14
shooting menu options, 35
Special Scene mode options, 52–55
Manual focus mode (MF)
about the use of, 8, 209–210
in Basic Zone mode, 60
defined/described, 265
focus ring control, 24
focusing options, 57
Live View Shooting mode, 198
macro photography, 182
options, 4–5
shooting movies and video, 39–40, 82
Manual mode (M)
aperture control, 5–6, 19–20
in Creative Zone mode, 56
exposure control, 142–144
shooting video, 210–211
manufacturing specifications, 46
megapixel. *See* pixels
memory card. *See also* downloading and storage
defined/described, 265
external card reader, 221, 262
formatting, 2, 44
installing, 2
viewfinder display, 27
Menu button (MENU), 2, 5, 18–19
metadata, 169, 237, 265
metering modes, 26, 36, 150–151, 194, 266
metering timer, 39–40
microphones, 13, 23–25, 173, 201, 206–208, 210–212, 254–255. *See also* noise; sound recording
midtone, 259, 265
Mode dial. *See* Main dial
monochromatic (image toning), 62, 202, 265
monochrome photography, 13, 26, 62–64, 147, 163–164
Movie (button/mode). *See also* Live View Shooting; Shooting menus; videos
about the functions and settings, 3–5, 198
accessing the menus, 18, 31
choosing the focus mode, 208–210
frame rate (FPS, frames per second), 202–203
lighting and sound, 205–208
menus, features and options, 39–41
saving video clips (snapshots), 211–212
shooting the video, 198–202, 210–211
shutter speed, 203–205
support equipment, 212–213
Movie Servo AF mode, 8, 39, 82, 198, 201–202, 208–209, 211
My Menu (Setup), 19, 48

N

natural light, 129, 138–139, 145
nature photography, 88, 97, 100, 131, 137, 176–179
night and low-light photography, 4, 45, 52–53, 113, 118, 183–186, 252
noise, 31, 37, 39, 77, 103, 194, 200, 239, 265. *See also* digital noise; microphones
NTSC (video format), 40, 45, 202–203

O

180-degree rule, 203
One-shot autofocus mode, 7–8, 21, 57–60, 197, 208
optical aberration, 86
overexposed (image), 265. *See also* underexposed (image)

P

painting with light, 111–114
PAL (recording format), 40, 45, 202
panning, 91, 106, 110, 170, 249, 255, 265
partial-metering mode, 36, 151, 194
Photo Gallery for Windows, 235
photo-editing. *See also* video-editing
  addressing software requirements, 234–235
  Digital Photo Professional, 222, 236–239
  downloading and storing images, 221–223
  downloading software, 235, 241, 246, 248–249
  Image Browser EX, 221, 239–241, 246–247
  in-camera options, 223–225
  iPhoto, 221, 235, 242–243
  Lightroom, 66, 79, 221–222, 236, 241–242
  Photomatix Pro, 120
  Photoshop, 66, 78–79, 91, 118, 120, 231, 235, 241, 243–245, 252
Picture Style. *See also* sharpness and contrast
  about the button functions, 21
  accessing the feature, 6
  movie information display, 29
  movie shooting options, 121
  selecting the options, 61–65
  shooting menu options, 35–36
  shooting video, 202
  using the button features, 145–146
  viewfinder display, 193–194
Picture Style Editor, 146–147, 163–164, 224–225
pincushion distortion, 265
Pinterest, photo sharing, 229
pixels, 6–7, 40, 78–80, 149, 226, 265
playback
  about the button functions, 5–6, 20–22
  accessing the menu, 18–19
  editing images, 223–225
  menu 1 options and features, 41–42
  menu 2 options and features, 42–43
  playing background music, 208
  reviewing images and videos, 9
  reviewing photos and videos, 28–29, 161, 218–219
  rotating and resizing images, 44, 78–79
  uploading images to the web, 226–227
  using a TV or smart device, 220
  viewing image histogram, 149
  viewing movies, 212
polarizing filter, 189, 265
pop-up flash. *See also* built-in flash
  achieving proper exposure, 71, 131
  activating and using, 16–17, 152–153
  Basic Zone modes, 50–51
  flash controls, 33–35, 47
  Live View display, 194
  red-eye reduction, 152–153
  triggering external speedlites, 74, 154–155
  use for fill flash, 73
  use in manual mode, 142
  viewfinder display, 27
portrait photography, 4, 50–51, 56, 61–62, 88–89, 99, 105, 114–116, 158–165, 258
postproduction. *See* photo-editing
Power button, 4, 13, 44
Premiere Pro CC, 246–247, 249
printing images from the camera, 225–226
Program AE (exposure mode), 4–5, 265
protecting images, 41

Q

Quick Control/Print button
  about the functions, 6, 22
  selecting exposure modes, 13–14
  selecting the options, 196, 199, 209
  shooting video, 211
  using the features, 29, 50–52, 54, 61, 74, 78, 154
  viewfinder display, 3, 194
  viewing and editing options, 219–220

R

RAW (file format)
  aberration correction, 33
  aspect ratio, 197
  defined/described, 265
  dust removal, 37
  editing software, 234–245
  image size and quality, 6–7, 78–79, 170
  monochrome conversion, 62
  resizing images, 42
red-eye reduction
  activating the feature, 16–17, 71
  defined/described, 33
  indicator lamp, 26
  in Movie shooting mode, 32
  photo editing for, 235, 240, 243
  use with pop-up flash, 152–153
  viewfinder display, 26
Reduce/Exposure Lock button, 5, 20

reflective light meter, 265
reflectors, 258, 265
remote controls/accessories
activating playback functions, 43
Bulb (exposure mode), 262
cables and wireless devices, 251–252
camera sensor, 16–17
camera terminal, 23
flash systems, 154–155
intervalometer, 184, 264
night photography, 111–112
tips for taking better photos, 183–186
triggering the shutter by, 17
Remote Switch (RS-60E3), 112, 253
remote terminal (side of the camera), 23
resizing images, 42, 78, 220, 225, 233, 235, 237–239
RGB color model, 220, 237, 247, 266. *See also* Adobe RGB; color space; histogram display; sRGB
rotating images, 41, 43–44, 219, 235, 237, 239
Rule of Thirds, 123–124, 162, 178

S

Scene Intelligent Auto Shooting. *See also* Autofocus
about the feature, 2, 4
in Basic Zone mode, 50–51, 54–55
default setting, 81
defined/described, 14
selecting the feature, 18, 32, 102, 104
setting ambience effects, 147
set-up options, 43
shooting video, 211
Select folder option (Setup), 43
self-portrait, 159
self-timer
activating the feature, 17
Basic Zone modes, 50–51
defined/described, 266
drive mode/countdown option, 21, 32, 65, 77, 114
Live View display, 195
taking portraits, 159
use with pop-up flash, 152–153
sensors
aperture and shutter speed, 56
auto cleaning, 37, 46
auto focus, 38
CMOS (image capture), 262
display off, 19
exposure, 102
flash, 8
LCD auto off, 45
lens, 84
remote control, 17
Settings button
about the function, 6, 20
adding background music, 208
assigning set-up functions, 46–48
changing autofocus options, 209
Live View shooting options, 60–61
printing images, 225–226
setting shooting menu options, 38–39
setting white balance, 205
using Playback, 9, 218–219
setup. *See also* getting started
about the options, 43
menu 1 options and features, 43–44
menu 2 options and features, 44–45
menu 3 options and features, 45–46
menu 4 options and features, 46–47
My Menu settings, 48
shadows. *See* highlight and shadow
sharing photos and videos, 225–231
sharp (image focus), 266
sharpness and contrast, 64, 224, 233, 237–241, 243, 263. *See also* light/lighting; sidelighting
Shooting menus. *See also* Live View Shooting; Movie
about the functions, 31
flash control options, 33–35
menus, options and features, 32–37
Shutter-priority AE (exposure mode), 4–5, 56
shutter/shutter button
about the use of, 5
activating the focus and exposure system, 12
defined/described, 266
flash sync options, 34
night photography, 111–114
setting shutter speed, 105–106
using fast speeds, 106
using slow speeds, 106–111
viewfinder display, 27
sidelighting, 131–133, 181, 266
slave unit/mode (flash), 34–35, 74, 154–155, 266
slide shows, 43, 208, 242, 249
Slow sync (flash mode), 71
social media, sharing images, 227–231
soft lighting, 129, 137–138, 159, 167
software. *See* photo-editing; video-editing
sound recording, 40, 207, 246
sound recording menu/options. *See* microphones
speaker (back of the camera), 20, 219
Special Scene mode, 4, 13–14, 49, 52–55, 105. *See also* Handheld Night Scene photography; HDR Backlight photography; night and low-light photography
Sports (exposure mode), 4, 14, 52, 55, 105
sports photography, 56, 59, 65, 88, 96, 99–100, 106–107, 116–117, 119, 169–172, 215
spot-metering mode, 26, 36, 150–151, 194, 266
sRGB, 36, 147, 266. *See also* RGB color model
storage/storing images. *See* downloading and storage
street photography, 100, 126, 183
studio portrait, 158, 160

T

telephoto lenses, 86, 88, 96, 99–100, 266
3-2-1 rule, 223
Through-the-Lens. *See* E-TTL/E-TTL II technology
TIFF (Tagged Image File Format), 236, 266
time-lapse photography, 184, 264, 266
tips from the professionals
  before and after the shoot, 10
  color calibration, 148
  event photography, 176
  family photography, 168
  night photography, 113
  portrait photography, 165
  shooting video, 216
  things to check after a shoot, 76–77
  travel photography, 190
tonal range, 266
touch (screen controls). *See* LCD touchscreen
tracking modes, 20, 37–39, 60–61, 82. *See also* Face Tracking
Transmit (FTP client), 226–227
travel photography, 99, 186–190
tripod, 213, 216, 251, 255–257
tripod socket, 15
tungsten light, 22, 51, 68, 144, 205–206, 266
Twitter, photo sharing, 229

U

underexposed (image). *See also* backlighting; bracketing
  defined/described, 104, 266
  exposure compensation, 118–119, 151
  flash control, 20
  lighting adjustment, 36, 56
  noise, 265
  viewfinder display, 26, 195
uploading images to the web, 226–227

V

video snapshots, 40–41, 211–212, 219, 241, 247
video-editing, 246–249. *See also* photo-editing
videos. *See also* Movie (button/mode)
  composition and exposure, 121
  image size and quality, 6–7, 82
  reviewing with Playback, 9
  setting the shooting mode, 3–4
  Setup options, 45
  shooting in Basic Mode, 81
  tips for taking better, 216
  types of, 214, 216
viewfinder, 25–27, 266
viewing images and videos. *See* playback
vignetting, 33, 86, 243–244, 266

W

watermark, copyright protection, 230
websites. *See also* sharing photos and videos
  equipment rental, 92
  free photo resizing tools, 235
White Balance. *See also* color temperature; light/lighting
  about the button functions, 22
  accessing the feature, 6
  Automatic White Balance (AWB), 261
  in Basic Zone modes, 50–55, 186
  benefits, 49
  bracketing, 36, 70, 145
  choosing the settings, 66–70
  Creative Zone modes, in, 55–56, 199
  customizing the setting, 36, 205–206
  daylight balance, 213, 263
  defined/described, 266
  editing and adjusting, 237
  flash exposure and, 139–140
  lighting adjustment, 144–145, 205, 212
  movie information display, 29
  tips for taking better photos, 77
  using a gray card, 259–260
  using color checker, 260
  using the Cross Keys, 6
  viewfinder display, 26, 194
wide-angle lens. *See also* barrel distortion; focal length
  aspheric lens, 86
  basic considerations, 84
  defined/described, 266
  depth of field, 115
  night photography, 112
  portrait photography, 158–160
  vignetting, 91
wildlife photography, 56, 59, 65, 88, 100, 106, 176–179
Windows Live Movie Maker, 248–249
Wireless (flash mode), 74
wireless functions/accessories, 17, 35, 252
WordPress (blogging platform), 227

Z

zoom lens/zoom ring, 25, 85–89, 96, 166, 173

Guides to go.

Digital Field Guides are packed with essential information about your camera, plus great techniques for everyday shooting. Colorful and easily portable, they go where you go.

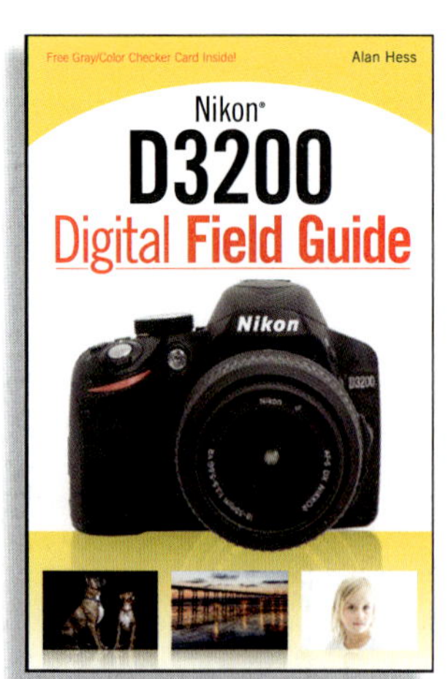

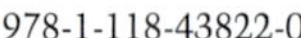
978-1-118-43822-0

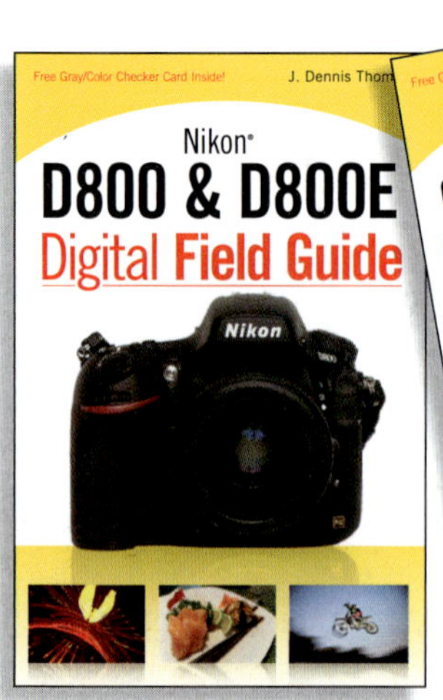

978-1-118-16914-8

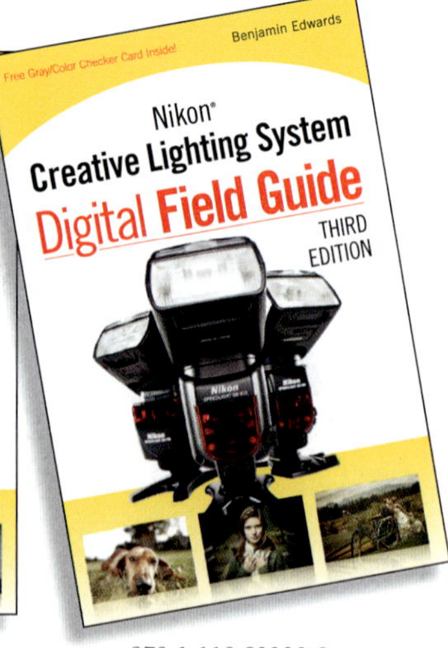

978-1-118-02223-8

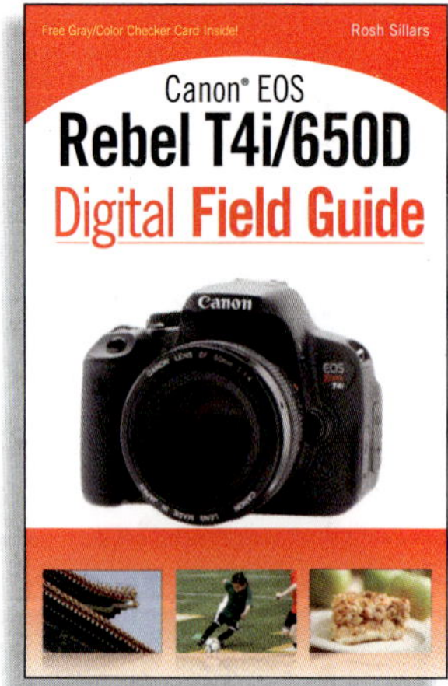

978-1-118-16913-1

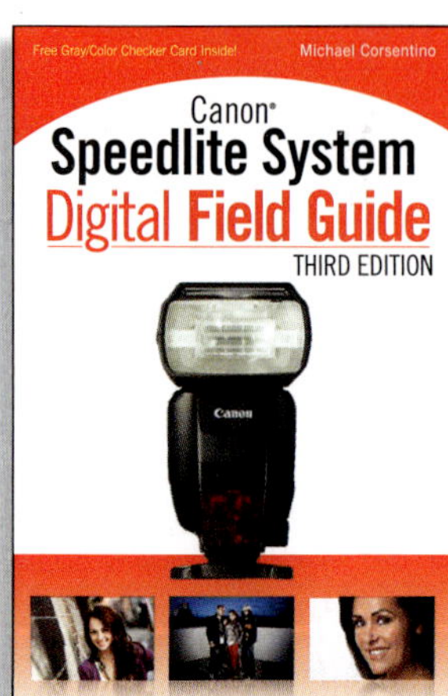

978-1-118-11289-2

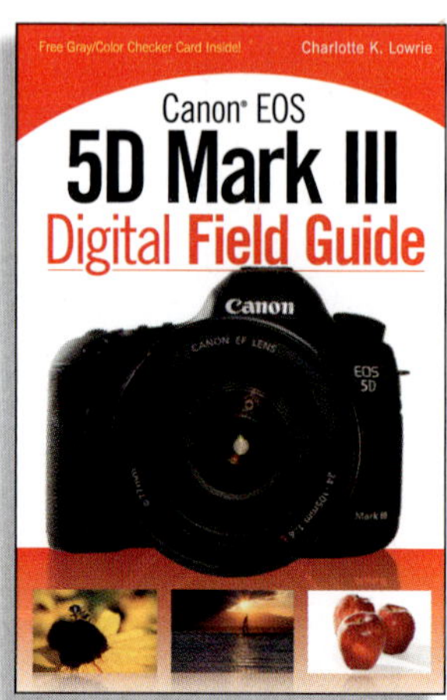

978-1-118-16911-7

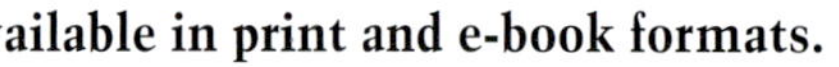
Available in print and e-book formats.

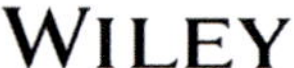